Performing the Renaissance Body

Law & Literature

Edited by
Daniela Carpi and Klaus Stierstorfer

Volume 11

Performing the Renaissance Body

Essays on Drama, Law, and Representation

Edited by
Sidia Fiorato and John Drakakis

DE GRUYTER

ISBN 978-3-11-046259-3
e-ISBN (PDF) 978-3-11-046481-8
e-ISBN (EPUB) 978-3-11-046448-1
ISSN 2191-8457

Library of Congress Cataloging-in-Publication Data
A CIP catalog record for this book has been applied for at the Library of Congress.

Bibliographic information published by the Deutsche Nationalbibliothek
The Deutsche Nationalbibliothek lists this publication in the Deutsche Nationalbibliografie; detailed bibliographic data are available on the Internet at http://dnb.dnb.de.

Printing: CPI books GmbH, Leck
♾ Printed on acid-free paper
Printed in Germany

www.degruyter.com

Table of Contents

John Drakakis

Foreword

> But since my soule, whose child love is
> Takes limmes of flesh, and lese could nothing doe,
> More subtile then the parent is,
> Love must not be, but take a body too,
> And therefore what thou wert, and who,
> I bid Love aske, and now
> That it assume thy body, I allow,
> And fix it selfe in thy lip, eye, and brow.
> (John Donne, *Aire and Angels*)

Donne's 'love' poem traverses the distance between a neo-Platonic spirituality on the one hand and a direct materiality that occupies a central place in the regime of 'sense' that elsewhere Donne thinks of as part of a 'dull sublunary' world. But that dull material world is not without its initial excitements, as well as its drawbacks, as the narrator of Shakespeare's Sonnet 129 laments; what promises 'joy', and what is recollected as 'dream' is "A bliss in proof, and proved, a very woe." (l.11) Neo-platonic desire is, in the final analysis, a delusion as the body returns from reverie to the permanent 'hell' of the fallen world: "All this the world well knows, yet none knows well / To shun the heaven that leads men to this hell." (ll.13–14)

The intellectual and analytical turn, during the last half-century to the materiality of history, has allowed us to 'read' the body as a text, and has encouraged us to regard it as a site or repository of all of the social and cultural forces that contribute to our definitions of what a 'society' is. Historically the shifts of emphasis that accelerated during the English Renaissance, including discoveries within the realm of the natural and biological sciences, along with the privileging of the human subject in its social environment that was part of the evolution of humanism, provided the substance for representations of the body within the fields of literature and drama. Early Modern accounts of the interpretation of dreams, the medical anatomizing of the human body, and the attempts to link the physiological account of bodily humours with the emotions, all found their way into imaginative writing during the period. Alongside established practices of torturing and dismembering the body as an essential part of the judicial process of punishment for crime, the slow transformation of legal procedures were also represented in the numerous 'trial' scenes that appeared in Elizabethan and Jacobean plays. To this extent, the inherently theatrical elements of the law found an analogy in the popular theatre, where juridical practices were represented, challenged, and occasionally subverted.

The present, specifically focused collection offers a range of topics that indicate both the variety and the ubiquity of the issues that are linked with the body as a resource of representation within the totality of the Renaissance social milieu. The inscription of the body within the discursive spheres of gender identity, sexuality, law, psychology, and politics during this formative historical moment are central to the discussions that follow. The issue is not simply a matter of representation, rather what is important is that the various ways, and the manner in which fictional narratives are deployed in order to articulate and resolve problems of ideology emerge and are developed at particular historical conjunctures.

As the verbal contortions of Donne, or the anxieties, and guilt of Shakespeare's radically divided lover caught between the demands of sexual pleasure and the constraints of a morally restrictive code of social behaviour demonstrate, the 'body' is more than simply a brute fact of material life. It is already textualised, and endowed with meanings that were contested in the Early Modern period. The embryonic individualism, and the interpretive practices that accompanied it rendered archetypal explanations of human behaviour, and the steps that were taken to curb its excesses, inadequate. Montaigne's essay "Of Age" might stand as a ready illustration of the kind of perplexing doubts that arise from the empirical observation of the socialised body:

> It is the body which sometimes yieldeth first unto age and other times the mind. And I have seen many that have had their brains weakened before their stomachs or legs. And forasmuch as it is a disease, little or nothing sensible unto him that endureth it and maketh no great show, it is so much the more dangerous. Here I exclaim against our laws, not because they leave us so long and late in working and employment, but that they set us a-work no sooner, and it is so late before we be employed. Methinks that considering the weakness of our life, and seeing the infinite number of ordinary rocks and natural dangers it is subject unto, we should not so soon as we come into the world allot so great a share thereof unto unprofitable wantonness in youth, ill-breeding idleness, and slow-learning prentissage.[1]

Here description accompanies judgement and opinion, but the perspective is governed by observation of the contradictions that emerge as the body passes through the process of ageing. Montaigne's observations are indicative of a culture turning its gaze on human idiosyncrasy and the body's momentary resistances to accepted social practice

Each of the following essays inscribes the body in a chosen textual field and teases out the implications of aligning its materiality with discourses whose ef-

---

1 Michel de Montaigne, "Of Age," in *Shakespeare's Montaigne: The Florio Translation of the Essays, A Selection*, eds. Stephen Greenblatt, Peter G. Platt (New York: NYREV, 2014): 86–89, 89.

fects are themselves material. The common ground that they all share is the emphasis that they place upon representations of the body, in law, in medical practice, and in art, highlighting the ways in which what we have come to think of as discreet discursive domains intersect and illuminate each other.

Sidia Fiorato

Introduction. Performances, Regulations and Negotiations of the Renaissance Body. Legal and Social Perspectives

In the Early Modern period the body becomes the focus of the social, legal and cultural imagination and the privileged metaphor for specific cultural discourses and political practices. Due to its ambivalent expressive force, it represents the seat and the means for the performance of normative identity, and it is an index of alterity, or the constitutive other. According to Michel Foucault, "[P]ower relations have an immediate hold upon it [the body]; they invest it, mark it, train it, torture it, force it to carry out tasks, to perform ceremonies, to emit signs."[1] During the Elizabethan and Jacobean periods, when law and power depended upon their "privileged visibility,"[2] these characteristics intersect with the aesthetic and performative dimension of law and inform the debates on the juridical constitution of authority, as well as its reflection on the formation and moulding of individual subjectivity.

Early Modern government is grounded on an aesthetic process which entails the acknowledgement of the rhetorical power of symbols, spectacle and theatre.[3] In the common law tradition, characterized by the absence of textual codification, the legitimacy of juridical institutions is established and actualized through

---

1 Michel Foucault, *Discipline and Punish* (New York: Knopf Doubleday Publishing Group, 2012), 25.

2 Stephen Greenblatt, *Shakespearean Negotiations* (Oxford: Clarendon Press, 1988), 64.

3 See Paul Raffield, *Images and Cultures of Law in Early Modern England: Justice and Political Power, 1558–1660* (Cambridge: Cambridge University Press, 2004), 89 and 88. King Henry VIII was the first English monarch to realize the binding effect of the aesthetic portrayal of political power on the subjects' imagination, which led to a public acceptance of authority. The age of Elizabeth I then witnessed the mutual dependence of art and government and the development of its spectacular dimension, a characteristic which her successor James I never mastered, differently from his wife Anna of Denmark. See also Paul Raffield, "Contract, Classicism, and the Common-Weal: Coke's Reports and the Foundations of the Modern English Constitution," *Law and Literature*, 17.1 (2005): 69–96, 78: "in cultural and social terms, law is an imaginative construct, dependent for its legitimacy on the successful reception of a multiplicity of diverse images. This is of particular relevance in the sixteenth and early seventeenth centuries, when government was conducted in an age of spectacle and, in relation to the authority of kingship, the medieval notion of symbolism as reality prevailed."

a carefully orchestrated system of representations and visual signs which is articulated at different social levels. The legal sphere thus constituted is inextricably linked with the visual in establishing complex mutually supporting social dynamics, between aesthetic representations and normative considerations. The resulting "art" of law[4] affects the perception of the representations of power in the legal imagination of the individual, an unconscious and psychological sphere where the legitimacy of the represented form of the law is acknowledged and where an identification with principles and juridically enforced constraints takes place. Its force and power depend precisely on the inscription on the soul of specific images, in an appeal to a collective unconscious.[5] Images and icons "speak directly to the senses and affect the psyche, [...] avoid[ing] the [...] intervention of logos, language and reason."[6] As Paul Raffield asserts, "[central] to the creation of this state is the Platonic notion of order as a symbol of perfection; its achievement, in the state or in the individual, depends upon the correct ordering of parts and the performance by each part of its allotted function."[7]

Within this context, central to the period is the metaphor of the body politic which in its multifarious articulations is inscribed at all levels of society. Such a metaphor is based on the analogy between the human body and the political order, divided into different parts and functions that correspond to the members or organs of the community "[c]onceived as a collective body, a supra-individual organically and internally divided whole and not the mere sum of the individuals composing it."[8] The body politic was often symbolized as a harmoniously articulated body: "each physical member, aware of 'degree,' knew its place and function"[9] and determined the well being and balance of the whole.

4 Raffield, *Images and Cultures of Law*, 2.

5 See Ian Ward, *Shakespeare and the Legal Imagination* (London: Butterworths, 1999), 1; Costas Douzinas, Lynda Nead, "Introduction" to *Law and the Image. The Authority of Art and the Aesthetics of the Law* (Chicago and London: The University of Chicago Press, 1999): 1–15, 9; Daniela Carpi, "Potere e legittimità in *King Lear, King John, Julius Caesar*," in *Iconologia del potere: rappresentazioni della sovranità nel Rinascimento*, eds. Daniela Carpi, Sidia Fiorato (Verona: Ombre Corte, 2011): 106–118, 109.

6 Costas Douzinas, "The Legality of the Image," *Modern Law Review*, 63.6 (2000): 813–830, 817.

7 Raffield, *Images and Cultures of Law*, 2–3.

8 Adriana Cavarero, *Stately Bodies. Literature, Philosophy and the Question of Gender* (Ann Arbor: University of Michigan Press, 2002), 99.

9 Mark Franko, *Dance as Text. Ideologies of the Baroque Body* (Cambridge: Cambridge University Press, 1993), 32.

At a jurisprudential level, "Calvin's case" in Plowden's *Reports* incorporated the conception of the king's two bodies into substantive law as the representation of the ordered state. The body natural of the king was

> subject to all Infirmities that come by Nature or accident, to the Imbecility of Infancy or Old Age, and to the like Defects that happen to the natural Bodies of other People. But his body politic is a Body that cannot be seen or handled, consisting of Policy and Government, and constituted for the Direction of the People, and the management of the public weal.[10]

The physical frailty of the body natural is transcended by the ethereality of the body politic, which cannot be seen or handled, but is represented through the image of the lawful authority of the state in a presentification of its ontological conception.[11] As Cavarero observes, politics curiously banishes the body from its foundational categories while it constantly figures its order precisely in terms of the metaphor of the body.[12] Actually, "the absence of systematic codification necessitated that common law manifested its corporeality in images other than texts"[13] and this seems to pave the way for a return of corporeality itself.

The Inns of Court regularly staged masque spectacles, whose allegories, music and dance were instrumental in the perception and acknowledgement of power and its incarnation,[14] and contributed to the creation of an elitist political conscience through the symbols, the images, the forms and representations of the law. Apart from the *corpus iuris*, the law requires for its own existence in history "a living body, who recites it and imposes it, as it possesses the keys to access it and reveal it."[15] The legal community of the Inns of Court was "the principal architect" in shaping and constructing the representations that were instrumental to the maintenance and perpetuation of the social order.

Within an aesthetic context, the sovereign's body natural was "transfigured in royal portraiture, where it became an icon: the monarch as *imago Dei*," and "lent visible, tangible form to the mystical basis of the law's authority."[16] This iconological system was however restricted to the sphere of the court and the no-

---

10 Edmund Plowden, *Commentaries or Reports* (London: Brooke, 1816), 212a.

11 See Raffield, *Images and Cultures of Law*, 57–58, and Cristina Costantini, "Representing Law: Narrative Practices, Poetic Devices, Visual Signs and the Aesthetics of the Common Law Mind," in *Liminal Discourses. Subliminal Tensions in Law and Literature*, eds. Daniela Carpi, Jeanne Gaakeer (Berlin: De Gruyter, 2013): 27–36.

12 See Cavarero, *Stately Bodies*, 7.

13 Raffield, *Images and Cultures of Law*, 58.

14 Cristina Costantini, "The Literature of Temple Bar," *Pólemos* 1 (2007): 169–178, 73.

15 Cristina Costantini, *La legge e il tempio* (Roma: Carocci, 2007), 21–22 (my translation).

16 Raffield, *Shakespeare's Imaginary Constitution*, 2.

bility. In the Early Modern period, playhouses were emerging as a parallel "visual context" which addressed large public audiences and could focus on a wide range of subject matter. As Raffield emphasises, sixteenth-century poetic drama proved capable of embodying "emergent political ideas through the synthesis of aural and visual imagery" and, at the same time, it staged the psychological complexities of the subject of law in the political context of the sovereign nation-state. The theatre became the seat for the dialogue of human ideas, for a communal relationship between audience and actors which relied on the poetic imagination as a vehicle that invited participation in its activities of both the legal and cultural imagination, and as the means to involve the subject within the narratives of the plays and of the law. According to Raffield, "English law provided a flexible juridical framework within which the intricacy and vibrancy of society could be expressed and regulated" in theatrical works; "[t]he performances in the Elizabethan playhouses mark the emergence of law from the formal arena of the legal institution into the imagistic and non-reverential sphere of the social and of the public."[17] At that time, theatre and law were evolving into increasingly secular institutions whose values and techniques were interchangeable.[18] The pervasive court-as-theatre metaphor referred to the theatricality of trials and to the emerging juridical structure of drama itself. Actually, the context of drama allows for the existence of multiple performative agencies and polyvocalities; it can stage aesthetically the effectiveness of legal normativity by rendering the social form and its codified roles manageable and tangible, but it can also expose society's fears and produce composite images of legal reality. Drama not only addresses but also exploits uncertainties and conflicts within legal procedure and discourse and can, within certain constraints, put into question the whole system. The poetics of Elizabethan power was indivisibly linked to a poetics of the theatre[19]; "figurative art speaks directly to the visual sense, but poetry also appeals to the visual imagination by its capacity to conjure pictures into the minds of its audience."[20]

The theatre becomes the privileged arena for the display of power and authority and the spectacle was experienced as a mediation and a representation of political reality; on the other hand, in a complementary relationship, the ju-

17 Raffield, *Shakespeare's Imaginary Constitution*, 8.

18 Dennis Kezar, introduction to *Solon and Thespis. Law and Theatre in the English Renaissance*, ed. Dennis Kezar (Notre Dame, Indiana: University of Notre Dame Press, 2007): 1–16, 2.

19 See Stephen Greenblatt, "Invisible Bullets: Renaissance Authority and its Subversion, *Henry IV* and *Henry V*," in *Political Shakespeare: Essays in Cultural Materialism*, eds. Jonathan Dollimore and Alan Sinfield (Manchester: Manchester University Press, 1994): 18–47, 44.

20 Raffield, *Shakespeare's Imaginary Constitution*, 1.

diciary and the state relied on the power of spectacle and were articulated in accordance with the registers of public performance.[21] In this context, the theatre undergoes a process of "aesthetic empowerment"[22] and enters into a dialectic relationship with the power it represents. If, as we suggested earlier, the law requires a *corpus* for its actualization which is both a physical *corpus* that "embodies" the law and a material corpus represented by the book of law,[23] it also needs a *corpus* over which it can exert its authority and control. The people of a community "embody" such a *corpus* in their behavior toward each other and their relationships (personal and/or professional) in everyday life.

In Early Modern England, the term "individual" suggests a series of relations "to a normative, pathological, or utterly elusive whole, or to other [...] parts, and to the range of symbolic structures that are based on those relations."[24] The tension between these body parts and corporeal wholes lies at the heart of social and symbolic structures. The family, conceived of as the mirror image of the state, was the foundation of the social status of its members; individuals were not perceived as having identities in themselves, but were subsumed into the one of the *pater familias*. They consequently belonged to a wider social dimension and became "epistemic fragment[s] in a collective message."[25] This is articulated on a bodily level through the establishment of a social body "finished, symmetrical, closed, its actions controlled and its dangerous passions contained"[26] in the crystallization of social norms.

The period is characterized by an "increased self-consciousness about the fashioning of human identity as a manipulable, artful process."[27] The verb "to fashion" indicates the forming of a self, and implies also the imposition of "a distinctive personality [...] a consistent mode of perceiving and behaving"[28]; it underlines outward appearance, the representation of a person's nature or intention in speech or actions. In the context of the court, where status depended

---

21 See Simon Barker, Hilary Hinds, "'The fashion of play-making': theatre, drama and society in Early Modern England," introduction to *The Routledge Anthology of Renaissance Drama*, eds. Simon Barker, Hilary Hinds (Routledge: London 2003): 1–13, 3.

22 Greenblatt, *Shakespearean Negotiations*, 4, 5, 40, 64.

23 Costantini, *La Legge e il tempio*, 215.

24 David Hillman, Carla Mazzio, "Individual parts," in *The Body in Parts: Fantasies of Corporeality in Early Modern Europe*, eds. Hillman, Mazzio (New York: Routledge, 2013): xi–xix, xv.

25 Skiles Howard, *The Politics of Courtly Dancing in Early Modern England* (Amherst: University of Massachussets Press, 1998), 2.

26 Howard, *The Politics of Courtly Dancing*, 49.

27 Stephen Greenblatt, *Renaissance Self-Fashioning. From More to Shakespeare* (Chicago and London: The University of Chicago Press, 1980), 2.

28 Greenblatt, *Renaissance Self-Fashioning*, 2.

upon display, the process of self-fashioning expressed the mastery of the court's social code, allowed participation in commonly accepted rituals, and implied the sharing of the values of a common culture. Such values were thus inscribed on the subject's body where they were preserved and at the same time transmitted; identity was created and communicated through the performance of the self, and became a discursive practice crucial to the negotiation of power relations, a visible and kinetic representation that was both internalized, and was also part of the social body. This process did not exhaust itself in a mere mirroring of political authority; there was a passage "back and forth in the production of mirror images"[29] through the persistent negotiation of social energy. The body becomes the focus of visual traces which produce, shape and organize collective physical and psychological experience, and at the same time it articulated the signs and structures of power and difference, reflecting social pressures and the potential for subversion.

The normative system of the law interposes

> a 'legal screen' between the subject and the social gaze, filtering the objects of vision and determining the way in which we see and are given to the world to be seen. The screen is a collection of authoritative images and material practices which offer a repertory of approved representations through which social identity is inscribed.[30]

Therefore, the "fleshy body" merges with "approved imagery" to form "the 'normative body' of the individual."[31] As Goodrich emphasises, "[a]t its strongest, the legal definition of the person (*ius personarum*) is determined by the theory of images as the form of human appearance, of human presence. The legal subject itself is in one respect to be understood or recognized as a visual fiction drawn upon the natural person."[32] In order to enter the realm of the law, it is necessary to be a legal subject, which involves by definition being both already a subject at law and wearing the mask, the sign, of the legal institution: it is only as a legal sign that one can enter the discourse of law. In instituting life, the law founds subjectivity as a place, a sign or a mark, from which the subject speaks. Without an appreciation of its visual and aesthetic forms, it is impossible to comprehend

---

29 Greenblatt, *Shakespearean Negotiations*, 8.
30 Costas Douzinas, "Sublime Law," *Parallax*, 14.4 (2008): 18–29, 18.
31 Douzinas, "Sublime Law," 18.
32 Peter Goodrich, "Specula Laws: Image, Aesthetic and the Common Law," *Law and Critique* 2.2 (1991): 233–254, 233.

the procedures by which Law as judgment and measure inscribes itself upon everyday life.[33]

Law has developed historically around figures of denial, prohibition and interdiction; juridical language aims at clearing reality of all its contradictions, reducing it to univocal categories, defined roles and behavior. However the repressed threatens inexorably to return and to expose what escapes the codification of the law, of what the law itself has repressed in order to impose its normative function on society and the subsequent creation of social individuals. "The threat of the repressed is [...] the threat of the unknown or, more precisely, the intimation of that which has not yet been determined, which is not mapped in advance by law's *regula* or calculus in the institutional form of knowledge as recognition."[34] The repressed presses against the barriers of consciousness and this leads, according to Goodrich, to a "displacement and deformation of that which could otherwise be reconstituted,"[35] a body and its drives.[36] The characteristic feature of the law is to set its own preconditions by inscribing and fixing the body in precise rules of conformity of manners and gestures, and by establishing clear-cut notions of identity. The suppressed intricacies of identity threaten to return as uncontrollable figures that will lead to a renegotiation of power by constantly threatening to undermine its binary structures and proving to be unassimilable forces.

'Woman' represents a particularly ambivalent juridical category within traditional Western discourse in view of her disruptive potential within the domain of the law. Women were allowed to perform in the masque, as they were essential for the legitimation of the patriarchal structure of society. Connected intrinsically with the body, women were considered bearers, and not creators, of allegorical significance. At the same time, however, their expressive force (conveyed precisely through their bodies) could be used to assert a feminine voice and the expression of a female identity instead of celebrating a patriarchal social order. In order to contain female self-fashioning and to maintain the patriarchal process of meaning creation, women were subjected to gendered performative codes.[37]

---

33 Goodrich, "Specula Laws," 235.

34 Peter Goodrich, *Oedipus Lex* (Berkeley: University of California Press, 1995), 13.

35 Goodrich, *Oedipus Lex*, 12.

36 Peter Goodrich, David Gray Carlson, "Introduction," in *Law and the Postmodern Mind*, eds. Peter Goodrich, David Gray Carlson (Ann Arbor: The University of Michigan Press, 1997): 1–12, 3.

37 See Clare McManus, *Women on the Renaissance Stage. Anna of Denmark and Female Masquing in the Stuart Court 1590–1619* (Manchester: Manchester University Press, 2002), 11.

The body on stage acquires different functions in its double dimension as both the body of the *dramatis persona* and the body of the performing actor, both furnishing considerable expressive potential. Theatre posits at the centre the body in all its meanings and conceptions; it is "an art of body and an art grounded in body,"[38] which becomes a site of negotiation. The body is shaped and made meaningful by culture whose structures and rules result in embodied practices. Parallel to the semiotic conception of the body which considers it as a symbolic and discursive object overdetermined by culture, phenomenological discourse considers culture as grounded in the human body. According to Merleau Ponty, individuals experience the world through perceptive awareness and the body comes to constitute our point of view on the world[39] (thus countering the Foucaldian vision of the body as a passive object, a material entity manipulated by institutions and structures of power). This embodied subjectivity sees the body not merely as a textual entity produced by discursive practices but as the active and perceptible vehicle of being. Onstage the body acquires multiple modalities of expression, it opens itself to play and display and at the same time enters the imaginative dimension of the audience: "[t]he performer/character's gaze [...] exceeds the containing parameters of representational space [...] Alone among the elements that constitute the stage's semiotic field, the body is a sign that looks back."[40] The subject thus opens itself to self-reinvention through play and display, in an art of bodily possibilities which is involved in social networks of established meaning and negotiations of power. Performance thus becomes the embodied enactment of cultural forces in the sense of "an engagement of social norms, [...] an ensemble of activities with the potential to uphold societal arrangements or, alternatively, to change people and societies."[41] Contemporary performance studies actually find their philosophical antecedent precisely in the Renaissance period, which vigorously expressed the idea of the

---

38 Simon Shepherd, *Theatre, Body and Pleasure* (New York: Routledge, 2006), 7.

39 See Maurice Merleau-Ponty, *Phenomenology of Perception* (London: Routledge, 2002), 94–95: "[t]he body is the vehicle of being in the world, and having a body is, for a living creature, to be intervolved in a definite environment, to identify oneself with certain projects and be continually committed to them. [... I]f it is true that I am conscious of my body via the world, that it is the unperceived term in the centre of the world towards which all objects turn their face, it is true for the same reason that my body is the pivot of the world."

40 Stanton B. Garner, *Bodied Spaces: Phenomenology and Performance in Contemporary Drama* (Ithaca: Cornell University Press, 1994), 49.

41 Jon McKenzie, *Perform or Else; From Discipline to Performance* (London and New York: Routledge, 2001), 30.

world as a stage, the *theatrum mundi:* "The world no longer appeared as a book to be read, but as a performance to participate in."[42]

The body thus enters the realm of the aesthetic through the articulation of identities by means of a language simultaneously written on the body and through the body: a performance act is interactional in nature and involves symbolic forms and the live bodies of a community. As Turner suggests, "if man is a sapient animal, [...] a symbol using animal, he is, no less, a performing animal, *homo performans*"[43] characterized by the urge for self-representation.[44] The turn to performance studies allows us to transcend the Foucauldian conception of the body as a passive object of discourses of power; "Our bodies cannot be understood as standing outside culture, as the ground or origin of our social identities. But that doesn't mean that bodies should therefore be understood as inert or passive surfaces on which culture inscribes its meanings."[45] Normativity creates a social dimension,[46] but at the same time it engenders the abjected, that is, it excludes the "bodies of those who define the limits of the norm by falling outside it."[47] Therefore, if the 'matter' or materiality of bodies is conceived as "an effect of power and signification, such that the matter of bodies will be indissociable from the regulatory norms that govern their materialization and the signification of those material effects,"[48] other bodies emerge, which claim their right to expression and to "matter" on their own terms. In this way, a mutual relationship is established between the dominant and its discursive other, which cannot be reduced to separate elements existing independently. "Just as the network of power relations ends by forming a dense web that passes through apparatuses and institutions, without being exactly localized in them, so too the swarm of points of resistance traverses social stratifications and individual unities."[49] Such points of resistance produce cleavages in a society, affecting the individuals and remolding them in their bodies and minds.

---

42 Richard Schechner, *Performance Studies: An Introduction* (London: Routledge, 2002), 19.
43 Victor Witter Turner, *The Anthropology of Performance* (New York: PAJ Publications, 1988), 81.
44 See Raffaele Cutolo, *Into the Woods of Wicked Wonderland* (Heidelberg: Winter, 2014), 56.
45 James Loxley, *Performativity* (New York: Routledge, 2006), 117.
46 See Loxley, *Performativity*, 121: "The various institutions and discourses that constitute the social are in Foucault's analyses instances of a productive or positive mode of power, and actually serve to constitute that which they merely claim to know."
47 Loxley, *Performativity*, 121.
48 Gill Jagger, *Judith Butler. Sexual Politics, Social Change and the Power of the Performative* (New York: Routledge, 2008), 54.
49 Michel Foucault, *History of Sexuality*, vol. 1. An Introduction, trans. Robert Hurley (New York: Pantheon Books, 1978), 96.

The normative body thus emerges as a fiction that falls apart in performance, where its ontological, social and political implications are investigated. By making reference to Greenblatt's questions "What is the effect of representation on the object or practice represented?" and "Above all, how is the social energy inherent in a cultural practice negotiated and exchanged?"[50] We can assert that the body that is culturally and socially embedded, and engaged with, on stage

> loses part of its earlier meaning and force, yet simultaneously gains new dimensions of signification, which, when the item is later again moved to its original zone, will not simply disappear. Indeed, having returned from the zone of the theatre, it may well have resulted in a complete re-articulation of the discursive subject that was acquired in the first place.[51]

Dramatic performance becomes a "performance of the threshold" which reveals the foundations of the community, the limits of its definition, and the extent of containment and control; "the liminal position of the theatre, which it shared with other forms of festivity, far from simply ventriloquizing the discourses of political domination, engaged in forms of representation through which other, potentially subversive voices could be heard."[52] With regard to this, we can adopt Punter's approach to the Gothic and apply it to the Renaissance *Weltanschauung:* "the law is a purified abstract whole [...] which can find no purchase in the doubled, creviced, folded world of the real by which it is in turn destined to be hunted."[53] The theatre stages the period's cultural anxieties and creates an "embodied mediation," in the sense that it stages "a transaction from physical bodies (including the Queen's Body) to aural representations, from phantasmatic characters to corporeal beings" and performs the presence of an absence.[54] This refers to a negotiation of the theorization of the body politic at all levels: juridico-theoretical in general as well as in the specific case of the sovereign's relationship with the judicial body; social in the questions about race; social and legal in the phenomenon of the witch hunt which called for an extension and adaptation of the law in order to include it, and familiar in the gendered construction of

---

50 Greenblatt, *Shakespearean Negotiations*, 11–12.
51 Jürgen Pieters, *Moments of Negotiations. The New Historicism of Stephen Greenblatt* (Amsterdam: Amsterdam University Press, 2001), 238.
52 John Drakakis, "Fashion it thus," in *Materialist Shakespeare*, ed. Ivo Kamps (London: Verso, 1995): 280–291, 282.
53 David Punter, *Gothic Pathologies. The Text, the Body and the Law* (Basingstoke: Macmillan, 1998), 2–3.
54 See Cristina Costantini's essay in the present volume.

women; iconological in the subversive staging of a female body politic. As Carpi asserts, the epistemological crisis of the Renaissance period expressed itself in the fragmentation and subversion of established discourses such as the organological metaphor of the body politic[55] and this in its turn is echoed through the different levels of Early Modern society. This is the perspective of the essays of the present volume, which contribute to the epistemological and legal debate of the period, and offers multiple aspects for further critical reflection. The topics addressed articulate themselves into the following theorical groups: the alien body (Neumeier, Tempera, Antor) also in its medical and legal articulations (Doerr), female sovereigns' bodies (Costantini, Fiorato, Velissariou), conceptions of the body politic (Raffield, Word, Baldissone), ontological liminality of the body (Carpi, Cutolo).

1 Trying "Other" Bodies: The Witch, the Black and the Old

Neumeier focuses on the witch's body as the site for the identification as well as for the enactment of transgressive desires. The works she takes into consideration are grounded in historical events such as the Witchcraft Act (1604), or witch trials such as those in Lancashire (1612[56] and 1634) and Edmonton (1621), and both underscore questions and implications related to the codification of the figure of the witch. The cases these works introduce focus on the cultural context which posited the witch as the symbol of female transgression and call for a negotiation of boundaries that establish the identity of the community. Proceeding chronologically, from Shakespeare's *Macbeth* to Middleton's *The Witch*, to Rowley, Dekker and Ford's *The Witch of Edmonton* and Heywood and Brome's *The Late Lancashire Witches*, Neumeier observes a progressive humanization of the witches which intensifies the focus on the body as the site of illicit sexual practices and the material space for punishment and control. Starting from a religious perspective, the works progressively assume a medical and

---

55 See Daniela Carpi, "Renaissance into Postmodernism: Anticipations of Legal Unrest," in *Liminal Discourses. Subliminal Tensions in Law and Literature*, eds. Carpi, Gaakeer: 177–189, 180.

56 The first English confession of a direct contract with the devil occurs in the 1612 trial in Lancashire. (See Clive Holmes, "Popular Culture? Witches, Magistrates, and Divines in Early Modern England," in *Understanding Popular Culture: Europe from the Middle Ages to the Nineteenth Century*, ed. Steven L. Kaplan (Berlin: Mouton, 1984): 85–111, 101).

legal one, and determine "a gradual shift towards an exploration of the witch's body as a readable sign"; from within this context, however, there remains an insistence "on the continuous threat of a transgressive and transformative monstrosity which cannot be contained."[57]

The first text that Neumeier considers is Shakespeare's *Macbeth* (1606), where the witches have a pivotal albeit ambiguous role; the tragedy focuses on the effects of their predictions, which affect the political and legal discourses of the play, as they prompt an act of treason and consequently provoke an imbalance in the body politic and its social order, while their motivations remain obscure. The witches remain distant from the human world, closed and inscrutable in their unreadable difference which seems to secure the boundaries between the supernatural and the human. Their ambiguity seems to require a displacement of the corporeal onto Lady Macbeth as agency in order to propel the action; however the woman's attempt at attaining their status as the fourth witch and Macbeth's own parallel attempt at metamorphosing himself into a devil provoke bodily dismemberment and mental fragmentation.

Middleton's *The Witch* is a tragicomedy which underlines the similarities between witches and humans who share the same sexual desires. The witches are portrayed as ordinary women of all ages and classes and they become examples of anarchic tendencies rather than of *maleficium*, although they do perform magic rituals. They seem to become the locus for the displacement of the desires and fears of the society of the court, as they are solicited by all characters for their charms and interventions in the human sphere in order to attain and /or maintain social position and power. Actually, Middleton relied on Scot's *Discoverie* as a source, a treatise which heretically located witchcraft belief "not in but as the imagination";[58] in his text, the witches still escape codification and are not called to account for their actions; they remain separated from the human world (they do not manifest themselves in human contexts, but the characters go in search of them), as they suggest the possible uncanny interference and penetration of boundaries between the two domains.[59]

---

57 See Neumeier's essay in the present volume.

58 Stephen Greenblatt, "Shakespeare Bewitched," in *New Literary Study: Essays on Reproducing Texts, Representing History*, eds. Jeffrey N. Cox, Larry J. Reynolds (Princeton: Princeton University Press, 1993): 108–135, 114.

59 Middleton's work was influenced by the recent events at the English court, in particular the murder by poison of Sir Thomas Overbury and the plot between the Countess of Essex and several cunning people to make her husband impotent, so that she might gain a divorce and marry her lover.

As Neumeier points out, the witch becomes concretized during the trials, where she is transformed from "imaginary/literary to literalized."[60] *The Witch of Edmonton* (1621) is grounded in the historical event of the trial and execution of Elizabeth Sawyer in the same year. Neumeier underlines how the play presents, and at the same time reflects upon, the authority of the law, raising questions about the legal power of verifying the truth, through fostering an interrogation of notions of witnessing and confession. Witchcraft and the law both rely on the power of language in connection to ritualized procedures. Only the return to a firm belief in the word of the law seems to be able to counter the spreading of evil. The empirical focus of the legal process is on the body of the accused, which is codified to incarnate transgressive behaviour and its punishment.

The Late Lancashire Witches (1634) is grounded upon the historical Lancashire trial of the same year. The witches are women firmly anchored in society and they prove capable of inflicting chaos and acting out their own desires (in particular transgressive sexual desires). The legal perspective focuses on the liter(e)ality of the witch as a precondition for court procedures. On the one hand, the witches are rendered less powerful than Shakespeare's weird sisters in order for them to be punishable; on the other hand, their demonic attributes affirm their difference and justify their expulsion from society. The body is still at the centre of the legal investigation first in the search for the evil mark, then, and most importantly, when its harming (for example the cutting of a paw/hand) enacts a reversal in the witch's nature and her return into her human body that can then be punished. The play ends once again underlining the superiority of the law, in the face of which the satanic power dissolves.

Tempera's essay shifts these legal perspectives and enlists as evidence the performances of the victim's bodies. She focuses on Potts' *The Wonderfull Discoverie of Witches in the Countie of Lancaster* (1612), a collection of legal documents (interspersed with dialogical moments) relating to trial procedures denouncing the activities of village witches. The relevant aspect of this text is the inclusion of victims' statements, that underline how their bodies have become affected by the *maleficium*; some of them no longer bear the traces of the physical suffering which is however evoked in physical terms such as the inability to quench one's thirst, or the suddenness of being taken ill. Others call the court's attention to their permanent disabilities, becoming real bodies of evidence and eliciting the audience's and the jury's sympathy. In this way the theatrical aspect of trials emerges, where the performance of a social evil takes place (actually, all allegations of wasting diseases could be attributed to the consequences of famine, epi-

60 Shamas, *We Three*, 92.

demics, or the vulnerability of children to illness). In particular the attention here shifts from the body of the supposed witch to the victim's body, to find trace of the effects of the *maleficium*. The major accusation pinpoints the victims' loss of strength creating the image of a languishing body which is allegorised as the suffering body politic. As Tempera observes, "The attack of the witches on the body natural of even the lowliest of the king's subjects is an attack on the body politic of the king: the private losses of the relatives of the individual victims are all subsumed under the king's loss of subjects."[61] This provoked and sanctioned harsh punishment in order to heal the body politic and make it whole again, and took place in connection within a displaced version of Paracelsus' medical paradigm: the theorization of the porousness of the human body consequently rendered it vulnerable to external attacks, and this increased the fear of witches.

Antor's analysis of Shakespeare's *Othello* focuses on the codification and negotiation of alterity through bodily attributes. Iago both epitomizes and underlines the inscrutability and unreliability of the body as a signifier, and perceives it in its ambiguous complexity as a means to attain his aims. By discursively acting upon bodies, he manages to submit them to processes of fashioning and in this way to act upon and determine the image of the characters' identity. At the opening of the tragedy, Iago underlines Othello's negative otherness through his physical trait of blackness, which inescapably defines him as evil and unnatural, and associates him with animality and moral inferiority in the context of white Venetian society. Iago contributes also to the stigmatization of gender alterity by associating Desdemona with animal imagery, in order to debase her status and emphasise the unnaturalness of miscegenation. In this first scene, however Iago merely amplifies Venetian attitudes; as a matter of fact, through their secret marriage, the two characters commit an act of rebellion against the acknowledged order of patriarchal society. Othello's threat to the Venetian body politic is iconologically symbolized by his possession in marriage of Desdemona's white body in a grave, and allegedly magical infringement of the laws of nature.

However, Desdemona removes Othello's body from the centre of attention when she emphasises his moral qualities; she loves Othello not in spite of but because of his alterity, as Antor underlines. Desdemona performs her role beyond the bounds of gender decorum and becomes the spokeswoman of a new aesthetic conception, while simultaneously articulating a transition from aes-

61 See Tempera's essay in the present volume.

thetic to ethical beauty.[62] As Drakakis observes, Brabantio is characterized by the fear of loss of patriarchal control,[63] which is manifest in a loss of linguistic control. His dream, that is, the unconscious patriarchal fear of miscegenation, does not receive redress but the problem remains ambiguously understated. The trial scene in the opening act of the play concludes ambiguously when the Duke resorts to the terms "fair" and "black" as moral epithets; his play on the semantic instability of the terms seems to confirm the unresolved cognitive dichotomy between black/evil and white/fair/good. He seems to play with bodily signifiers in the same way as Iago, and in conclusion leaves them suspended.

Iago's self-fashioning relies on a conception of the body as a devious tool for the realization of his plans; already in the first act, almost in an act of self-denunciation, he actually declares "I am not what I am" (1.1.64). In the course of the tragedy he often (and ironically) tells Othello that bodies and bodily outward appearances can deceive, and bases his allegations on Desdemona's behaviour in rejecting her father's control. During the trial scene, Othello had tried to base his defence upon the coincidence between his inner and outer aspect "My parts, my title, my perfect soul shall manifest me rightly" (1.2.31–1–32), but, Iago manages to subvert his mental categories and to direct him into his own distorted vision of reality. Othello's attempts at reading Desdemona's body are guided by Iago's perception of the body as an unreliable signifier, whose interpretive openness is turned against Desdemona herself. In a shifting of planes, Othello fully interiorised his ensign's normalization of anti-black xenophobic stereotypes and fears of miscegenation, which become the lens through which he reads his wife and believes the allegation of her possible infidelity with Cassio. Othello's attitude is epitomized in the final scene of the tragedy when Desdemona's body comes centre-stage as the symbol of the discrepancy between appearance and reality, the "cunning'st pattern of excelling nature" (5.2.11). In the final disclosure of Iago's responsibility for, and orchestration of, the whole course of events, the categories of othering become blurred and the moral valorization of skin colour and physical attributes are put into question. The fact that the white Iago is revealed as the author of "the heathenish, satanic and therefore

---

62 See Daniela Carpi, "Law and Aesthetics in *Othello*," in *Le Cabinet du Curieux. Culture, Savoirs, Religion de l'Antiquité à l'Ancien Régime*, eds. Witold Konstanty Pietrzak, Magdalena Kożluk (Paris: Classiques Garnier, 2013): 79–90.

63 John Drakakis, "Il sogno di Bramanzio: *Othello* e il potere del patriarcato," in *Iconologia del Potere*, eds. Carpi, Fiorato: 141–163, 144.

'black' plan" lays bare "the ambivalence of conceptualizing categories of identity and alterity in an Early Modern world of growing racial and ethnic diversity."[64]

Doerr focuses her analysis on Jonson's interest in the body as the site for legal and physical inquiry. The protagonist of Jonson's *Volpone* is portrayed by means of his feigned legal and physical frailty; his heirless status and his advanced age would render him prey to the claims of many suitors who try to comply with his requests in order to be officially declared his heirs. The activity of the potential heirs is articulated within a legal and medical perspective, which strictly focuses on bodily exploitment and analysis; Corbaccio seeks the restoration of his bygone youth and he seems to draw strength from Volpone's perceived weakness. Corvino agrees to offer Volpone his own wife as a cure for his malady, thus subjecting her disempowered body to patriarchal violence and control. Celia refuses to comply with her husband's wishes even in the face of the threat of physical danger and humiliation in order to maintain her moral integrity and this event leads to a trial scene in which Volpone stands accused of rape. Volpone's body, described as aged, bed-ridden and weak, becomes the site of the investigation and the agency for the falsification of the report that leads to his initial acquittal. In an attitude parallel to Corbaccio's, Voltore seems to draw his judicial strength from Volpone's weakness and feigned incapacity to speak for himself.

The final unmasking of Volpone's lies allows the performative punitive action of the law to be exercised upon the culprit's bodies in ways redolent of the Dantesque *contrappasso* which replicates men's crimes on their bodies.

2 Codification of the Body Politic and Common Law Jurisprudence

Raffield explores the use and the development of the metaphor of the human anatomy as a representation of the State, as well as of the relationship between governor and governed, in Early Modern English jurisprudence. He underlines how in such context there emerged a hybrid image of the body politic derived from classical and biblical texts emphasising natural law theory and Judaeo-Christian jurisprudence;[65] a juridical line of thought from Fortescue to Coke

---

64 See Antor's essay in the present volume. It can be observed that Iago tries to project upon others his own black and perverted personality and in so doing puts under discussion fixed aesthetic codifications of identities.

65 See Raffield, "Contract, Classicism, and the Common-Weal," 73: "The resultant literary constitution became indissolubly associated with common law orthodoxy [...] The Reports are there-

(with its roots from Aristotle and Cicero) asserts the divine provenance of laws and their source in natural law as facets of the common law. In the light of this theoretical background, Raffield reflects upon the balance between temporal and spiritual powers, and the constitutional relationship between governor and governed. Kantorowicz traces the mystical nature of the king's two bodies as the basis of Elizabethan juridical thought in Fortescue's works, as well as in Plowden's earlier texts. However, instead of supporting the connection between two widely separated works which ascribe the continuity over time of the body politic to its similarity with angelic nature, Raffield reverses the connection and argues that spiritual imagery provided the means through which temporal objectives were attained. In particular, the poetic imagination of the judiciary was instrumental in establishing and spreading the constitutional theory of limited monarchy. In his *De Dominio* (1715), Fortescue links the idea of the mystical quality of the figure of the king to his capacity for good and therefore his obligation to act at all times in the interests of *res publica*. In Raffield's opinion, Kantorowicz ignored Fortescue's fundamental tenet of the parity between "regal" and "political," and his secular turn in his assertion that ideal kingship is predicated upon *dominium politicum et regale*, rather than on *dominium regale* alone. By "political" Fortescue does not imply only the authority of the Parliament, but also the judiciary, thus theorizing something approaching supreme constitutional authority. This conception of monarchy is antithetical to the theory of mystical kingship, i.e., of a monarch endowed with divine and irrefutable power, expounded by Richard II and his Tudor (and early Stuart) successors. Actually, Raffield observes how Richard II's emphasis on the divinity of kingship "must be seen to a great extent as a response to the various rebellions and incursions upon the royal prerogative, which threatened his reign and eventually led to his deposition"[66] in 1399. Kantorowicz's statement of the commitment of Elizabethan judges of the common law to the theory of the king's two bodies is belied by the fact that they actually followed the doctrine of equity, which is directed to the ideal good of society. As a proof of the power of the judiciary, Raffield reports how, contrary to the identification of the body natural with the body politic of the king as expressed in the concept that *Rex* is *Lex loquens*, and which characterized Charles I's royal conception, in 1649, the parliament tried, convicted, and sentenced to death "the king's body natural without affecting se-

---

fore of unique semiotic importance, demonstrating the manipulative power of the image to effect the attachment of the subject to the legal institution."

66 See Raffield's essay in the present volume.

riously or doing irreparable harm to the King's body politic."[67] Through these elements Raffield emphasises how the image of the body was crucial to the development of the idea of the State, whether that State was conceived in exclusively temporal or spiritual terms, or as a combination of both.

Ward focuses on the constitutional relevance of the character of Lord Chief Justice in Shakespeare's *Henry IV, part 2.* In *Henry IV, part 1,* he had imprisoned Prince Hal for violent assault; after the king's death, he has to justify his decision before the newly crowned king. The Lord Chief justice's defence is based on the common law doctrine of constitutional sovereignty and on the well known distinction between the public and private body of the king. He says that when exercising his functions, he acted as a representative of the King's justice and that the Prince's misbehaviour had been directed at King's public image. According to this principle, if Hal now seeks vengeance, he will undermine the very law upon which his own authority is ultimately based. The young King acknowledges his mistake, recognizes the importance of their respective offices and re-invests the Lord Chief Justice in his function as the administrator of the law. In a magisterial jurisprudential and performative exchange of reciprocal investiture, the new King pledges himself to a *dominium politicum et regale* over *dominium regale.* He openly commits himself to summoning the parliament and to choosing noble counsel. The common weal is here presented as distinct from its embodiment in the king and at the end of the play the newly crowned Henry V acknowledges the law as an embodiment of his royal authority. In the subsequent play *Henry V,* the king tells Katharine that "nice customs curtsy to great kings" (5.2.3252), thus showing how the king is both above the law and the guarantor of its authority.

Baldissone focuses on Ethienne De La Boétie's *On Voluntary Servitude* (probably written in 1548 and circulated in various posthumous editions from 1574 onwards) and emphasises its original and radical construction of the relation between nature, body and power. Power is seen by Boetie as the result of a series of practices in which one body is put at the service of another. By reiterating their commitment, the donors become subjects and exemplify the power of the tyrant (a word that La Boétie uses to indicate any wicked ruler) as a paradoxical effect of the will of his subjects. La Boétie emphasises the unnatural character of the popular will claiming that subjects continue to offer their bodies and the products of their bodily activities out of habit, as if their servitude were part of a natural human condition. As Baldissone observes, the appeal to

67 Ernst H. Kantorowicz, The *King's Two Bodies. A Study in Medieval Political Theology* (Princeton: Princeton University Press, 1957), 23.

nature opens a gap between the supposed natural human inclination – actually La Boétie presupposes an originary human freedom into which all are born – and the actual practice of millions of men carrying the burden of subjection not by force, but under the spell, as it were, of the name of just one man – while the rejection of the status of servitude would likewise be the result of a mere act of will.[68]

Many scholars have criticized LaBoetie's treatise on the grounds that he does not investigate the ultimate consequences of passive resistance, nor propose a description of a just state according to his belief in the possibility of a power which does not imply the servitude of its subjects. Baldissone goes beyond La Boetie's polemical analysis of the mechanisms of power, perceiving how he actually offers an alternative to the absolute organization of the despot in a plural collective subject, "which he describes with his astounding neologism *tous uns* [all ones]. This grammatical pluralization of the One produces a different subjectivation path, which is immune to the spell of the Western *reductio ad unum*, both in its monarchical and democratic version."[69] The shift of the source of political authority to the seemingly powerless (although in negative and self-defeating terms) grounds La Boetie's disregard for the notion of the divine origin of sovereignty (in modern terms) and his analysis of a non-theological construction of political power. Moreover, he does not conceive of servitude and domination as enduring entities or permanent conditions, but as relations that have to be constantly reconfirmed, because they are the effect of iterated practices.

3 Liminal Bodies: The Life/Death Edge on Stage and in the Body Politic

Carpi's essay focuses on the concept of power in *Julius Caesar* and on the problem of legality/legitimacy in relation to the threat of tyranny; Caesar's emergence as sole ruler, and his identification with Roman government threatens to upset

---

68 With regard to this, see Josè Gil, *Metamorphoses of the Body* (Minneapolis: The University of Minnesota Press, 1998), 20: "In the final analysis, "voluntary servitude" contains belief that only brings about subjection because a pseudosubjection brings about belief. It is not an "appearance" that is offered up as reality, an "illusion of freedom" that comes from the outside to entrap an individual or a group. But the conditions of production of the appearance that invite allegiance should be such that they oblige the subject to become him or herself producer of the appearance, only to be all the better subjected, rather than to be reduced to vulnerable passivity."

69 See Baldissone's essay in the present volume.

the balance in the body politic. As Carpi observes, the rhetorical strategies of Brutus and Marc Antony, when they appear after the assassination of Caesar, is connected with a very contemporary theme, namely the manipulation of the masses. The theme of rejection and rebellion is interwoven with the problem of sedition and with the process of securing the consent of the masses in order to attain legitimation.

Brutus's oration focuses on abstract values and rational argument; he appeals to an abstract love of Roman republican institutions, and underlines the value of liberty, but he "joins them to no story of the nation, no particular symbols or memories around which people's passions might crystallize."[70] As Carpi elsewhere argues, "the link between cultural beliefs, ideals and values and the law cannot be undervalued and dispensed with."[71] If Brutus justifies Caesar's death exclusively in terms of a benefit to the body politic, Antony emphasises the laceration of the body politic, and the anxiety it produces. He appeals to the Roman populace's emotions and chooses to emphasise his personal affection for the man Caesar, "for the fallen leader, seen not as an abstraction but as a unique embodied individual."[72] At this point, the forms of verbal communication are augmented and strengthened by non-verbal means of communication, such as body language and proxemics, thus demonstrating Antony's skill as a consummate orator.

Antony posits Caesar's murder as a political fact[73] but he reinterprets the meaning of the assassination. He chooses to speak through Caesar's body, giving voice to Caesar's wounds, as symbols of the wounded body politic; in so doing, he attains a "physical and verbal fusion with the corpse."[74] It is as if "the opened body of Caesar summons Antony to enter and occupy it, to speak for it"[75] in a

---

70 Martha C. Nussbaum ""Romans, Countrymen, and Lovers": Political Love and the Rule of Law in *Julius Caesar*," in *Shakespeare and the Law. A Conversation among Disciplines and Professions*, eds. Bradin Cormack, Martha C. Nussbaum, Richard Strier (Chicago and London: The University of Chicago Press, 2013): 256–281, 263, and 256: "Brutus prefers emotions resolutely fixed on an abstract object, which reason can justify and commend."

71 Carpi, "Potere e legittimità in *King Lear, King John, Julius Caesar*," 107.

72 Nussbaum, "Romans, Countrymen and Lovers," 263.

73 Differently from Brutus, whose argument is a self-referential construct, Antony does not present and/or sustain a political programme, nor does he incite violence against the conjurors: he focuses on the unsettling gravity of the corpse. (See Daniel Juan Gil, "'Bare Life.' Political Order and the Specter of Anti-social Being in Shakespeare's *Julius Caesar*," in *William Shakespeare's Julius Caesar*, ed. Harold Bloom (New York: Infobase Publishing, 2010): 147–162).

74 Lloyd Davis, "Embodied Masculinity in Shakespeare's *Julius Caesar*," in *William Shakespeare's Julius Caesar*, ed. Bloom: 115–130, 126.

75 Gil, "Bare Life," 150.

material expression of the body politic. Carpi underlines how Antony's oration transfigures itself and becomes a disembodied logos through its focus on corporeal detail; first his toga, symbol of his military success and now lacerated, then his wounds, each of which is assigned the name of one of the assassins and which gape wide in silent speech, and finally the blood, still flowing from the wounds. This transition initiates a process of sacralization of Caesar's body, which loses its materiality, transcends its finite corporeality and becomes "a body purified by death, sanctified by intentions, salvific in its outcome of sacrifice for the common good."[76] Antony uses the power of the theatre to perform an act of metaphoric totalisation in which Caesar's spirit symbolizes the greatness of Rome[77]; from this perspective, the body politic is shown to transcend the limitations of the body natural and incorporates into itself the entire Roman populace.

Cutolo's essay underlines the original Shakespearean exploration of the unstable boundary of the life/death opposition in plays such as *Romeo and Juliet*, and *Cymbeline*. This issue is connected to Shakespeare's ongoing interest in the analogy between sleep and death which in these plays permits the postulation of a liminal state. Cutolo starts by observing how Hamlet's monologue challenges the Cartesian conception of man as a mind-body duality and the termination of the *res cogitans* in death; Hamlet's words imply a continuity of human consciousness as "in that sleep of death [...] dreams may come" (3.1.65). Such dreams point to an existential after-life and thus to an equivalence between being and doing, between the existential and the active. "The 'figure in words' of the sleep-death duality realizes itself as a 'figure in action – and situation.'[78] Shakespeare here creates and exploits the dramatic and imaginative possibilities of a renowned literary *topos*.

Through the performance of phenomenological death, Shakespeare moves between ontology and phenomenology. His two characters Juliet and Imogen are and are not dead/alive at the same time, thus achieving the unity of to be *and* not to be through their motionless bodies. The Shakespearean state of apparent death creates and reaches a new in-between state that is immanent and transcendent at the same time; through a process of temporary disembodiment, the self reaches a metaphysical dimension which blurs the distinction between what *is* and what *appears*, between what is known and what is unknowable. This dimension recalls the inner abandonment of the poetical journey towards

76 See Carpi's essay in the present volume.
77 Betteridge, *Shakespearean Fantasy and Politics*, 119
78 Meera Sushila Viswanathan, *Exploring Shakespeare: The Dynamics of Playmaking* (New Delhi: Orient Longman Private Limited, 2005), 37.

the divine origin of the self, with a new appreciation and understanding of the theatrical imagination, and its capacity to produce art.

4 Staging the Queenly Body: The Performance of a Female Body Politic

Costantini analyzes the subtle link between Queen Elizabeth's corporeality and sovereignty as instrumental for the juridical imagination of a national past and the creation of English national identity. As Raffield observes, following the Act of Supremacy, the authority of crown and state became coextensive and "common law acquired much of the jurisdiction previously associated with ecclesiastical law."[79] The theorization of the presence of the body of law or *corpus iuris* recalled Eucharistic recognition; "as authority moved from church to state, from theology to jurisprudence, so presence was predicated not on the recognition of deity but on the recognition of the body politic"[80] as *verba visibilia*. Costantini presents another implication of this analogy, one that exploits religious imagery in order to reinforce English jurisprudential claims. The transubstantiation of the flesh into the body of sovereignty recalls the Christian dogma and is based on a possible division between self-presentation (the ways in which Royalty and Queenship were portrayed and promoted by the sovereign herself and the court) and re-presentation (the figurative and narrative presentation of the image of authority) in a theo-political re-reading and reinterpretation of the concept of the king's two bodies.

Costantini's assumption is that Elizabeth's natural and physical body was transfigured not only into a sovereign political body, but also into a theological *katéchon* and thus represented one of the most significant foundations of the ancient English constitution. Her virginal flesh was transformed into a salvific body: in the context of the assertion of the early Christianization of Britain and the illegitimate usurpation by the Bishop of Rome of the power of the English crown, Elizabeth came to represent the godly force providentially destined to fight the Antichrist (the assumed universality of the Church of Rome) and at the same time defined a precise geopolitics of power. In this way, the history of the Common Law jurisdiction was transfigured into a nationalized sacred ontology. The inclusive depiction of the Sovereign Body within the pages of the Henrician and Elizabethan Bible marked the undivided integrity of the two *corpora iuris*

79 Raffield, *Images and Cultures of Law*, 1.
80 Raffield, *Images and Cultures of Law*, 15.

(the secular and the divine law) as the main figuration and defence of the autonomous jurisdiction of the English Tradition. Actually Foxe associated Elizabeth with the emperor Constantine, who established the union of Church and Empire in the name of true Christianity. Costantini highlights how "[t]he body of law is shaped by an indissoluble concurrence of ontological questions, aesthetical responses and narrative accounts." Representations and performances connect the present to an actual and imagined past, mingling images from different sources (classical and religious) that act upon the body as the theatre for the encounter of autonomous discursive fields (in particular from theology to law) and upon its transfiguration into the body of sovereignty as the theatre for contending political and theological interests. "The wise and learned composition of claims and pretensions forged a new order (both political and juridical) by heralding Elizabeth as a godly champion, defender of the nation and founder of the English Empire, within whose boundaries the theatricalization of monarchy was combined with a history of salvation."[81]

Fiorato's essay focuses on Queen Anna of Denmark and her significance as a queen consort who, after the forty-four-year reign of a single female monarch (Elizabeth I), introduced a royal duality and a royal "other" in the monarchical constituency. King James I's patriarchal body politic codified the dependent status of his queen by incorporating her into the monarchical political ideology, thus emphasising the question of gender. However, Anna refused a purely symbolic role and appropriated the artistic genre of the masque in order to articulate her own independent conception of queenship. In this context she was able to exploit and anticipate many elements of performance theory, the most important of which was the privileged visuality of the body on stage and its implications. In order to understand the importance of her attainment, it is necessary to reflect on the masque tradition that confronted Anna when she opened the stage to female performance. The Inns of Court masques traditionally represented women negatively, as the antithesis of law and reason; by exploiting the bifurcation of the interpretation of images into icons and idols, the positive depiction of masculine archetypes posited the ordered structure of law. Raffield observes how this provided a means of understanding the law through its exceptions but also highlights how in a period founded upon female subordination, the prevalent female presence in the masque provided a powerful image of the potential for disruption of the status quo. This attitude responded to the need of strengthening the iconic signs of institutional authority by vividly depicting and contrast-

81 See Costantini's essay in the present volume.

ing images of reason and anti-reason.[82] In my opinion, this characteristic foregrounds the female potential for subversion which will be later exploited by Queen Anna.

As a matter of fact, the queen's active engagement in masques strove to articulate a specific political plan. By opening the masque stage to noblewomen she codified a female body politic, whose members were formed by the women of her court. In *The Vision of the Twelve Goddesses* she entered the stage as Bel-Anna, thus creating a character to signify her queenship (with an actual enthronement on stage) and in *Cupid's Banishment*, she substituted the absent King as privileged spectator and addressee of the masque. In the latter case, the masque sanctioned the existence of a separate Queen's court at Greenwich, the establishment of female rule and of an independent female body politic. It can therefore be asserted that Anna attained the creation of her own queenly identity through performance, defined as a cultural practice that "conservatively reinscribe[s] or passionately reinvent[s] the ideas, symbols and gestures that shape social life."[83] Even if Anna did not and could not concretely alter her position at King James's court, she managed to appropriate the rituals which should have imposed a gendered identity on her person and use them in order to assert her own difference. She managed to subvert the sanctioned female performative acts and attain the dimension of a "body that matters" according to her own system of value.

Velissariou analyses female rulers in Jacobean tragedies within the context of Jacobean gendered sexual politics and shows how female desire and sexual transgression – although finally punished – facilitate the powerful emergence of the resistant female subject and reveal the permeability of the body politics to interior and exterior disruption.

Whereas Elizabeth I had subsumed her body natural to her body politic, and through her virginity had symbolized the immutability and impenetrability of the body politic, the female protagonists of the Jacobean tragedies disprove the utility of such a union, showing instead how "the unity of the natural and mystical bodies of a king posed a danger to the state: the identification of the two implied the disintegration of the body politic,"[84] as it exposed the vulnerability of the king's natural body.

---

82 See Raffield, *Images and Cultures of Law*, 148–150.

83 Elin Diamond, "Introduction," to *Performance and Cultural Politics*, ed. Elin Diamond (New York: Routledge, 1996): 1–14, 2.

84 Rebecca Bushnell, *Tragedies of Tyrants: Political Thought and Theatre in the English Renaissance* (Ithaca: Cornell University Press, 1990), 38–39, quoted in Velissariou in the essay in the present volume.

Webster's Duchess of Malfi is a noblewoman who emphasizes the natural power of her body and articulates through it her own two-bodied concept of status. She rules the duchy in her capacity as regent for her young son, therefore her authority derives from her once pregnant body, a literalization of two bodies in the construction of governance which links her role to that underpinned by the philosophy of the king's two bodies. This first characteristic posits the political resonance of the female pregnant body, which the duchess manages to transcend in order to transform herself from regent, ruling for her son, to regnant, ruling in her own right.[85] Velissariou emphasises how, relying on her position of power, the duchess chooses to assert her independent corporeality through the free expression of her sexuality against familial and dynastic interests; she chooses to marry below her status, thus allowing the private claims of her body natural to prevail over the public claims of her body politic, and also subverting the period's established primacy of the husband/head over the wife/body in the family context (which mirrored the state structure). Her decision implies a divorce of her natural body from her political body; her private marriage exists simultaneously with her public life as a ruler but it remains separate and hidden from it. In this way, her private life emerges as constitutive of subjectivity, but as it is the subjectivity of a political ruler, this situation also implies the construction of "a shadowy body politic that improperly duplicates the proper one, since it coincides with her bedroom and with the night," as Velissariou observes. However, the duchess' re-gendering of marital roles disrupts the patriarchal social order; for this reason, her body natural finally suffers public punishment and becomes "crystallised in its death."

Velissariou proceeds in her analysis to demonstrate how Beaumont and Fletcher's Evadne in *The Maid's Tragedy* and Chapman's Tamyra in *Bussy d'Ambois* undermine the image of the body of the king as the "social plenum" that demands dependency and incorporation as the subject's only available position.

---

85 See Sid Ray, *Mother Queens and Princely Sons: Rogue Madonnas in the Age of Shakespeare* (New York: Palgrave Macmillan, 2012), 71 and 74: "as the regent for the Amalfi duchy, the duchess functions as both a 'head' and a 'body', just as she functions as a keeper if both the body natural and the body politic. When she was married to the former duke, now deceased, she was the 'body' to the 'head'. In that role, she gave birth to her son, who will rule the duchy when he comes of age. Until that time, however, she is both her son's and the duchy's head. She is therefore a ruler who integrates the head and the body, which were so oddly separated and hierarchized in Early Modern political discourse. Her authority is not based on the grotesque image of a disembodied head but rather on the powerful image of a maternal superbody. Thus the duchess offers a different model of governance from the absolute monarchical model; her model is feminine, whole, capacious and regenerative, a corporate entity where head and body work together cohesively."

Evadne commits tyrannicide on stage by profiting from the collapse of the king's body politic into his corrupted body natural because of his uncontrollable sexual indulgence; through a performance of female sexual desire, she penetrates the male body, stabbing and therefore symbolically raping and killing the King. Her resistance to her own objectification and loss of honour relies on the corruptibility and desecration of the king's body natural; however, her subversive act is finally contained by being presented as a means to secure patriarchal power on the part of her brothers.

Sexual transgression enacts female resistance against a double subjection, both to the patriarchal power of the husband and to the political power of the prince, and for this reason is considered a public crime, the equivalent of treason, punished through (public) torture and death.[86] The wife's assertion of power against her husband is understood in relation to the subject's assault upon the sovereign's power; whatever attacks the law of the sovereign also attacks him physically, since the force of the law is the force of the prince. The crime is imprinted on the subject's body, thus rendering legible and allowing the display of the state's power over that body through physical punishment, in an analogy with the procedure applied to the witches' bodies, as analyzed by Neumeier and Tempera.

The description of the essays contained in the present volume demonstrates how the body is positioned centre-stage in the Elizabethan and Jacobean period as the ideological focus of the articulation of power and, at the same time, as a repertoire of infinite (cultural and historical) possibilities.

---

86 See Foucault, *Discipline and Punish*, 55: "If torture was so strongly embedded in legal practice, it was because it revealed truth and showed the operation of power. It assured the articulation of the written on the oral, the secret on the public, the procedure of investigation on the operation of confession; it made it possible to reproduce the crime on the visible body of the criminal; in the same horror, the crime had to be manifested and annulled. The nature of the threat posed by the criminal can only be intensified when the crime is a crime against the aristocratic body itself."

I Trying “Other” Bodies: The Witch, the Black and the Old

Beate Neumeier

(Disciplining) Monstrous Renaissance Bodies: Staging the Witch

"The monstrous body, more than an object, is a shifter, a vehicle that constructs a web of interconnected and yet potentially contradictory discourses about his or her embodied self."[1] The monstrous as "embodied difference" (Rosi Braidotti) or "boundary creature" (Haraway)[2] evokes a disconcerting ambivalence between the de- and restabilization of boundaries.

> Monsters, then, are deeply disturbing; neither good nor evil, inside nor outside, not self or other. On the contrary, they are always liminal, refusing to stay in place, transgressive and transformative. They disrupt both internal and external order, and overturn the distinctions that set out the limits of the human subject.[3]

Authors from Margrit Shildrick to Jack Halberstam[4] have emphasized the central role of the cultural production of the monstrous as articulation of a (radically ambivalent) affective and cognitive challenge oscillating between horror and fascination, repulsion and attraction, the material and the symbolic.

The monstrous foregrounds the interrelation between scientific discourses and cultural and political practices,[5] as shifts within the significations of the

1 Rosi Braidotti, "Signs of Wonder and Traces of Doubt: On Tetralogy and Embodied Differences," in *Between Monsters, Goddesses and Cyborgs: Feminist Confrontations with Science, Medicine and Cyberspace*, eds. Nina Lykke, Rosi Braidotti (London and New Jersey: Zed Books, 1996): 135 – 152, 150.

2 Donna Haraway, *Simians, Cyborgs, and Women: The Reinvention of Nature* (New York: Routledge, 1991), 2.

3 Margrit Shildrick, *Embodying the Monster: Encounters with the Vulnerable Self* (London and Thousand Oaks and New Delhi: Sage Publications, 2002), 4.

4 Judith Halberstam, *Skin Shows: Gothic Horror and the Technology of Monsters* (Raleigh: Duke University Press, 1995).

5 See Birgit Stammberger, *Monster und Freaks: Eine Wissensgeschichte außergewöhnlicher Körper im 19. Jahrhundert* (Bielefeld: transcript, 2011), 48–51; Iris Mendel and Nora Ruck, "Das Monster als verkörperte Differenz in der Moderne: De-Monstrationen feministischer Wissenschaftskritik" in *Von Monstern und Menschen: Begegnungen der anderen Art in kulturwissenschaftlicher Perspektive*, eds. Gunther Gebhard, Oliver Geisler and Steffen Schröter (Bielefeld: transcript, 2009): 117–135; Beate Neumeier, "Engendering the Monstrous: Kulturelle Transformationen im Theater der Frühen Neuzeit" in *Gender in Bewegung: Aktuelle Spannungsfelder der Gender und Queer Studies*, eds. Elke Kleinau, Dirk Schulz and Susanne Völker (Bielefeld: transcript, 2013): 197–213.

monstrous as norm-constitutive other (see Michel Foucault) accompany the historically specific processes of the production of norm and difference within societies.[6] The English Renaissance as a period of the Early Modern shaping of cultural boundaries between human and animal, male and female, matter and spirit, natural and supernatural was a particularly productive time in terms of the monstrous. Notions of monstrous transgression and transformation figure prominently in a wide range of Renaissance texts, from political and religious pamphlets to medical and psychological treatises, to poetry and theatre, which obsessively thematize and enact foundational questions about notions of identity and reality. In the context of this epistemological crisis, corporeal and metaphorical, empirically verifiable and imaginative notions of the monstrous often coexist and intermingle within an intricate discursive web, whose complexities Stuart Clark has traced in his analysis of *Vanities of the Eye* (2007) in connection to "the major historical developments [...]: the vogue for visual artifice, the exploration of demonology, religious reformation, and philosophical skepticism."[7]

The theatre as the most visible visual medium of the Early Modern period gives shape to witches and fairies, to devil-dogs, lycanthropes, and ass-headed humans, using these monstrous bodies 'to make visible' the cognitive and affective horrors of "uncertainty and unreliability,"[8] which are fundamentally linked to questions about the act of seeing, the nature of perception and its relation to knowledge.[9] However, Renaissance theatre not only functions as a complex discursive network and as a space where these issues are being negotiated, but is

6 See Michel Foucault, *Abnormal: Lectures at the Collège de France 1974–75* (London and New York: Verso, 2003); Mendel and Ruck, "Das Monster als verkörperte Differenz," 119.

7 Stuart Clark, *Vanities of the Eye: Vision in Early Modern European Culture* (Oxford and New York: Oxford University Press, 2007), 5.

8 "For between the fifteenth and seventeenth centuries European visual cultures suffered some major and unprecedented shocks [...] in one context after another, vision came to be characterized by uncertainty and unreliability, such that access to visual reality could no longer be normally guaranteed" (Clark, *Vanities of the Eye*, 2).

9 See Reynolds: "The Early Modern English theatre was dangerous [...] because it demonstrated an understanding of identity as transformational." Bryan Reynolds, *Performing Transversally: Reimagining Shakespeare and the Critical Future* (New York: Palgrave Macmillan, 2003), 159. For an analysis of the monstrous in English Renaissance theatre see also Mark Thornton Burnett's study of the construction of monsters (*Constructing 'Monsters' in Shakespearean Drama and Early Modern Culture* (Basingstoke and New York: Palgrave Macmillan, 2002)), Susan Zimmerman's analysis of the abject in conjunction with the religious shift of the Reformation (*The Early Modern Corpse and Shakespeare's Theatre* (Edinburgh: Edinburgh University Press, 2005)) and Maurizio Calbi's mapping of uncanny, abject and monstrous bodies in connection to Early Modern anatomical science (*Approximate Bodies: Gender and Power in Early Modern Drama and Anatomy* (London and New York: Routledge, 2004)).

itself being shaped and transformed in the process. Moreover, the impact of the theatre is often cast in terms of these "boundary disputes,"[10] particularly in Puritan pamphlets cautioning against the monstrous transformations of spectators entering the theatre as devout Christians, and coming forth "possessed of the Diuell" (John Greene 1615), or "transformed into dogges" (John Rainoldes 1600) through the infernal art of players who "metamorphose [...] into Monsters" themselves (William Prynne 1633).[11]

The witch as paradigmatic monstrous shape-shifter enacts the epistemological crisis of the Early Modern period, a crisis which can be played out over her body. The increasing obsession with the witch's body as matter to be deciphered and disciplined, discernible during this time, is linked to a growing interest in the legal body and its intersection with religious, political, social and medical/humoral bodies.[12] In this context the fascination with shape-shifting marks the interrelation of issues of gender, age and class, evident in the prototypical witch of the fairy tale, Snow White's (step)mother, who is transformed from the beauty and innocence of the courtly positioned lady posing in front of the mirror, to the ugliness and evil of the socially marginalized old hag selling her poisonous merchandise.[13] As such, she embodies the secret link between the ideal of femininity and its dark underside, and thus stages the impossibility of maintaining a binary distinction between truth and falsity, unity and division. The shape-shifting of the witch signals a fundamental anxiety about female

---

10 Stephen Greenblatt, *Hamlet in Purgatory* (Princeton and Oxford: Princeton University Press, 2001), 244.

11 For further reference see Bryan Reynolds, *Transversal Subjects: From Montaigne to Deleuze After Derrida* (New York: Palgrave Macmillan, 2009).

12 On witchcraft in the Early Modern period see Keith Thomas, *Religion and the Decline of Magic: Studies in popular beliefs in sixteenth- and seventeenth-century England* (London: Weidenfeld and Nicolson, 1971); Alan MacFarlane, *Witchcraft in Tudor and Stuart England: A Regional and Comparative Study* (London: Routledge, 1999); Marion Gibson, *Reading Witchcraft: Stories of Early English Witches* (London: Routledge, 1999); Stuart Clark, *Thinking with Demons: The Idea of Witchcraft in Early Modern Europe* (Oxford: Oxford University Press, 1997). For comprehensive studies on witchcraft and law see Barbara Shapiro, *A Culture of Fact: England, 1550–1720* (Ithaca: Cornell University Press, 2000); Orna Ayagon Darr, *Marks of an Absolute Witch: Evidentiary Dilemmas in Early Modern England* (Farnham and Burlington: Ashgate, 2011) and Laura Stokes, *Demons of Urban Reform: Early European Witch Trials and Criminal Justice, 1430–1530* (Basingstoke: Palgrave Macmillan, 2011). See also Edward Bever, "Witchcraft Prosecutions and the Decline of Magic," *Journal of Interdisciplinary History* 40.2 (2009): 263–293 and Todd Wayne Butler, "Bedeviling Spectacle: Law, Literature, and Early Modern Witchcraft," *Yale Journal of Law and the Humanities* 20.2 (2008): 111–129.

13 See Heidi Breuer, *Crafting the Witch: Gendering Magic in Medieval and Early Modern England* (New York: Routledge, 2009), 96–97.

changeability and deception as well as the need for its containment, as the witch incorporates the female transgressions of the Renaissance ideals of chastity, silence and obedience. She functions as exemplary symbol of "the monstrous regiment of women" (John Knox' *First Blast of the Trumpet Against the Monstrous Regiment of Women* 1558) repeatedly evoked in Early Modern pamphlet literature, which calls upon the literal and metaphorical link between *whore*, *shrew* und *witch* as configurations of female monstrosity. In this context the debate about gender in terms of "nature" or "custom" from the mid-sixteenth century onwards up until the Pamphlet War in 1621[14] – the year of the staging of *The Witch of Edmonton* after her historical trial and execution – is marked by a gradual turn from the importance of clothing as social and cultural gender marker to an increasing insistence on the body as unchangeable marker of norm and norm transgression, and thus as apt site of discipline and punishment.

Consequently, the bodily search for the witch's mark gains decisive importance, as it seems to promise unambiguous information about the shape-shifting witch. In the English context the witch's mark allows for a blending of the European idea of the devil's mark sealing the witch's satanic pact with the English tradition of the witch's relation to her animal companion, that stand-in for the devil, the familiar. The notion of the familiar draws on folk beliefs about shape-shifting, such as "the capacity of the Devil to adopt an animal form, of witches to change themselves into animals empowered by the Devil, and of witches to turn people into animals."[15] Even if the metamorphosis of humans into animals was highly contested during the English Renaissance and predominantly not seen as actual shape-shifting, but only as the creation of its illusion,[16] it was highly influential in the popular imagination and effectively used in theatrical production.

The image of the familiar sucking on the witch's mark or teat in particular marks the intersection of the maternal and the erotic with evil.[17] This deviant

---

14 For an analysis of the Pamphlet War see Sandra Clark, "Hic Mulier, Haec Vir, and the Controversy over Masculine Women," *Studies in Philology* 82.2 (1985): 157–183.

15 Philip C. Almond, *The Lancashire Witches: Persecution, Politics and Murder in Early Modern England* (New York: Palgrave, 2012), 77.

16 See Almond, *The Lancashire Witches.*

17 On witchcraft and gender see Anne Barstow (*Witchcraze: A New History of European Witch Hunts* [San Francisco: Pandora, 1994]); Deborah Willis (*Malevolent Nurture: Witch-Hunting and Maternal Power in Early Modern England* [Ithaca and London: Cornell University Press, 1995]) and Diane Purkiss (*The Witch in History: Early Modern and Twentieth-Century Representations* [London: Routledge, 1996]). On the witch's mark in particular see Orna Alyagon Darr, *Marks of an Absolute Witch*; Darr, "The devil's mark: a socio-cultural analysis of physical evidence,"

and demonic sexuality is inseparable from the witch's criminal acts ranging from spells causing impotence to murder and cannibalism. At the same time, the possible projection of shape-shifting onto the devilish familiar seems to allow for a fixation of the witch's body as a stable and accessible sign, and thus to permit a containment of the subversive threat of the witch as an embodiment of an emasculating female empowerment.

The witch and her persecution as a central, multi-layered indicator of the larger epistemological crisis of the time is particularly evident in the fascination with the witches' sabbath as indicator of gender upheaval, as sign of political and social rebellion and of religious tensions. This is particularly apparent in the conflation of witchcraft and Papism, which is to be found in actual trial records, and is taken up ambivalently in witch plays of the early seventeenth century.[18] The rise of the witch thus can be read as an ambivalent articulation of anxieties about, and a desire for the catholic presence of, the supernatural at a time of "the decline of magic"[19] in the Early Modern period. The attempts to contain the threat of the witch coincide with the rise of legal and medical discourses, which build on and surpass religious and social discourses by claiming authority over the witch's body and mind, and which result in the respective punishments of prison or madhouse.[20]

In the theatre, the rise of the witch goes along with the rise of tragicomedy in the first half of the seventeenth century, an ambivalent new genre which allows for the articulation of the wish fulfillment of a containment of the crisis in question, while at the same time highlighting the persistence of doubt as well as the secret desire for the transgression of boundaries. The theatre thus resembles the courtroom presenting the case (often in conjunction with medical expertise) and turning the spectator into judge and jury, while at the same drawing attention to the limits of medical diagnosis and legal judgment, insisting on ambivalences and uncertainties and their monstrous embodiment.

Continuity and Change 24.2 (2009): 361–387 and Malcolm Gaskill, "Witchcraft and Evidence in Early Modern England," *Past and Present* 198.1 (2008): 33–70.

18 See Richard Wilson, "The pilot's thumb: *Macbeth* and the Jesuits" in *The Lancashire Witches: Histories and Stories*, ed. Robert Poole (Manchester and New York: Manchester University Press, 2002): 126–145 and *Region, Religion and Patronage: Lancastrian Shakespeare*, eds. Richard Dutton, Alison Findlay and Richard Wilson (Manchester and New York: Manchester University Press, 2003).

19 Thomas, *Religion and the Decline of Magic.*

20 See Darr, *Marks of an Absolute Witch*; Darr, "The Devil's Mark" and Yvonne Petry, "'Many Things Surpass our Knowledge': An Early Modern Surgeon on Magic, Witchcraft and Demonic Possession," *Social History of Medicine* 25.1 (2011): 47–64.

1 Tragedy's Mad Bodies: *Macbeth* (1606) and the Natural/Supernatural Boundary

Macbeth sets the stage for Jacobean-Caroline witch drama at the intersection of religious, medical, political and legal discourses about witchcraft, drawing upon topical historical events and issues discussed in King James' *Demonology* (1597; repub. 1603), put into legal action in the *Witchcraft Act* (1604), and connected to the Gunpowder plot (1605). According to Richard Wilson's persuasive analysis, Shakespeare's play prefigures the wider public discussion about witch congregations in England, which took shape in the context of court cases like the Lancashire trials of 1612 and 1634, taken up in Middleton's *The Witch* (1612–16) and in *The Late Lancashire Witches* (1634).[21] The weird sisters' introductory scenes in the play combine references to popular witchlore about familiars (Grimalkin, Paddock 1.1.7–8)[22] and *maleficium* (from "killing swine" to "a pilot's thumb" 1.3.2 and 1.3.26) with current legislation about the handling of body parts and topical historical events, such as references to the ship, The Tiger (1.3.6), which had just returned from an unfortunate voyage.[23] Although the exchanges between the witches can be read as "condensed stories" in a "process of metaphorisation,"[24] what is striking, is their placement on the threshold in-between literal and figurative readings, calling upon the urge for, and resistance to, imaginative narrativization and explanatory closure. This monstrous in-betweenness is mirrored in Banquo's and Macbeth's initial fragmented contradictory reading of the weird sisters between human and supernatural, male and female, matter and spirit, before their individually colored process of narrativization sets in.

The witches' predictions about future rulership and its implications lay bare the intersections between religious, political and legal discourses. The truth of the first prediction prompts the political discourse of treason. The process set in motion will change Macbeth's initial reading of the witches as "imperfect speakers" (1.3.68) who leave him with a "suggestion whose horrid image doth

---

21 See Richard Wilson's discussion of *Macbeth* as the first English play staging the congregation of the weird sisters in terms of a "satanic confederacy" which "may have influenced the contemporary criminalization of witchcraft as political conspiracy" (127), revealing the links between the "quasi-catholic witches" of the play and "the traumatic events of 1605" as well as the "author's own proximity to the gunpowder conspirators" (Wilson, "The pilot's thumb," 134).

22 All quotes from William Shakespeare, *Macbeth* in *The Norton Shakespeare*, ed. Stephen Greenblatt, Second Edition (New York and London: Norton, 2008), 2569–2632.

23 For a detailed analysis see Wilson, "The pilot's thumb."

24 Purkiss, *The Witch in History*, 210.

unfix my hair" and "thought, whose murder yet is but fantastical" (1.3.133–134, 138), to his belief in their "perfect'st report" (1.5.2) in the letter to his Lady. Despite the witches' warning that "the charm's wound up" (1.3.35), and Banquo's musings about them as "instruments of darkness" (1.3.123) which will draw them into madness, the play will now follow Macbeth's logic of the murderous necessity to prove the truth of the prophecy.

Only when Lady Macbeth enters the stage does evil take over. The witches vanish as the Lady carries on their part by conjuring the spirits, complementing Banquo's evocation of the image of the marginalized old village witch-hag ("each one at once laying her choppy finger / Upon her skinny lips" 1.3.43–45) with the beautiful wicked witch-queen, whose evil power seems more horrifying as it suggests the secret alliance of a pervasive monstrous regiment of women. Consequently it is the Lady who evokes witchlore images of infanticide (1.7.54–59), and – like the murderer of old Hamlet – pours poisonous spirits in Macbeth's ear ("that I may pour my spirits in thine ear" 1.5.24), which will simmer in his head as in a witch's cauldron, a process echoed later by Macbeth himself, when he describes his mind as a witch's cauldron, "full of scorpions" (3.2.37).

The limits of the Lady's empowerment, however, ironically already surface in the banquet scene, which is the last exhibition of her strength as she covers up for Macbeth, before her sleepwalking madness and his decision to seek a second meeting with the witches. Although she appears the strongest in contrast to Macbeth in this scene, accusing him of being "quite unmanned in folly" (3.4.7), denouncing his visions as "a woman's story at a winter's fire" (3.4.64), the Queen's helpless rationalization of Macbeth's fears already indicates her distance from the weird sisters, before their queen, Hecate, makes her powerful entrance. Lady Macbeth, the would-be witch, is revealed as bewitched herself, and, consequently, will be punished.

According to the gendered logic of the play Lady Macbeth's power signals Macbeth's weakness, and it is thus only by the 'wading' further into bloody evil without her mediation and knowledge ("be innocent of the knowledge dearest chuck" 3.2.46) and by attempting to play the devil to the witches, that Macbeth can reaffirm a masculinity which seems strangely drained of meaning at the end, "signifying nothing" (5.5.27). If at the outset of events the Lady presented herself as witch calling upon the spirits, Macbeth in his second meeting with the weird sisters tries to perform the role of satanic witch-master threatening them with an "eternal curse" (4.1.121). The ridiculous futility of this attempt turns his vision of omnipotence into a display of impotence. In the context of Early Modern gender anxieties the emasculating implications of Macbeth's encounter with the witches can only be dissimulated by emphasizing the insurmountable difference between the supernatural world of the witches and the human protagonists.

Throughout the play Macbeth and his Lady are associated with bodily dismemberment and mental fragmentation.[25] From the initial reference to the bloody killing of his enemy ("Till he unseamed him from the nave to th'chops / And fixed his head upon our battlements" 1.1.22–23) to his own beheading Macbeth is linked to aspects of bodily and mental fragmentation. Contrasting King Edward's healing touch (4.3) to Macbeth's dissociating evil touch, the play traces the process of the protagonist's disintegration from his first reaction to the weird sisters shaking his "single state of man" (1.3.139), to his experience of the division between eye and hand ("the eye wink at the hand" 1.4.52) taken up in his vision of hands plucking out eyes ("What hands are here! Ha, they pluck out mine eyes" 2.2.57) and of the "dagger of the mind" (2.1.38) which can be seen but not touched, to his desperate demand "let the frame of things disjoint" (3.2.18), up until his acknowledgment that all past certainties of solidity and wholeness ("whole as the marble, founded as the rock" 3.4.21) are shattered ("stones have been known to move, and trees to speak" 3.4.122).[26] Macbeth's imagery of bodily and mental disintegration is complemented by the Lady's imagery of a dissolution of ego boundaries, prefigured in her appeal to the spirits for a transformation of bodily fluids ("Make thick my blood / [...] / And take my milk for gall" 1.5.41–46), and later played out in her state of "slumbery agitation" (5.1.9–10), in which her senses of vision, smell and touch take over in the bodily enactment of her repressed memory of the bloody deed.

Throughout the play the weird sisters seem to generate these divisions. This is visualized in the cauldron (4.1), whose ingredients consist of body parts, organs and liquids of "abject animals" (like snake, worm, and adder, lizard and frog, bat and dog, owl and baboon etc.) and "marginalised humans" (Jew, Turk, Tartar, red-haired wench and birth-strangled babe).[27] At the same time, however, the weird sisters seem to promise a union between the word and the flesh, the literal and the metaphorical. They remain monstrously ambivalent, evoking the (catholic) belief of the past while foregrounding its irretrievable loss. The play thus spells out the "crisis of vision" and its religious as well as political and psychological underpinnings, positioning Macbeth and the Lady

---

25 For a detailed analysis of witchcraft and bodily fragmentation see Anna Rosner, "The Witch Who Is Not One: The fragmented Body in Early Modern Demonological Tracts," *Exemplaria* 21.4 (2009): 363–379.

26 See Wilson, "The pilot's thumb," 135–136.

27 See Richard Wilson on "the abuse of dead bodies in witchcraft to the worship of body parts by Catholic congregations" ("The pilot's thumb," 129).

at its center, torn between the belief in the prophecies and suspicions about their deceptiveness. Faced with the liminal witches, whose predictions are true and false at the same time, it is the human need for "certainty," which ironically brings forth the truly monstrous birth of murder.

Shakespeare's *Macbeth* stages the tragedy of the desire to master the epistemological crisis by marking the limits of human desire for omnipotence in gendered terms: the attempt at a willful metamorphosis into witch and devil ends with the Lady succumbing to a somatized madness, and with Macbeth to what could be called a paranoid hysteria.[28] While the Lady loses control over her mind in the sleepwalking re-enactment of her sinful deed – because the body does not forget what the mind tries to repress ("These deeds must not be thought / After these ways" 2.2.32–33) –, Macbeth maintains the mental control over his body, but loses his capacity to feel ("I am in blood / Stepped in so far that should I wade no more, / Returning were as tedious as go o'er" 3.4.135–37), hysterically oscillating between obsessive desires to confirm his vision of the prophecy ("I'll make assurance double sure" 4.1.94) and its inevitable falsifications ("Then comes my fit again. I had else been perfect. / [...] / Now I am cabined, cribbed, confined and bound / To saucy doubts and fears" 3.4.23, 26–27), between fantasies of omnipotence and recognitions of an empty self.[29] Ironically, at the end of the play the fundamental uncertainty of vision, the inability to establish a stable connection between sign and meaning, is countered by a reaffirmation of gender boundaries in the final transformation of Lady Macbeth from the witchlike heroine into the madwoman and of Macbeth from the demonic hero into the despairing but unrelenting warrior.[30] Their respective deaths, her presumably mad suicide and his beheading, thus assert a gendered body/mind split.

---

28 See also Beate Neumeier, "Engendering the Monstrous" and Neumeier, "Vision and Desire: Fantastic Renaissance Spectacles" in *Gothic Renaissance*, eds. Elisabeth Bronfen and Beate Neumeier (Manchester: Manchester University Press, 2014): 95–112.

29 See Juliet Mitchell, *Madmen and Medusas: Reclaiming Hysteria* (London: Penguin Books, 2000). For an analysis of witchcraft and hysteria in *Macbeth* see Joanna Levin, "Lady Macbeth and the Daemonologie of Hysteria," *English Literary History* 69.1 (2002): 21–55.

30 For an analysis of madness and gender see Janet Adelman, *Suffocating Mothers: Fantasies of Maternal Origin in Shakespeare's Plays, 'Hamlet' to 'The Tempest'* (New York and London: Routledge, 1992) and Carol Neely, *Distracted Subjects: Madness and Gender in Shakespeare and Early Modern Culture* (Ithaca: Cornell University Press, 2004). See also Beate Neumeier, "Inszenierungen des Wahnsinns im Theater der englischen Renaissance: Gender und Genre" in *Wahnsinn in der Kunst: Kulturelle Imaginationen vom Mittelalter bis zum 21. Jahrhundert*, eds. Susanne Rohr und Lars Schmeink (Trier: Wissenschaftlicher Verlag Trier, 2011).

Taking up current debates about demonology, madness and gender, the tragedy participates in the cultural shift towards a naturalization of gender boundaries and a gradual separation of the spiritual from the material world. From an initial focus on religious, political and legal discourses about the nature of witchcraft, the play moves to the exploration of medical-psychological discourses providing a gendered reading of and control over the human body and mind. However, despite the deadly closure for Macbeth and his Lady, the weird sisters remain disconcertingly beyond control and without recognizable motivation, vanishing from the play unpunished. The focus, thus, is still on the uncertainties of the weird sisters' monstrous in-betweenness, defying the demarcation of boundaries between natural/supernatural, male/female, matter/spirit, literal/metaphorical.

2 Tragicomedy's Sexed Bodies: *The Witch* (1613–16) and the Male/Female Boundary

Defined by contemporaries as a monstrous conjunction of incompatible effects and affects, ("grief and laughter are so very incompatible, that to join these two copies of nature together, would be monstrous,")[31] tragicomedy can be read as a response to the described cultural crisis and the anxieties it produced, simultaneously offering solutions and doubts about their adequacy. At a time when the increasing focus on individual interiority and psychopathology in Jacobean-Caroline tragedies offers explanations to secure the boundaries between human/animal, male/female, matter/spirit, tragicomedy emerges as a "diseased" liminal genre evoking contradictory emotional responses, in which the containment generated by the ending can be effectively unsettled by a destabilizing emphasis on theatrical self-reflexivity and affective/cognitive ambivalence. Tragicomic witch plays as diverse as Middleton's *The Witch* (1613–16) and Rowley, Dekker and Ford's *The Witch of Edmonton* (1621) stage, albeit differently, the gradual shift towards an exploration of the witch's body as readable sign, while at the same time insisting on the continuous threat of a transgressive and transformative monstrosity which cannot be contained.

---

31 George Sewell, "An Essay on the Art, Rise and Progress of the Stage" in *The Works of William Shakespeare*, eds. Alexander Pope and George Sewell, Vol. 7 (London, 1725), vii. See also *Renaissance Tragicomedy: Explorations in Genre and Politics*, ed. Nancy Klein Maguire (New York: AMS Press, 1987), 1.

Recently editors have linked Shakespeare's *Macbeth* with Thomas Middleton's *The Witch* to the point where Middleton himself is claimed to have contributed more than just the songs from his play to that of Shakespeare. Like Shakespeare's *Macbeth,* Middleton's *The Witch* is informed by a political and legal subtext, as it draws on the court scandal concerning Frances Howard's annulment of marriage to Robert Devereux on the grounds of impotence and her subsequent marriage to Robert Carr in conjunction with the murder of Thomas Overbury, who had tried to prevent the second marriage (1613). The sensational details of the trials included Devereux's claim to be incapable of performing sexually with his wife, though not with others, as well as the bodily inspection of Howard's virginity evoking associations with the search for the witch's mark, and finally the confession of Howard's waiting woman, Anne Turner, to the poisoning of Overbury in terms of a deadly *maleficium.* When in the murder case Anne Turner was sentenced as "a whore, a bawd, a sorcerer, a witch, a papist, a felon and a murderer,"[32] this conflation of sources of evil and their respective religious, political and social overtones illustrates the blending of variations of female transgressiveness and proves the female body as a screen onto which these issues are projected.

In contrast to the historical Anne Turner, who was hanged in 1615, Middleton's witch Hecate, whose *maleficium* is the cause of impotence in the play, and her satanical sisterhood remain as unpunished as Shakespeare's weird sisters. Critics have argued that the "fantastical"[33] or "grotesque and farcical"[34] presentation of Middleton's witches works towards a "reduction of the witch to a symbolic figure"[35] rendering the witch "provocative but ultimately not threatening."[36] At the same time, the tragicomedy seems to play on the links between the Howard/Overbury case and the actual Lancashire witch trials (1612), reminding the audience of the ambivalences between literal and metaphorical readings of the figure of the witch.

In contrast to *Macbeth* Middleton's play opens with the introduction of the humans rather than the witches, thus emphasizing from the start that it is human behavior – betrayal, whoredom, desire and cruelty – which is at stake. The witches' agency is predominantly sought after in relation to male desire (Sebastian, Almachildes) for (sexual) possession of women, and to female revenge

---

32 Quoted from Purkiss, *The Witch in History,* 221.

33 Julia Garrett, "Witchcraft and Sexual Knowledge in Early Modern England," *Journal for Early Modern Cultural Studies* 13.1 (2013): 32–72, 46.

34 Purkiss, *The Witch in History,* 217.

35 Purkiss, *The Witch in History,* 219.

36 Garrett, "Witchcraft and Sexual Knowledge," 46.

(Duchess) on cruel men. However, in contrast to Almachildes' wish for a love charm, Sebastian's demand for a parting charm is supposed to re-establish his hold over his former beloved (Isabella), who is now married to another man (Antonio). The comic potential of the working of these charms stands in stark contrast to the potentially horrifying effect of the Duchess' wish for a murderous spell over Almachildes, her accomplice in the vengeful murder plot against her husband. All major characters seem to be governed by a potentially destructive desire "to have possession" of an other, who is consequently reduced to a mere tool in the process of the realization of this desire (Fernando: "You see she's gone: / Another has possession" 1.1.5–6).[37] This objectification is embodied in the stage presence of the whore Florida as well as enacted in Almachildes' use of a love charm in order to turn a young woman's disgust into desire, and most horribly literalized in the ghastly cup, made out of the Duchess' father's skull, which the Duke forces upon his wife to assert his dominance. This notion of a desire of bodily objectification and fragmentation seems disturbingly associated with the use of body parts in evil witchcraft rituals.

Consequently, the three witch scenes of the play foreground the witches' similarity to the humans, although they openly display the sensational horrifying witchlore scenarios, which are only hinted at in the fragmented stories referred to in *Macbeth*. Thus the first witch scene (1.2) aims to confirm and surpass popular fantasies about the witches' sexual and criminal transgressions in its detailed description of incest, murderous charms and cannibalism including the boiling of an "unbaptised brat" (1.2.18), whose orifices are stuffed with "magical herbs" (1.2.38). At the same time a close contact between witches and humans is emphasized in Almachildes' voluntary and well-prepared contribution of a number of herbal ingredients to the hellish cauldron.

Whereas Shakespeare's *Macbeth* focuses on the effect of the weird sisters whose motivations remain disturbingly obscure, Middleton's tragicomedy immediately centers on Hecate's own excessive sexual desires for her son, as well as for other young men, including Almachildes. The incestuous relation between Hecate and her son Firestone and the pet-like relation to her familiars, as well as the son's fantasies of matricide, foreground the monstrous link between the maternal and the sexual, which serves as a subtext of *Macbeth*'s "fantasy of escape from the maternal matrix."[38] However, the grotesqueness of Hecate's sexual encounters, enhanced by references to her old age (1.2.70–75), can be read as a

37 All quotes from Thomas Middleton, *The Witch* in *Three Jacobean Witchcraft Plays: Sophonisba, The Witch, The Witch of Edmonton*, eds. Peter Corbin and Douglas Sedge (Manchester: Manchester University Press, 1986). Further references are given in the text.
38 Adelman, *Suffocating Mothers*, 140.

sign of cultural anxiety about female sexuality and as a strategy of its containment.

In this context the witches' appearance in the third act (3.3) of Middleton's play, with the mock-religious spectacle of Hecate mounting her familiar Malkin descended from above, is not just an interpolation without plot relevance, but serves as central ingredient in the play's hellish recipe, as it demonstrates that the witches are now ready to fly and "able to putrefy [...], to infect a whole region" (3.3.18). The final appearance of the witches (5.2) focuses on the cauldron as central symbol and realization of the (un)homely brew which has been in the making throughout the play. The play's central concern is thus the social threat to the community posed by the witches' realization of desire without fear of consequences. At the end of the play the witches remain unpunished like Shakespeare's weird sisters, indicating a permanent powerful presence within the community.

Despite the spectacular display of the witches' transgressive desires and practices, a horrifying similarity between the demonic and the human world has been emphasized throughout the play. Thus the presentation of the Duke's desire to make his wife drink from her father's skull calls up associations with cannibalistic incorporation, while the secret delivery and abandonment of Francesca's new-born child casts doubts upon women's maternal feelings. By the end of the play the humans, whose desire seems without boundaries, appear ultimately more threatening than the witches, who seem to acknowledge rules and regulations, such as the inability to "disjoin wedlock" (1.2.172), and the limitations put on death spells ("His picture made in wax [...] / [...] /Will waste him by degrees" 5.2.4–6).

However, according to genre conventions, a potentially tragic outcome is averted either by fate or by human intervention. Moreover, the accidental death of Sebastian's rival enables a reunion with his former beloved, while the Duchess' display of "grief and honour" seems to make amends for her sinful murderous intent (5.3.129–130). Whether Almachildes will die from the spell cast by the witches now seems irrelevant. The focus is on the happy ending and on the uneasy contention that monstrous desires can be pardoned, because it is only the act, which counts.

Accordingly, whereas Shakespeare's tragedy *Macbeth* explores desire and action in terms of moral conscience and psychological upheaval, such concerns have little relevance in Middleton's tragicomedy. The radical ambivalence about the relation between desire, thought, language and action in *Macbeth*, played out in the protagonists' inner turmoil, gives way to the insistence upon the gap, which allows for the happy reunions rather than punishments. The emphasis on the act and its bodily evidence goes along with a shift from the importance of language as ambivalently literal and metaphorical in *Macbeth* towards the material ingredients of the hellish recipes.

In this context the question of the witches' enigmatic nature between supernatural/natural, female/male, corporal/imaginative posed in *Macbeth* does not arise. In Middleton's sexualized power play it is the threat of a distinctly emasculating femininity, which is played out in scenarios of spell-induced impotence and potential death. The witches' transgressive female empowerment can be feared and celebrated at the same time,[39] because its threat is contained with reference to their limitations as well as through their presentation as theatrical spectacle set off from the action in three scenes. However, as neither human intervention nor fate are explored as a moral counter force or a sign of heavenly order, the happy ending self-consciously presents itself as part of a fairy tale machinery. The definition of this form of tragicomedy as "desire without act" is ironically foregrounded in the play's impotence charm.

Despite the genre-dependent evasion of questions of discipline and punishment, the feminization of the monstrously ambivalent demonic witch goes along with an increasing focus on the body as a material space for control. The body, as a site of containment of the transgressive witches' social threat to infect the whole community in early seventeenth century texts, shifts the witchcraft debate from a predominantly religious discourse into legal and medical discourses, which partake in the cultural movement towards disambiguation, identifying and effectively eliminating the witch – and increasingly the madwoman – from the community, while successfully essentializing woman as "perfect in her own sex."[40] However, this process remains bound to "saucy doubts and fears" (*Macbeth* 3.4.27) and to ambivalent articulations of an irrepressible monstrous femininity.

---

39 See Julia Garrett: "In many respects the play's portrait of the witches' sexuality conforms quite seamlessly to anti-feminist ideology and its attendant anxieties. [...] And yet the play also invites a celebratory appreciation of these figures of excess" ("Witchcraft and Sexual Knowledge," 48 and 49).

40 "[B]y arguing that woman is 'equally perfect in her own sex' as the male is in his, late Renaissance Galenists [...] disunite the physiology and anatomy of male and female in matters of sex." (Ian MacLean, *The Renaissance Notion of Woman: A Study in the Fortunes of Scholasticism and Medical Science in European Intellectual Life* (Cambridge: Cambridge University Press, 1980), 45).

3 Tragicomedy's Legal Bodies: *The Witch of Edmonton* (1621) and the Debate about Discipline and Punishment

In contradistinction to Middleton's fairy tale version of tragicomedy, Rowley, Dekker and Ford's *The Witch of Edmonton* (1621) pushes the form to its limits towards domestic drama and the poetic justice of two executions and a wedding, foregrounding the social, moral and legal implications of boundary issues about the human and the demonic.[41] The play by William Rowley, Thomas Dekker, and John Ford does not refute the existence of witchcraft, but rather tries to differentiate between superstitious popular beliefs and serious demonological considerations, focusing on the historical event of the trial and execution of Elizabeth Sawyer in the same year (1621) and drawing on Henry Goodcole's pamphlet about the court case and the culprit's confession *The Wonderful Discovery of Elizabeth Sawyer, A Witch.*[42] In the play *The Witch of Edmonton* the willed transformation of the title character Elizabeth Sawyer, presented as an old isolated mistreated woman, falsely accused of witchcraft, into a witch taking revenge on the community ("Cause I'm poor, deformed and ignorant [...] Must I for that be made a common sink / For all the filth and rubbish of men's tongues / To fall and run into?" 2.1.3–8), is enacted with the embodied assistance of a dog-shaped blood sucking "thing called Familiar" (2.1.36), forcing her into the devil's pact.[43]

In contrast to Middleton's play, the power in this relation lies not with the witch, but with the familiar as devilish incarnation, on whose compliance and sexual attention Elizabeth Sawyer depends to satisfy her "black lust" (5.1.4).

---

41 See my argument in "Engendering the Monstrous" and "Vision and Desire." On domestic tragedy see Viviana Comensoli, "Witchcraft and Domestic Tragedy in *The Witch of Edmonton*" in *The Politics of Gender in Early Modern Europe*, eds. Jean R. Brink, Allison P. Coudert and Maryanne C. Horowitz (Kirksville: Sixteenth Century Journal Publications, 1989): 43–59 and Larry S. Champion, "'Factions of Distempered Passions': The Development of John Ford's Tragic Vision in *The Witch of Edmonton* and *The Lover's Melancholy*" in *'Concord in Discord': The Plays of John Ford, 1586–1986*, ed. Donald K. Anderson (New York: AMS Press, 1986): 109–130.

42 See Garrett, "Witchcraft and Sexual Knowledge," Todd Wayne Butler, "Swearing Justice in Henry Goodcole and *The Witch of Edmonton*," *Studies in English Literature 1500–1900* 50.1 (2010): 127–145 and Katherine O'Mahoney, "The Witch Figure: *The Witch of Edmonton*," *The Seventeenth Century* 24.2 (2009): 238–259.

43 All quotes from William Rowley, Thomas Dekker and John Ford, *The Witch of Edmonton* in *Three Jacobean Witchcraft Plays: Sophonisba, The Witch, The Witch of Edmonton*, eds. Peter Corbin and Douglas Sedge (Manchester: Manchester University Press, 1986). Further references are given in the text.

However, even after her transformation, the play maintains the ambivalence between the perception of, and sympathy for her, as a scapegoat for every evil within the village, and as an abhorred threatening witch intent on evil doings. The play increases the tension between those conflicting perspectives to the very end, when Sawyer appears most helplessly human and most witch-like at the same time, desperately conjuring her devil-dog companion.

In this context the corporeal stage presence of the devil-dog is used for an insistence on contradictory perceptions and evaluations of him as a dog, a supernatural being, and a theatrical device evoking onstage reactions between terror and desire, repulsion and attraction, fear and – most disturbingly – pity, creating a multiplicity of images and readings which resist all attempts at closure. In the tragic plot about the bigamist Frank Thorney, who turns into a murderer, the devil-dog's supernatural agency is emphasized, while in the comic plot about the young villager Cuddy Banks, who needs a love charm in order to fulfill his desires, the doggish potential is foregrounded, whereas the witch-plot capitalizes on both readings.[44] However, at the same time these clear-cut distinctions are undermined as all narrative strands focus on ambivalent intersections between social coercion, psychological disposition, and evil power in shaping notions of identity and reality.

Thus the appearance of the devil-dog in the bigamy-plot just before the murder raises questions about whether the devil-dog is a materialization of Frank's evil thoughts, as the devil-dog's remark, "the mind's about it now," (3.3.2) seems to suggest, or an embodiment of satanic power planting murder in his innocent mind, as Frank's utterance, "'Tis done now, what I ne'er thought on," (3.3.16) seems to imply. However, all attempts to mark the boundaries between the psychological and the demonic only lead back to their inseparability. Yet, in contradistinction to the witch-plot, Frank's public repentance at least enables the forgiveness of all of those whom he had wronged before his execution takes place.

It is the protagonist of the comic plot, Cuddy Banks, however, who despite his awareness and enjoyment of the devilish side of the devil-dog, treats the creature like a dog, whom he even pities at the end, suggesting alternative lives for him as "an honest dog" (5.1.153) who might "serve in some nobleman's, knight's, or gentleman's kitchen, [...] Or [...] translate [himself] into a lady's arming puppy" (5.1.167–172). This attitude seems to empower him to finally drive the devil-dog offstage, encouraging the creature's last transformation from supernatural agency into an actual barking dog that can be chased away.

---

44 For a detailed analysis see David Nicol, "Interrogating the Devil: Social and Demonic Pressure in *The Witch of Edmonton*," *Comparative Drama* 38.4 (2004): 425–445.

The Witch of Edmonton can thus be read as an exploration of the attempts to exorcise uncertainties about the intersections of the supernatural and the natural, the human and the demonic by incorporating the supernatural into a "realistic" depiction of a world which, despite its social deficiencies, is governed by providence. This is foregrounded by the transformation of the black devil-dog into the white dog of divine retribution towards the end, urging Elizabeth Sawyer to confess her crimes, putting her in mind of the "winding sheet" (5.1.37). Her rejection of this "puritan paleness" (5.1.53) and her insistent preference for his former "black colour" serve to justify her execution ("'Tis the black colour or none, which I fight under" 5.1.51–52). Ironically, the satanic power of the devil-dog can thus be revealed as part of the providential plan, while the eroticized discourse of old Elizabeth Sawyer's "black lust" for her "sweet Tom-boy" (5.1.81) renders her a radical outsider ("O my best love! / I am on fire, even in the mid'st of ice, / Raking my blood up till my shrunk knees feel / Thy curled head leaning on them. Come then, my darling. / If in the air thou hover'st, fall upon me / In some dark cloud" 5.1.9–14). However, the nurturing emotional attachment of the lonely Sawyer to her familiar still calls upon the audience's empathy. Moreover, the reassuring closure of her removal from the play is effectively counteracted by the obvious injustices and questionable moral behavior within the community.

Thus, almost all characters in the play are "guilty of illicit or criminal behavior" including "bigamy, adultery, sexual coercion, assault, slander, arson, deceit, theft, cross-dressing, murder and suicide."[45] Accordingly the play's emphasis is on the authority of the law, impersonated by Justice and assisted by Constable and Officers, as solution for the communal disorder ascribed to Elizabeth Sawyer. In contrast to the public call for vigilance (All: "Hang her, beat her, kill her!" 4.1.30), the representative of Justice remains an impartial observer and judge, warning against the "abuse [of] an aged woman!" (4.1.35), and listening to Sawyer's powerful accusation of evil witchery within society referring to princes and lordships, as well as city-witches, men-witches and – significantly – men of law.

The play invites the audience as witness and jury to sympathize with Sawyer as mouthpiece of social satire, but also to abhor her responsibility for a woman's death (Anne Ratcliffe), who wanted to testify against her, in the lines immediately following her diatribe. At the end of the play, when Sawyer is asked to confess and repent and thus to accept her punishment, only the audience recognizes the

45 Julia Garrett, "Dramatizing Deviance: Sociological Theory and *The Witch of Edmonton*," *Criticism* 49.3 (2007): 327–375.

lie of her denial of any involvement in the woman's death. This seems necessary to justify her execution to the spectator, but it also may throw doubt upon the legal power of verifying the truth. Accordingly *The Witch of Edmonton* has been called "one of the most radical dramatic challenges to the legal and cultural production of witches in the Renaissance."[46]

Throughout the play references to legal procedures are used and explored with regard to their implications for personal and communal relations. Thus notions of witnessing, confession, and trial are presented, highlighting different personal, cultural and legal viewpoints. The binding power of the vow in religious, legal and personal terms in particular is repeatedly discussed with reference to the lovers' oath between Frank Thorney and his secret bride (Winnifride), and the marriage vow between him and his official wife (Susan), as well as with regard to Elizabeth Sawyer's sealing of the devil's pact. In his detailed analysis of the "transformative power" of "efficacious speech," Todd Butler has shown how "Sawyer's curses bring forth first the devil and then her revenge upon the village."[47] Ironically, the oath's power guaranteed by a belief in the presence of truth in the (holy) word, seems to have lost its impact within the community, as Frank Thorney's betrayal of his beloved and his wife proves, while it seems most potent in Elizabeth Sawyer's turn to witchcraft. Moreover, even if the magic of the word is no longer acknowledged by the community, its efficacy is ironically reasserted by the very fact that Sawyer's demonic transformation seems to be generated by ascriptions of witchcraft. Only the return to a firm belief in the word of the law seems to be able to counter the spreading evil. Witchcraft and the law both rely on the power of language in connection to ritualized procedures. But by the end of the play the superiority of the law has to be acknowledged even by the demonic power, in the symbolic change of the devil-dog's colour from black to white. The emphasis on the limitations of Elizabeth Sawyer's empowerment facilitates the ambivalent construction of her as pitiful wronged old woman *and* evil witch to the very end, when her bodily punishment is contrasted with her spirit of defiance. Like Cuddy Banks, who reads the devil-dog both as powerful demon *and* harmless pet, the spectator as witness/juror remains aware of the dependence of all judgments upon perception and evaluation, without however, ever denying the "real" threat of the demonic.

The Witch of Edmonton participates in a cultural movement attempting "to reconcile the new focus on the empirical world with traditional Christian cosmol-

---

46 Dennis Kezar, "*The Witch of Edmonton* and the Guilt of Possession" in *Solon and Thespis: Law and Theater in the English Renaissance*, ed. Dennis Kezar (Notre Dame: University of Notre Dame Press, 2007): 124–160, 127.
47 Butler, "Swearing Justice," 129.

ogy" through what has been called an "experimental" or "empirical demonology."[48] The printed version of the play, dating from 1658, coincides with a remarkable return of the fascination with the supernatural in mid-seventeenth-century texts as part of a "politically conservative" project to counter the threatening implications of an increasing erosion of belief in manifestations of the supernatural in the context of the rise of empiricism.[49] The emergence of an "empirical supernaturalism" can thus be read as mediation, "bridg[ing] the gap between the empirical and non-empirical within a recognizable aesthetic framework,"[50] satisfying the demand for a belief in the providential workings of poetic justice. Tragicomedy as a genre of monstrous in-betweenness does attest to the desire for certainty while still insisting on the tensions involved in this transformational process.

4 Comedy's Theatrical Bodies: *The Late Lancashire Witches* (1634) and the Literal/Metaphorical Boundary

Staged witchcraft is inevitably always contained witchcraft. Witch plays tend to foreground the theatricality of the figure of the witch by including songs and dances, often in connection to the witches' secret congregations. At the same time, extremely topical plays like *The Witch of Edmonton* and *The Late Lancashire Witches*, which were written in the context of current court cases like "pieces of dramatic journalism,"[51] exploit the theatrical potential of the trials, casting the spectator as ambiguously implicated observer, witness and/or jury of the witches' secret celebrations as well as their public sentencing at court. At the same time, as pointed out before, the theatre itself was seen as a space of bewitchment and monstrous transformation.

The Late Lancashire Witches by Thomas Heywood and Richard Brome takes up these issues in terms of a comedy with a difference, inviting the audience to

---

48 Ricardo Capoferro, *Empirical Wonder: Historicising the Fantastic, 1660–1760* (Bern: Peter Lang, 2010), 105.

49 See Andrea Brady, "Gothic Authorities and the British Popular Press" in *Gothic Renaissance*, eds. Elisabeth Bronfen and Beate Neumeier (Manchester: Manchester University Press, 2014): 180–196, 193.

50 Capoferro, *Empirical Wonder*, 69 and 70.

51 A.M. Clark on *The Late Lancashire Witches* in his *Thomas Heywood: Playwright and Miscellanist* (Oxford: Basil Blackwell, 1931), 120.

follow events from the witches' mayhem in the community culminating in a disruptive wedding feast, to the witches' persecution, conviction and prospective punishment. Written in the context of the historical Lancashire witch trial of 1634 and informed by religious politics, the play – according to critics from Herbert Berry to Alison Findlay – was presumably commissioned "by members of the Privy Council keen to condemn the women,"[52] particularly as Lancashire had been considered as "a nest of both Papists and witches"[53] for a long time. The historical court case ended with a pardoning of the alleged witches after an unsuccessful search for witch marks under the supervision of the King's physician, followed by the eventual confession of the child accuser to having provided a false former testimony. However, the fact that in 1637, three years after the trial "five women, one with a child were still detained,"[54] testifies to the necessity of exorcising these women from society.

The play foregrounds the intersection of the religious, political and legal discourses about witchcraft and its gender implications, using witchcraft "as a metaphor for threats posed by unruly subjects,"[55] while still insisting on the witches' liter(e)ality, necessary to justify punishment and contain the threat on a plot level. However, although the play was supposedly written in favor of witchcraft beliefs, it keeps a significant ambivalence about its metaphorical and/or literal readings. From the beginning onwards the satirical comedy is mostly directed against the victims of witchcraft, while the grotesquely pain- and even pitiful punishment of the shape-shifting witch's cut-off paw/hand and the deathly prospect of the witch's beheading is emphasized towards the end. The play's ending in particular foregrounds the futility of all efforts to contain the witches' monstrous bodies in comedic boundaries by pushing the genre to its limits towards a "monstrous" tragicomic effect as expression of insoluble affective and cognitive incongruities.

The play opens on the central question of ocular proof in the current witchcraft debate, and comically explores the paradoxical claim of the witches' vanishing from sight as an empirical proof of magic (Arthur: "what I see / [...] / To

---

52 Herbert Berry, "The Globe Bewitched and El Hombre Fiel" in Herbert Berry, *Shakespeare's Playhouses* (New York: AMS Press, 1987): 121–148 referred to by Alison Findlay, "Sexual and Spiritual Politics in the Events of 1633–34 and *The Late Lancashire Witches*" in *The Lancashire Witches: Histories and Stories*, ed. Robert Poole (Manchester: Manchester University Press, 2002): 146–165, 150.

53 Quoted from Findlay, "Sexual and Spiritual Politics," 159.

54 Findlay, "Sexual and Spiritual Politics," 151.

55 Findlay, "Sexual and Spiritual Politics," 153.

that will I give credit" 1.1.48–51).[56] The discussion between a fundamental skeptic (Shakstone) and a rational believer (Arthur) about a hare's sudden disappearance during a hunting event remains unresolved, as the complexity of the debate is enhanced by its association with questions about the literal versus the metaphorical through the introduction of the foolish Whetstone, whose firm belief in witchcraft is associated with his inability to understand figurative speech (when he is called a "WitchMaster" 1.1.108–109). Although this makes him the butt of satire, his belief in witchcraft is soon substantiated by the appearance of the witches and by his close relation to them. The play thus paradoxically proves the liter(e)ality of witchcraft to the skeptics, but at the same time foregrounds its metaphorical function as sign of social disorder. The witches only appear onstage (in 2.1) after the audience has been presented with the "distraction [they] have set in Seelyes house," (2.1.550–551) where children rule over parents, servants over masters and women over men. What seems like madness is caused by the witches, as the play seems to favor a supernatural over a medical-psychological discourse about witchcraft. At the same time, there is no exploration of the witches' evil demonic powers, nor of specific motivations for their pranks. Instead there is a fairly general emphasis on their anarchic spirit ("which shall beget / Wonder and sorrow mongst our foes, / Whilst we make laughter of their woes" 2.1.551–553), which is put to effect most spectacularly at the wedding festivity of the servants of the Seely family and the successive witches' sabbath.

Both events serve as a communal celebration of the witches' power to inflict chaos and to act out their own desires, amongst which transgressive sexual desires figure most prominently. The power of the witches is connected to their ability to cross the human/animal boundary by shape-shifting into hares (1.1.27), greyhounds (2.1.923–927), or – more often – cats (2.1.790–811 and 5.1.2289–2330), as well as to their knowledge of transvection to overcome limitations of time and space (as in the miraculous transportation of wine from London 3.1.1199–1200). But despite these supernatural abilities the late Lancashire witches are women firmly anchored in society, varying in age and social standing, united in a "Satanicall sisterhood," (3.1.1507) which is presided over by Mistress Generous, the respectable wife of Master Generous, and assisted by Mal Spencer, the young lover of Master Generous' servant Robin.

Their empowerment is inevitably presented as sign of an emasculating gender upheaval, which leaves the men as helpless victims, incapable of regaining

56 All quotes from Thomas Heywood and Richard Brome, *An Edition of The Late Lancashire Witches by Thomas Heywood and Richard Brome*, ed. Laird H. Barber (New York and London: Garland Publishing, 1979). Further references given in the text.

control (see Robin: "my Wench and her friends the Fiends, will teare me to pieces" 3.1.1266–1267). The witches' power resides not only in their connection to the demonic, but decisively in their sisterhood, which the play focuses on, contrasting the communal joyful celebration of the witches' sabbath to the chaotic disharmony of the wedding festivity. The latter event seems to turn the inside out of an intoxicated brain, as the Seely family is now transformed again (3.1. 1291), while the music stops or is discordant, the wine disappears, and "all the meat is flowne out o'the chimney" to be replaced by the ingredients of a witch's cauldron, "Snakes, Batts, Frogs, Beetles, Hornets, and Humble-bees" (3.1.147, 148).

The real feast, spied upon by Robin ("ile peep in at some cranny or other, and try if I can see what they are doing" 4.1.1513–1514), is transferred to the witches, who wine and dine, sing and dance together. The scene explicitly addresses the voyeuristic overtones of contemporary witch-hunts. Even if the sexual excess of the witches' sabbath is left to the audience's imagination, it is implicitly evoked in contrast to the disrupted wedding night of Seely's servants, marred by his impotence and her public abuse of him, which in turn provokes a parodic skimmington paraded before the newly-weds by the community. However, social punishment proves to be an ineffective remedy of disruptive behavior, as the enraged servant couple successfully beats up the impersonations of a shrew and her husband intended to shame them. The play thus foregrounds the links between the shrew, the whore and the witch, only to then insist on the witch as the source of all evil.

After the witches' sabbath as the play's climactic moment of utmost empowerment, the action inevitably turns to methods of discipline and punishment of the unruly women, offering two consecutive 'trials.' The first is Master Generous' private trial of his wife after he has been informed about her secret double life. Acting as jury and judge he pardons her, because of her confession and seeming tearful repentance ("when I looke towards Heaven / I beg a gracious Pardon" 4.1. 1792–1793). This is possible because it is not her nature which defines the witch, but the disruptive effects of her behavior on family and community. This legalistic attitude towards witchcraft as human crime rather than as expression of demonic power and insurmountable otherness allows for a more successful containment of the cultural anxieties which were projected onto the figure of the witch. However, Master Generous' private forgiveness has to fail, as despite his repeated use of legal terms his judgment is marred by his emotional attachment and his inability to recognize Mistress Generous' scheming use of "passionate words mixt with forc't tears, /[which] Did [s]o inchant his eyes and eares" (4.1.2046–2047). As her trickery raises disconcerting suspicions about all women's display of feelings as deceitful witchcraft, the detection and punishment of the witch as a reassertion of her difference in spite of her likeness to other women is all the more important.

In this context the play advocates a legal discourse, which centers on the ocular proof of a bodily inscription of innocent virginity or satanic sexuality. This emphasis on bodily evidence is first addressed by the call for a jury of women (4.1.1949) to search the body of the still virgin bride after the servants' wedding night as a proof of her accusation of the husband's impotence. The gendered anxieties about female honesty are also taken up in the witches' prank played upon the young gents, whose pride is shamed by visions of their supposedly biological lower class fathers (a tutor, a tailor and a servant). Despite the immediate resolution of the issue and the confirmation that "'Tis all for mirth, we mean no hurt," (4.1.2081) the notion of a fundamental uncertainty about paternity raises deep-seated fears and doubts about female virtue and trustworthiness, which can only be resolved on a public level involving the whole community and legitimized by unquestionable bodily evidence.

Consequently the last act is devoted to the hunt and punishment of the witches culminating in a court-like situation. It is only now that the satanic side of the witches is foregrounded as a justification for the actions against them. Significantly it takes a Soldier to meet and beat the "company of Hell-cats" (5.1.2417) by cutting off one of the cats' paws with his sword. Cultural and bodily markers coincide as "most infallible markes" (5.1.2444) to identify the witch, when Master Generous finds the bloody paw transformed into an all too familiar hand wearing his wedding band ("Is this the hand once plighted holy vowes, / And this the ring that bound them?" (5.1.2445–2446). When Mistress Generous is discovered hiding in bed, aptly turning the place of marital union and order into a sick-bed, her dismemberment leaves no room for doubt or pardon (Master Generous: "My heart hath bled more for thy curst relapse / Than drops hath issu'd from thy wounded arme" 5.1.2526–2527). The witches' "Covenant with the greatest enemy of mankind" (5.1.2551–2552) calls for harsh punishment as prerequisite for a restoration of order. Significantly the audience is reassured that despite their evil powers, "Witches apprehended under hands of lawfull authority, doe loose their power; / And all their spells are instantly dissolv'd" (5.1.2631–2633).

Like *The Witch of Edmonton*, Heywood and Brome's play foregrounds the dilemma inherent in the double-edged stratagem of legal procedure, which has to emphasize the witches' evil power in order to justify their punishment, but at the same time has to diminish their demonic status in order to affirm the power of the law over them. Consequently, the depiction of the witches oscillates between demonization and humanization, between difference from and similarity to all women, between metaphorical likeness and literal otherness. The ensuing ambivalences are most apparent in Master Generous, who is cast as judge intent on punishing the witch and as husband pitying his wife. However the end of the play insists on the necessity of a legalistic view of witchcraft, enforcing her expulsion from society. This is justified because of the solidarity of the satanic sisterhood and their refusal of confession, while the single testimony of one old woman functions as comical confirmation of common witchlore about sexual intercourse with the devil (Peg. "He pleas'd me well Sir, like a proper man. [...] Only his flesh felt cold" 5.1.2753–2755).

The play's ambivalence between the witches as metaphor for unruly women and as literal demonic otherness enables their function as satiric 'masterminds', renders credibility to the reaction of pity and ensures the necessity and possibility of their elimination from society. The ineffectivity of attempts to counter the gender upheaval and restore order through private confession or public shaming rituals reveals the need for a legal solution, which insists on the potential liter(e)ality of the witch as precondition for the court procedures to be put into effect. As in *The Witch of Edmonton* the effective containment of the threat to social order relies on the double strategy of rendering the witches more ordinary and less powerful than Shakespeare's weird sisters in order for them to be punishable, while at the same time insisting on their demonic affiliations in order to justify their deadly expulsion from society. In this context the body guarantees the witch's identification through the witch mark or through the loss of her shape-shifting power when bodily harmed or arrested by the law. It is thus the knowledge and use of the limitations of the witch's power inscribed onto her body, which enable her punishment and expulsion and prove the law as reassuringly more powerful. However, the grotesque presentation of the cut-off hand of the 'master'-witch and the emotional disturbance of the husband emphasize the ambivalence between the distancing effect of the satiric comedy and the affective involvement of the horror of the 'real,' even if only as part of a theatrical spectacle, generating the monstrously mixed feelings ascribed to tragicomedy ("Perhaps great Mercy may / After just condemnation give them day / Of longer life" Epilogue 2807–2809).

Like *The Witch of Edmonton* Heywood and Brome's *The Late Lancashire Witches* participates in a cultural movement attempting to incorporate the demonic witch into an empirical world view. However, both plays, while attesting to the desire to contain the threat of the unruly witch, still insist on the tensions involved in this process, oscillating ambivalently between celebration and condemnation of the satanic sisterhood, metaphorical and literal readings, comedy and tragicomedy. The audience is left with a promise of the witches' execution, but at the same time with the lasting impression of the play's central celebration of the witches' sabbath as a powerfully joyful, yet illicit alternative to the licensed wedding festivity, and with a powerful final statement of their unrelenting spirit refusing confession and repentance (Mistress Generous: "I will say nothing, but what you know you know, / And as the law shall finde me let it take me" 5.1.2726–2727).

5 Staging Monstrous Renaissance Bodies: The Witch and the Negotiation of Boundaries

The staging of the witch during the first decades of the seventeenth century foregrounds the epistemological crisis in Early Modern European culture, highlighting its religious, political and social implications. As a monstrous creature *par excellence*, the figure of the witch embodies the negotiation of boundaries in-between supernatural/natural, human/animal, male/female, matter/spirit. In this context the gender anxieties addressed in the witch plays discussed here are linked differently to the discussion of other uncertainties, indicating discursive intersections. Moreover, the plays are written in the context of historical events like the *Witchcraft Act* of 1604, or actual court cases like the Lancashire witch trials of 1612 and 1634, or the trial of the witch of Edmonton 1621, thus taking active part in the shaping and changing of ideas about the witch and her cultural significance.

5.1 Likeness and Difference: The Metaphorical and the Literal

All witch plays discussed here participate, albeit differently, in the debate about the characterisation of the witch in relation to human nature, and focus in this context on her supernatural powers as the most distinctive differential characteristic. Shakespeare's *Macbeth*, in which "everything is on the border between fantasy and reality,"[57] sets the scene for this discussion by staging the witches' uncertain nature as most radical embodiment of in-betweenness. Ambivalently conjoining aspects of the old village hag, the demonic witch and the prophetess, the weird sisters always remain without reach of the protagonists, whose attempt to 'metamorphose' into witch and devil acting out the desire for omnipotence is inevitably countered by returning hauntings about and experiences of absolute powerlessness. Reading the witches' difference as likeness, which can be emulated, inevitably leads to a reaffirmation of their inexplicable unreadable differ-

57 Greenblatt, *Hamlet in Purgatory*, 193.

ence, reestablishing the boundaries between the supernatural and the human in gendered terms via Macbeth's death in battle and the Lady's mad suicide.

Cultural anxieties about female empowerment and their containment, which are played out in Lady Macbeth's association with and dissociation from the weird sisters, take center stage in Middleton's *The Witch*, in the emphasis on a likeness between witches and humans, who share the same sexual desires. At the same time, however, the witches' world remains clearly different, separate from the human world of the play. This ambivalence between likeness and difference is enabled through the genre-dependent insistence on the gap between desire and act, which ensures the return to human order despite the close interaction with the world of the witches. At the same time, the artificiality of the ending foregrounds the persistence of the witches' threat of an unruly sexualized femininity and its power "to infect" the whole community. At the other end of the tragicomic spectrum *The Witch of Edmonton's* title character is presented like any other old mistreated woman, but also as unmistakably different through the devil's pact. In contrast to Shakespeare's and Middleton's witches, however, she always remains human, and consequently subservient to the demonic powers, which she cannot control.

Heywood and Brome's *The Late Lancashire Witches* illustrates the continuity of these concerns, foregrounding the 'infection' of the community by the witches who are not only indistinguishable from, but actually are, ordinary women representing all ages and classes. The play thus emphasizes the witch as metaphor for transgressive femininity as emasculating threat, illustrating their sexual desires and satirical pranks as examples of an anarchic spirit rather than of murderous *maleficium*. At the same time, however, the liter(e)ality of the witches and their ineradicable difference is evoked as necessary precondition for their effective punishment and expulsion from society. Despite the insistence on the inevitability of their damnation, the discrepancy between the comic pranks and the deathly punishment raises doubts about the justification of the measures taken, rendering the boundary between condemnation and celebration, fear and pity and laughter disturbingly ambivalent. The debate about the witch as metaphorical or literal threat of the boundaries in questions thus remains unsettled, as plays like *The Witch of Edmonton* and *The Late Lancashire Witches* probe into attempts at integrating the supernatural witch into an empirical world view.

5.2 Body and Mind: Desire and the Act

If "the witch becomes a somatic intermediary between humanity and the Devil,"[58] the witch's body functions as preferred site of the witch's identification. The voyeuristic gaze onto the witch's body as a site of transgressive sexual practices is particularly evident in an obsession with ocular proof in religious as well as medical and legal discourses discussed in Renaissance art and theatre[59] and can be seen in conjunction to the 'crisis of vision' and the rise of empirical sciences legitimizing an "'opening' to the eye's inspection what had been secret, closed, or hid."[60] At the same time the deceptiveness of ocular proof, highlighted in many of the texts and plays of the period, requires increasingly diversified methods and procedures.[61]

The witch plays discussed here unfold a wide spectrum of approaches to the corporeality of the witch as site of the enactment of transgressive desires. Thus the radical ambiguity of Shakespeare's weird sisters ("what seemed corporal / Melted as breath into the wind" 1.3.79–80) seems to necessitate a displacement of the corporeal onto Lady Macbeth as would-be witch, whose descent into a somatized madness and her subsequent death forestall the law's bodily punishment and emphasize the distance between witches and humans.

By contrast, the humanization or rather feminization of the witches in the later witch plays from *The Witch* to *The Witch of Edmonton* and *The Late Lancashire Witches* coincides with an increasing focus on the witch's body as a site of illicit sexual practices, particularly in descriptions of the relation with their familiars foregrounding the horrifying link between the maternal and the erotic. In this context references to the witches' old age – most prominently in *The Witch* and *The Witch of Edmonton* – can be read as a satirical reduction of the witches' threat, but also as a reminder of the unrelenting power of female transgressiveness. In this context the shape-shifting of the familiar rather than the witch in *The Witch of Edmonton* can be read as limitation of the threat of the witch, while her unrelenting spirit in contrast to the transformation of the

---

58 Rosner, "The Witch Who Is Not One," 371.

59 For the emergence of the voyeuristic gaze in Renaissance art see Sigrid Schade and Silke Wenk, "Inszenierungen des Sehens: Kunst, Geschichte und Geschlechterdifferenz" in *Genus: Zur Geschlechterdifferenz in den Kulturwissenschaften*, eds. Hadumod Bußmann and Renate Hof (Stuttgart: Kröner, 1995): 340–407, esp. 383–384.

60 Patricia Parker, "Fantasies of 'Race' and 'Gender': Africa, *Othello* and bringing to light" in *Women, "Race," and Writing in the Early Modern Period*, eds. Margo Hendricks and Patricia Parker (London: Routledge, 1994): 84–100, 87.

61 See Darr, *Marks of an Absolute Witch* and Darr, "The devil's mark."

devil dog into “the white dog of retribution” at the end of the play emphasizes her continuous threatening otherness.

In *The Late Lancashire Witches* the emphasis on the bodily proof of virginity (bride) as well as witchery (witch’s paw) is linked to an emphasis on the witches’ shape-shifting, but balanced by a reassurance of the superiority of the law, in front of which the satanic power of the witches has to dissolve. Significantly, the play does not rely on the bodily search of the witch’s mark, but prefers the cutting off of the paw/hand, enforcing a return of the witch into her human body, as an even more effective form of punishing bodily identification. The hand as site and symbol of human action with the wedding band as sign of the matrimonial vow has to be cut off to cure the community from the witches’ evil infection in an effort to reassert the union between the literal and the metaphorical body.

5.3 Vision and Language: Legal and Medical Investigation

The noticeable scopophilic obsession witch the witch’s body in Early Modern culture is connected to “a visual language of espial”[62] in cross examinations as well as in eye witness accounts in witch trials, revealing the intersection of the epistemological and the erotic in the search for the truth. The figure of the witch signals both the unreliability and deceptiveness of vision and language, and the insistence on the belief in the union between word and meaning, speech and act. The power of the witches’ language resides in its specific code, apparent in its vocabulary, rhyme, and rhythm in connection to particular rituals, gestures, movements, actions. This secret language is decisive for the witches’ magic power, as it conveys and commands vision, transforms or even kills through charms and spells. The horrifying portrayal of the witches’ satanic imitation of catholic rites in the plays can not only be read as an expression of anti-papist anxieties, but also of a secret desire to compensate for what has been lost in the wake of the Reformation. This ambivalence enhances the dramatic depiction of the witches, who are feared and celebrated at the same time.

While in *Macbeth* the unreadability of the witches’ utterances emphasizes their proximity to the supernatural, the humanization of the witches in the other plays coincides with an emphasis on the linguistic rules and rituals they are subordinated to. But although the witches in Middleton’s play follow the prescriptions of spells and recipes of the cauldron, their secret sisterhood is still pre-

62 Parker, “Fantasies of ‘Race’ and ‘Gender’,” 88.

sented as powerful, while the witch of Edmonton seems as much perpetrator as victim of her own doing, praying "the devil's *pater noster*," (2.1.186) but never quite in command of the magic she exercises.[63] By comparison, the satanic sisterhood of *The Late Lancashire Witches* is presented as a more anarchic congregation intent on bodily pleasures, whose language seems not discernibly different from ordinary language, and thus easier to overrule.

The attempts to counter the witches' linguistic power indicate the rise of legal and medical discourses in the Early Modern period, which provide an explanatory reading and a bodily discipling of the unruly witches. Shakespeare's *Macbeth* takes up the debate about the distinction between witchcraft, bewitchment and madness, setting off the indisputable superiority of the witches' unreadable discourse against a medical discourse of rationalising readability, which however, remains limited and insufficient. Ironically, the madness of Macbeth and his Lady results from their belief in the magical power of the word as truth. The inability to understand the double meaning of the witches' words, in turn, is played off against the couple's necessary reliance on a deceptive discourse to carry out their murderous plans. The play follows the protagonists' movements in-between a quasi-religious desire to believe in the word as truth and the acknowledgment of a functional use of language emptied out of magic. Lady Macbeth's madness appears as a loss of command over language and body, which ironically reasserts the unity of word and act. The figure of the witch in the plays discussed exploits the desire for truth, but offers deception, causing a madness which may infect everyone, from the ruling elite of the country (*Macbeth*) to a whole region (*The Late Lancashire Witches*).

In the context of the use of the witch "to dramatise crises in gender order and in contemporary religious politics"[64] the question of the witch's confession as proof of guilt and sign of acceptance of punishment, gains decisive importance. Confession and penitence turn the deathly punishment of the witch into a symbolic reintegration into the community. Because of their close connection to actual witchcraft trials, legal procedures are foregrounded in *The Witch of Edmonton* and *The Late Lancashire Witches*, where the power of the witch is limited. But even these plays emphasize the defiance of the witches, who (for the most part) resist confession, although the law is increasingly presented as an effective counter force relying on linguistic strategies to examine testimonials and to attain confession as well as on medical inspections to obtain bodily proof. In

63 See also Sarah Johnson, "Female Bodies, Speech and Silence in *The Witch of Edmonton*," *Early Theatre* 12.1 (2009): 69–92.

64 Findlay, "Sexual and spiritual politics," 152–153.

The Witch of Edmonton it is the personified authority of the Constable and the Justice, on whose effective and impartial enforcement of the law the community has to rely to contain the witch's threat. In *The Late Lancashire Witches* the occasional use of legal terms by major characters seems to justify an examination of the witches before the actual court case takes place (Arthur: "shall we try if we can by examination get from something that may abbreviate the cause unto the wiser in Commission for the peace before wee carry them before'em." 5.1.2702–2705). However, the repeated emphasis on the fact that "the Witches must expect their due / By lawfull Justice," (Epilogue 2802–2803) and that the community "dare not hold it fit, / That we for Justices and Judges sit," (Epilogue 2801–2802), illustrates anxieties about vigilantism.

The authority of the law depends upon its separateness from the community, guaranteed by the specificity of its ritualized procedures and its language, founded upon the belief in the performative power of the word, as in the testimonial oath. The theatrical spectacle can ironically foreground associations between the holy vow in front of the court and the secret sealing of the devil's pact. In the context of the religious crisis of the early seventeenth century and its gender implications the turn to a legal discourse seems to encourage the possibility of an "empirical demonology," which counters the threat of the witch without denying its power.

5.4 Tragic and Comic: Horror, Pity and Laughter

The theatrical appearance of the witch in tragedies, comedies and tragicomedies is connected to widely differing genre-specific affective appeals. Although many Jacobean tragedies, from Webster's *Duchess of Malfi* and *The White Devil* to Middleton and Rowley's *The Changeling* take up the discourse about witchcraft, the horror of the literal embodiment of the witches' monstrous in-betweenness prevalent in *Macbeth* seems to give way to metaphorical evocations of witchcraft in the context of psychological explorations of the horror of female transgressions which foreground a medical-psychological discourse of madness which only gradually disentangles itself from a discourse of bewitchment.

While the figure of the witch inevitably remains on the margins of tragedy, she can take on a more prominent role in comedy and tragicomedy, where she is linked to both rule and ridicule, as a powerful witch in command and as an old mistreated village hag. The discourse of madness in skeptical texts about witchcraft from Reginald Scot's *Discoverie of Witchcraft* (1584) onwards in particular, allows for an emergence of the witch as an old, poor and often melancholic woman[65] whose delusions of power can be ridiculed. Traces of this concept are particularly evident in the descriptions of old witches engaging in transgressive sexual encounters with the devil, the familiar, or with young men of the community. While the age difference in these encounters functions as a means of ridicule, this potential reduction of the threat of the witch is balanced by illustrations of her power of *maleficium* over the community, and its male members in particular.

At the same time the figure of the powerful witch emerges as a source of satire, ridiculing the helpless victims of her *maleficium*, either in terms of sexual subjugation (Almachildes in *The Witch*), or in relation to anarchic pranks (the Seely household in *The Late Lancashire Witches*). In this context the ambivalent ending of *The Late Lancashire Witches* illustrates the difficulties of reconciling the powerful witch as tool of criticism of social disorder with her deathly punishment. In *The Witch of Edmonton* this ambivalence that represents Elizabeth Sawyer as pitiable old woman, source of justified criticism of the community, and evil witch is evident throughout the play. Both plays' endings foreground this ambivalence by conjoining the prospective execution with a defiance of confession, which justifies the deathly punishment, but also celebrates the witches' unrelenting spirit and even calls upon notions of pity.

Tragicomedy as a mixed genre can accommodate feelings as diverse as horror, pity and laughter. Foregrounding the witch as expression of cultural fears and desires, as threat to social order and its containment, tragicomedy addresses cultural 'boundary work' proposing solutions and questioning their validity at the same time. This pertains, albeit differently, to the tragicomic fairy tale of *The Witch*, as well as to the domestic realism of *The Witch of Edmonton*, while *The Late Lancashire Witches* begins as a satirical comedy but ends raising questions about the relation of laughter to horror and pity. In the last two plays (written in the 1620s and 1630s) the emphasis on providence and poetic justice seems to encourage the conjunction of these seemingly "incompatible" feelings, while foregrounding the fact that pity seems to come at the price of lethal punishment. At a time when boundaries are being reassessed according to new premises, tragicomedy insists on a both/and instead of an either/or solution, foregrounding a persistence of monstrous ambiguities, which will never be resolved.

---

65 See Scot: "old, lame, bleare-eied, pale, fowle, and full of wrinkles; poor, sullen, superstitious, and papist" (Reginald Scot, *The Discoverie of Witchcraft* (London: Henry Denham for William Brome, 1584), 7).

Mariangela Tempera

"…Languished…, and then died": Courtroom Drama and the Bodies of the Victims in Thomas Pott's *The Wonderfull Discoverie of Witches* (1612)

In 2012, the fourth centenary of a witch trial was celebrated in Lancaster and in Pendle Forest with a series of events aimed primarily at attracting and entertaining tourists.[1] Historically, the tragic events of 1612, followed by another witch scare in 1633, had attracted national attention in the seventeenth century and their fame has since been kept alive by the work of minor playwrights and novelists.[2]

The 1612 events have also attracted considerable critical attention because they are far better documented than most English witch trials. In November 1612, Thomas Potts published the first edition of his *The Wonderfull Discoverie of Witches in the Countie of Lancaster*,[3] thus fulfilling a task that had been assigned to him by the judges themselves. As an Associate Clerk on the Northern Circuit, he would have had access to all the legal materials concerning the case and would have been an active participant in the Assizes. Of course, his report is far from transparent. He relies heavily on pre-trial depositions, while trying to convey the impression that he is faithfully describing the courtroom proceedings; he extolls the wisdom and learning of the judges in the loftiest terms while verbally attacking and ridiculing the defendants. More disturbingly, for scholars attempting to reconstruct the events, he "blinds us with ceremony, and silently edits out sections of procedure against the Lancashire witches."[4]

1 See: http://lancashirewitches400.org

2 For book-length studies of the two trials and their afterlives in literature, see Mariangela Tempera, *The Lancashire Witches: Lo stereotipo della strega fra scrittura giuridica e scrittura letteraria* (Imola: Galeati, 1981), and *The Lancashire Witches: Histories and Stories*, ed. Robert Poole (Manchester: Manchester University Press, 2002). I have incorporated brief extracts from my 1981 book in the present article.

3 All the quotations in my text are taken from the second edition of *The Wonderfull Discoverie* (1613), which is reprinted in: Marion Gibson, *Early Modern Witches: Witchcraft Cases in Contemporary Writing* (London and New York: Routledge, 2000): 173–265.

4 Marion Gibson, *Reading Witchcraft: Stories of Early English Witches* (London and New York: Routledge, 1999), 54.

Potts's *Discoverie* portrays the activities of village witches that resort to *maleficium* (harmful magic) because they have seen their requests for alms refused (it is the "charity denied" paradigm that was identified and studied by Keith Thomas[5]), but also because of enmity among neighbours and of souring relationships between folk-healers and their customers. The witches attract all the attention of the author, the readers and the critics, because of the fascinating ambiguity of their figures and of their tragic fate. But the legal documents edited and presented in the *Discoverie* also include the statements of their victims, whose stories are far less colourful, but still worth examining in detail. In fact, being less shocking and controversial than those of the witches, their depositions may have been less heavily edited by Potts and therefore closer to what they actually said. The victims play important roles in the courtroom drama of the Assizes, because ascertaining what happened to their bodies is at the core of the trial.

1 The Lancaster Assizes of August 1612

At the beginning of April 1612, following a series of complaints about witchcraft-induced illnesses and deaths in the neighbourhood of Pendle Forest, Richard Nowell, a Justice of the Peace based in Lancaster, examined and arrested the eighty-year-old doyennes of two clans of local witches, Elizabeth Southerns (aka 'Old Demdike') and Anne Whittle (aka 'Chattox'), Demdike's grandchild Alizon Device and Chattox's daughter Anne Redferne. A few days later, the other witches met at Malkin Tower allegedly for the purpose of naming a familiar spirit and finalizing plans for blowing up Lancaster Castle in order to free the prisoners. The group included Demdike's daughter, Elizabeth, and her grandchild, James, who admitted the conspiracy to Nowell. Thanks also to the testimony of Elizabeth's nine-year-old daughter, Jennet, the participants in the meeting were arrested and questioned throughout the summer. One of the accused, Jennet Preston, was tried in York on a separate charge (the murder of Thomas Lister).[6] All the others (except Old Demdike who had died in custody) were tried at the Lancaster Assizes on 18–19 August. Ten of the defendants were found guilty and executed on 20 August. The Assizes also examined the accusa-

---

5 Keith Thomas, *Religion and the Decline of Magic: Studies in Popular Beliefs in Sixteenth- and Seventeenth-Century England* (Harmondsworth: Penguin, 1973).

6 Her story is told in a 16-page pamphlet appended to the *Discoverie*. On the controversy surrounding the authorship of this short pamphlet, see Philip C. Almond, *The Lancashire Witches: A Chronicle of Sorcery and Death on Pendle Hill* (London: I.B. Tauris, 2012), 83–87.

tions of Grace Sowerbutts against a group of women from Salemsbury. Her outlandish claims of possession and cannibalism failed to convince the judges. Grace eventually admitted to having been suborned by a Jesuit, and the defendants were acquitted.

2 The Courtroom and the Stage

Although no longer dominated, as in Roman times, by the star advocate celebrated in Cicero's *Brutus*, Jacobean trials still bore some resemblance to a theatrical performance.[7] Even the Assizes, where the plaintiffs had no representation and the reading of their previous confessions took the place of *viva voce* depositions, would have attracted a large, sometimes unruly audience: "[t]he tradition, still alive today, that criminal trials constitute a public spectacle, also contributed to the unseemly nature of assize proceedings."[8] The spectators could look forward to some lively, unscripted moments that are carefully preserved by Potts, who repeatedly refers to what is unfolding under his eyes as a "tragedy":

> [...] who were the principall authors and actors in this late woefull and lamentable *Tragedie*, wherein so much Blood was spilt. (182)
> [...] the next in order was her sonne *James Device*, whom shee and her mother, old *Dembdike*, brought to act his part in this wofull Tragedie. (206)
> [...] and then to discover his [the Catholic Priest's] plotted Tragedie (225)
> Here then is the last that came to act her part in this lamentable and wofull Tragedie, (249)

"Witch-trials [...] were intricately plotted human dramas with a large, but often historically invisible, supporting cast."[9] Potts does his best to inject some life into members of the "supporting cast." The "Jurie of Gentlemen for life and death" (190) forms the privileged audience for whose benefit (and the Judge's) the proceedings are held. Judge Bromley makes sure they have more than enough evidence, complementing the written records with *viva voce* examination

---

7 "The adversarial nature of English law necessitated that, in every action, two conflicting interpretations of the same events were offered by the plaintiff and the defendant, each of whom employed a narrator to convince the court that his interpretation of events was the most convincing." Paul Raffield, *Images and Cultures of Law in Early Modern England: Justice and Political Power, 1558–1660* (Cambridge: Cambridge University Press, 2004), 24.

8 J.S. Cockburn, *A History of English Assizes, 1558–1714* (Cambridge: Cambridge University Press, 1972), 110.

9 Malcolm Gaskill, "Witchcraft, Politics, and Memory in Seventeenth-Century England," *The Historical Journal* 50.2 (2007): 289–308, 306.

of witnesses (209). He is very cautious: "being very suspitious of the accusation of this yong wench *Jennet Device* [...] tooke great paines to examine her of every particular point" (235). He shares the doubts of the jurors: "My Lord *Bromley*, and all the whole Court not a little wondering, as they had good cause, at this liberall and voluntarie confession of the Witch" (244).

Judge and jurors, in turn, become part of the show for the much larger audience of witnesses and onlookers. Bromley "drew the eyes and reverend respect of all that great Audience present" (253). The "great Audience" is made up of the local people, whose "crie" has brought Anne Redferne, previously acquitted, to a second trial (229). These people are the "good Neighbours" who demand "to be delivered from the companie of such a dangerous, wicked, and malicious Witch [Margaret Pearson]" (249). They respond in various ways to the events that unfold before their eyes in the courtroom: they empathize with the victims: "Oh, who was present at this lamentable spectacle, that was not moved with pitie to behold it!" (246); they show "contempt" for Anne Whittle (191), whose crimes "[take] away all sense of humanity" (191). They show surprise for the "marke" of Elizabeth Device: "as the best that were present in that Honorable assembly, and great Audience, did affirme, they had not often seene the like." (202) They compare and contrast witches: "All men that knew her [Anne Redferne] affirmed, shee was more dangerous then her Mother" (232). Some of them are called upon to testify about what they know at first hand.

Like his fellow pamphleteers, Potts reproduces the written depositions that were taken prior to the Assizes rather than *viva voce* exchanges between defendants and witnesses; he does, however, insert a couple of highly theatrical moments involving Jennet Device, the nine-year-old star witness for the prosecution. Subjected to verbal abuse by her mother (understandably unhappy with the role her child is about to play in condemning her to the gallows), Jennet bursts into tears. The solicitous judge has Elizabeth removed from the courtroom and then orders "the Maide to bee set upon the Table in the presence of the whole Court." It is from this stage that Jennet spins her damning tales for a rapt audience. Later on, when she is requested to pick out from an identity parade the witches who attended the Malkin Tower banquet, "she went and tooke *Alice Nutter*, this prisoner by the hand, and accused her to be one" (235). She then proceeds to do the same with other prisoners (241).

The author inserts a modest disclaimer in his *Discoverie:* "It is no part of my profession to publish any thing in print, neither can I paint in extraordinarie tearmes." (256) And yet, he manages to let fragments of lively dialogue slip into a text that relies almost entirely on legal documents. Some witnesses report Thomas Preston's deathbed denunciation of a witch in unusually melodramatic terms: "*Jennet Preston* lyes heavie upon me, [...] helpe me, helpe me: and so departed, crying out against her." (260). Alizon Device is moved to tears when she is addressed directly by John Law, a cripple who makes his entrance supported by his son and tells the court how, on meeting the defendant in a country lane, he fell out with her over some pins, was struck down and has never recovered: "which with weeping teares in great passion turned to the Prisoner; in the hearing of all the Court hee said to her, *This thou knowest to be too true:* and thereupon she humblie acknowledged the same, and cried out to God to forgive her; and upon her knees with weeping teares humbly prayed him to forgive her that wicked offence; which he very freely and voluntarily did" (244). The witch on her knees in front of her crippled victim is a powerful *tableau* that is offered for the entertainment and instruction of the onlookers.

Potts does not openly acknowledge it, but comedy as well as tragedy finds its way into the courtroom and from there into his work. He records the words of meddlesome gossips: John Robinson "had chidden and becalled this Examinate [Elizabeth Device], for having a Bastard child with one *Seller.*" (201) He describes small episodes of personal hostility that should be considered endemic in a community and should not attract the attention of the law: John Nutter's son, "misliking her [AnneChattox's] doings, put the said Kan and milke over with his foot" (198). Mrs Towneley, thinking that James Device and his mother had "stolne some Turves of her, bade him packe the doores: and withal as he went forth of the doore, [...] gave him a knock betweene the shoulders" (208). From these petty quarrels, he occasionally salvages a fragment of conversation that is ready for replaying on stage: Richard Baldwyn tells Demdike and Alizon: "get out of my ground Whores and Witches, I will burne the one of you, and hang the other. To whom this Examinate [Demdike] answered: I care not for thee, hang thy selfe" (184).

One of the victims, Robert Nutter, is portrayed as a slightly ridiculous young master who can only threaten in the future, since at present he has no control over his father's land. He (allegedly) tried to force himself upon Anne Redferne and, being rejected, "in a great anger tooke his Horse, and went away, saying in a great rage, that if ever the Ground came to him, shee shoul never dwell upon his Land" (193); on leaving the estate to go on a journey, Robert tells Anne's husband that "if ever he came againe he would get his Father to put the said *Redferne* out of his house, or he himselfe would pull it downe" (195). Actually, his father, Christopher Nutter, is quite dismissive of his profligate offspring. When a languishing Robert peevishly insists that he has been bewitched, Christopher does not believe him: "Thou art a foolish Ladde, it is not so, it is thy miscarriage." To which his tearful son replies with another one of his empty threats: "I am sure I am bewitched by them [Chattox and Redferne], and if ever I come againe [...] I will procure them to be laid where they shall be glad to bite Lice in two with their teeth." (231) The son eventually dies but this skeptical father is only prepared to admit that his family may have been targeted by witches when he himself lies on his deathbed.

The Chaddocks too are the stuff comic characters are made on. The wife keeps nagging at her sick husband, who refuses to believe that he has been bewitched. She tells a friend "I thinke that my husband will never mend until hee have asked her [Isabel Robey's] forgivenesse, choose him whether hee will be angrie or pleased, for this is my opinion; to which he answered, when he did need to ask her forgivenesse, he would, but hee thought hee did not need, for any thing hee knew" (252). Actually, Peter Chaddock's statement at the arraignment shows that he has finally embraced his wife's position and is fully convinced of Isabel's responsibility; like a comedy husband, however, he is not prepared to admit that she was right all along.

The dramatic and comic moments that occasionally enliven Potts's dull assemblage of legal documents could make us forget that "legal spectacle differs from theatrical spectacle precisely because it makes an explicit claim to the real."[10] By foregrounding the suffering and death of the victims, the author makes sure that we do not.

3 The Bodies of the Victims

As one would expect in courtroom proceedings, the victims of the Lancashire witches are meticulously identified. However, three skulls remain anonymous, leaving the onlookers to wonder which graves had been desecrated to provide the ingredients for black magic. James Device testifies that in 1600 Anne Chattox "did take three scalpes of people, which had been buried, and then cast out of a grave [...]; and tooke eight teeth out of the said Scalpes, whereof she kept foure to her selfe, and gave the other foure to the said *Demdike*" (196). It is not, as we might expect, the skulls but the teeth that are precious enough to be carefully guarded for twelve years and are now produced as evidence against old Demdike. Gruesome as it may seem, this magic is a far cry from digging up the corpse of a child, boiling it and then eating the rotting flesh (219–220), a crime of which the Salemsbury witches are accused, and then – to prove how fair the court was – acquitted.

10 Todd Wayne Butler, "Bedeviling Spectacle: Law, Literature, and Early Modern Witchcraft," *Yale Journal of Law and the Humanities* 20.2 (2008): 111–129, 120.

Through the written depositions of those who survived the attacks of the witches and are in court to tell their stories of woe we can catch glimpses of bodies that have endured a lot of pain and discomfort but have not been permanently damaged. Peter Chaddock volunteers a detailed account of recurring sick spells that coincide with disagreements with Isabel Robey, and of temporary returns to good health which occur whenever he makes peace with her. The first episode of being "sore pained in his bones" (250) is followed by a "paine and starknesse" in his neck (250), then by a high temperature that triggers an unquenchable thirst: "hee would have given any thing he had, to have slacked his thirst, having drinke enough in the house, and yet could not drinke" (251), then again "great warch in his bones, and all his limes" (251). In her deposition, Jane Wilkinson maintains that, having denied Isobel Robey some milk, on her way to a neighbouring village, she "was suddenly pinched on her Thigh as shee thought, with foure fingers & a Thumbe twice together, and thereupon was sicke, in so much as shee could not get home but on horse-backe, yet soone after shee did mend" (251). The bodies of these victims bear no visible trace of their close encounters with the forces of evil, and yet their narratives contain elements with which their audience in the courtroom can easily empathize: the inability to quench one's thirst, the frightening experience of being taken ill while away from the comfort zone of one's home.

The exhibition of the victims' bodies reaches its climax when Alizon Device comes face to face with John Law, the pedlar "deformed by her Witch-craft, and transformed beyond the course of Nature" (243). Potts takes great pains to ensure that his readers share the horror felt by the courtroom audience at the sight of his devastated body. John Law's confrontation with Alizon is followed by the deposition of his son, that gives us further details of this victim's plight: the pedlar "lay in Colne speechlesse, and had the left-side lamed all save the eye: and when this Examinate came to his father, his said father had something recovered his speech, and did complaine that hee was pricked with Knives, Elsons and Sickles and that the same hurt was done unto him at Colne-field [...]" (245). We are also told that John Law had been "a verie able sufficient stout man of Bodie, and a goodly man of Stature." But now "his head is drawne awrie, his Eyes and face deformed, His speech not well to bee understood; his Armes lame especially the left side, his hands lame and turned out of their course, his bodie able to endure no travel" (246).

Today's readers do not need medical training in order to come to the conclusion that the unfortunate pedlar had suffered a stroke (perhaps triggered by the frightening confrontation with a notorious witch). However, in a seventeenth century courtroom, the sight of his disabled body, the contrast between his previous robust health and his present helplessness, the loss of income caused by his inability to travel would have concurred to turn the jury against his attacker, thus sealing her fate. Potts is far less interested in the plight of another able-bodied young man, Elizabeth Device's son James, who had been arrested with the rest of his clan and testifies for the prosecution at the Assizes. Other than an unsubstantiated hypothesis of attempted suicide, no explanation is given by the clerk for the decline of this youth who has become "so insensible, weake, and unable in all things, as he could neither speake, heare, or stand, but was holden up when hee was brought to the place of his Arraignement" (206). Again, today's readers would come to their own conclusions as to the causes of James's physical decline while he was in the hands of gaolers who, in theory, should not have used coercive methods to turn him against his family.[11] In Potts's "tragedie" the crippled bodies of John Law and James Device are a stark reminder of the ultimate difference between the stage and the courtroom. These "actors" will not stretch out their limbs and bow for the applause at the end of their performance.

Those who were allegedly killed by the witches cannot speak for themselves or parade their ailing bodies. If the depositions of their surviving family members are to be trusted, quite a few of them identified and denounced their tormenters in their final moments, but only one managed to corroborate his accusation after death. When Jennet Preston is forced to face Thomas Lister "after hee was dead, & layd out to be wound up in his winding-sheet, the said *Jennet Preston* coming to touch the dead corpes, they bled fresh bloud presently, in the presence of all that were present" (261). The belief that a corpse would start bleeding in the presence of its murderer was commonly held in Early Modern England, where suspects dreaded the ordeal of being forced to touch the corpse in front of witnesses.[12]

The vast majority of the victims seems to have suffered from wasting diseases. In Potts's formulaic language, they all "languished and then died":

---

11 For evidence of a very limited use of torture in order to gather evidence in Elizabethan and Jacobean England, see John H. Langbein, *Torture and the Law of Proof: Europe and England in the Ancien Régime* (Chicago and London: The University of Chicago Press, 2006 [1976]), 73–139.

12 For examples of Early Modern scholarly opinions on this point and for accounts of two Scottish trials involving bleeding corpses, see James Crossley's "Notes" to his edition of Potts's *Discoverie* in *Remains Historical and Literary Connected with the Palatine Counties of Lancaster and Chester*, vol. VI (Manchester: The Chetham Society, 1845), 47–50. In *Richard III*, Shakespeare himself refers to this belief when Lady Anne asks the bearers of Henry VI's corpse to witness that, in the presence of Richard of Gloucester, "[d]ead Henry's wounds / Ope their congealed mouths and bleed afresh." (1.2.55–56, *The Norton Shakespeare*, New York: W.W. Norton & Co., 1997).

> [...] a woman Child of the sayd *Richard Baldwins* was fallen sicke; and [...] the sayd Child did languish afterwards by the space of a year, or thereabouts, and dyed [...] (187)
> [...] a child of the said *John Moores*, called *John*, fell sicke, and languished about half a yeare, and then died: (198)
> [...] the said [Hugh] *Moore* presently fell sicke, and languished about halfe a yeare, and then died. (198)
> *Robert Nutter* [...] fell sicke, and so languished until about Candlemas then next after, and then died. (231)
> *Christopher Nutter*, about Maudlintide next after following fell sicke, and so languished, until Michaelmas then next after, and then died (231).

In a rural community, where cattle rearing was a vital source of income, the death of a cow is described in the same words employed for the loss of a loved one: "[...] a Cow of the said *John Nutters* fell sicke, and so languished three or foure dayes, and then died" (198). Along with other, less frequent, phrasings of the same concept, "languished and then died" attributes to witchcraft the slow, unstoppable loss of strength that might easily be due to other causes, such as: the vulnerability to disease of small children that resulted in a very high rate of infant mortality; famine (the trial took place while Lancashire was in the grip of a major agriculture crisis); venereal disease (whose symptoms were described by physicians in similar terms[13]).

In attributing the slow decline and death of so many people to *maleficium*, the Jury could rely on long-held beliefs supported by the depositions of both defendants and victims. In the late 1550s, the preacher John Jewel had described to Queen Elizabeth the pitiful spectacle offered by the bodies of the bewitched: "Your grace's subjects pine away even unto death, their colour fadeth, their flesh rotteth, their speech is benumbed, their senses are bereft."[14] Sixty years later, the Lancashire witches still knew how to cause the same symptoms in their victims.

In her deposition, Elizabeth Demdike explains that

> [...] the speediest way to take a mans life away by Witchcraft, is to make a Picture of Clay, like unto the shape of the person whom they meane to kill, & dry it thorowly: and when they would have them to be ill in any one place more then an other: then take a Thorne or Pinne, and pricke it in that part of the Picture you would so have to be ill: and when

13 See, for example, William Clowes's 1596 description of a man suffering from *Gonorrhea faetida:* "his body greatly pined and wasted, as it were in a lingering consumption." (*Selected Writings of William Clowes 1544–1604*, F.N.L. Poyntner ed. (London: Harvey & Blythe Ltd., 1948), 93).

14 The sermon is quoted in: George Lyman Kittredge, *Witchcraft in Old and New England* (New York: Russell & Russell, 1956 [1929]), 252.

> they would have any part of the Body to consume away, then take that part of the Picture, and burne it. And when they would have the whole body to consume away, then take the remnant of the sayd Picture, and burne it: and so thereupon by that meanes, the body shall die. (184)

Introduced at the beginning of the pamphlet with the authority of a major witch (who, however, does not admit to having personally used the technique she describes in so many details), this step-by-step recipe for *maleficium* sets the tone for the rest of the narrative. Pictures of clay resurface throughout the *Discoverie.* Every description of sudden pains and pinches suggests that somewhere, out of sight, a witch is manipulating a home-made doll, thus slowing down or speeding up at will the decline and death of her target: "[...] about a weeke after the Picture was crumbled or mulled away; the said [John] *Robinson* dyed"(201); "[...] and within two daies after all was crumbled away; the said Mistris *Towneley* died" (208).

In no other account of English witchcraft does image magic play such an important role. It knits together the victims as one single languishing body, thus helping the reader go beyond the individual suffering to look at the greater picture – a picture which is inspired by a well-known political metaphor.

4 The King's Subjects and the Body Politic

At the beginning of his lengthy account of the trial, Potts reminds his readers that the authorities were spurred into action by "the complaint of the Kinges subjects for the losse of their Children, Friendes, Goodes, and cattle" (182). In exchange for their allegiance, the subjects are entitled to the king's protection, and Potts is there to share with the readers his wonder at how well James's law enforcers discharged their duties. Towards the end of his pamphlet, once the readers have had ample opportunity to empathize with the misfortunes of so many common people powerless in the face of *maleficium*, the author elaborates on another reason why the king is not only an ideal addressee but also a protagonist of the *Discoverie:* what the humble clerk is recording is a tragedy "wherein his Majestie hath lost so many Subjects, Mothers their Children, Fathers their Friends, and Kinsfolkes the like whereof hath not been set forth in any age" (249). The attack of the witches on the body natural of even the lowliest of the king's subjects is an attack on the body politic of the king: the private losses of the relatives of the individual victims are all subsumed under the king's loss of subjects. And this king has expert knowledge of witchcraft.

In 1603, King James's *Daemonologie*, which had first appeared in Edinburgh in 1597, was reprinted in London. It was followed, the next year, by a tightening of the existing edict on witchcraft which would have signalled to ambitious judges like Bromley that the prosecution of crimes connected with witchcraft had high priority for the king, and that major trials would have attracted his attention. The new legislation had a major impact on the 1612 trial: for example, the unburying of skulls and removal of teeth would not have damned Anne Chattox as a witch prior to the 1604 Act. As for the *Discoverie*, its debt to the *Daemonologie* is quite evident and proudly acknowledged by the author: "What hath the Kings Majestie written and published in his *Daemonologie*, by way of premonition and prevention, which hath not here by the first or last been executed, put in practice or discovered?" (249–250).[15]

According to James, the devil teaches witches to make images of wax of clay "[t]hat by the rosting thereof, the persones that they beare the name of, may be continuallie melted or dryed awaie by continuall sicknesse."[16] He goes on to specify that the "instrumente of waxe haue no virtue in that turne doing" but the devil himself may intervene "to weaken and scatter the spirites of life of the patient" so that "he at last shall vanish awaie, euen as his picture will doe at the fire."[17] In the same way, the devil and his agents, the witches, stealthily erode the body politic, whose health can be restored only if they are cut off.

The victims of the Lancashire witches could hardly have been expected to interpret their own wasting bodies within the framework of the shifting scientific paradigms that, at the time, engaged the learned men of Europe in heated debates. The ideal, royal addressee of the *Discoverie* and the better educated among its potential readers would have been well aware that Galen's humour-centered medicine was being complemented, if not entirely superseded, by the theories of Paracelsus and his followers. Paracelsus maintained that "disease [...] is an entity in its own right, whose origins lie outside the body in a foreign invader which he variously termed a 'homunculus' or a 'seed'."[18] The emphasis

---

15 For Potts's indebtedness to the *Daemonologie*, see: Stephen Pumphrey, "Potts, Plots and Politics: James I's *Daemonologie* and *The Wonderfull Discoverie of Witches*," in *The Lancashire Witches*, ed. Robert Poole: 22–41.

16 James VI and I, *Daemonologie, in Forme of a Dialogue, Divided into Three Bookes* (Edinburgh, 1597), 44.

17 James VI and I, *Daemonologie*, 46.

18 Jonathan Gil Harris, *Foreign Bodies and the Body Politic: Discourses of Social Pathology in Early Modern England* (Cambridge: Cambridge University Press, 1998), 22. See also Charles Webster, "Alchemical and Paracelsian Medicine" in *Health, Medicine and Mortality in the Sixteenth Century*, ed. Charles Webster (Cambridge: Cambridge University Press, 1979): 301–334.

on the porousness of the human body and its vulnerability to external attacks did, of course, heighten the fear of witches and trigger requests of harsher measures against them. Such requests were promptly satisfied by the authorities: after all, the execution of eight women and two men outside the city gates of Lancaster was a small price to pay in order to protect the body natural of the king's subjects and make the body politic whole again.

Heinz Antor

Constructing Alterity: Race, Gender, and the Body in Shakespeare's *Othello*

When *Othello* was first staged in 1604, this was the third time Shakespeare dealt extensively with racial alterity as a main theme in one of his plays, his depiction of Aaron in *Titus Andronicus* ten years earlier being the first example of such an undertaking and Shylock in *The Merchant of Venice* another. While Aaron in the first play was the embodiment of evil,[1] this cannot be said of Othello whose racial otherness is negotiated in a more subtle and differentiated way.

Othello was written in a period of marked cultural and political change, and one of the most important factors in the new dynamics of Early Modern culture was the expansionist development of England as a trading nation and the beginning of its establishment as a colonial power. This also led to an influx of foreigners into the British Isles and to a greater visibility of racial and ethnic diversity in English society. And although black people had been a presence in England ever since the arrival of black Roman legionnaires, by the time that Shakespeare wrote *Othello*, the presence of visibly different racial others had become an issue,[2] as Andrew Hadfield has shown with reference to late Elizabethan society:

> Othello may [...] make allusion to contemporary political events and pronouncements. In 1596 Elizabeth ordered Edward Baines to have ten 'blackamoors' sent out of the realm, 'of which kind of people there are already here too many'. A week later she announced that 89 English prisoners were being released from Spain and Portugal in return for an equivalent number of 'blackamoors'. English subjects were told to behave like good Christians, get rid of black servants and 'be served by their own countrymen rather than with those kind of people'. In 1601, just before *Othello* was first performed, Elizabeth published an edict banishing 'the great number of niggers and blackamoors which (as she is in-

1 Bartels refers to him as "the consummate villain." See Emily C. Bartels, "Making More of the Moor: Aaron, Othello, and Renaissance Refashionings of Race," *Shakespeare Quarterly* 41.4 (1990): 433–454, 435.

2 According to Emily Bartels "England's increasing stake in overseas expansion and colonization made the need to clarify and classify cultural others more urgent" (Emily C. Bartels "Shakespeare's view of the world," in *Shakespeare: An Oxford Guide*, ed. Stanley Wells and Lena Cowen Orlin (Oxford: Oxford University Press, 2003): 151–164, 162). Cf. Aebischer who points out that "the construction of race in *Othello* and *Titus* can be explained as a feature of their origin in an England engaged in early colonial enterprises." (Pascale Aebischer, *Shakespeare's Violated Bodies: Stage and Screen Performance* (Cambridge: CUP, 2004), 110).

> formed) are crept into this realm ... who are fostered and relieved here to the great annoyance of their own liege people, that want the relief which those people consume.'[3]

During the period, the union of the kingdoms of Scotland and England, along with Britain's increasing involvement as an emerging world power in international affairs,[4] resulted in a focus upon national identity. Alterity, as the flipside of identity, also became an issue.[5] One of the most prominent sites for the negotiation of otherness was race, and *Othello* is one of the most striking contemporary examples of the depictions of racial alterity in Early Modern England.[6]

Right from the beginning of the play, Othello is othered by the Iago and Roderigo onstage, and this emphasis on his alterity is closely linked to his physical blackness. In the opening scene of the play, even though Othello has yet to make an appearance, he is constructed as a negative other in the conversation between Roderigo, Iago, and – later – Brabantio. Although he is the focus of the conversation, Othello is not once referred to by his name in this scene, but always as "the Moor" (1.1.39, 57, 118, 127, 149, 166, 179)[7], and by reference to his skin colour and physical traits, all of which suggest stereotypical associations of cultural

3 Andrew Hadfield "Contextual Overview," in *A Routledge Literary Sourcebook on William Shakespeare's Othello*, ed. Andrew Hadfield (London: Routledge, 2003): 7 – 14, 11.

4 Neill points out that "it can hardly be accidental that it [i. e. *Othello*] belongs to the very period in English history in which something we can now identify as a racialist ideology was beginning to evolve under the pressures of nascent imperialism" (Neill, Michael, "Unproper Beds: Race, Adultery, and the Hideous in *Othello*," *Shakespeare Quarterly* 40.4 (Winter 1989): 383–441, 394. Cf. David Schalkwyk, "Race, Body, and Language in Shakespeare's Sonnets and Plays," *English Studies in Africa* 47.2 (2004): 5–24, 5 and Eve-Marie Oesterlen, "(Re)Covering the Bla(n)ck Presence: Race and Gender Representations in Shakespeare's *Othello*," in *CorpoRealities: In(ter)ventions in an Omnipresent Subject*, ed. Body Project (Königstein: Helmer, 2004): 259–274, 262.

5 Bartels points out that "[g]iven England's [...] belated entry into the expansionist scene where its European rivals were charting their empires, for the English to position themselves literally or figuratively, [...] for them to advance an English nationalist self over and against an ethnic 'other' [...] was no easy matter" (Bartels, "Shakespeare's view of the world," 158). With reference to Early Modern England, Traub also refers to "nationality as an implicitly gendered, erotic, as well as incipiently racial, phenomenon" (Valerie Traub, "Mapping the Global Body," in *Early Modern Visual Culture: Representation, Race, and Empire in Renaissance England*, eds. Peter Erickson and Clark Hulse (Philadelphia: University of Pennsylvania Press, 2000): 44–97, 46.)

6 Even though *Othello* is set in Venice, the play is to be read with the English situation in mind because "Shakespeare [...] looks outward to 'the world', even as he keeps his eye on England" (Bartels, "Shakespeare's view of the world," 151–152). Moreover, Shakespeare chose Venice for the setting of *Othello* because it was "a place defined by its ethnically and religiously diverse population" (Bartels, "Shakespeare's view of the world," 154).

7 William Shakespeare, *Othello*, in *The Complete Works*, eds. Stanley Wells and Gary Taylor (Oxford: Clarendon Press, 1986). All subsequent quotations will be taken from this edition

and moral inferiority.[8] Iago's xenophobic attitude towards Othello is already evident in his sarcastic use of the term "his Moorship" (1.1.32) for the black general, the bitterly ironic tone of which hinges on an allusion to the phrase "his lordship" and its implied incompatibility with blackness. If Iago's thoughts appear to be racist, this is due to the fact that he is incapable of accepting being thwarted by others in the execution of his plans and wishes. We do not hear of any prior resentment or animosity of Iago's against Othello, and yet, as soon as his aspirations for advancement to the post of lieutenant are disappointed, he accentuates Othello's blackness in order to transform his general into an outsider. To the ambitious egomaniac Iago, then, Othello's black body was only invisible and the outsider strategically acceptable so long as he was useful to the ensign's career. But, in what can only be seen as a racist turn whereby hitherto suppressed sentiments come to the fore, Othello's blackness becomes the sign of a negative otherness that is to be used to stigmatize him.[9] This falls on fertile ground with Roderigo, who, as a suitor of Desdemona, has his own grudge against Othello and refers to him as "the thick-lips" (1.1.66), yet again stressing a bodily feature that others Othello by emphasizing his racial origins.

Both Iago and Roderigo, in a classical racist manoeuvre, thus draw a discursive borderline between white and non-white with the purpose of literally 'denigrating', that is, blackening and denouncing Othello. When they wake Brabantio and tell him that his daughter Desdemona has eloped with Othello, this stigmatisation is repeated by means of a strategy that stresses Othello's racial and moral alterity, his blackness thus being associated with animality and evil. It is the physical aspect of Othello as a black body that is stressed rather than

---

8 Bartels, in this context, mentions that "the Moor [...] stands out in Shakespeare's oeuvre as the non-European 'other' residing, literally and figuratively, closest to home. Etymologically, the term indicates a native of Mauritania [...] Moors are grouped with non-African peoples, Arabians, Turks and Spaniards among them. In addition, geography and ethnicity often serve to register moral or behavioural traits" (Bartels, "Shakespeare's view of the world," 160). That Iago's use of the epithet 'Moor' does indeed refer to Othello's skin colour although the term 'Moor' could also mean "simply to be a Muslim" (Bartels, "Shakespeare's view of the world," 161) is made clear by the fact that Othello has already converted to Christianity so that this latter meaning of Moor does not apply here. Loomba explains that "black-skinned people were usually typed as godless, bestial and hideous, fit only to be saved (and in Early Modern Europe, enslaved) by Christians" (Loomba, Ania, *Shakespeare, Race, and Colonialism.* [Oxford: OUP, 2002], 91). For warnings against an over-simplified use of categories of 'race' with reference to Early Modern culture cf. Traub, "Mapping the Global Body," 57.

9 Cf. Bartels, "Making More of the Moor," 448: "[T]he demonization of an Other [...] is, in fact, a defensive move to avert the potential disempowerment of the self."

the general's character. Iago others Othello in fundamental terms by declaring him to be outside the community of humans when he tells Brabantio:

Even now, now, very now, an old black ram
Is tupping your white ewe. Arise, arise!
Awake the snorting citizens with the bell,
Or else the devil will make a grandsire of you. (1.1.88–91)

Othello is here constructed as an animal rather than a human, and the contrast between him as the "old black ram" and Desdemona, who is only marginally more flatteringly referred to as "your white ewe," stresses the unnaturalness of a miscegenation between white and black.[10] Iago's reference to the devil[11] clearly serves the purpose of designating Othello as a moral inferior and thus further contributes to the negative characterization of the general as an outsider whose alterity – in Iago's warped logic – is based on his black skin colour.

Iago engages in a pattern-building process here in which he draws a clear line that separates the black, morally inferior other from the white, Venetian self. However, the borderline between white and black is not the only one drawn by Iago. After all, Desdemona is here compared to an animal just as much as Othello, and indeed Iago is not only insensitive to what he perceives to be the ethical imperatives of racial alterity but also to the otherness of gender.[12] His misogynist tendencies are palpable not only here, in his demeaning

---

10 Cf. Singh on Iago's use of "bestial imagery to denote the supposedly unnatural marriage between the Moor and Desdemona": Jyotsna Singh, "Post-colonial criticism," in *Shakespeare: An Oxford Guide*, eds. Stanley Wells and Lena Cowen Orlin (Oxford: Oxford University Press, 2003): 492–507, 493. Howard rightly points out that "[f]rom the start her [i.e. Desdemona's] 'whiteness' is privileged as something precious that can be sullied by the touch of the 'lascivious Moor'" (Jean E. Howard, "Feminist Criticism," *Shakespeare: An Oxford Guide*, eds. Wells and Orlin: 411–430, 426).

11 Five years before the first staging of *Othello*, Thomas Dekker had presented the Moor Eleazar in *Lust's Dominion* (1599) as a "black devil." Ian Smith observes that "the significant number of references to 'devil' in *Othello* is directly related to the overdetermined racial identity of the title character, given that black was the conventional corporeal color used in the medieval and Early Modern representations of devils. [...] the devil's black color has a racializing function that permeates the play, extending beyond Othello to reiterate the profoundly racial ethos of the drama," Ian Smith, "Othello's Black Handkerchief," *Shakespeare Quarterly* 64.1 (Spring 2013): 1–25, 12.

12 This is why "feminists have increasingly insisted that satisfactory answers depend on simultaneously probing the gender and the racial dimensions of the play as they unfold in the charged arena of Renaissance Venice" (Howard "Feminist criticism," 424). For example, Bartels points out that "[a]s *Othello* centers on the issue of both racial and sexual difference, it

comparison between Desdemona and a white ewe owned by Brabantio ("*your* white ewe," my emphasis), but already in his earlier invective against Cassio, whom he hates for having been promoted to the post of lieutenant, and who he refers to as "One Michael Cassio, a Florentine, /A fellow almost damned in a fair wife" (1.1.19–20). The blackness of racial others, then, is marginalized, rejected and stigmatised just as much as the female beauty of women, bodily attributes thus being turned into discursive weapons of discrimination. Significantly, Cassio is here referred to as a Florentine, as a member of a rival city state, and therefore othered himself. Iago can only think in binary terms in which a clear-cut conceptual line separates him and all those who are useful to him; they occupy a negative sphere that contains everybody and everything that might thwart his ambitions and counter his personal interests. He thus others humans on grounds of race, ethnicity, gender, religion and sexuality.

The issue of racial othering, however, is the one the play is most intensely concerned with, which is why, in the scene in which Brabantio is alerted to his daughter's relationship with Othello, this is repeatedly stressed. For example, Iago extends his animal comparison by mockingly telling the old man that "you'll have your daughter covered with a Barbary horse, you'll have your nephews neigh to you, you'll have coursers for cousins and jennets for germans. [...] I am one, sir, that comes to tell you your daughter and the Moor are now making the beast with two backs." (1.1.113–115, 117–119). Othello has now turned from a black ram into a Barbary horse, the word Barbary not only pointing to Othello's

---

draws attention to the conflation of such differences in previous discourse on the Moor; [...] Shakespeare brings them together to betray the circumscription of racial and sexual difference as an issue neither of race nor of sexuality but of power" ("Making More of the Moor," 447). Similarly, Dympna Callaghan states that "[i]n the Renaissance, the spectacle of absolute racial otherness [...] is staged via the trope of gender difference" (Dympna Callaghan, "'Othello Was a White Man': Properties of Race on Shakespeare's Stage," in *Alternative Shakespeares. Volume 2*, ed. Terence Hawkes (London: Routledge, 1996): 192–215, 204). Cf. Schalkwyk, "Race, Body, and Language," 8: "[T]he 'otherness' of racial and gender difference are predicated upon a shared, projective vilification." To Oesterlen, *Othello* is "a tragedy that is so obviously and obsessively concerned with fantasies of race and gender" (Oesterlen, "(Re)Covering the Bla(n)ck Presence," 261). Rippy states that in *Othello* "blackness and femininity are used not as binary opposites, but as interrelated and mutually oppressive constructions" (Marguerite Hailey Rippy, "All Our *Othellos:* Black Monsters and White Masks on the American Screen," in *Spectacular Shakespeare: Critical Theory and Popular Cinema*, eds. Courtney Lehmann and Lisa S. Starks (Madison, NJ; Fairleigh Dickinson UP, 2002): 25–46, 26). Stallybrass also points out that "the discourses of racism and misogyny are deployed and interrogated in the play" (Peter Stallybrass, "Patriarchal Territories: The Body Enclosed," *Rewriting the Renaissance: the Discourses of Sexual Difference in Early Modern Europe*, eds. Margaret W. Ferguson, Maureen Quilligan and Nancy J. Vickers (Chicago: The University of Chicago Press, 1986): 123–142, 136).

African origin, but also being etymologically related to the concept of the 'barbarian' and its associations with primitivism. Moreover, Iago's emphasis on the sexual act, the physical coupling of a white female and a black male body, shows the physicality and 'body-fixation'[13] of his xenophobic and misogynist imagination, while the grotesqueness[14] of the idea of neighing nephews and animal relatives serves to accentuate the division that Iago draws between black and white thereby rejecting the notion of any form of hybrid coming together of others.

Roderigo's own speech to Brabantio is based on similar assumptions about race. He contrasts Brabantio's "fair daughter" (1.1.124) with "the gross clasps of a lascivious Moor" (1.1.128) and in doing so he objects in particular to the physical union of white and non-white bodies while at the same time slanderously associating blackness with coarseness and a lack of sexual discipline.[15] Roderigo tries to forestall any possible liberal reaction by Brabantio by formulating his own evaluative narrative of Desdemona's liaison with Othello:

> Your daughter, if you have not given her leave,
> I say again hath made a gross revolt,
> Tying her duty, beauty, wit and fortunes
> In an extravagant and wheeling stranger
> Of here and everywhere. (1.1.135–139)

Roderigo here not only others Othello as a stranger, but – even worse – he objects to his non-identity as being "of here and everywhere," both part of the Venetian state and yet again not part of it.[16] Not only does Roderigo refuse here to accept Othello's integration into the social order of Venice, but Othello is also turned into a dangerous source of infection from outside, an outsider

13 This is also one of the main reasons why Lux can refer to *Othello* as "a body-intensive text" (Mary F. Lux, "'Work on my medicine': Physiologies and Anatomies in *Othello*," *Othello: New Critical Essays*, ed. Kolin, Philip C. (New York: Routledge, 2002): 379–390, 379).

14 Oesterlen points out that "the white man's fear of miscegenation [is] staged in the play as monstrous sexuality" (Oesterlen, "(Re)Covering the Bla(n)ck Presence," 262).

15 Iago here takes up a contemporary prejudice because "Moors on the Early Modern stage, and in other kinds of texts, were often depicted as treacherous, cruel, and sexually rapacious" (Howard "Feminist criticism," 426).

16 Bartels draws our attention to the fact that "while stereotypical Moors, such as Shakespeare's Aaron, were indeed taking shape within renaissance discourse, the Moor emerged simultaneously as a highly complex subject, unlikely to fit any single mould, more likely to carry the signs of a number of cultural traditions" (Bartels, "Shakespeare's view of the world," 161), and it is this complexity that Roderigo objects to here.

who has managed to breach the defences of Venetian identity and who now becomes a hazard by lasciviously clasping its fair daughter Desdemona.

Brabantio easily falls prey to Iago's and Roderigo's ploy because of his latent racist prejudice which is brought to the fore by the accusations levelled against Othello. He may have been a good host to the black general on many occasions but it turns out that this was only due to Othello's usefulness as a defender of Venetian interests against the Ottomans rather than to a genuine appreciation of the black man as a fellow human being. Confronted with the notion of marriage and sexual intercourse between Desdemona and Othello, he rails against both his daughter and her lover:

> [...] O unhappy girl! –
> With the Moor, say'st thou? – Who would be a father? –
> [...] O she deceives me
> Past thought! [...]
> [...]
> [...] O, treason of the blood!
> Fathers, from hence trust not your daughters' minds
> By what you see them act. Is there not charms
> By which the property of youth and maidhood
> May be abused? Have you not read, Roderigo,
> Of some such thing?
> [...]
> [...] O, would you had had her. (1.1.165–177)

What Brabantio objects to here is not merely a daughter's disobedience, but rather her act of crossing racial boundaries which turns her elopement into a "treason of the blood" threatening the white Venetian family with the shame and pollution of miscegenation. That Brabantio's objection is indeed an ultimately racist one is underlined by his wish that Roderigo should have gained Desdemona's favour rather than Othello. Earlier in the scene, Brabantio still chided Roderigo for his attempts at wooing Desdemona and told him that

> I have charged thee not to haunt about my doors.
> In honest plainness thou hast heard me say
> My daughter is not for thee (1.1.97–99)

Brabantio's change of mind is due to Desdemona having entered into a relationship with "the Moor" – like Iago and Roderigo, he uses this term only to refer to Othello – and is thus clearly racially motivated. From Brabantio's point of view, a white Venetian is the only possible candidate for the double role of Desdemona's husband and father to his grandchildren. The blood-nexus in Brabantio's argument uncovers his racist prejudice.

This is the reason why, dissatisfied with his daughter's behaviour as he may be, Brabantio ultimately puts most of the blame on Othello and literally tries to 'whitewash' Desdemona by constructing her as a victim of the black general's seductive, allegedly satanic rhetoric. This also allows Brabantio to accuse Othello by using the negative stereotypes of Orientalist discourse:[17]

> O thou foul thief! Where hast thou stowed my daughter?
> Damned as thou art, thou hast enchanted her,
> For I'll refer me to all things of sense,
> If she in chains of magic were not bound,
> Whether a maid so tender, fair, and happy,
> So opposite to marriage that she shunned
> The wealthy curlèd darlings of our nation,
> Would ever have, t'incur a general mock,
> Run from her guardage to the sooty bosom
> Of such a thing as thou – to fear, not to delight.
> Judge me the world if 'tis not gross in sense
> That thou hast practised on her with foul charms,
> Abused her delicate youth with drugs or minerals
> That weakens motion. I'll have't disputed on.
> 'Tis probable and palpable to thinking.
> I therefore apprehend and do attach thee
> For an abuser of the world, a practiser
> Of arts inhibited and out of warrant. (1.2.63–80)

Brabantio's speech here is infused by a white racist Eurocentrism that normalizes his own Orientalist prejudice that identifies Venice with "all things of sense," and excludes Othello as a practitioner of 'non-sense'. The reference to Othello's "sooty bosom" betrays the racist sentiment of Brabantio's harangue, and maligns him on religious (he is "damned"), anthropological (he is a mere non-human "thing"), ethnic (he is not "of our nation") aesthetic (he is "to fear, not to delight") and moral (he has "practiced on her with foul charms") grounds.

---

17 That Shakespeare does indeed refer to the discourse of Orientalism in his play is also pointed out by Edward Said who states that "in Shakespeare's *Othello* (that "abuser of the world"), the Orient and Islam are always represented as outsiders having a special role to play *inside* Europe. (Edward Said, *Orientalism: Western Conceptions of the Orient* (London: Penguin Books, 1995 [[1]1978]), 71). Othello is not of Turkish or Asian but of African descent, but this includes him in the Western category of the Oriental other because "[y]ears of conquest meant that Ottoman subjects included Africans [...]" (Bartels "Shakespeare's view of the world," 2003, 154).

In the face of these insults, however, Othello is remarkably calm. In his conversation with Iago and in the following confrontation with Brabantio, he is confident that he will be judged on his merits, that it will be "My parts, my title, and my perfect soul" (1.2.31), and not his body and its skin colour that will "manifest me rightly" (1.2.32). The thought of the possibility of racist discrimination does not even seem to occur to him.

Brabantio, however, wants the case to be referred to the Duke because he sees in this situation a threat of a more fundamental kind:

> For if such actions may have passage free,
> Bondslaves and pagans shall our statesmen be. (1.2.99–100)

In other words, according to Brabantio, what is at stake here is much more than a daughter's disobedience to her father or her love affair with a black general, but the welfare of the whole state. The mingling of Desdemona's white and Othello's black bodies is constructed by an incensed Venetian father as a threat to the body politic, which will no longer be safe against social upheavals once the borderlines that separate master from slave and Christian from pagan have become porous and can be penetrated.[18] The penetration of Desdemona's white body by black Othello here becomes symbolic of the dangerous infiltration of the culturally other into the Venetian state.

That Venice is indeed threatened by a non-white and jeopardizing other is confirmed in what immediately follows when we learn about "A Turkish fleet, and bearing up to Cyprus" (1.3.8), a Venetian colony now in danger of being invaded by Venice's Ottoman rivals. Because Venice is now in need of Othello's military skills he is referred to by a Senator as "the valiant Moor" (1.3.47) and even as "Valiant Othello" (1.3.48) by the Duke himself, in direct contrast to earlier appellations. In this context his skin colour is of no importance.

Into this different discursive field, Brabantio now approaches the Duke with his complaints against Othello. However, knowing how much the Duke values Othello, at first he only describes the offence without naming the offender. He constructs Desdemona as a victim who has been lured into behaving irrationally by means of malevolent supernatural forces:

---

18 Bartels observes that Othello is "situated in a potentially threatening position near the 'inside' of authority and power" and points out that "he uses that situation […] as a means of questioning the difference nonetheless imposed upon the Moor" (Bartels, "Making More of the Moor," 442). It is this destabilization Brabanzio objects to here.

She is abused, stol'n from me, and corrupted
By spells and medicines bought of mountebanks.
For nature so preposterously to err,
Being not deficient, blind, or lame of sense,
Sans witchcraft could not. (1.3.60–64)

Desdemona becomes a type of Eve "corrupted" by a satanic power and her behaviour is now seen as an infringement of the laws of nature. In this way Brabantio's own position is normalised and in an orientalizing gesture Othello is presented as a depraved other in league with the forces of evil. The violation which has supposedly been committed against his daughter is effected through interference with Desdemona's body, i.e. by the dispensing of some evil substance or medicine whose physiological effects have impaired the proper functioning of her mind. Significantly, when the Duke promises to use "the bloody book of law" (1.3.67) against whoever may have committed this apparent violation, Brabantio now identifies the supposed culprit not by naming him as Othello, but yet again through designating him by the use of the collective racial epithet: "Here is the man, this Moor" (1.3.71). That this is no coincidence becomes apparent in Brabantio's next speech in which he once more tries to make his case by claiming in a racist argument that a white young girl's love for a black man is a physical and psychological monstrosity that can only be explained through recourse to the powers of evil:

A maiden never bold,
Of spirit so still and quiet that her motion
Blushed at herself – and she, in spite of nature,
Of years, of country, credit, everything,
To fall in love with what she feared to look on!
It is a judgement maimed and most imperfect
That will confess perfection so could err
Against all rules of nature, and must be driven
To find out practices of cunning hell
Why this should be. I therefore vouch again
That with some mixtures powerful o'er the blood,
Or with some dram conjured to this effect,
He wrought upon her. (1.3.94–106)

Once again, Brabantio here essentializes the borderline that, in his racist thought, others and separates the black man from his white daughter. He complains about Desdemona's present lack of xenophobia when he refers to Othello as "what she feared to look on," her fear (φόβος or phóbos) of the foreigner or stranger (ξένος or xenos) having been replaced by love. Yet again, the blood and thus the body, in Brabantio's speech, becomes the gateway to the corruption of the white girl.

The Duke, however, is not impressed by Brabantio's arguments and, in a remarkably anti-racist and clear-headed way rejects such accusations by pointing out that

> To vouch this is no proof
> Without more wider and more overt test
> Than these thin habits and poor likelihoods
> Of modern seeming do prefer against him. (1.3.106–109)

The Duke here criticizes racist thinking as a recent but widespread and popular prejudice which is to be rejected as unfounded. Apparently, the multicultural elements of Venetian society have made some Venetians – such as the Duke – quite cosmopolitan and unprejudiced in their thinking while the presence of racial and cultural alterity has so unsettled other Venetians like Brabantio and made them so insecure that their suave and urbane tolerance and hospitality can quickly degenerate into racist xenophobia.

Othello denies nothing and admits the force of his own desire: "I do confess the vices of my blood" (1.3.123). However, he goes on to describe the course of his courtship as the result of the charm and power of his character, expressed in the exotic stories of his adventures, featuring "cannibals," "Anthropophagi" and "men whose heads / Do grow beneath their shoulders" (1.3.142–144):

> She swore in faith 'twas strange, 'twas passing strange,
> 'Twas pitiful, 'twas wondrous pitiful.
> [...]
> She loved me for the dangers I had passed,
> And I loved her that she did pity them.
> This is the only witchcraft that I used. (1.3.159–68)

Desdemona, it would appear, does not love Othello in spite of his alterity but rather *because of it*. Like her father, she notices Othello's otherness, but unlike Brabantio, the confrontation with alterity does not make her retreat xenophobically into the shell of her white identity, but rather allows her to turn empathetically towards that which is ἐξωτικός or exotikos, i. e. alien, foreign, strange. Also, Desdemona does not judge Othello by his outward, bodily appearance: "I saw Othello's visage in his mind" (1.3.252).

Othello's version of their budding love is confirmed by Desdemona who declares her loyalty to both Brabantio as her father and to Othello as her husband. Speaking to her father, she refers to Othello as "the Moor my lord" (1.3.188), and in doing so she takes over the generic racial term Brabantio uses for Othello but also combines it with "my lord," thus signalling her subjection to the patriarchal authority of her husband. Desdemona thereby crosses a conceptual borderline by allowing a black other to become her lord, a notion that is completely unacceptable within the framework of Brabantio's bipolar racist thought. This is also why, in what follows, Brabantio only grudgingly gives his assent to his daughter's union with Othello, not really "with all my heart" (1.3.92). Consequently, he refuses to allow Desdemona to remain at his house during Othello's absence in Cyprus (1.3.240) because as far as he is concerned, she is now "dead" (1.3.59). Desdemona pleads with the Duke to let her accompany her husband to Cyprus by once more declaring a love that Brabantio has declared to be so unnatural:

> That I did love the Moor to live with him,
> My downright violence and storm of fortunes
> May trumpet to the world. My heart's subdued
> Even to the very quality of my lord.
> I saw Othello's visage in his mind,
> And to his honours and his valiant parts
> Did I my souls and fortunes consecrate;
> [...]
> Let me go with him. (1.3.248–259)

Moreover, she also justifies her love for Othello by inverting the terms of the antiracist argument, declaring the body to be of secondary importance to the mind when it comes to judging a person's character. She says that when she chose Othello as her husband she was totally aware of "the very quality of my lord" and she declares his blackness to be irrelevant. For his part the Duke is convinced by Desdemona's and Othello's arguments and grants their wish to go to Cyprus together. He even tries to assuage Brabantio's unhappiness by declaring that

> If virtue no delighted beauty lack,
> Your son-in-law is far more fair than black. (1.3.289–290)

The rhyming couplet here suggests closure just as much as the Duke's attempt at reconciling Brabantio with his new state as father-in-law to a black man does, but the very ambiguity of these two lines immediately alerts us to the instability of such a supposed re-establishment of harmony. "Fair" and "black" here may be used as moral epithets by the Duke, but his linking them to Othello's skin colour uses the semantic instability of these words and thus opens up an interpretive space in which the Duke's words can also be read as indirectly and involuntarily reconfirming the racist categorizations produced by Brabantio. The play on words produced by the Duke is only possible through his insinuation that black-bodied Othello can still be his fair-minded general, which in turn is based on the persistence of the cognitive borderline that divides black from white/fair and evil from good. Had this cognitive pattern already been dissolved, the Duke's words would not have made any sense.

The first act thus does not end on a harmonious note. Rather, we are presented yet again with the point-of-view taken by Othello's enemies. Brabantio is not convinced by the Duke's words, and he tries to spoil the joy Othello takes in Desdemona by issuing a warning to him:

> Look to her, Moor, if thou hast eyes to see.
> She has deceived her father, and may thee. (1.3.292–293)

While Desdemona and the Duke have argued that outward appearances may be deceptive and that a good soul may have a black face, Brabantio here shows himself dissatisfied with the opaque inscrutability of a world that is more complex than his simplistic binary and essentialist patterns of interpretation would allow.[19] At the same time, Brabantio raises the issue of trust, and that the gulf between being and appearances[20] may indeed be dangerously deceptive is immediately brought home to us when Othello not only vouches for Desdemona's faithfulness, but, in the very same line (1.3.290), addresses his ensign as "Honest Iago." The discrepant awareness between what Othello knows and what we know makes us wary of any premature attempts to stabilize the situation.

Before Act 1 ends, however, Iago still has a surprise in store for us. Having used Othello's body as the basis of a discourse of racist discrimination, he now makes a U-turn by conceptualizing the body in a totally different way, when Roderigo moans about his hopeless love for Desdemona and declares that "it is not in my virtue to amend it" (1.3.318). Iago is incensed by this and replies:

> Virtue? A fig! 'Tis in ourselves that we are thus or thus. Our bodies are our gardens, to the which our wills are gardeners; so that if we will plant nettles or sow lettuce, set hyssop and weed up thyme, supply it with one gender of herbs or distract it with many, either to have it sterile with idleness or manured with industry, why, the power and corrigible authority of this lies in our wills. If the beam of our lives had not one scale of reason to poise another of sensuality, the blood and baseness of our natures would conduct us to most preposterous

19 Rippy also stresses the play's problematizing of essentialism by pointing out that "*Othello* [...] is a story of conflict between essential and represented identity, manifested in the crossing over of race" (Rippy, "All Our *Othellos*," 30).

20 Aebischer even argues that "Shakespeare's first act is entirely dedicated to questions of evidence, the difference between being and seeming – a question of the sign" (Aebischer, *Shakespeare's Violated Bodies*, 127).

> conclusions. But we have reason to cool our raging motions, our carnal stings, our unbitted lusts; whereof I take this that you call love to be a sect or scion. (1.3.319–332)

The determinism that linked Othello's black body to an existence of mere physicality is here replaced by a constructivist self-determinism according to which humans are rational beings who can channel and curb their bodily desires.[21] Significantly, the voluntaristic conceptualization of the body produced here by Iago is explained by means of a gardening metaphor that Shakespeare had used earlier in *Richard II* [2.1 and 3.4] whose significance extended to the body politic. Once again, the negotiation of alterity and the construction of the body in *Othello* is relevant not only with regard to the characters on stage, but with reference to the polity as a whole.

Iago indirectly concedes that Othello is not determined by his black body when he tries to encourage Roderigo by telling him that Othello and Desdemona will soon tire of each other:

> It cannot be long that Desdemona should long continue her love to the Moor [...] nor he his to her. It was a violent commencement in her, and thou shalt see an answerable sequestration [...].These Moors are changeable in their wills [...]. The food that to him now is as luscious as locusts shall be to him shortly as bitter as the coloquintida. She must change for youth. When she is sated with his body, she will find the error of her choice. [...] If sanctimony and a frail vow betwixt an erring barbarian and a super-subtle Venetian be not too hard for my wits and all the tribe of hell, thou shalt enjoy her [...]. (1.3.341–356)

Iago continues to other Othello here, and he continues to engage in negative stereotyping, but it becomes clear that the black general, too, has a will and is not entirely prone to the stirrings of his body. Consequently, that will, in turn, needs to be constructed into the position of a negative alterity and is thus declared to be changeable by Iago. Othello, then, is othered both with reference to his body and to his will because what now counts for Iago is Othello's promiscuity that is a by-product of the racial stereotype that Iago invokes. All of these manoeuvres are tools in the hands of the villain who is only interested in the power of imposing his own will.

However, Iago's final soliloquy in Act 1 shows that he is also affected by the physical aspects of existence which emerges through a jealousy of possession

---

21 Cf. Ian Smith who points out the man-made constructedness specifically of the non-white body when he observes that "[t]he black body in the Early Modern theatre is the body of artistic and artisanal creation – conceived [...] according to [...] the ideological demands of race" (Smith "Othello's Black Handkerchief," 22).

that adds to his hatred of Othello, and that he will ultimately project onto the tragic hero:

> I hate the Moor,
> And it is thought abroad that 'twixt my sheets
> He's done my office. (1.3.368–370)[22]

Iago's sexual jealousy is unfounded, but it turns into a major factor that motivates him in his activities against Othello. Male proprietorial attitudes towards the female other then are used by Iago in his ploy of bringing about Othello's downfall just as much as his strategies of racial othering. Act 1 thus ends with Iago having conceived his devilish plan to make Othello suspect Desdemona of marital infidelity with Cassio:

> I ha't. It is ingendered. Hell and night
> Must bring this monstrous birth to the world's light. (1.3.395–396).

Iago's choice of words here is significant in as far as his intrigue has not only been "engendered" in the sense of 'conceived of,' but it has literally been created through a linking of black Othello with gender attitudes, counting on the black general's dormant patriarchal suspicion of female fragility and infidelity. Both the black body and the female body are used by Iago, then, in his perfidious Machiavellian game, in which he negatively others and (ab)uses whoever does not function according to his will. Iago's plan, as we know, is a "monstrous birth" indeed, and the play here, in an instance of dramatic irony, has Iago unwittingly deconstruct his negative and prejudicial categorization of Othello, while inadvertently revealing the discrepancy between his own external appearance – he is, after all, an 'ensign' – and his devilish interior.

Othello's ancient ('ensign'), then, not only abuses his general for his blackness, but he also constructs humans with female bodies as negative others. Iago is a racist and a misogynist to boot. His negative attitude towards women is apparent not only in the unscrupulous way in which he plans to slander Desdemona as an adulteress, but also in his disparaging treatment of his wife Emilia. When, after their arrival in Cyprus, for example, Cassio greets Emilia and gives her a welcome kiss of courtesy, Iago comments:

---

22 This quotation is taken from the Cambridge School Shakespeare edition of the play and cannot be found in the Oxford Shakespeare (William Shakespeare, *Othello*. The Cambridge School Shakespeare (Cambridge: CUP, 1992 [1984])).

> Sir, would she give you so much of her lips
> As of her tongue she oft bestows on me
> You would have enough. (2.1.103–104)

The wife Emilia is here othered as a shrew, with Iago once again reverting to his strategy of the construction of a negative alterity whenever it suits his purposes. That this is not merely due to some marital quarrel between Iago and Emilia, but emanates from the former's misogynist attitudes, becomes clear when Desdemona protests against Iago's depiction of Venetian women:

> IAGO Come on, come on. You are pictures out of door,
> Bells in your parlours; wildcats in your kitchens,
> Saints in your injuries; devils being offended,
> Players in your housewifery, and housewives in your beds.
> DESDEMONA O, fie upon thee, slanderer!
> IAGO Nay, it is true, or else I am a Turk.
> You rise to play and go to bed to work. (2.1.112–118)

It is Iago's inclusive condemnation of women that Desdemona justly challenges. Unimpressed by Desdemona's defence, Iago proceeds to add even more slander by declaring all women to be prostitutes. Be it the black bodies of the Turks or the bodies of women, physical otherness is used by Iago to construct a negative alterity against which he can position himself and over which he can claim supremacy. Both women and Turks are here represented as transgressors that have to be kept at bay, and they are used by Iago as justifications for the imposition of his will. The exchange between Iago, Emilia and Desdemona here may present an appearance of playful banter, but it nevertheless raises serious issues which characterize Iago and prepares the audience for what is to come.[23]

In the humorous exchange that follows between Desdemona and Iago (2.1.120–167), triggered by her question "Come, how woulds't thou praise me?" (2.1.120), the concept of fairness (2.1.132, 137–138, 145, 151) becomes the central epithet for describing women and, through its being contrasted with the notion of blackness (2.1.134–136), it is to be interpreted also as a marker of race. M. R. Ridley, in his 1958 Arden edition of the play, all but ignored the references to race and gender in this passage, which is why, in a footnote, he calls it "one of the most unsatisfactory passages in Shakespeare." But this ignores that – however playful the exchange may be – it is anything but "a long piece of cheap

23 This is made clear by Desdemona herself who, in an aside, refers to the serious subtext of the situation by declaring that "I am not merry, but I do beguile / The thing I am by seeming otherwise." (2.1.125–126)

backchat."[24] Rather, it focuses our attention once more on Iago's disdain for racial and sexual others, i. e. for blacks as well as for women. Women are yet again shown in a negative light by Iago who declares them to be scheming minxes who use their wit to put their fairness to their own advantage:

> If she be fair and wise, fairness and wit,
> The one's for use, the other uses it. (2.1.132–133)

Even worse, he insinuates that black people either scheme to find themselves a white partner or try to pass as white, both possible readings of the following lines reflecting badly on Othello:

> If she be black, and thereto have a wit,
> She'll find a white that shall her blackness fit. (2.1.135–136)

When chided by Desdemona for praising "the worst best" (2.1.146–147) and asked to produce praise for "a deserving woman indeed" (2.1.147–148), Iago proffers an image of a woman negatively defined through self-denial, "who [is] never proud," "never loud," "never gay" (2.1.151–153). Iago's ideal woman suppresses her own emotions ("her displeasure fly," 2.1.156) and thoughts ("ne'er disclose her mind," 2.1.159) and is of course immune to attentions from other men ("See suitors following, and not look behind," 2.1.160). According to Iago, then, women are there to do nothing but "suckle fools and chronicle small beer" (2.1.164), a "most lame an impotent conclusion" (2.1.158) indeed, as Desdemona points out. She consequently warns Emilia not to heed Iago's words: "Do not learn of him, Emilia, though he be thy husband." (2.1.164–165)

This exchange between Iago and Desdemona fulfils a humorous function in the play, which is why Ridley comments that "[p]erhaps the passage was just a sop to the groundlings, for whom otherwise – the Clown being negligible – there is little comic entertainment; this is just the sort of interchange that might occur between the great lady and the professional jester" (Ridley, 54, fn. for ll. 109–166). True as this may be, it underestimates the serious subtext of this passage, which once again shows us Iago as a misogynist racist who uses the bodily otherness of blacks as well as women to construct a discourse of negative alterity that marginalizes and subjects them to his own masculine authority. The scene is thus prepared for Iago's devious plot that he describes to Roderigo:

---

24 William Shakespeare, *Othello*, The Arden Shakespeare, ed. M.R. Ridley (London, New York: Methuen, 1979 [1958]), 54, fn. for ll. 109–66.

> Mark me with what violence she first loved the Moor, but for bragging and telling her fantastical lies. To love him still for prating? – let not thy discreet heart think it. Her eye must be fed, and what delight shall she have to look on the devil? When the blood is made dull with the act of sport, there should be again to inflame it, and to give satiety a fresh appetite, loveliness in favour, sympathy in years, manners, and beauties, all which the Moor is defective in. (2.1.223–231)

In Iago's materialist discourse of the body here, it is merely physical desire that initially triggers affection, a feature that augments his characterisation of Othello as a 'devil' of whom Desdemona will ultimatetely tire.

Iago others Othello and Desdemona and Cassio, his rival, now needs to be othered within the framework of his egomaniac world picture. This is effected by Iago's constructing of the newly appointed lieutenant as inauthentic in the etymological sense of the word. Cassio, to Iago, is not αὐθεντικός ('authentikos') or 'reliable,' inasmuch as he combines an attractive external appearance with an evil interior, which is why, he makes Roderigo believe that Desdemona was attracted to him. Iago characterizes Cassio as

> a knave very voluble, no further conscionable than in putting on the mere form of civil and humane seeming for the better compass of his salt and most hidden loose affection. Why, none; why, none – a slippery and subtle knave, a finder of occasions, that has an eye can stamp and counterfeit advantages, though true advantage never present itself; a devilish knave! Besides, the knave is handsome, young, and has all those requisites in him that folly and green minds look after. (2.1.238–247)

Once again, as in his earlier description of Desdemona's cooling passion for Othello, Iago here refers to outward appearance. In Iago's speeches, the wished-for authenticity of the reliable match between the outward appearance of the body and the interiority of the subject becomes problematic in the cases of both Othello and Cassio because Othello as a black man does not occupy the role of a subaltern subject; indeed he has the power to ignore Iago's wishes for promotion. Cassio, however, needs to be constructed as a morally doubtful, equivocating philanderer, confirming his view of the construction of the body as an inauthentic, unreliable signifier.[25]

He reiterates his racist objection to miscegenation when countering Roderigo's claim that Desdemona is "of most blest condition" (2.1.249–250) by pointing out that "If she had been blest, she would never have loved the Moor" (2.1.252–253). Cassio's allegedly incipient affair with Desdemona, in turn, is reaffirmed by

---

25 This allows Lux to discuss *Othello* within a modern critical framework of "the body as text" (Lux, "'Work on my medicine'," 379).

Iago through his over-interpretation of supposed bodily signs of affection which are nothing but symptoms of his own censorious prudery that obscures his obsession with patriarchal possession and that is turned into a tool for the disparagement of others:

> Dids't thou not see her paddle with the palm of his [i. e. Cassio's] hand? [...] Lechery, by this hand; an index and obscure prologue to the history of lust and foul thoughts. (2.1.253–258)

The only character filled with lust and foul thoughts is of course Iago himself whose obsession with others' bodies, be they female or black, is of almost pathological proportions. In his final soliloquy in Act 2 Scene 1, he admits to himself "That Cassio loves her, I do well believe it" (2.1.285), and he concedes that Othello "Is of a constant, loving, noble nature, [...] A most dear husband" (2.1.288, 290). And yet, he forges an intrigue against both of them from motives that are related to his fixation on the body and his obsession with sexual possession:

> Now I do love her [i. e. Desdemona] too,
> Not out of absolute lust – though peradventure
> I stand accountant for as great a sin –
> But partly led to diet my revenge
> For that I do suspect the lusty Moor
> Hath leaped into my seat, the thought whereof
> Does, like a poisonous mineral, gnaw my inwards;
> And nothing can or shall content my soul
> Till I am evened with him, wife for wife – (2.1.290–298)

Iago's suspicion of *all* men as potential rivals, no matter whether they are black or white, fuels his sexual jealousy that makes him conceive of the plan of making Othello jealous in turn, "Even to madness" (2.1.310).

Iago is a cunning lecher who sets out to realize his plan and who, at the same time, indulges in sexual fantasies concerning Desdemona in his conversation with Cassio. In that dialogue he tries to lure Cassio into a discussion of Desdemona's sexual attractiveness. He calls her "sport for Jove" (2.3.17), the most sexually potent of the Greek gods, and "full of game," sexually experienced and full of sexual tricks (2.3.19).[26] His preoccupation with others' bodies does not stop there, however. In this exchange he refers to his general for the first time by his real name rather than by the epithet 'the Moor', but he cannot refrain from foregrounding the man's racial otherness by calling him "black Othello"

26 Ridley paraphrases the expression as meaning "expert love-play" (M.R. Ridley "Introduction" to William Shakespeare, *Othello*, 69).

(2.3.29). Nor does he shrink back from actively interfering with the bodies of others, such as when he makes Cassio drunk in order to make him lose control of body and mind and thus become "full of quarrel and offence" (2.3.46). After Brabantio's unfounded allegations of Desdemona having been "corrupted / By spells and medicines" (1.3.60–61), we are here confronted with a real attempt at such corruption, this time through the spell of alcohol. Iago, then, manipulates the body both discursively, by constructing it as a negative female or black other, and by materially and physically interfering with it.[27]

Iago's plot against Cassio is successful and the latter becomes so drunk that Othello is called for:

> Are we turned Turks, and to ourselves do that
> Which heaven hath forbid the Ottomites?
> For Christian shame, put by this barbarous brawl. (2.3.163–165)

Othello here casts himself in the role of the defender of Christian decorum while the combatants are constructed as Turkish others who have come to do that which "heaven hath forbid the Ottomites." However, the incident jeopardises Othello's own 'judgement' in that in his response he allows his 'blood' to 'rule' and 'passion' to gain the upper hand:

> Now by heaven,
> My blood begins my safer guides to rule,
> And passion, having my best judgement collied,
> Essays to lead the way. (2.3.197–200)

The blood as the seat of the passions in the taxonomy of humoural physiology,[28] now takes over from the mind, and reason is replaced by passion. Not only are we confronted here with an implicit affirmation of an orientalist prejudice,[29] but

27 He has similarly interfered with "Three else of Cyprus – noble swelling spirits, / That hold their honours in a wary distance, / The very elements of this warlike isle –" (2.3.51–53), whom he has not only made drunk as well but whom he also here constructs as a negative stereotypical other.

28 Cf. Bruce R. Smith, "Studies in Sexuality," in *Shakespeare: An Oxford Guide*, eds. Stanley Wells and Lena Cowen Orlin (Oxford: Oxford University Press, 2003): 431–450, 432. On the use of blood in *Othello* cf. also Lux, "'Work on my medicine'," 383. On the "Ecology of the Passions" in *Othello* cf. Gail Kern Paster, *Humoring the Body: Emotions and the Shakespearean Stage* (Chicago: The University of Chicago Press, 2004), 25–76.

29 Indeed, "an excessive internal heat or passion" (Bartels 2003, 159) was considered to be a possible cause of blackness at the time. Bruce Smith states that Othello's "Venetian compeers would have expected a dark-skinned Moor, a denizen of the hot, moist climes of the southern

the audience is also provided with a first instance of Iago's scheme bearing fruit. In the dichotomy of body and mind, it is implied, the balance between the two might be disturbed and the wrong side might dominate. The construction of Othello as a unity of exterior and interior is exactly what Iago has aimed for, despite the bifurcation of his own subjectivity.

The notion of the self being made up of a physical body and of a metaphysical element is manipulated in the conversation between Cassio and Iago following the former's disgraceful dismissal as Othello's lieutenant.

> CASSIO: Reputation, reputation, reputation – O, I ha' lost my reputation, I ha' lost the immortal part of myself, and what remains is bestial! My reputation, Iago, my reputation.
> IAGO: As I am an honest man, I thought you had received some bodily wound. There is more sense in that than in reputation. Reputation is an idle and most false imposition, oft got without merit and lost without deserving. You have lost no reputation at all unless you repute yourself such a loser. What, man, there are more ways to recover the general again. (2.3.256–266)

Iago, in his affirmation of the priority of the body over such "impositions" as reputation, again shows himself as a materialist since, for him, the body provides but the material to be used by the subject in a process of self-fashioning. This is a necessary prerequisite to Iago's plan of revenge.

Cassio, however, is not convinced by this argument and bemoans his misfortune:

> O thou invisible spirit of wine, if thou hast no name to be known by, let us call thee devil.
> [...]
> O God, that men should put an enemy in their mouths to steal away their brains! That we should with joy, pleasance, revel, and applause transform ourselves into beasts!
> [...]
> To be now a sensible man, by and by a fool, and presently a beast! O strange! Every inordinate cup is unblessed, and the ingredient is a devil. (2.3.275–277, 283–286,298–301)

In this complaint about the effects of a craftily induced inebriation, the audience recognizes a number of themes used before by Iago. If he referred to Othello as a devil in his speech to Brabantio in 1.1.92, he is indirectly characterized as the evil one himself here by Cassio because we know that it is Iago who is responsible for his drunkenness. Once again, Iago is shown to be the engineer of the reduction

---

Mediterranean, to be dominated by blood, at the expense of the other three 'humours', and to the detriment of reason" (Smith, "Studies in Sexuality," 433).

of a human being to an animal, a strategy he pursued with reference to Othello in his dialogue with Desdemona's father (1.1.117–118).

Iago uses bodies as instruments in his devious scheme of arousing Othello's sexual jealousy. Desdemona's body is to become the lever that disturbs Othello's position within white Venetian society, as evidenced in Iago's equivocating soliloquy at the end of Act 2, in which he tries to justify his advice to Cassio to ask Desdemona to intercede with Othello:

> She's framed as fruitful
> As the free elements; and then for her
> To win the Moor, were't to renounce his baptism,
> All seals and symbols of redeemèd sin,
> His soul is so enfettered to her love,
> That she may make, unmake, do what she list,
> Even as her appetite shall play the god
> With his weak function. (2.3.332–339)

Bodily attraction is to become the means through which Iago's intends his plan to work, and Desdemona unwittingly plays Iago's game when she promises to plead Cassio's case. Indeed, she naively tells the dismissed lieutenant that "His [Othello's] bed shall seem a school" (3.3.24), thereby implying that she will indeed use her own sexual powers to convince Othello to change his mind.

That bodies and bodily outward appearances can deceive, however, is cleverly chosen by Iago as the topic of the long conversation he has with Othello in Act 3 scene 3, in the course of which he manages to raise the general's suspicions against Cassio and Desdemona. Iago's dark insinuations and his cleverly performed reluctance to become more explicit allow Othello to supplement his allusions to Cassio's and Desdemona's alleged infidelity and again make use of imagery that has the body appear as an unreliable and opaque signifier. Iago's assertion that "Men should be what they seem, / Or those that be not, would they might seem none" (3.3.131–132) alerts Othello to the possibility of a discrepancy between outward appearance and interior psychological reality. This is then emphasised by his use of a combination of legal and body imagery designed to justify an affected hesitancy:

> Why, say they are vile and false,
> As where's that palace whereinto foul things
> Sometimes intrude not? Who has a breast so pure
> But some uncleanly apprehensions
> Keep leets and law-days, and in session sit
> With meditations lawful? (3.3.141–146)

As the image of the inwardly tainted but outwardly pure breast shows, we are once again confronted with the problem of the unreliability of the body as a signifier.

Iago himself turns out to be just as unreliable,[30] however, when he tells Othello that he would not suspect Cassio of anything untoward because he would not risk damaging his reputation:

> Good name in man and woman, dear my lord,
> Is the immediate jewel of their souls. (3.3.160–161)

In a moment of dramatic irony, we realize that Iago here contradicts his own earlier words to Cassio when he claimed that all that counts is that the body remains unharmed because "Reputation is an idle and most false imposition" (2.3.262–263). In such a world as this, then, reality has become difficult to discern, and neither the body nor a person's words are to be trusted. The ground is thus prepared for Othello's misjudgement of Desdemona based on observations of outward appearances that obscure the truth.

Iago even sanctimoniously warns Othello against the possible ravages of jealousy, and in doing so, he chooses an image which is characterized by its explicitly corporeal quality when he refers to jealousy as "the green-eyed monster which doth mock / The meat it feeds on." (3.3.170–171) In its stress on the consumption of flesh, this image not only graphically refers to the substance of the body in order to describe a state of the mind, but it also hints at the consumption of specifically human "meat," thereby allowing Iago implicitly to connect Othello with notions of cannibalism and the monstrous.

Iago thus prepares the ground for Othello performing the racist and orientalist script of the non-white subject as a primitive barbarian.[31] What this amounts to is a yoking of Othello to the logic of white racist discourse, a strategy which bears fruit almost immediately when, having been reminded by Iago that "She did deceive her father, marrying you" (3.3.210), he turns an affirmation of Desdemona's honesty into doubt: "And yet how nature erring from itself –" (3.3.232). This is immediately taken up by Iago who now clinches the matter by once

---

30 Aebischer, then, is right, when she points at Iago's "quality of en*sign*" and states that he "presents himself as an incomplete sign in need of interpretation" (Aebischer, *Shakespeare's Violated Bodies*, 131).

31 Howard refers to "the gradual transformation of Othello into a stereotypically jealous, irrational, and murderous Moor" (Howard, "Feminist Criticism," 428), but the potentially condemning effect of such a transformation is relativized by the play's emphasis on the fact that Othello is actually being scripted by Iago and, almost like a puppet, performs his stereotypical role.

again making sure that Othello thinks about his marriage to Desdemona as an act of miscegenation:

> Ay, there's the point; as, to be bold with you,
> Not to affect many proposèd matches
> Of her own clime, complexion, and degree,
> Whereto we see in all things nature tends.
> Foh, one may smell in such a will most rank,
> Foul disproportions, thoughts unnatural!
> But pardon me. I do not in position
> Distinctly speak of her; though I may fear
> Her will, recoiling to her better judgement,
> May fall to match you with her country forms
> And happily repent. (3.3.233–243)

This is a remarkable moment in the play because, rather than object to Iago's racist presuppositions and reject his conclusions, Othello here fully interiorises his ensign's normalization of anti-black xenophobic stereotypes and fears of miscegenation and thus makes it possible for Iago to insinuate Desdemona's possible infidelity and her consequent rejection of her husband in favour of a white suitor that becomes the source of Othello's jealousy.[32] Iago has succeeded in making Othello colour-conscious by 'whitening' his mind in so far as the latter now perceives his black skin to be a possible reason for Desdemona's alleged infidelity: "Haply for I am black" (3.3.267).

Iago is very much aware of the effect his strategy has already had on Othello, and once again, he expresses this by using body imagery:

> The Moor already changes with my poison.
> Dangerous conceits are in their natures poisons,
> Which at the first are scarce found to distaste,
> But, with a little act upon the blood,
> Burn like the mines of sulphur. (3.3.329–333)

These insinuations are likened to a drug having an effect on Othello's blood so that the ensign according to this logic, interferes with his general's body, the latter being the seat of the dangerous emotions that will procure his downfall.

Othello is indeed unhinged by Iago's ominous hints and asks for ocular, visible proof (3.3.369) that can transform doubt into certainty, although he is also

---

32 Singh also points out that "[p]erhaps what is most tragic is how Othello himself internalizes some of the racist stereotypes deployed by Iago and Brabanzio" (Singh, "Post-colonial Criticism," 493).

gradually overcome by the suspicions Iago has planted on his mind. It is significant that in describing Desdemona's supposed moral downfall due to her alleged infidelity, he projects onto her the physical marker of his own race:

> I'll have some proof. Her name, that was as fresh
> As Dian's visage, is now begrimed and black
> As mine own face. (3.3.391–393)

This is important because since Iago will not be able to provide Othello with actual proof – he says himself that "It is impossible you should see this" (3.3.407) –, his plan depends on Othello following his logic of insinuation. This is why he invents the tale of Cassio's dream in which the discredited lieutenant is alleged to have mistaken Iago for Desdemona (3.3.423–430), thus conjuring up a more graphic image of Othello's wife's infidelity.[33] Significantly, this is also the moment when Iago first mentions Desdemona's handkerchief (3.3.439–440), which thus stands in for Desdemona's chastity and extends metonymically to the claim that all women are promiscuous. Through this clever ploy, Iago manages to provide the ocular and the bodily[34] proof of Desdemona's adultery with Cassio. Othello is convinced by Iago's arguments and the ensign's plot takes its course when the general begins to think of a revenge whose physical contours reflect his own appearance: "Arise, black vengeance, from the hollow hell." (3.3.451)

Desdemona, who is, of course, totally unaware of Iago's plot immediately realizes the potentially incriminating effect the loss of her handkerchief might have on the mind of a jealous man but regards her 'noble' husband as an exception:

> my noble Moor
> Is true of mind, and made of no such baseness
> As jealous creatures are [...]

33 Iago's fiction of Cassio's dream works because "it reifies existing assumptions about a white woman who disobeys her father to marry a black man" (Stephanie Moss, "Transformation and Degeneration: The Paracelsan/Galenic Body in *Othello*," in *Disease, Diagnosis, and Cure on the Early Modern Stage*, eds. Stephanie Moss and Kaara L. Peterson. (Aldershot: Ashgate, 2004): 151–170, 156).

34 Jenstad similarly talks about "the metonymic connection between handkerchief, wedding sheets, and Desdemona's body" (Janelle Jenstad, "Paper, Linen, Sheets: Dinesen's 'The Blank Page' and Desdemona's Handkerchief," in *Approaches to Teaching Shakespeare's "Othello,"* eds. Peter Erickson and Maurice Hunt. (New York: MLA, 2005): 194–201, 196). Ian Smith less convincingly refers to the handkerchief as Othello's "substitute self" (Smith, "Othello's Black Handkerchief," 14).

> [...]
> [...] I think the sun where he was born
> Drew all such humours from him. (3.4.26–31)

Using the logic of humoural physiology and the psychology based upon it, Desdemona here argues that it is due to his very identity as a 'noble Moor' that Othello will not fall victim to jealousy.[35] This is, of course, contradicted by the stereotype, and as the audience knows, this has already happened. But this does not automatically turn the play into a racist one, for the implied conclusion here is not that Desdemona is wrong because all Moors are in thrall to their passions. Rather, we are made aware of the fact that Desdemona's logic hinges too exclusively on the workings of the body. It is true that Iago persistently uses body imagery in his dealings with Othello, but nevertheless, the play makes us aware of how deviously and carefully he constructs his words so that ultimately it is not his race or his body that makes Othello jealous, but the racist pattern of the discriminatory discourse produced by Iago.

The ensign has thus manipulated his general's horizon of understanding which has negative effects on Othello's attempts at reading the body that becomes an unreliable signifier whose interpretive openness he now turns against Desdemona;[36] for example when he notices that she has a hot and moist hand. Albeit superficially lighthearted, he seriously interprets this as a sign that "here's a young and sweating devil here / That commonly rebels" (3.4.42–43), thereby hinting at the propensity to marital infidelity of his wife. The ground having thus been prepared for Iago's intrigue, the missing handkerchief can have its full effect. When Othello describes the handkerchief, he claims that "There's magic in the web of it" (3.4.69) and that "it was dyed in mummy, which the skilful / Conserved of maidens' hearts" (3.4.74–75), explaining that the use of such substances taken from dead human bodies[37] can cast a spell over a woman and make her fall in love with its owner. Othello here clearly and blatantly contradicts his earlier claim made to the Duke that his storytelling and his own love

---

35 Desdemona's reference to the sun is no coincidence because "Renaissance writers were particularly interested in knowing what produced 'blackness'" and considered "overexposure to the sun" as one possible explanation (Bartels "Shakespeare's view of the world," 159).

36 Cf. Oesterlen who points out that "[u]nder Iago's guidance, woman is [...] constructed as an unreliable body of signs" (Oesterlen "(Re)Covering the Bla(n)ck Presence," 267).

37 This reference to "medicinal cannibalism" associates Othello with anthropophagism and thus with the stereotype of the black barbarian other (cf. Smith "Othello's Black Handkerchief," 16 and 20). On medicinal cannibalism in *Othello* cf. Noble (Louise Noble, *Medicinal Cannibalism: Early Modern English Literature and Culture* (Houndmills: Palgrave Macmillan, 2011), esp. 127–159).

for Desdemona was the only witchcraft he used on her (1.3.168), and the play here once again opens up space for ambivalence.[38] A racist might find all his or her prejudices confirmed in Othello's inconsistency, while there is indeed no reason why one should have to read it in this way.

When Othello asks Desdemona to produce the handkerchief he has given her and she responds by asking him to rehabilitate Cassio, the two argue for the very first time. After Othello, enraged and jealous, has abruptly exited Emilia characterizes male-female relations by means of body imagery:

> 'Tis not a year or two shows us a man.
> They are all but stomachs, and we all but food.
> They eat us hungrily, and when they are full,
> They belch us. (3.4.101–104)

Men generally are here constructed as cannibals, but her remark may also apply to the particular case of Othello, and inadvertently adopts an element of racial stereotyping. Here the annihilation and discarding of the other's body confirms that woman is an alterity to be subjected in order to guarantee the dominance of the self. But even more, sexual jealousy is a by-product of patriarchy that effectively erodes the dominant patriarchal power from within: "a monster / Begot upon itself, born on itself" (3.4.158 – 159). Othello, then, here is certainly associated with the monstrous, the grotesque and the abnormal, which, to some extent places Emilia's statement within the discourse of negative racist othering, but she also discloses a female subjectivity that is an *effect* of the 'ills' of patriarchy.

Othello is othered in the sense of not being himself any longer. Desdemona herself states that "My lord is not my lord, nor should I know him / Were he in favour as in humour altered" (3.4.122–123), and we know that, in terms of contemporary humoural psychology, Iago has poured the poison of his treacherous words into Othello's ear and thus disturbed his blood, i. e. his emotions. Othello therefore is no longer master of himself, and he even loses control of his body when he falls into an epilectic fit in Act 4, scene 1. This fit is used immediately by Iago to depict him as a transgressive and barbarous other:[39]

---

38 Cf. Howard who points out that "it is not just the handkerchief itself that is important, but also the stories Othello tells of its origin" (Howard, "Feminist Criticism," 426).

39 Moss points out that Othello's epileptic fit "embeds the cultural values of Early Modern polemics against Mohammed in Shakespeare's play. Christian revision of Mohammedanism labeled its founder as an epileptic rather than a prophet" (Moss, "Transformation and Degeneration," 159) so that Othello here is othered yet again: "Epilepsy in *Othello* [...] alludes to the founder of Islam and thereby becomes a cultural marker of the Moor's degeneration from Christian warrior into infidel" (Moss, "Transformation and Degeneration," 160). To Vozar, Othello's

> The lethargy must have his quiet course.
> If not, he foams at mouth, and by and by
> Breaks out to savage madness. (4.1.51–53)

The black general here is associated with savagery and lunacy in a rhetorical move that refers both to a medical condition and also to the discourse of racist discrimination with its orientalist construction of alterity. The condition of Othello's epilectic body augments Iago's strategy of negative othering.

The notion of Othello as a monster[40] hinted at by Emilia is unwittingly taken up again by himself when he wakes from his trance and refers to himself as "A hornèd man's a monster and a beast" (4.1.60). Without knowing it, Othello here takes up again Iago's animal comparison from Act 1, in which he described the black general as "a Barbary horse" (1.1.113–114) and, referred to his sexual relation with Desdemona, as " making the beast with two backs" (1.1.118). The play thus turns into an echo chamber reverberating with Iago's racist othering devices, which produces such a powerful effect.

The success of Iago's strategy is underlined by his conversation with Cassio about Bianca, which Othello overhears, and which he claims will be about Desdemona. Iago speculates on his general drawing wrong conclusions from Cassio's body language:

> Now will I question Cassio of Bianca,
> [...]
> He, when he hears of her, cannot restrain
> From the excess of laughter. [...]
> [...]
> As he shall smile, Othello shall go mad;
> And his unbookish jealousy must conster
> Poor Cassio's smiles, gestures, and light behaviours
> Quite in the wrong. (4.1.92–102)

---

epileptic fit also symbolizes his estrangement from white Venetian culture and constitutes "his failure to abide by his adopted Venetian ideal of stoic self-Mastery" (Thomas M. Vozar, "Body-Mind Aporia in the Seizure of Othello," *Philosophy and Literature* 36.1 (April 2012): 183–186, 184). Similarly, Lux says that "Othello's epileptic disorder [...] may have cultural/geographical causes/roots" (Lux, "'Work on my medicine'," 387).

40 On monsters and notions of the monstrous in *Othello* cf. Mark Thornton Burnett, *Constructing 'Monsters' in Shakespearean Drama and Early Modern Culture* (Houndmills: Palgrave Macmillan, 2002): 95–124.

We are confronted here with another instance of the inscrutability and unreliability of the body as a signifier, which is turned into a devious tool for the realization of Iago's plans.

When Othello determines to kill both Cassio and Desdemona, he does not realize that his conclusions are based on a misreading of outward appearances but he is aware of the body's potential to exert an unwanted influence on him when he says, "I'll not expostulate with her, lest her body and beauty unprovide my mind again" (4.1.199–201). Othello is afraid of another misreading of the body, as Desdemona's body cannot, he thinks, harbour a deceitful adulteress. In other words, Othello, at the very moment when he has already unknowingly fallen victim to the pitfalls of the ambiguity of the body as a signifier displays a certain epistemological scepticism with regard to his possible reading of Desdemona's body. When he loses his temper and strikes Desdemona in the presence of Lodovico, the latter begins to doubt Othello's reputation as "the nature / Whom passion could not shake" (4.1.267–268) and he even asks himself: "Is he not light of brain?" (4.1.271), thus echoing Iago's claim earlier. What follows is another quarrel between Othello and Desdemona, the former this time openly accusing his wife of being a whore (4.2.35–90). Emilia is infuriated by this act of injustice and comments:

> Hath she forsook so many noble matches,
> Her father and her country and her friends,
> To be called whore? Would it not make one weep? (4.2.129–131)

Emilia's reference to Desdemona's having forsaken her country in order to marry Othello reactivates the miscegenistic logic of Act 1. And this permits us to view Othello's following actions through an orthodox racist lens as those of a black negative other. Such a perspective is not enforced, though. It is even questioned when Emilia immediately realizes that Othello must be "abused by some most villainous knave / Some base, notorious knave, some scurvy fellow" (4.1.143–144). Even so, Emilia's words are not completely free from orientalising prejudice because when she wishes heaven to punish the knave that is the source of Othello's behaviour

> And put in every honest hand a whip
> To lash the rascals naked through the world,
> Even from the east to th'west! (4.2.146–148)

she places the origin of evil in the east and thus in the imagined realm of the non-white other.

As the scene of Desdemona's murder at the hands of Othello approaches we are constantly reminded of the intercultural and interracial context of the story. Thus, as Desdemona prepares to go to bed, she tells Emilia the story of the death of her mother's maid Barbary (4.3.25) the very name of whom conjures up notions of barbarian otherness.

Before the murder scene, however, the outcome of Iago's intrigue against Cassio and Roderigo is shown to miscarry, and Iago kills Roderigo in order to silence him. Cassio, however, is only wounded, and in order to deflect suspicion from himself, Iago has immediate recourse to a further othering strategy by constructing Bianca as a prostitute who, because she sells her body, cannot be trusted and is to be suspected of involvement in the attack on Cassio (5.1.86–103).[41]

In the final scene of the play the body is of central importance again. On the one hand, Othello sees his wife's body and 'blood' as the source of the passions as the cause of her infidelity and his dilemma (5.2.1–3), but on the other hand he vows not to destroy its beauty (5.2.3–5). He decides to kill her anyway, though, because her body has become the "cunning'st pattern of excelling nature" (5.2.11) and thus cannot be trusted; because Desdemona's skin, "whiter [...] than snow, / And smooth as monumental alabaster" (5.2.4–5), hides her infidelity and is thus the cause for the discrepancy between appearance and reality. The misogynist racist Iago has managed to infect Othello with the suggestion that a woman's beauty must condemn her. The result is that Othello is trapped in an impossibly paradoxical situation:

> I will kill thee
> And love thee after. One more, and this the last.
> So sweet was never so fatal. (5.2.18–20)

At the point when Desdemona realizes that Othello is about to kill her, the description of his demeanour reflects elements of the very stereotype that earlier she had rejected: "you're fatal then / When your eyes roll so" (5.2.39–40) and "why gnaw you so your nether lip? / Some bloody passion shakes your very frame." (5.2.46–47) Desdemona unwittingly alludes to the othering of Othello along racial lines.

Desdemona defends herself by pleading that she never loved Cassio nor gave him her handkerchief, but Othello interprets her words as part of a larger

41 As Howard points out, there is indeed "no textual indication that Bianca is attached to a number of men simultaneously, and her loyalty to Cassio is unswerving" (Howard, "Feminist Criticism," 425).

female rhetorical strategy designed to divert him from what he is convinced is a necessary and 'sacrificial' action:

> Thou dost stone my heart,
> And makes me call what I intend to do
> A murder, which I thought a sacrifice. (5.2.68–70)

Desdemona, whose skin is earlier described as 'alabaster' is now accused of turning Othello's own 'heart' into stone. The living human body thus becomes, in the couple's speeches, defamiliarized and 'petrified.'

When Emilia realizes what has happened and Othello admits to having killed his wife, she addresses the general as "the blacker devil" (5.2.140) and thus has recourse to the same equation between blackness and the devil that Iago himself had deployed in his speech to Brabantio in Act 1.1.192. When she calls for help, she refers to "The Moor" who "hath killed my mistress. Murder, murder!" (5.2.174) – and we are reminded of the discursive system of reference we already know from the first scene of the play.

Emilia by now has realized that it was Iago who manipulated Othello and she questions and harangues her husband for it. The latter, committed to a patriarchal and misogynist frame of reference, still thinks that he can silence her, but Emilia resists. When he tells her to be silent she replies:

> Good gentlemen, let me have leave to speak.
> 'Tis proper I obey him, but not now.
> [...]
> 'Twill out, 'twill out. I peace?
> No, I will speak as liberal as the north.
> Let heaven, and men, and devils, let 'em all,
> All, all cry shame against me, yet I'll speak. (5.2.202–203, 225–280)

While in the case of Othello a racial other has been lured to commit a gratuitous murder, Emilia, now the subversive female other rebels against this patriarchal construction and claims a voice of its own, thus triggering Iago's downfall. For his part, Iago has no other means to defend himself than reverting to familiar strategies of slander, calumny and denunciation, which have now lost their power. When Emilia discloses the truth of how the handkerchief found its way to Cassio, Iago calls her a "Villainous whore," (5.2.236) thus invoking another negative gender stereotype but this proves to be ineffective as an othering manoeuvre on this occasion. The villain Iago stabs his wife (5.2.242), and as she dies, she condemns Othello in racist terms "Moor, she was chaste. She loved thee, cruel Moor" (5.2.256).

Othello, now full of remorse, refers to himself as a "cursèd, cursèd slave" (5.2.283) and is addressed by Lodovico as "O thou Othello, that was once so good / Fall'n in the practice of a cursèd slave" (5.2.297–298). This slide from 'Noble Moor' to 'slave' serves to point up the difficulty that the play as a whole seeks to negotiate: the *difference* that resides in the figure of the tragic hero himself: he is a 'black' man with a 'white' heart, and the result is a bifurcated identity that the play cannot satisfactorily resolve.

Similarly, when Iago's plot against Cassio is uncovered the latter calls it "Most heathenish and most gross!" so that the borderline between white Christendom and non-white heathendom is blurred because it is the white Iago who turns out to have been the originator of the heathenish, satanic and therefore 'black' plan.[42] The moral valorization of skin colour and, by implication, of other physical attributes is thereby put in question. The categories of othering have become blurred. It is only fitting, then, that Iago, too, is ultimately referred to as "this slave" (5.2.341) by Lodovico.

It is typical of the ambivalence of the play that, despite the de-essentializing of the construction of alterity based on bodily features such as skin colour, Othello in his final soliloquy, immediately before he stabs himself, reaffirms the white Venetian categories of cultural othering when he describes himself as "one whose hand, / Like the base Indian, threw a pearl away / Richer than all his tribe" (5.2.355–357). At the same time, in his final words before his death, he performatively casts himself in the role of slayer of the non-white Oriental threatening white Venice:

> Set you down this,
> And say that in Aleppo once,
> Where a malignant and a turbaned Turk
> Beat a Venetian and traduced the state,
> I took by th'throat the circumcisèd dog
> And smote him thus.
>
> *He stabs himself* (5.2.360–365)

Othello here reaffirms the categorization of Venice's enemies as evil others, and in doing so he stresses moral ("malignant"), cultural ("turbaned") and bodily

42 In fact, Iago's attempts at drawing a distinct borderline between white and black have been spurious all along because "clear lines of ethnicity and race were not easy to draw in this period" (Bartels "Shakespeare's view of the world," 159). Iago's strategy of doing so anyway in order to reduce the complexity of the situation and establish a simple dichotomy between white self and black other has failed.

("circumcisèd") features that serve to construct a discourse of negative alterity for the Turks. Thus, on the one hand, the familiar categories are re-affirmed. But, on the other hand, by 'smiting' himself in the same way that he "smote" the Turk in Aleppo, Othello also places himself in the role of the Turk, he becomes both slayer and slain, Venetian defender and Turkish enemy. He thus performs two contradictory and supposedly mutually exclusive roles at the same time.[43] Othello thus makes us aware of the instability and constructed nature of concepts of alterity and of the constitution of meaning so that Graziano's shocked comment, "All that is spoke is marred" (5.2.367), can also be read as a warning against a literal understanding of any such discursive concepts. That they are unavoidable, and that othering is a strategy we all engage in all the time, can also be observed in Lodovico's final words that de-humanize Iago by calling him a "Spartan dog" (5.2.371) and by referring to Othello as "the Moor" once again (5.2.376).

In *Othello*, then, Shakespeare not only engaged with contemporary issues concerning the influx into England of non-white people, but he also produced a play which, in a very differentiated and subtle way, uncovers and problematizes mechanisms of othering by laying bare the essentializing discursive strategies that underlie constructions of racial alterity. Shakespeare also provides many examples that show how the racial and gendered body signifies in this context in the discourse of othering.[44] The play's history of reception has often been marked by debates as to whether or not *Othello* is a racist play.[45] Such debates, however, tell us more about those engaging in them than about the play itself because the latter neither takes up a racist position nor ignores the presence and the mechanisms of racist thinking.[46] Rather, it lays bare the ambivalence of conceptualizing categories of identity and alterity in an Early Modern world of growing racial and ethnic diversity.

---

43 Cf. Howard who points out that "Othello divides himself" (Howard, "Feminist Criticism," 428) here. Oesterlen also refers to this scene and observes Othello's "sense of a split subjectivity" (Oesterlen, "(Re)Covering the Bla(n)ck Presence," 272).

44 Howard thus justly claims that "the gender and racial ideologies of the play intersect" (Howard, "Feminist Criticism," 429).

45 See Aebischer, *Shakespeare's Violated Bodies*, 123.

46 Bartels very aptly expresses this when she states that "[i]t is Iago and not the play itself that attempts to fix the terms of difference, and Iago's terms and not Othello's difference that come under fire" (Bartels "Making More of the Moor," 448).

Roxanne Barbara Doerr

Staged and Staging Bodies as Legal and Medical sites in *Volpone*

1 Introduction

In the light of numerous studies on the representation of law and justice, Early Modern drama has become an increasingly important field of inquiry, due to the mutually beneficial exchange between the theatre and the courtroom.[1] Ben Jonson's works – especially his comedies of humour, focused on fictional social classes and their typifying traits – are characterized by particularly strong connections to the law and to diverse legal issues and contexts for satirical, forensic and moral purposes. His studies of, and problems with, the law[2] because of his theatrical work, his literary skirmishes with publishers and his extra-professional entanglements with the law, allowed him to learn so much about legal technicalities and limitations that John Donne claimed "If counsellors in the law[s] of men and God would dare follow and emulate what you have dared here in your art, Poet, O we all should have the wisdom needed for salvation."[3] *Volpone*, in particular, is a very "legal" and "performative" text that incorporates within its structures a metanarrative element. As Sam Thompson points out in connection with the play, Jonson's insistence on adhering to literary rules, except those concerning final outcomes, makes him a "keeper of the laws."[4] The laws he upholds or breaks are decided on the basis of what is necessary in order to convey his ultimate moral lesson through references to legal and medical matters, and

1 Antoine Masson, for instance, argues that "Justice is a system of representation: Representation of truth by litigating parties in their arguments and embodiment by legal system themselves of their own powers," "Introduction to the Interactions between Law and Representation of Justice," in *Representations of Justice*, eds. Antoine Masson and Kevin O'Connor (Brussels: P.I.E. Peter Lang S.A., 2007), 15.

2 For more on this, see Frances Teague, "New Directions: Ben Jonson and Imprisonment," in *Volpone: a Critical Reader*, ed. Matthew Steggle (London: Bloomsbury, 2011), 125–143. Here Teague outlines Jonson's spotted criminal record and traces a peculiar resemblance between the Gunpowder Plot and *Volpone*. See also Lorna Hutson, "Law, crime and punishment," in *Ben Jonson in Context*, ed. Julie Sanders (Cambridge: Cambridge University Press, 2010): 221–228.

3 Sam Thompson, "The Critical Backstory," in *Volpone: a Critical Reader*, ed. Matthew Steggle: 8–30, 9.

4 Thompson, "The Critical Backstory," 10.

to the theatrical imperatives of genre. Therefore, by outlining an array of affinities and intersections between performative, legal and medical activity, the present study endeavours to demonstrate how *Volpone* is a representation of its age and of Jonson's interest in the body as both site and object of legal and physical inquiry. In the play in fact, events are staged and directed as in a theatre and centred on the body both as a pivotal element and, more importantly, as representations of physical and legal selfhood in accordance with some of the most common and significant legal and medical practices of the Early Modern period. As Dara Van Den Berg observes,

> Throughout his career, Jonson celebrated and mocked the human body, a case that can and cannot be altered. The body became for him the necessary representation of the self. Two models of self contended in the Early Modern era: self as moral essence and self as social construction. In Jonson's works, both are figured as the body, and are set in tension through tricks of naming, deformity, cross-dressing, disguise and projection, all designed to augment the body and to satisfy its desires.[5]

The corporeal and legal complexities of the play are emphasised in the play's "Argument": Volpone is immediately labelled as "childless, rich" and one who "feigns sickness." He "[o]ffers his state to hopes of several heirs / Lies languishing." However, in order to dispel any suspicion of his being impotent or undesirable, Mosca points out that the children his master supposedly fathered are numerous but entirely illegitimate from a legal (and a moral) standpoint:

> Bastards,
> Some dozen, or more, that he begot on beggars,
> Gipsies, and Jews, and black-moors, when he was drunk.
> Knew you not that, sir? 'tis the common fable.
> The dwarf, the fool, the eunuch, are all his. (1.5.44–47)[6]

---

5 Sara Van Den Berg, "True relation: the life and career of Ben Jonson," in *The Cambridge Companion to Ben Jonson*, eds. Richard Harp and Stanley Stewart (Cambridge: Cambridge University Press, 2000): 1–14, 12. In another, more pessimistic study on Ben Jonson and the body, this time in reference to his poetry, Ben Morgan sustains that "the body was not only a vehicle for Jonson: it is also a subject. The body's constant potential for baseness, disease and obscenity is also part of his passionately asserted, neo-classicist aesthetic credo. At crucial moments, especially in his poetry, the body's baseness becomes identified with everything he despises in literary production itself: that it might merely cater to the appetites of its audience, and that its sheer physical presence in the world makes it part of the – for Jonson – filthy transactions of advertising and crowd-pleasing in the nascent library and theatrical marketplace," "The Body," in *Ben Jonson in Context*, ed. Julie Sanders: 212–220, 212.

6 All quotations from Ben Jonson's *Volpone* are from the following edition: Ben Jonson, *Volpone and Other Plays*, ed. Michael Jamieson (London: Penguin Books, 2004).

Such conduct also recalls Volpone's claim that he is affected by consumption, known today as tuberculosis, which was thought to be transmitted through sexual contact. The low standards of the women he supposedly associated with, and the deformation of his alleged but unrecognized children, make it impossible for them to inherit. This, as well as his being affected by a serious disease, draws attention to the artificial precariousness of Volpone's fortune and its destiny after his seemigly imminent death. Instead of seeing this situation as a threatening one where many would take advantage of him in order to benefit from his heirless state and profit from his age, he exploits his legal and medical frailty in order to gain from his suitors:[7] "I have no wife, no parent, child, ally, / To give my substance to; but whom I make / Must be my heir: and this makes men observe me" (1.1.72–74).

Volpone thus takes on the role of a director who fabricates and engineers the plot, as well as the elements that will support his role as an incurably sick person who must receive the "birds of prey / That think me turning carcass" (1.2.89–90). His strategy is to mount a performance of his own that will always include changing costumes, utilizing props, and interacting with supporting actors. These ancillary characters either employ their own bodies or those of others to put on a theatrical performance to reach their goals, or seek to expose and prevent such performances from leading to miscarriages of justice. Performances in *Volpone* thus reinforce the bond between the body, the law and the stage in the execution and resolution of conflict: in fact, the law assumes different positions and intervenes in different ways based on the corporeal subject's legal and social standing, age and state of health. This will become apparent in the course of an intersectional analysis, such as the present one, of the play's legal and medical representation, scrutiny and treatment of the body.

2 Corbaccio and the Law's Conquest Over Body and Ageing

A first example of the intersection between the body and the law may be seen in the neediest of Volpone's suitors. Corbaccio represents an earthier and physically competitive victim for Volpone and a character whose scenes "are always the

7 See also Stella Achilleos, "New Directions: Age and Ageing in *Volpone*," in *Volpone: a Critical Reader*, ed. Matthew Steggle: 144–167, 158–160. It is thus possible to state that through his false illness, Volpone encourages the illegal practice of legacy-hunting that is mentioned in classical literature.

most physically engaging of those featuring the three gulls, and [...] provides room for stage business."[8] In the list of "The Persons of the Play" he is only described as "an Old Gentleman," with no indication of his profession but simply defined by his age and his social status as a "gentleman." His first appearance is announced by Mosca in a sarcastic aside: "Now we shall see / A wretch who is indeed more impotent / Than this can feign to be, yet hopes to hop / Over his grave" (1.4.2–5). Corbaccio, like the crow whose name he bears, is seen as an unwelcome omen that mediates between life and death and feasts on carcasses.[9] More than that, he seems to be deluded in his pursuit of a bygone youthfulness, as Achilleos suggests:

> Indeed, Corbaccio's ludicrous desire to become Volpone's heir seems to be triggered not simply by greed, but by a desparate attempt to recapture youth. His tenacious hope to inherit Volpone gives him a strangely powerful hold on life. [...] [T]he mere fantasy of outliving Volpone and inheriting his fortune functions for Corbaccio as an elixir of life, an alchemical essence the attributes of which make him feel rejuvenated.[10]

Corbaccio's association with the body is confirmed by his gift to Volpone, an "opiate here, from mine own doctor" (1.4.13) that he claims will make him sleep. He is even "transformed" into medicine when Mosca calls him "half dust" whose only use could be to be turned into "mummia" (4.4.15) and used as a drug. In accordance with common fears of the time, however, Mosca claims that "He [Volpone] has no faith in physic: he does think / Most of your doctors are the greater danger, / And worse disease t'escape" (1.4.20–22). Such a dire vision of the medical profession – which at the time was experiencing a crisis of authority – is connected to the period's inconsistent regulations of medical practice[11] because, as Mosca indicates,

> Mosca: they do it by experiment,
> For which the law not only doth absolve 'em,
> But gives them great reward: and he is loath
> To hire his death so.
> Corbaccio: It is true, they kill

8 Matthew Steggle, "Introduction" to *Volpone: a Critical Reader*, ed. Matthew Steggle (London: Bloomsbury, 2011): 1–7, 6.
9 Voltore (the vulture), Corvino (the raven) and Mosca (the flesh fly) also carry the names of carrion birds or – in Mosca's case – of parasitic insects, but their "feeding" on Volpone is more linked to wealth and social standing.
10 Achilleos, "New Directions: Age and Ageing in *Volpone*," 149.
11 For more on this see, William Kerwin, *Beyond the Body: the Boundaries of Medicine and English Renaissance Drama* (Amherst and Boston: University of Massachusettes, 2005), 134–137.

> With as much licence as a judge.
> Mosca: Nay, more;
> For he but kills, sir, where the law condemns,
> And these can kill him too. (1.4.29–34)

A further complication results from Mosca's disclosure of a fictional quasi-medical diagnosis of Volpone's alleged condition to Corbaccio, designed to lend authenticity to the deception. Whereas Voltore feigns concern over Volpone's health, Corbaccio responds to each statement and symptom with a recurrent and approving "good." Moreover, he seems to draw his own strength from the other man's seemingly gradual weakness when saying "Excellent, excellent! Sure I shall outlast him! / This makes me young again, a score of years" (1.4.55–56). He thus takes on an almost vampiric persona that contrasts with his earlier offer of medical "help" to Volpone. The old gentleman is deluded by a fantasy of rejuvenation that, as Stella Achilleos argues, articulates a "much broader set of social and cultural anxieties concerning age and ageing in the Early Modern period."[12]

Corbaccio perceives wealth and luxury as a panacea and connects abundance of possession with abundance of health. The legal power, financial appeal, and hope sparked by the aspiration to Volpone's inheritance are considered a source of medical relief and physical strength. Corbaccio's quest both for financial well-being and bodily health is made all the more urgent by his desperate race against time, which is alluded to in Mosca's and Volpone's private conversation in which they are sure that the latter, while certainly not in the prime of his life, will surely outlive his suitor. Corbaccio's precarious condition is further emphasised by means of numerous references to his physical frailty and by the stark contrast that is implicitly created with his young and vigorous son Bonario.[13]

This conflict between a weak body and a strong will, which cannot be denied or secured at a physical level, must be translated into different, i.e. legal, terms to allow the old gentleman to assert some power of action. Corbaccio, therefore, does not hesitate to turn to the law, disinheriting his son Bonario. A further aggravating detail consists in the fact that Bonario is seen by all – avocatori included – as a virtuous person. As a matter of fact, Bonario is the only character to

12 Achilleos, "New Directions: Age and Ageing in Volpone," 144.

13 Celia is also referred to by her bodily youthfulness (even in contrast with her husband) and, interestingly, she and Bonario are the ones to be totally innocent and initially beguiled and defeated in court by older and more knowing, albeit ill-intentioned, people of high social and financial standing.

doubt Mosca's intentions from the very beginning, something that Mosca notices and articulates in legal terms:

> You are unequal to me, and howe'er,
> Your sentence may be righteous, yet you are not,
> That ere you know me, thus proceed in censure.
> St Mark near witness 'gainst you, 'tis inhuman. (3.1.14–17)[14]

Corbaccio's action of disinheritance has a particularly powerful legal implication, in that it would convert the hitherto legitimate and guiltless son into a "written bastard" (3.2.65) although he has done nothing to deserve it. The trust that the elderly gentleman reposes in the law, and more precisely in the deception implied in Volpone's will, requires a legalistic reciprocity, but his own 'will' will be part of what is, in effect, an unequal exchange.

The decaying of the body therefore reflects a certain painful and gradual degeneration of morality and of the soul, all of which is further corrupted by unfair legal actions in a vicious cycle. Indeed, throughout the play "the body constantly changes – growing, decaying – and responds to the body politic that surrounds and constructs it."[15] Because of his greed and the play's moralizing discourse, Corbaccio and his unwitting son (the latter merely by association) are referred to as "two old, rotten sepulchres" (3.9.38). The hypocrisy of such criticism is enforced by the fact that Mosca says this only in order to dissemble his association with Corbaccio when justifying his actions to a very suspicious Voltore who has overheard the two consorting. Moreover, after paying very little for Voltore and Mosca's services, the latter reacts indignantly by identifying Corbaccio with his age and bodily conditions, thus reflecting his "culture's obsession with youth and its anxiety concerning the ravages of time on human nature" by wondering: "Bountiful bones! What horrid, strange offence / Did he commit 'gainst nature,

14 The same association between Bonario and justice is made by Bonario himself when he prevents Volpone from ravishing Celia: "Free the forced lady, or thou diest, impostor. / But that I am loath to snatch thy punishment / Out of the hand of justice, thou shouldst yet / Be made the timely sacrifice of vengeance, / Before this altar, and this dross, thy idol. / Lady, let's quit the place, it is the den / Of villainy; fear nought, you have a guard: / And he ere long shall meet his just reward. (3.7.268–275)

15 Van Den Berg, "True relation: the life and career of Ben Jonson," 12. Another example of the correspondence between decay of the body and that of the law, and in this case of legal property, may be found in Act 5, when a disguised Volpone tells an angered Voltore about "a handsome, pretty, customed bawdy-house" (5.7.12) that "fell with him. His body and that house / Decayed together" (5.7.14–15).

in his youth, / Worthy this age?" (4.6.89–90). Volpone also voices this shared opinion when he claims that

> So many cares, so many maladies,
> So many fears attending on old age.
> Yea, death so often called on as no wish
> Can be more frequent with 'em. Their limbs faint,
> Their senses dull, their seeing, hearing, going,
> All dead before them; yea, their very teeth,
> Their instruments of eating, failing them;
> Yet this is reckoned life! Nay, here was one,
> Is now gone home, that wishes to live longer!
> Feels not his gout, nor palsy; feigns himself
> Younger by scores of years, flatters his age
> With confident belying it; hopes he may,
> With charms, like Æson, have his youth restored:
> And with these thoughts so battens, as if fate
> Would be as easily cheated on as he,
> And all turns air! (1.4.145–158)

Volpone rehearses some of his feigned symptoms[16] while ridiculing Corbaccio's authentic desire to imitate Aeson and regain his youth through miraculous "charms" and trickery. Moreover, he claims that the causes of his suitor's future and imminent ruin are to be found in the avarice that accompanies his ungraceful ageing and in his desire for Volpone's death rather than in any unfair action on his own part. Degenerate conduct is therefore physically mirrored in Corbaccio's and – as is pronounced at the end of the play by means of the avocatories' final verdict – Volpone's decaying bodies, justifying the misfortune that eventually is believed to befall them. This karmic return of the illnesses Volpone has been simulating is already anticipated, for instance, during Lady Politic Would-be's exasperating visit, when, in order to prevent her from recounting her dream he feigns sickness. As the lady describes the ingredients for a specific remedy and tries to convince him to use it, he complains "before I feigned diseases, now I have one" (3.2.63) as he is forced to listen to her unneeded advice.

Volpone attempts to "demonstrate" false ageing and sickness (as well as his death[17] later on) while Corbaccio wants to regain his feigned youth regardless of

---

16 These include "my feigned cough, my phthisic, and my gout, / My apoplexy, palsy, and catarrhs" (1.2.125–126).

17 Significantly, this happens at the beginning of Act 5, which is the moment of Volpone's greatest triumph and corruption of soul, represented by his faked decease. Mosca however asks him how to proceed if someone were to ask to see the body. Lorna Hutson points out that "in English

the long term damage it would bring others. Both therefore dissemble their physical conditions – although in opposite ways – to fool those around them: such fraudulent conduct and staging of themselves leads to illegal actions, which, in their turn, lead, almost by accident, to judicial sentences that inflict both bodily and legal punishment on the perpetrators of the fraud.

3 Mountebanks, Performers on the Brink of Recognized Law and Medicine

The legal standing of different kinds of medication is also analysed in juridical terms: at one point Mosca voices Volpone's complaint about legally approved medicines which "flay a man" (1.4.26) because of their cost, despite their being legitimate because they are administered by a licensed physician. Different however, is the case of those who operate outside official boundaries, the most telling case in point being the mountebanks. As far as medical studies were concerned, the sixteenth and seventeenth centuries were characterized by an ongoing conflict between licensed physicians, who had studied at the university and who practiced medicine as their sole profession, and mountebanks, professionals from other fields who were not formally qualified and who exercised their medical duties part time. As Sarah Knight states:

> the type of the scholar-mountebank is rooted in medical polemic of the early seventeenth century. Educated physicists worked to damage the reputation of the mountebanks and figured their rivals in the marketplace as complete antitheses to the learned practice taught by the medical faculties at Oxford, Cambridge, and the Royal College of Physicians in London. As mountebanks became increasingly conspicuous on the margins of medical practice, the College in particular strove to cast doubt on their qualifications.[18]

law, the coroner was required to inquire into unexplained deaths *super visum corporis*, on the viewing of the corpse." Lorna Hutson, *The Invention of Suspicion: Law and Mimesis in Shakespeare and Renaissance Drama* (Oxford: Oxford University Press, 2007), 14 (original emphasis). In this case, although Volpone's supposed death was not unexpected since, as mentioned previously, Volpone claimed he suffered from consumption, the coroner's inspection of the body could have been requested because of the high possibility of contestation. Accordingly, Volpone answers Mosca's question with "Say it was corrupted" (5.1.77) and the latter adds "I'll say it stunk, sir; and was fain t'have it / Coffined up instantly and sent away" (5.1.78–79).

18 Sarah Knight, "'He is indeed a kind of Scholler-Mountebank': Academic Liars in Jacobean Satire," in *Shell Games: Studies in Scams, Frauds and Deceits (1300–1650)*, eds. Margaret Reeves, Richard Raiswell and Mark Crane (Toronto: Center for Reformation and Renaissance Studies, 2004): 59–80, 61.

Their different status in society and their manner of deploying their knowledge confirm William Kerwin's claim that "drama, in its agnostic structure, highlights the conflicts and the social competitions that shape medicine."[19] Such a conflict was prompted by the transition in medical knowledge from the Galenic tradition to a more modern empirical alternative requiring the need for licensed physicians to maintain their medical competence as well as their cultural and professional authority. Significantly, Kerwin also observes that this medical conflict took a metatheatrical turn by also becoming a contest over control of the medical marketplace between mountebanks' theatricality and conservative physicians' antitheatricality. Indeed, the distinguishing sign of physicians was that they were not implicated in theatrical representation but rather that their authority was rooted in their knowledge of established current medical texts. To them, the more liberal mountebanks were dangerous because of their willingness to employ, as Knight suggests, both traditional and more experimental forms of medicine and their consequent "appearing as a sign of social disorder and illegitimacy and making a dangerous confusion [...] between outer appearance and genuine authenticity:"[20]

> During the Jacobean period, a variety of writers anatomized the mountebank, from medical polemicists in their tracts against unorthodox practitioners to Ben Jonson in his comedy *Volpone* (1605), and from Francis Bacon in his pioneering educational treatise, *The Advancement of Learning* (1605), to Inns of Court satirists in their prose and plays. These writers use various strategies to dissect the mountebank's origins, professional tactics, and social function, yet their works overlap as they relate the mountebank to learning, language, and deceit. When mountebanks entered the sociological landscape of Early Modern England, they were appropriated as an apt template for portraying a kind of scholarship that relied on false claims of knowledge.[21]

Volpone's decision to disguise himself as a mountebank as a stratagem to seduce Celia without being recognized recalls the unquestionable illegality of his actions and allows him to "Maintain mine own shape still the same" (1.5.129). It also echoes the connection that professional physicians made and promoted between mountebanks and the Elizabethan underworld,[22] as well as the strong bond between actors and mountebanks. As Sarah Knight observes, "[a]ll mountebanks perform since [...] they only feign medical know-how, but theatrical characters ('Juglers' and 'Stage Players') are especially prone to becoming moun-

19 Kerwin, *Beyond the Body*, 2.
20 Kerwin, *Beyond the Body*, 133.
21 Knight, "'He is indeed a kind of Scholler-Mountebank,'" 59.
22 For more on this, see Kerwin, *Beyond the Body*, 141 and 144.

tebanks. [...] Both mountebanks and actors performed on a stage and relied on the force of their words to convince an audience."[23] Mountebanks therefore dealt with matters of the body but as charlatans they enacted a "burlesque cure"[24] that parodied their claimed professional competence. The ambiguity of Italian mountebanks', and in particular of Scoto of Mantua's activity, is proposed as the object of a heated discussion between Sir Politic Wouldbe and Peregrine. While the former naively considers them "Great general scholars, excellent physicians, / Most admired statesmen, professed favourites / And cabinet counsellors to the greatest princes!" (2.2.10–12) the latter claims that

> And I have heard they are most lewd imposters,
> Made all of terms and shreds; no less beliers
> Of great men's favours, than their own vile med'cines;
> Which they will utter upon monstrous oaths:
> Selling that drug for two-pence, ere they part,
> Which they have valued at twelve crowns before. (2.2.14–19)

Peregrine and Sir Pol become judges of Scoto's authority and Volpone must protect himself from exposure of his methods, which depend upon "rhetorical and intellectual knavery as well as a show of academic expertise."[25] He does this by distancing himself from unreliable mountebanks, justifying his business in legal terms, and attempting to place himself within the law's protection by defending his case as if he were in court. His answer to Peregrine's objections to his prices and his work in general includes a self-legitimizing "countless catalogue of those I have cured" (2.2.129) with his *Oglio de Scoto*, as well as mention of "the patent and privileges of all the princes and commonwealths of Christendom" (2.2.130–131), the "depositions of those that appeared on my part, before the signiory of the Sanita and most learned College of Physicians," (2.2.132–133) and his official authorization to work "in all the territories that happily joy under the government of the most pious and magnificent states of Italy" (2.2.137–140). All of these titles and accomplishments allow Scoto to occupy a liminal position between common mountebanks and recognized physicians. Moreover, his *unguento* is described by means of ostentatious rhetorical flourishes in specific Latin medical terms. Interestingly, after his own performance and praise of the *unguento's* virtues, Volpone further markets the product by having his Nano per-

23 Knight, "'He is indeed a kind of Scholler-Mountebank,'" 62.
24 Achilleos, "New Directions: Age and Ageing in *Volpone*," 153.
25 Knight, "'He is indeed a kind of Scholler-Mountebank,'" 66.

form his own ode to the elixir, thus undermining his own claims to its effectiveness.

In this scene, Volpone openly speaks of medicine while pretending to be a mountebank who is in possession of the necessary legal qualifications even if he is not. This recalls the way in which he defended the legal validity of his lies and performances in his room while continuing to ponder how to defraud the people who approach him in search of his fortune. Such actions demonstrate that his activity is, in fact, illegal and that his credibility is thus impaired. While in the guise of Scoto, he also claims that those who try to take advantage of him by imitating his unique *Oglio di Scoto* are destined to fail, to *become* "poor wretches" just like the three suitors who try to gain Volpone's trust and fortune in vain. This is because in neither case have they earned it honestly or through "study" as he claims he did. In both cases therefore they are fools, and "to be a fool born is a disease incurable" (2.1.151): such "ill" people are therefore open and vulnerable to (and deserving of) the treatment they get – even if they become the victims of a healthy but dishonest creator of wealth who feigns illness or of a "quack doctor" who presents himself as a qualified physician. In fact, their fault lies in their true intentions and on their greedily taking up Volpone's provocations to feign their loyalty. "Righteousness" therefore, according to Volpone, is on the side of those who craftily and artfully claim and perform their roles, even if they are untrue, rather than on that of those who are hesitant or careless, even if they are truthful or if their actions do not surpass the boundaries of illegality. This is even more obvious in the case of those who are truly innocent like Bonario and Celia, as will emerge in the trial scenes. Since the wily can control legal justice, true justice is not to be found in human agency, but rather in providence or in unpredictable changes in circumstance.

3 Corbaccio, Celia, and the Culture of Dissection

The status of the much vaunted will[26] changes according to the suitor who is speaking to Mosca: in Voltore's case "The wax is warm yet, and the ink scarce dry / Upon the parchment" (1.3.47–48) which is a legal guarantee indicating knowledge of the validity of a signed and sealed will. To Corbaccio on the other hand, whose main interest is to outlive Volpone, time is of the essence:

26 For more on this, see Richard Allen Cave, "Patrilineal Law and the Plays of Ben Jonson," in *Property Law in Renaissance Literature,* ed. Daniela Carpi (Frankfurt am Main, Berlin, Bern, Bruxelles, New York, Oxford, Wien: Peter Lang, 2005): 117–130.

therefore, in his case the will remains incomplete and the lawyer's presence is simply promisory rather than a threat to his claim, providing a stimulus for him to go home immediately to "frame a will" (1.4.95) of his own. The will is mentioned again later on, when Mosca tells Corbaccio that Bonario had heard of the change of detail of the will and been provoked into wanting to kill his father as a consequence (3.9.3–7).

Even more haste is shown in Corvino's case, where the miser is "Not dead, sir, but as good" (1.5.6), only possessing the energy necessary to grasp the pearl that the merchant had brought him. In Corvino's case, the fake diagnosis reflects the merchant's extremely violent nature; as a matter of fact, Mosca encourages him to verbally abuse Volpone in order to transform his body into the physical consequences of the symptoms he feigns through an obscene rhetoric. In this way Mosca proves capable of extending the same linguistic creative strategies of his master by turning them upon the latter[27]:

> Mosca: [...] Those filthy eyes of yours that flow with slime
> Like two frog-pits, and those same hanging cheeks,
> Covered with hide instead of skin (Nay, help, sir)
> That look like frozen dish-clouts set on end.
> Corvino (aloud): Or like an old smoked wall on which the rain
> Ran down in streaks
> Mosca: Excellent! Sir, speak out [...](1.5.56–62)

Each time the medical assessment reflects the person to whom the diagnosis is reported: in fact, while Corbaccio is well acquainted with medical symptoms and conditions as a patient, Corvino is rash, anxious, and therefore in need of a colourful and extreme description. Accordingly, for Corvino, Volpone's will designating him as his heir is even more hurried and elusive, since it is penned by Mosca and based on a tacit verbal agreement, emanating from his own alleged interpretation of Volpone's responses:

> [...] but I,
> Taking the vantage of his naming you,
> 'Signior Corvino, Signior Corvino,' took
> Paper, and pen, and ink, and there I asked him,
> Whom he would have his heir? 'Corvino.' Who
> Should be executor? 'Corvino.' And,
> To any question he was silent to,

27 Rhetoric will also be used to transform Volpone's body later on, although in the attempt to do the opposite, i. e. embellish and rejuvenate him, when Volpone tries to seduce Celia through his words.

> I still interpreted the nods he made,
> Through weakness, for consent: and sent home th' others,
> Nothing bequeathed them but to cry and curse. (1.5.21–37)

The imaginary threat to Corvino's claim however is sustained when Mosca mentions others who were "so many – / All gaping here for legacies" (1.5.27–28) that Corvino would have to contend with following Volpone's death. This also allows the servant to suggest a means of postponing Volpone's death, by proposing Corvino's wife as a "cure" for his master.

In truth Celia is the character who is most constrained in the play because of her body; she is young, female, and attractive, and, according to the law of matrimony, under her husband's complete control. Because she commits to a commercial transaction with Scoto di Mantua by purchasing his "oil" without his knowledge or consent, she is accused of infidelity, further confined in her own home and threatened by her husband to be turned into "an anatomy," allowing him to "Dissect thee mine own self, and read a lecture / Upon thee to the city, and in public" (2.3.71–72). There is an allusion here to the practice of anatomization and dissection which could often only be carried out through physicians' attainment of the bodies of executed criminals. In his reference to the *OED*, Jonathan Sawday observes that the word "dissection" has two meanings: that of a "methodological division of an animal body for the purposes of 'critical examination'" and the more drastic metaphorical one of "a more violent 'reduction' into parts: a brutal dismemberment of people, things, or ideas. This violent act of dissection tends to be associated with the related term of 'anatomization.'"[28] Furthermore, the literary counterpart of dissection is satire, which is largely present in *Volpone* for "A literary/satirical dissection, then, may be undertaken in order to render powerless the structures within which the dissector's knife is probing."[29] Whereas the play seeks to deconstruct, satirize, and expose many social and legal ills of Venetian society where medicine and the body are concerned, Corvino wishes to control his supposedly disobedient wife by turning her body – and therefore her entire essence – into a subservient object. Moreover, since the bodies that were used for dissection, anatomy lessons and studies usually belonged to marginal members of society such as "the criminal, the poor, the insane, suicides, orphans, even, simply 'strangers,'"[30] Corvino's threat is not only to harm her but to degrade her as an individual and a social/legal subject

28 Jonathan Sawday, *The Body Emblazoned: Dissection and the Human Body in Renaissance Culture* (London and New York: Routledge, 1996), 1.
29 Sawday, *The Body Emblazoned*, 1.
30 Sawday, *The Body Emblazoned*, 3.

by associating her with such marginalized categories; in this way Corvino pushes the demands of patriarchy to extreme conclusions, so that an innocent woman stands accused of behaving like a daughter of Eve.

Nevertheless, Celia is a complicit object of judgement and scrutiny by her husband, others and – later – the court as she attempts to "prove" her innocence:

> [...] if you doubt
> My chastity, why, lock me up for ever:
> Make me the heir of darkness. Let me live,
> Where I may please your fears, if not your trust. (3.7.25–28)

Celia's invoked framing and incarceration through legal means is physical and had in fact already been anticipated through her imprisonment in her own home by Corvino's threats, which mirror the period's strong patriarchal constraints on women.[31] Her plea also reinforces the omnipresent but here exasperated "culture of dissection" that Sawday, following Foucault, suggests also "promoted the beginnings of [...] the 'surveillance' of the body within regimes of judgement and punishment."[32]

The only time Celia displays any sort of power is when she does not act, i.e. when she refuses to satisfy her husband's request to sleep with Volpone. In the scene of her attempted seduction, when confronted with Volpone's speech on love, she is just as unmoved by Volpone's words as Bonario is with Mosca's. Their lack of self-interest and love for the truth allows them to see through the flattery and lies of others. Celia therefore becomes the judge that Volpone cannot sway by words or promises:

> [S]he represents that uncorrupt part of nature which refuses to be transmuted by the alchemy of Volpone's art. It is worth noting that in this episode the prevailing roles have

---

31 Frances Teague, for instance, points out that her very first "appearance" in the form of Mosca's description, portrays her as an available object of desire and that her acquiescing to Scoto's request for a handkerchief seems to confirm this, "New Directions: Ben Jonson and Imprisonment," 133–134. It is only when she speaks in her defense – as she will do throughout the entire play – that it becomes apparent that she is a perpetually manipulated and abused subject who, even after her absolution, will never be able to have an active legal or social role of her own, for she is simply sent back home and entrusted to her father's care and control again.
32 Sawday, *The Body Emblazoned*, 4. Furthermore, in quoting Peter Stallybrass, Sawday goes on to specify that: "in the Renaissance, women were the subject of 'constant surveillance,' since the female body seemed, in some way, 'naturally grotesque' – a body that escaped any boundary or limit," 9–10. This lack of control however later works against Celia when she faints in court, an excessively emotional reaction that the avocatori frown upon.

> been reversed, and, instead of controlling the dupes who beg favours from him, Volpone finds himself in the unwonted position of petitioner at the feet of the fair Celia.[33]

The failure of his plan leads him to resort to physical masculine violence towards her and the later rhetorical manipulation of those who are not immune to his power and arguments, including her husband. Therefore, her demonstration of female virtue is manipulated through masculine power and rhetoric in court, and is distorted into its very contrary. Corvino denounces her infidelity and aggressively alludes to the public humiliation that he will himself inflict upon her in accordance with the full force of the law. In this Corvino replicates the law of the time in his contemplation of the practices of dissection and gibbeting as punishment for serious offences:[34]

> Heart! I will drag thee hence home by the hair,
> Cry thee a strumpet through the streets; rip up
> Thy mouth unto thine ears; and slit thy nose,
> Like a raw rotchet! – Do not tempt me, come.
> Yield, I am loth – Death! I will buy some slave
> Whom I will kill, and bind thee to him, alive;
> And at my window hang you forth, devising
> Some monstrous crime, which I, in capital letters,
> Will eat into thy flesh with aquafortis,
> And burning cor'sives, on this stubborn breast.
> Now, by the blood thou hast incensed, I'll do 't! (3.7. 96–106)

According to Frances Teague, such punishments were the prerogative of the jurisdiction of the state, and Corvino acts here as if he were a formal representative of the law.

In the play, the virtuosity of the two defendants is renown and acknowledged by the avocatori at the beginning of the trial yet, in light of the performances, denials and manipulation of words, actions and evidence by Volpone and

33 Alexander W. Lyle, "Volpone's Two Worlds," *The Yearbook of English Studies* 4 (1974): 70–76, 72.

34 For more on this see Chapter 4 "Execution, Anatomy and Infamy," in Sawday, *The Body Emblazoned: Dissection and the Human Body in Renaissance Culture*, 54–84, where interestingly, it is stated that such provisions anticipated the 1752 'Murder Act', which reintroduced penal dissection as a response to a "perceived break-down in law and order on the part of the authorities," 54. Although dissection was already practiced, the added perceived mark of infamy of having one's body dismembered in public after death for medical and utilitarian reasons was intended as a further deterrent for criminals.

the suitors, not only their claims but also their reputations are obfuscated and unconvincing, leading to their injust incarceration.

4 Voltore's Use of the Body as Evidence in Court

The first trial in Act 4 is a performance in its own right, as are all trials in the play, for two main reasons. First, trials such as these were "quite literally intended as show trial[s]"[35] and as the culmination of the process of confirmation of evidence, information, and decisions that had already been decided before the weighing of empirical evidence. As in Jonson's real life trial connected to Guy Fawkes, the fact that "The real trial had already taken place [...] before the Privy Council,"[36] may be mirrored in the play in the avocatori's reference to and reliance on written statements and documents during the trial scene in the final act. The trial process therefore attributed great importance to the gathering and elaboration of various information and accounts, which were integrated with the later findings. Also, the concept of the courtroom was based on the trial as a ritual, where the truth would emerge by forensically asking the right questions and recounting – and therefore reacting to – the events at hand. This method of investigating, as Lorna Hutson explains, is based on the sixteenth century use of the word "invention" in its rhetorical sense, i.e. as the "processing of 'finding' [...] the most appropriate arguments, figures of speech, and topics to use in a particular kind of oration, or persuasive discourse."[37] In light of this, the "truth" was seen as the natural result and conclusion of the combination of the interrogation of witnesses with the advocate's ability to employ such information in order to state "facts" and tell a "story," or as Hutson terms it, "forensic narration"[38] that was considered credible when filtered by the judges' judicial discretion. Such a development in epistemological inquiry found its legal counterpart and validation in the ongoing increase in "the exercise of discretion, judgment, and a sense of how to weigh evidence."[39]

35 Fraser, quoted in Teague, "New Directions: Ben Jonson and Imprisonment," 128–129.
36 Fraser, quoted in Teague, "New Directions: Ben Jonson and Imprisonment," 129.
37 Hutson, *The Invention of Suspicion: Law and Mimesis in Shakespeare and Renaissance Drama*, 1.
38 Hutson, *The Invention of Suspicion: Law and Mimesis in Shakespeare and Renaissance Drama*, 146.
39 Hutson, *The Invention of Suspicion: Law and Mimesis in Shakespeare and Renaissance Drama*, 3.

Forensic narration, in turn, involves emphasis on the rhetorical shaping of the narrative in order to reach the desired verdict. This makes a process that was supposed to be fair into something manipulable, where the criterion of efficacy is the extent to which the narrative harmonises with the judicial authority's expectations and the inferences that could be plausibly attained through the narrative procedures of evidence gathering, inference and detection. This is decisively demonstrated in *Volpone* by the manner in which Volpone's party (and Voltore in particular as an insider of the court) conducts itself in court, especially during the first trial scene. As part of the Venetian legal structure in fact, Voltore is aware and confident of the importance of persuasion and rhetoric even in a fraudulent case such as theirs, for he claims that "I know this place most void of prejudice, / And therefore crave it, since we have no reason / To fear our truth should hurt our cause" (4.4.25–27). His case draws together the judicial and literary trends of the time, for its structure has much in common with that of the "comedy of intrigue," based on deception, disguises, conspiracies and stratagems.

Interestingly, Voltore is never referred to as an individual or in relation to his private life, but as the prototype of his profession, which is in turn described as a tongue, a form of speech that is capable of determining and creating the legality or illegality of an act by means of rhetorical and narrative skills. This becomes even more relevant when considering the fact, as Hutson notes, that at the time the word "judgment" was being used "in contexts suggestive of the refinement of an individual's eloquence and social skills through the interactions of what was being called, in certain handbooks on the art, 'conversation.'"[40] Voltore, as a lawyer, is therefore typified by his rhetorical abilities, which constitute the basis of his professional activity, as suggested when Mosca flatters him on Volpone's account:

> [Mosca] He [Volpone] ever liked your course, sir; that first took him.
> I oft have heard him say, how he admired
> Men of your large profession, that could speak
> To every cause, and things mere contraries,
> Till they were hoarse again, yet all be law;
> That, with most quick agility, could turn,
> And re-turn; make knots, and undo them;
> Give forkèd counsel; take provoking gold
> On either hand, and put it up. These men,
> He knew, would thrive with their humility.

40 Hutson, *The Invention of Suspicion: Law and Mimesis in Shakespeare and Renaissance Drama*, 304.

> And, for his part, he thought he should be blessed
> To have his heir of such a suffering spirit,
> So wise, so grave, of so perplexed a tongue,
> And loud withal, that would not wag, nor scarce
> Lie still, without a fee; when every word
> Your worship but lets fall, is a chequin! (1.3.51–66)

Voltore's initial success in court is accomplished precisely through calculated performance and convincing speeches in the courtroom which may be traced back to the "artificial proofs"[41] that emerged in classical rhetoric but were also well known to sixteenth century lawyers as a fundamental tool in forensic narration. He therefore uses his knowledge of the judicial system's workings to his own advantage, preparing the terrain for Volpone's dramatic entrance and presentation to the court. His way of dramatically selecting those he wishes to support his case is also a way of turning them into props and proof (which are presented as "inartificial proofs"). Voltore then openly appeals to the court's demand to reveal the truth, emphasising the importance of collective and collaborative detection:

> [...] Wherein, I pray your fatherhoods
> To observe the malice, yea, the rage of creatures
> Discovered in their evils; and what heart
> Such take, even from their crimes. But that anon
> Will more appear. (4.5.49–52)

Here the court's mechanisms work in reverse because the theatrical performance of most of those present are directed towards the concealment of the truth and the accreditation of an alternative fictitious story that has been prompted by the machinations of Mosca. As a result, the court is not primarily responsible for engineering a miscarriage of justice, but becomes an unwitting perpetrator of injustice and therefore another victim of Volpone and Mosca's plotting. Such an outcome, which may be found in other comedies of the time, had however been revived from the ruthless but successful forensic arguments found in classical comedy, where the judicial procedure was considered "purely strategic, without moral authority or divine sanction."[42] The avocatoris' well-meaning questions and decisions are reasonable and objective as they consider the "inartificial" proof and testimonies that are presented, but Bonario and Celia's cases are char-

41 For more on this, see Hutson, *The Invention of Suspicion: Law and Mimesis in Shakespeare and Renaissance Drama*, 158–159.

42 Hutson, *The Invention of Suspicion: Law and Mimesis in Shakespeare and Renaissance Drama*, 159.

acterized by an unconvincing "constancy" (4.4.1) and a lack of rhetoric. In the case of the conspirators, by contrast, each man bears his own "burden" (4.4.4) of the collective or "formal tale" (4.4.7) that Mosca fabricates for the occasion and that Voltore must represent in court. Moreover, the defendants' story "is unlikely in several ways. It is unprecedented. It is also improbable because it goes against reasonable expectations about human behaviour."[43]

In the face of such calculated interventions, Bonario's indignant retorts and Celia's swooning, which are perfectly plausible responses, have the paradoxical effect of making them appear even more guilty in the eyes of the court. In fact, they are associated with emotion and irrationality, which the court confuses with artifice and regards as the expected reactions of a guilty person whose malevolent acts have been exposed by the trial's forensic proceedings.[44] Moreover, the defendants appeal to other forms of justice – "mercy," "consciences" (4.4.15) and "heaven" (4.4.16) – which are however instantly discounted as "no testimonies" (4.4.17) and are therefore considered legally worthless. In fact, as Bonario points out, these appeals are not permissible "in your courts" (4.4.17). Hence, the defendants' spontaneous reactions and disillusion in the juridical process are but two further unanticipated "pieces" in the falsified forensic narration crafted by their accusers.

In order to close his case, Voltore uses Volpone's physical body and state of health as evidence by introducing him as "The aged gentleman, that had there lain bed-rid / Three years and more" (4.4.80–81) who is "so weak / So feeble" (4.4.14–15). In doing so, he draws his own legal strength from Volpone's apparent incapacity to speak for himself. But because Volpone is not ill, this claim is illegal, along with Voltore's perjury and conscious misuse of the court's trust in him as a professional. The deceitful narration also involves the fake (and therefore illegal) and sarcastic diagnosis that Voltore performs and reports in court:

> Here, here
> The testimony comes, that will convince,

---

43 Lisa Klotz, "Ben Jonson's Legal Imagination in *Volpone*," *SEL* 51.2 (Spring 2011): 385–408, 393. Klotz then explains how the conspirator's testimonies are faulty in truth: Corbaccio and Lady Would-Be, because of Mosca's manipulation, give untrue testimony without realizing it, while Corvino and Volpone purposely lie in court. The latter moreover, is "the most false but, paradoxically, it is also reasonable for the avocatori to believe it," 399. For more on oaths and alternative equivalent speech acts in *Volpone*, see Andrew N. Adler, "Can Formalism Convey Justice? – Oaths, 'Deeds,' & Other Legal Speech Acts in Four English Renaissance Plays," *St John's Law Review* 72.2 (Spring 1998): 237–290.

44 Hutson, *The Invention of Suspicion: Law and Mimesis in Shakespeare and Renaissance Drama*, 149.

> And put to utter dumbness their bold tongues.
> See here, grave fathers, here's the ravisher,
> The rider on men's wives, the great impostor,
> The grand voluptuary! Do you not think
> These limbs should affect venery? Or these eyes
> Covet a concubine? Pray you, mark these hands.
> Are they not fit to stroke a lady's breasts?–
> Perhaps he doth dissemble![45] (4.6.20–27)

The "torture" methods that Bonario proposes following these claims, i.e. "goads, or burning irons; / Put him to the strappado" (4.6.31) that have "cured the gout" (4.4.32) in the past and would "help [him] of a malady" (4.4.33) offer a contrast and represent yet another way in which the law may actively coerce the body as a means of restoring social order. In fact, these practices seek to contest Volpone and Voltore's performances through a further assessment of bodily conditions; moreover, these measures, as Teague points out, were well known to Ben Jonson from a legal perspective because Guy Fawkes, with whom Jonson was accused to have consorted, was discovered while guarding the gunpowder to be used for the attack and tortured *et sic per gradus ad ima tenditur* to extract information concerning his fellow conspirators until he finally confessed.[46] The body is therefore a site of investigation and – if deemed guilty – it could be considered the temple of guilt and therefore be branded (like Jonson was) by legal authorities as a means of reminding the felon of his deed and as a warning to others of the kind of punishment the felon could expect. In contrast, Bonario and Celia do not, and cannot, perform their defence by presenting forensically collected evidence, but, instead, base their case entirely on their assertions of innocence. Therefore, although Bonario also contests that "vicious persons, when they are hot and fleshed/ In impious acts, their constancy abounds: /Damned deeds

45 Although Volpone is not a rogue because of his social standing, his and Mosca's actions have a lot in common with those narrated in rogue literature. In this case, the idea of dissembling and self-invention could be associated with Robert Greene's claim that the reason for his activities is that "He that cannot dissemble cannot live," Craig Dionne and Steve Mentz, "Introduction" to *Rogues and Early Modern English Literature*, eds. Craig Dionne and Steve Mentz (Michigan: University of Michigan Press, 2006), 2. Moreover, "these narratives echo the peculiar Renaissance anxiety over the difference between inward and outward shows," 7. Later on, Dionne specifies that "This science of 'dissemblance,' [...] is a ghoulish parody of humanism's rhetorical emphasis on the grammar of self-advancement, the instrumentalization of the linguistic codes needed to fashion a niche in the affairs of state by construing the 'mind' of one's addressee," 54.

46 Fawkes too, like other accused criminals, was afraid of bodily disfigurement and therefore purposely jumped from the scaffold in order to break his neck and avoid public mutilation. For more on this, see Teague, "New Directions: Ben Jonson and Imprisonment."

are done with greatest confidence" (4.4.50–52), his and Celia's lack of evidence in their favour and their lack of any performing skill make his protests worthless, leading to their arrest and the possibility of conviction.

In contrast, during the second trial scene in Act 5, in order to reveal the truth Voltore must justify the glaring contradictions in his previous evidence and performance. Hence his rhetorical appeal to an alternative form of legal thinking, the same one called upon by Celia: the court's mercy, which must "Once win upon your justice, to forgive –" (5.10.5). This is a less certain and convincing performance because it is one that Voltore is much less familiar with. He is, in fact "distracted" (5.10.5) and knows not "which t'address myself to first" (5.10.7) but claims that this is because he has been "struck in conscience" (5.10.11), yet another concept mentioned by Celia in the course of the previous perverted trial. He then affirms this position of humility – whether it is sincere or not we do not know – by physically kneeling before his learned colleagues. Although this was intended as a means of escaping the law, Corvino immediately claims that "The man is mad!" (5.10. 8), thus locating the lawyer's performance outside any sort of legally valid reasoning. He then proceeds to attribute Voltore's confession to envy and to demonic possession by the devil, rendering his physical conduct legally inadmissible. Upon learning that Volpone is alive, he performs just such a devilish possession, turning his previous but truthful hesitation into "firm" (5.12.18) falsity.[47] This outrageous enactment is again legitimized through a diagnosis of his physical symptoms, as if he were being scrutinized on medical grounds:

> [Volpone] God bless the man!
> – Stop your wind hard, and swell – see, see, see, see!
> He vomits crooked pins! His eyes are set,
> Like a dead hare's hung in a poulter's shop!
> His mouth's running away! Do you see, signior?
> Now it is in his belly!
> [Corvino] Ay, the devil!
> [Volpone] Now, in his throat.
> [Corvino] Ay, I perceive it plain.
> [Volpone] 'Twill out, 'twill out! Stand clear. See, where it flies!
> In shape of a blue toad, with a bat's wings!
> Do you not see it, sir? (5.12.24–32)

---

47 This could recall the "fake epileptics," a category of criminal beggars of the time. For more on this, see Arthur F. Kinney's "Introduction" to *Rogues, Vagabonds & Sturdy Beggars: a New Gallery of Tudor and Early Stuart Rogue Literature*, ed. Arthur F. Kinney (Amherst: The University of Massachusetts Press, 1990): 11–57, 26–27.

The moral and legal significance of such a state renders the lawyer's earlier arguments inadmissible. This performance therefore automatically negates both the previous one and his written statement, uniting the body's supposedly altered physical condition with what is now a retrograde change in the validity of legal documentation and liability.[48]

5 The Law's Rulings over the Body

Volpone's fraudulence takes many forms, all of which prompt the contenders' illegal actions, for Voltore, Corbaccio, and Corvino are all deceived but also have no problem in either deceiving others, or in compromising positions they had hitherto held dear. This, along with their false testimonies and illegitimate performances in court, marshals them into the criminal law, and leads to their legal punishments. As a result, the conspirators' sentences are equally varied and tailored as a species of Dantesque *contrappasso*. Mosca is sentenced first and most heavily, losing everything he had worked for and undergoing whipping[49] and lifelong imprisonment, which reproduces the legal and physical constraints he claimed to impose on his former master. Voltore loses the right to practice his legal profession, and therefore both his professional and social status. Corbaccio loses his wealth to the son he initially disinherited and is forced to enter a monastery where his hopes of rejuvenation will be frustrated since he will have to concentrate on how to "die well" (5.12.132). Corvino is sentenced to the public humiliation with which he threatened his wife followed by divorce, which entails his total loss of control over her. Celia, however, does not gain as much as Bonario, since she simply returns to her father, albeit with an enlarged dowry and her pre-marital integrity restored.

---

48 Klotz also mentions examinations of suspected witches at this point, "Ben Jonson's Legal Imagination in *Volpone*," 401–402, another very similar circumstance in which the body, and more precisely any abnormal signs, markings, or manifestations, could be considered legal proof and grounds for sentencing.

49 Whipping, along with the stocks, clogs, shackles, and public executions, were introduced by Elizabeth's 1572 Act, and "was more than a public show of judicial might: it symbolically linked in the cultural imaginary the idea [...] to a carnal contagion," Dionne, "Fashioning Outlaws: The Early Modern Rogue and Urban Culture," in *Rogues and Early Modern English Culture*, eds. Craig Dionne and Steve Mentz: 33–61, 44. It was mostly intended for rogues and idlers but also, among other categories, for those who "fayninge themselves to have knowledge in Pisnomye [physiognomy] Palmestry or other abused sciences," which leads to the conclusion that, should Volpone's disguise as a mountebank have emerged in the course of the trial, he could have been obligated to serve the same sentence as Mosca.

Volpone's sentence is particularly cruel and is described as the "mortifying of a Fox" (5.12.125), since it recalled the bodily humiliation that the power of the court could implement:

> [1st avocatore] [...] thy substance all be straight confiscate
> To the hospital of the *Incurabili.*
> And since the most was gotten by imposture,
> By feigning lame, gout, palsy, and such diseases,
> Thou art to lie in prison, cramped with irons,
> Till thou be'st sick and lame indeed. (5.12.119–124)

He must relinquish his wealth to a hospital, from which he will receive no ultimate benefit, and he will then be imprisoned. The harsh irony of the punishment consists in the fact that it puts him in the position to truly become that which he initially feigned. As a result, according to Frances Teague, "[t]he concluding punishments that strike us as unduly harsh also make more sense in Foucault's terms [on torture and imprisonment] since they attempt to replicate the men's crimes on their bodies."[50]

These sentences do not follow the theatrical and generic conventions of the time with regard to "poetic justice,"[51] since "the final punishments imposed on Volpone and Mosca could be seen as breaking general decorum, because they are too harsh for a comedy."[52] The "swift ruthlessness of [the] moral judgement"[53] and the law administered by the Jacobean judicial system overrides the law of the theatre that prescribed the proportionality of the villain's final punishment. Paradoxically, Jonson does this to "vindicate theatre"[54]: as a playwright and poet he becomes a judge who passes judgement on his characters according to a theatrical and moral equity, in a manner that reflects the actions of judges in court. He believed, in fact, that "some laws are 'needful' and others disposable, and the poet assumes the liberty to keep or break laws as he sees fit [...] in the service of higher principles"[55] whose application "depended on his changing assessment of which laws were valid and which were not for any

---

50 Teague, "New Directions: Ben Jonson and Imprisonment," 139.

51 For more on this, see Wolfgang Zach, *Poetic Justice: Theorie und Geschichte einer literarischen Doktrin, Begriff – Idee – Komödienkonzeption* (Tübingen: Max Niemeyer Verlag Tübingen, 1986).

52 Thompson, "The Critical Backstory," 10.

53 Klotz, "Ben Jonson's Legal Imagination in *Volpone*," 393.

54 James P. Bednarz, "New Directions: Jonson's Literary Theatre: *Volpone* in Performance and Print (1606–1607) in *Volpone: a Critical Reader*, ed. Matthew Steggle: 83–104, 96.

55 Bednarz, "New Directions: Jonson's Literary Theatre," 96.

given play."[56] Volpone's only remaining consolation therefore is theatrical practice and the audience's appreciation: thus he "doubtful stands" (5.12.156) awaiting his second, and possibly more merciful, judgement by the audience. The unmasking of Volpone's lies and his new and declining condition are determined by the rule of law, thus reinforcing the strong tie between medicine, law, and performance which all take place around, and within, the body. This is also in line with Jonson's intent in writing the play, as specified in the epistle accompanying the 1607 folio, in which he states that "it being the office of a comic poet to imitate justice, and instruct to life" he had endeavoured, for "instruction and amendment, to reduce not only the ancient forms, but manners of the scene: the easiness, the propriety, the innocence, and last, the doctrine, which is the principle end of poesie, to inform men in the best reason of living."[57] He therefore aims at educating the audience while entertaining it and, as opposed to the "poetasters" of the time, thus making a strong intellectual and moral statement. In fact, despite human error and malice, in the end the innocent and virtuous will be redeemed as in the case of the wronged Celia and Bonario, while those who act immorally and commit injustice will be judged and punished.

One of the elements that particularly evades the traditional poetic laws of the genre however is the intensity, detail, and extreme nature of Volpone's punishment.[58] Although the inflicted pain is not direct or sharp like Mosca's because of his status as a 'gentleman,' the fact that he is to languish in a prison reflects and drastically precipitates the bodily decline and infirmity that is now the physical embodiment of his moral depravity and lack of respect or compassion for others. Ageing and disease are not contemplated among possible legal punishments but this decision does demonstrate that the law can regulate the body's physical conditions and environment and therefore influence its future, albeit indirectly. The allusion to Volpone's future infirmity implicates the body's becoming subject to legal scrutiny and change, as well as an object on whose surface is inscribed the sign of the crime, making it a site of its punish-

---

56 Bednarz, "New Directions: Jonson's Literary Theatre," 97.

57 Jonson, "Epistle" in *Volpone* and Other Plays, ed. Michael Jamieson: 41–45, 44.

58 Lisa Klotz also points out and outlines the Venetian legal system's and judges' ambiguity and reputation for severity with historical examples (see Klotz, "Ben Jonson and Legal Imagination in *Volpone*," 388–389). See also Richard H. Perkinson, "'Volpone' and the Reputation of Venetian Justice," *The Modern Language Review* 35.1 (1940): 11–18.
This could be coupled with Jonathan Kertzer's view that "Justice is conceived not as arithmetical balance or reciprocity, but as excess, not as a remedy for heretical conduct but as itself impatient, outrageous, even lawless," *Poetic Justice and Legal Fictions* (Cambridge: Cambridge University Press, 2010), 17.

ment. It also reflects the period's need to isolate and contain evasions of the law through immobility and confinement.[59] From this perspective, to keep the body still and, in this case, clad in irons, is to keep illegal activity at bay and to exert absolute and total control over the human subject.

In conclusion, the Jacobean stage could be seen as a place where a story is acted out in its entirety and, as may be found in Jonson's other comedies, the unravelling of a fictitious and illegal plot occurs inadvertently by means of unpredictable "accidents" that lead to a more just conclusion. However, the situation at hand is particularly complicated in *Volpone*. As Lisa Klotz asserts:

> it is not the judge but judicial decision making in general that Jonson exposes for comic effect and serious consideration. Jonson broadens the aim of his satire beyond the easy targets of corrupt judges or inane enforcement of laws, and instead achieves a more general exposition of the limits of forensic investigation, including the evaluation of witness credibility, the measuring of the plausibility of testimony, and the pressures of quick judicial decision making done with incomplete information and little time for reflection.[60]

Forensics, the law and the body are intertwined, and such intersections that occur are often complicated by fictitious and illegal deviations, and entanglements that the characters themselves cannot see. It is therefore up to the audience to challenge and dismantle the fictional narrative of those who are both deceivers and deceived by seeking a solution to the problem while watching or reading the events unfold, although they are guided by the play's satiric investments. In fact, only the audience has access to all the characters' asides and knows the true reason for all of their actions, thus becoming the true detainers of "discretion" and unclouded judgment, "a 'proper judge of what he sees' because 'all faults lie open to discovery.'"[61] This allows further metanarrative reflection on the righteousness – or lack thereof – of the solutions to the various "cases" presented throughout the play and generates further forensic investigations of the ways in which such situations can be resolved, morally, ethically and professionally.

---

59 For more on this, see Linda Woodbridge, *Vagrancy, Homelessness, and English Renaissance Literature* (Urbana: University of Illinois Press, 2001).

60 Klotz, "Ben Jonson's Legal Imagination in *Volpone*," 387.

61 Hutson, *The Invention of Suspicion: Law and Mimesis in Shakespeare and Renaissance Drama*, 317. The quotes within the quotes are John Dryden, "Of Dramatic Poesy" (1668) in *John Dryden: Selected Criticism*, ed. James Kinsley and George Parfitt (Oxford: Clarendon Press, 1970), 60.

II Codification of the Body Politic and Common Law Jurisprudence

Paul Raffield

Representing the Body of Law in Early Modern England

"A publike weale is a body lyvyng."[1] So claimed Sir Thomas Elyot on the opening page of *The Book Named the Governor*, published in 1531; the "Public weal" here meaning the common-weal or commonwealth: the *res publica*. Elyot's political theories were heavily influenced by Aristotelian ideals of civic republicanism. Indeed, the anatomical metaphor with which to describe the nature and formulation of the State, and the relationship therein between governor and governed, is traceable at least as far back as *The Politics* of Aristotle, in Book V of which he cautions against the exponential growth of any part of the State: "The body consists of parts, and all increase must be in proportion, so that the proper balance of the whole may remain intact, since otherwise the body becomes useless."[2]

My concern in this essay is to explore the development and manipulation of the anatomical image in the context of Early Modern English jurisprudence. I am especially interested in the apparent fusion of classical, natural law theory with the tenets of Judaeo-Christianity, thereby creating a hybrid image of a body politic, derived as much from classical texts as it is from the pages of the Bible. To borrow a phrase from Foucault (discussing the tragic fate of Actaeon, as related in Book III of Ovid's *Metamorphoses*): "in the complicity of the divine with sacrilege, some of the Greek light flashed through the depths of the Christian night."[3] In creating such an image, simultaneously Christian and pre-Christian, the English jurists of the Early Modern period were demonstrably adhering to the Ciceronian maxim (quoted by Sir Edward Coke on the title page to Part I of *The Reports*): "law is unerring reason, adhering to a divine purpose."[4] Reason and divinity were perceived by Coke and his judicial brethren to be coextensive and indivisible facets of the common law.

I am grateful to Hart Publishing for granting me permission to incorporate brief extracts from Paul Raffield, *Shakespeare's Imaginary Constitution: Late Elizabethan Politics and the Theatre of Law* (Oxford: Hart Publishing, 2010).

1 Sir Thomas Elyot, *The Boke Named the Governour* (London: T. Bertheleti, 1531), sig, Ar.
2 Aristotle, *The Politics*, trans. T.A. Sinclair (London: Penguin, 1992), 303, Bk V.III.1302b33.
3 Michel Foucault, *Aesthetics: Essential Works of Foucault, 1954–1984*, ed. J.D. Faubion, 3 vols. (London: Penguin, 2000), 2:125.
4 *"Lex est certa ratio e mente divina manans,"* Part 1 (1602) of *The Reports of Sir Edward Coke, Knt. In English*, ed. George Wilson, 7 vols. (London: Rivington, 1777), 1:title page.

Sir John Fortescue, the Lancastrian Chief Justice (and Lord Chancellor in exile) during the turbulent reign of King Henry VI, located the source of law's creation in the Judaeo-Christian deity, claiming in his *De Laudibus Legum Angliae* (written around 1470, but not published in English until 1567),[5] that "Laws which are made by Men, (who for this very End and Purpose receive their Power from GOD) may also be affirmed to be made by GOD."[6] The claim to divine provenance notwithstanding, Fortescue was adamant that English law is derived simultaneously from the law of nature. He quotes from Book V of Aristotle's *The Nicomachean Ethics* as authority for his claim that the law of nature is the ultimate fount of English law: "'The Law of Nature is the same, and has the same Force all the World over'."[7] Of equal relevance to Fortescue's claim that the foundations of common law are rooted in natural law is the assertion of Cicero that "True law is right reason in agreement with nature; it is of universal application, unchanging and everlasting [...]."[8] Cicero's encomium to the immutable within time, to the congruency of nature and human reason, and therefore to the primacy of natural law, was adopted by Early Modern common lawyers as a dictum which validated the claim to jurisdictional hegemony for a legal system predicated not upon statute, but upon *recta ratio* or right reason, as reflected in the customary laws of England.

Fortescue describes in considerable anatomical detail the form of the English body politic, noting the linguistic and symbolic connection between laws and ligaments:

> [t]he Law, under which the People is incorporated, may be compared to the Nerves or Sinews of the Body Natural; for, as by these the whole Frame is fitly joined together and compacted, so is the Law that Ligament (to go back to the truest Derivation of the Word, *Lex à Ligando*) by which the Body Politic, and all its several Members are bound together and united in one entire Body.[9]

Coke used identical imagery in his report of *Postnati. Calvin's Case*, published in Part 7 of *The Reports* in 1608, in order to describe the relationship between king and subject: "As the ligatures or strings do knit together the joints of all the parts

---

5 Robert Mulcaster's English translation of *De Laudibus Legum Angliae* was published in 1567 under the title *A Learned Commendation of the Politique Lawes of England.*

6 Sir John Fortescue, *De Laudibus Legum Angliae*, ed. John Selden (London, R Gosling, 1737), 5.

7 Fortescue, *De Laudibus*, 29; Aristotle, *The Nicomachean Ethics* Bk V.VII.1134b18–20.

8 "*Est quidem vera lex recta ratio naturae congruens, diffusa in omnes, constans, sempiterna...*": Marcus Tullius Cicero, *De Republica* in *De Re Publica, De Legibus*, trans. Clinton W. Keyes (Cambridge, Mass.: Harvard University Press, 1928), 211, Bk. III.XXII.33.

9 Fortescue, *De Laudibus*, 22.

of the body, so doth ligeance join together the Sovereign and all his subjects."[10] The Italian jurist, Giambattista Vico, also noted in *La Scienza Nuova* (published in 1725), that the words for law derive from those for tendons or cords. Commenting on Vico, George Hersey observed that the Italian word "corda" translates variously as a tendon, a harmonious musical sound, and the string of a lyre.[11] The Greek *nomos* means both "tune" and "law," and Plato employed the pun on *nomos* throughout *The Laws*, for example in his assertion that "After the 'prelude' [the preliminary analysis of the State] should come the 'tune', or (more accurately) a sketch of a legal and political framework."[12] There is much to say about the correlation between musical harmony and the constitution of the ideal State, of the relevance to the origins of law of the myth of Orpheus, and of Cicero's insistence that "What the musicians call harmony in song is concord in a State, the strongest and best bond of permanent union in any commonwealth."[13] But that is for another essay. For now, I wish merely to observe the correlation between musical harmony and the Platonic idea of justice (or *dikaiosunê*) as being inextricably linked to the notion of harmonious relations between the State and the individual, and between fellow citizens of the State. The relationship between musical harmony and the making of good laws is a recurring theme in *The Laws*. Writing about the legal regulation of music in the Athenian democracy, Plato describes a "kind of song too, which they thought of as a separate class, and the name they gave it was this very word that is so often on our lips: 'nomes' ('for the lyre', as they always added)."[14]

The association of the lyre with the harmonious governance of society remained a central image in the iconography of common law during the Early Modern period. The musical metaphor of the stringed instrument was employed by the Elizabethan divine, Richard Hooker, with reference to the nature of kingship. In *Of the Laws of Ecclesiastical Polity*, Hooker aligned Christian theology with an Aristotelian model of community.[15] The co-existence of Church and State is a central tenet of Hooker's communitarian ethos. In the ideal commonwealth

10 Coke, *Postnati. Calvin's Case*, 7 *Reports* (1608), 4:1a, at 4b.
11 George Hersey, *The Lost Meaning of Classical Architecture: Speculations on Ornament from Vitruvius to Venturi* (Cambridge, MA: MIT Press, 1988), 5.
12 Plato, *The Laws*, trans. Trevor J. Saunders (London: Penguin, 2004), 156, Bk V.IX.734e; see also, Plato, *The Laws*, 513, n 1.
13 Cicero, *De Re Publica*, 183, Bk II.XLII.69.
14 Plato, *The Laws*, 107–108, Bk III.V.700b.
15 On the influence of Aristotle over the political theory of Hooker, see Tod Moore, "Recycling Aristotle: The Sovereignty Theory of Richard Hooker," *History of Political Thought* 14.3 (1993): 345–359.

that Hooker describes, the monarch is the unifying figure that links the Church in an indivisible bond with the people. Crucially, the subject of power in Hooker's commonwealth is not the monarch in person but the "body of the commonwealth."[16] In such a polity, "where the King doth guide the state and the law the King, that commonwealth is like an harp or melodious instrument."[17] Hooker's allusion to the musical harmony of Orpheus's lyre demonstrates the potency of classical mythology and the resonance of its images in the imaginations of Early Modern writers. As Hersey has noted, the myth of Orpheus and the lyre "records the moment when law was first introduced into the society that invented that myth."[18]

It is axiomatic of any discussion concerning the Early Modern body politic that reference is made to Ernst H. Kantorowicz's magnum opus: *The King's Two Bodies*. Respectful though I am of the depth of scholarship exhibited by Kantorowicz, of the magisterial scope of the book, and of its lasting influence over the work of subsequent generations of scholars, I must take issue with some of the claims made by Kantorowicz in the interests of discerning the true balance between temporal and spiritual powers, and in configuring the constitutional relationship between governor and governed. Kantorowicz quotes from Fortescue's *De Dominio Regali et Politico*[19] in support of his thesis that the Lancastrian Chief Justice was proposing that the king shared with "the holy sprites and angels" certain mystical powers. Kantorowicz claims that "Elizabethan jurists 'borrowed' from Fortescue," in elucidating the theory that the king was possessed of two bodies: the body natural and the body politic.[20] In particular he makes an explicit link between Fortescue's assertion that the angels do not "grow old" and Plowden's report of the *Case of the Dutchy of Lancaster*, in which the great law-reporter wrote that the body politic of the king "is ut-

---

16 Richard Hooker, *Of the Laws of Ecclesiastical Polity*, ed. Arthur S. McGrade (Cambridge: Cambridge University Press, 1989), 179, Bk VIII.6.1.

17 Hooker, *Of the Laws*, 146, Bk VIII.3.3; on Hooker's subjection of the monarch to the interests of society, see Peter Lake, *Anglicans and Puritans? Presbyterianism and English Conformist Thought from Whitgift to Hooker* (London: Unwin Hymen, 1988), 109, 201.

18 Hersey, *Lost Meaning of Classical Architecture*, 5. George Puttenham wrote that "Orpheus assembled the wilde beasts to come in heards to harken to his musicke, and by that meanes made them tame, implying thereby, how by his discreete and wholsome lessons uttered in harmonie and with melodious instruments, he brought the rude and savage people to a more civill and orderly life." George Puttenham, *The Arte of English Poesie* (London: Richard Field, 1589), 4.

19 *De Dominio Regali et Politico* was published in 1715 as *Difference Between an Absolute and Limited Monarchy*, and in 1885 under the title *The Governance of England*.

20 Ernst H. Kantorowicz, *The King's Two Bodies: A Study in Medieval Political Theology* (New Jersey: Princeton University Press, 1957), 8.

terly void of infancy, and old age."[21] Arguably, it is conjectural in the extreme to correlate an Elizabethan law report with a work written approximately ninety years earlier, purely on the basis that both texts refer to the process of ageing. Insofar as the power of the king resembles *character angelicus*,[22] the mystical quality of kingship is reflected in its suggestive capacity for good: the king acts at all times in the interests of *res publica*. This observation should be central to any discussion of Fortescue's delineation of positive powers and what he terms impotent "non-powers":[23] kings and angels exercised only the former. Nowhere in *De Dominio* does Fortescue claim for the king the metaphysical status of *character angelicus*. At most he asserts that, like the angelic choir, the institution of monarchy is a power for good; as such, it is incapable of sin, ageing or sickness. Using a Biblical analogy, with appropriate references both to Old Testament sources and St. Thomas Aquinas's *On Princely Government*, Fortescue attributes to the judiciary a level of dominion within the constitution that was antithetical to the absolutist pretensions of Richard II and his Tudor (and early Stuart) successors:

> [t]he children of Israel, as Saint Thomas says, after God had chosen them as 'his own people and holy realm', were ruled by Him under Judges 'royally and politically', until the time that they desired to have a king such as all the gentiles, which we call pagans, then had, but they had no king but rather a man who reigned upon them 'only royally'. With which desire God was greatly offended, as well for their folly, as for their unkindness since they had a king, which was God, who reigned upon them politically and royally.[24]

Fortescue concludes his republican meditation in *De Dominio* with the thought that, according to Aquinas, the prince who rules in accordance with political and royal dominion is less likely to "fall into tyranny" than one who rules by royal dominion alone.[25]

---

21 Sir John Fortescue, "The Governance of England" in *On the Laws and Governance of England*, ed. Shelley Lockwood (Cambridge: Cambridge University Press, 1997): 81–123, 95; *Case of the Dutchy of Lancaster* in *The Commentaries or Reports of Edmund Plowden*, 2 vols. (Dublin: H. Watts, 1792), 1:212, 213.

22 Kantorowicz cites only one Biblical source for the claim to monarchic *character angelicus:* the reference is less than authoritative, being the opinion expressed by the woman of Tekoah to King David, i.e. "for as an angel of God, so is my lord the king to discern good and bad" and "my lord is wise, according to the wisdom of an angel of God," 2 *Samuel* 14.17, 20 (Authorised King James Version of The Bible).

23 Fortescue, "The Governance of England," 95.

24 Fortescue, "The Governance of England," 84.

25 Fortescue, "The Governance of England," 84.

While Fortescue's political thought was undoubtedly informed by prevailing ideas in late medieval theology, Kantorowicz ignores the fundamental tenet of *De Dominio*, which is the secular observation that the ideal of kingship is predicated upon "*dominium politicum et regale*," rather than on *dominium regale* alone.[26] The parity between "regal" and "political" establishes Fortescue's work as a Bractonian interpretation of limited monarchy: "The king must not be under man but under God and under the law, because law makes the king."[27] Noting the similarity to Bracton, Alan Cromartie notes that "What readers found in Fortescue, however, was unimpeachable authority – the word of a Chief Justice – for a range of near-republican opinions."[28] I would go farther than Cromartie, and argue that Fortescue's opinions were not "near-republican," but totally republican – if by "republican" we mean not anti-monarchist (which Fortescue patently was not), but rather that which represents the best interests of the common-weal or *res publica*. The word "political" is used by Fortescue to imply not only the consent of Parliament, but also the guidance and wise counsel of the judiciary, who perform a rabbinical or didactic role. Fortescue described the judges of the common law as "*Sacerdotes*, (Priests): The Import of the Latin Word (*Sacerdos*) being one who gives or teaches Holy Things."[29] *De Laudibus*, an impassioned *apologia* for the English legal profession and the common law, ensured Fortescue's lasting talismanic status among common lawyers. But it was his elevation of the judiciary to something approaching supreme constitutional authority, which probably endeared him most to lawyers of the Elizabethan period. Insofar as the common law was, according to Fortescue and all Early Modern jurists, of divine origin, then it is fair to state that the judiciary gave or taught "Holy Things." But in their application of municipal law, they were more concerned with what Sir Edward Coke described as "the artificial reason and judgment of law,"[30] than with metaphysical speculation over the mystical quality of monarchic authority. This is demonstrated most clearly in those cases from the 1560s, reported by Plowden, in which the matter of the king's two bodies was discussed in court, and to which Kantorowicz refers in his book.

---

26 Fortescue, "The Governance of England," 83.

27 "*Ipse autem rex non debet esse sub homine sed sub deo et sub lege, quia lex facit regem.*" Henry de Bracton, *De Legibus et Consuetudinibus Angliae* (c. 1235), trans. Samuel E. Thorne, 4 vols. (Cambridge, Mass.: Belknap Press, 1968–77), 2:33.

28 Alan Cromartie, *The Constitutionalist Revolution: An Essay on the History of England, 1450–1642* (Cambridge: Cambridge University Press, 2006), 21.

29 Fortescue, *De Laudibus*, 4–5.

30 Coke, *Prohibitions del Roy*, 12 *Reports* (1655), 7:64a, 65a.

The selective use of quotations from Fortescue and (especially) Plowden serves well the argument of Kantorowicz that the mystical nature of the king's body politic came to dominate judicial thought in Elizabethan England, but this is not an accurate picture of the juridical landscape in relation to the resolution of disputes concerning real property (the cases on which Kantorowicz concentrates in *The King's Two Bodies*). It is more accurate to suggest that spiritual imagery provided the means through which temporal ends were attained. In the *Case of the Dutchy of Lancaster*, heard in 1561, the salient issue of law was whether the Crown was bound by the terms of a lease made by King Edward VI during his minority. The decision of the court that Elizabeth I could not avoid the terms of the lease made by her half-brother, "by reason of his nonage," was based upon the metaphysical phenomenon of the king's two bodies: "what the king does in his body politic cannot be invalidated or frustrated by any disability in his natural body."[31] But commentators tend to overlook the fact that the judges in this case employed the religious imagery of the conjoined bodies as a means of representing the secular principle that, like her subjects, the Queen was accountable to law, as interpreted by her judges. In *Willion v Berkley* (another case involving the grant of land by Edward VI), heard only a few months before the *Case of the Dutchy of Lancaster*, the argument that the body natural of the king was subsumed by the body politic was rejected by a majority of the judges; Justice Anthony Brown stated that "the person of the king shall not rule the estate in the land, but the estate in the land shall rule the person of the king."[32] These cases illustrate the manner in which the poetic imagination of the judiciary was directed towards representing the constitutional theory of limited monarchy.[33]

In *Willion v Berkley*, the Bractonian principle of a king subject to the law was firmly restated. Chief Justice Dyer argued there that the king's subjects were

---

31 Plowden, *Case of the Dutchy of Lancaster, Commentaries*, 1:213.

32 Plowden, *Willion v Berkley, Commentaries*, 1:223, 245. Kantorowicz fails to note that in the earlier case of *Hill v Grange* (1556), "the argument of the king's eternity, which he chooses to cite as an impressive ending to his chapter on Plowden, was actually rejected by the lawyers," Lorna Hutson, "Not the King's Two Bodies: Reading the 'Body Politic' in Shakespeare's *Henry IV, Parts 1 and 2*," in *Rhetoric and Law in Early Modern Europe*, eds. Victoria Kahn and Lorna Hutson (New Haven: Yale University Press, 2001), 166–198, 177; Plowden, *Hill v Grange, Commentaries*, 1:164.

33 Given the exaggerated juridical importance with which Kantorowicz invests the theory of the king's two bodies, it is noteworthy that in a later work he describes pre-modern judges in terms of their sovereignty and poetic judgments: see Ernst H. Kantorowicz, "The Sovereignty of the Legal Artist: a Note on Legal Maxims and Renaissance Theories in Art," in Ernst H. Kantorowicz, *Selected Studies* (New York: J.J. Augustin, 1965), 118.

"members" of the body politic: together with the king, "he and his subjects compose the corporation [...] and he is incorporated with them, and they with him."[34] Of course, Dyer's definition of the body politic can be read as a secular interpretation of the *corpus mysticum*, but it must be conceded that he placed great emphasis on the status afforded the subject in determining the form of the "corporation" of the State. As Plowden reports unequivocally, "the whole court was of opinion [that] every subject has an interest in the king."[35] Dyer's definition of an inclusive body politic implies a level of popular consent. In this respect, the body politic as defined in *Willion v Berkley* is more directly related to the consensual body politic described (more than 40 years later) by Coke in *Calvin's Case* than to the more absolute model described by Plowden in the *Case of the Dutchy of Lancaster*. In the latter, the body politic is "constituted *for* the direction of the people"; while in the former "it is framed *by* the policy of man."[36]

At the heart of Dyer's judgment is the tacit assumption that conscience is an integral facet in the ideology and application of the common law. The influence of Christopher St. German's *Doctor and Student* in particular, and the equitable tenets of renaissance humanism in general, are evident features of his judgment. He is describing an equitable system of justice, not necessarily in terms recognisable to the Court of Chancery (this was, after all, the Court of Common Pleas), but in the Aristotelian sense of judges as poets and sovereign artists applying the imaginary precepts of natural law to the tangible pragmatics of common law. The first of these precepts is that of doing good and avoiding evil. *Willion v Berkley* is especially notable for the moral distinction, made by Justice Anthony Brown, between right and wrong: his judgment embodied Aquinas's first precept of law, outlined above, that "good is to be done and pursued, and evil is to be avoided."[37]

The theory of mystical kingship, of a monarch endowed with divine and irrefutable power, was one that the Plantagenet King Richard II had expounded. The religious devotion of Richard II and his emphasis on the divinity of kingship – "The deputy elected by the Lord" in Shakespeare's *Richard II*[38] – must be seen to a great extent as a response to the various rebellions and incursions upon the

34 Plowden, *Willion v Berkley, Commentaries*, 1:234.
35 Plowden, *Willion v Berkley, Commentaries*, 1:231.
36 Plowden, *Case of the Dutchy of Lancaster, Commentaries*, 1:213; Coke, *Postnati. Calvin's Case*, 7 *Reports* (1608) 4:10a (emphasis added).
37 St. Thomas Aquinas, *Summa Theologica (Pars Prima Secundae)* (Teddington: The Echo Library, 2007) 421, Q94, "Of the Natural Law."
38 William Shakespeare, *King Richard II*, ed. Charles R. Forker (London: Arden Shakespeare, 2002), 3.2.53.

royal prerogative, which threatened his reign and eventually led to his deposition. But to argue as Kantorowicz does that the Elizabethan judges of the common law were united in their professional commitment to the theory of the king's two bodies, and that such unity was represented in their various judicial decisions, is inaccurate. In all of the cases in which the theory of the king's two bodies is discussed, a majority of judges demonstrate adherence to an equitable doctrine, predicated upon the classical principle of *epieikeia*. Aristotle's idea of equity was not bound by formalism: *epieikeia*, with its implications of fairness and equability, envisages the ideal good of society, in much the same way as Platonic *dikaiosunê* envisages right relations between men.[39] Above all, most of the judges in the cases considered here demonstrated adherence to St German's injunction:

> that thou do justice to every man as much as in thee is: and also that in every general rule of the law thou do observe and keep equity. And if thou do thus, I trust the light of the lantern, that is, thy conscience, shall never be extincted.[40]

Of course, certain judges stood in awe of the king's divine majesty, according the monarch a level of supra-legal power, which was antithetical to the limited powers invested in the king by Bracton and Fortescue. If, by way of conclusion, we jump forward from the 1560s to the 1630s, and to the trial of John Hampden in November 1637 for his refusal to pay ship-money, we hear Sir Robert Berkeley declaring in judgment that "I never read nor heard that *Lex* was *Rex*, but it is common and most true that *Rex* is *Lex*, for he is *Lex loquens*, a living, a speaking, an acting law."[41] It was the characterisation of Charles I as the actual embodiment or personification of law, to which common lawyers and Parliamentarians were opposed: in the judgment to which I refer above, Berkeley had appeared to mistake the body natural of Charles Stuart for the body politic of Charles I. In January 1649, eleven years after Hampden's trial, the King found himself the defendant at his own trial in Westminster Hall. The indictment stated that he had been "trusted with a limited power to govern by and according to the laws of the land"; a trust which he had betrayed in favour of "a wicked design to erect and uphold in himself an unlimited and tyrannical power to rule according to his will, and to overthrow the rights and liberties of the people [...]" The King

---

39 Aristotle, *The Nicomachean Ethics*, Bks V.X.1137a30–1138a3, VI.XI.1143a19–1143b17.

40 Christopher St. German, *Dialogues Between a Doctor of Divinity and a Student in the Laws of England*, ed. William Muchall (Cincinnati, Ohio: Robert Clarke, 1874), 44.

41 Quoted in Samuel R. Gardiner, *History of England*, 10 vols. (New York: AMS, 1965), 8:278.

asked the court "by what authority he was brought thither?"[42] Such a question returns us inevitably and finally to the matter of the king's two bodies: the answer to the question posed by Charles I being that the king's body natural was tried in the name of the king's body politic. As Parliament declared in May 1642, even though judgment were given in the King's courts "against the King's Will and Personal command, *yet are they the King's Judgments*."[43] To use the words of Kantorowicz himself: in January 1649 Parliament tried, convicted, and sentenced to death "the king's body natural without affecting seriously or doing irreparable harm to the King's body politic."[44] Whether it was St. Paul, in 1 *Corinthians*, describing the Christian commonwealth on earth as "many members, yet but one body,"[45] or Thomas Hobbes in 1651, invoking the image of the Biblical Leviathan with which to represent "The Matter, Forme, and Power of A Common-Wealth Ecclesiasticall and Civil"[46] – "His heart is as firm as a stone; yea, as hard as a piece of the nether *millstone*"[47] – the image of the body was crucial to the development of the idea of the State; whether that State be exclusively temporal or spiritual, or composed of both temporal *and* spiritual parts.

---

42 *The Trial of Charles the First, King of England, before the High Court of Justice*, ed. John Nalson (Oxford: R. Walker and W. Jackson, 1746), 24, 25, 28.

43 Quoted in Kantorowicz, *King's Two Bodies*, 21.

44 Kantorowicz, *King's Two Bodies*, 23.

45 *The First Epistle of Paul the Apostle to the Corinthians* 12.20. Coke adapted a passage from 1 *Corinthians* 2.9, with which to describe the momentous juridical status of *Postnati. Calvin's Case:* "... such a one as the eye of the law (our books and book-cases) never saw, as the ears of the law (our reporters) never heard of, nor the mouth of the law (for *judex est lex loquens*) the Judges our forefathers of the law never tasted," Coke, *Postnati. Calvin's Case*, 7 *Reports* (1608) 4: 4a. The relevant passage from 1 *Corinthians* reads: "Eye hath not seen, nor ear heard, neither have entered into the heart of man, the things which God hath prepared for them that love him"; see Raffield, *Shakespeare's Imaginary Constitution*, 147–149.

46 Thomas Hobbes, *Leviathan, or, The Matter, Forme, and Power of A Common-Wealth, Ecclesiasticall and Civil* (London: Andrew Crooke, 1651), title page.

47 *The Book of Job*, 41.24; this verse is cited on the title page of the first edition of *Leviathan*.

Ian Ward

The Image of Power: Shakespeare's Lord Chief Justice

It is perhaps unsurprising that the figure of the Lord Chief Justice in Shakespeare's *Henry IV part 2* has, at least until very recently, received relatively scant critical attention.[1] Like almost every other character in the play, he is destined to play a supporting role to the voracious character of Sir John Falstaff. Indeed, as we shall see, it might be argued that the Chief Justice's principal dramatic role is to serve as Falstaff's foil. He is not written to entertain. He is written to instruct. And he is certainly not given to whimsy, or to poetry. The Lord Chief Justice, as we shall also see, is a man given to recommending "cold consideration."[2] He is not intended to vie with Falstaff for attention. His is the voice of reason.[3] But this does not diminish its significance. It simply makes it more elusive.

The audience encounters the Lord Chief Justice on four occasions during *Henry IV part 2*. The first occasion is as early as Act 1 Scene 2, where he encounters Falstaff in the street and challenges him to explain why he failed to attend a summons "when there were matters against you for your life" (1.2.131). The summons alludes to an incident in *Henry IV part 1* where Falstaff took part in a robbery at Gads Hill. Falstaff first tries to feign deafness. When this fails he then deploys rhetorical trickery in the hope of distracting the Lord Chief Justice. It proves to be fruitless. Indeed, the problem is precisely Falstaff's facility for deception. His greatest crime is to have "misled the youthful Prince" (1.2.143). He will not however mislead the Lord Chief Justice. For now Falstaff escapes justice, able to plead "land-service": a doctrine recognised in common law whereby someone on military service could defer a court summons. But this contest, between the reason of the Lord Chief Justice of England and the whimsy of the Prin-

---

1 The two most significant recent commentaries being Paul Raffield, *Shakespeare's Imaginary Constitution: Late Elizabethan Politics and the Theatre of Law* (Oxford: Hart, 2010), 173–178, and Kenji Yoshino, "The Choice of Four Fathers: Henry IV, Falstaff, the Lord Chief Justice and the King of France in the *Henriad*," *Yale Law Journal* 22 (2010): 417–439, affirming at 417 and 427 the relative critical neglect.

2 William Shakespeare, *Henry IV part 2*, ed. A. Humphreys (London: Routledge, 1967), 5.2.98. All subsequent references are taken from this edition, which is abbreviated as H. IV 2.

3 According to Daniel Kornstein, the Lord Chief Justice is Shakespeare's "most unqualifiedly, unmistakably complimentary portrait of a sober, solid, fair-minded lawyer." See his *Kill All the Lawyers? Shakespeare's Legal Appeal* (Princeton UP, 1994), 135.

ce's "ill angel" will be rejoined (1.2.163). And there can only be one winner, for England, as Shakespeare so frequently reminds his audience, like its dying king is "foul" and diseased (3.1.39). The "times are wild," and it is in such times that the need of reason is greatest (1.1.9).

The Lord Chief Justice appears on stage again in Act 2 Scene 1, and again it is as a foil to Falstaff. This time he alights upon the Hostess of the Boar's Head Tavern in Eastcheap trying, with the uncertain help of two officers, to attach Falstaff for debt. Here again Falstaff manages to talk himself out of trouble, at least for now. But it is notable, in passing, that Shakespeare should have his Lord Chief Justice, the majesty of his high office notwithstanding, descend to the streets of Eastcheap in order to ensure that justice is done to all the king's subjects no matter how low their station, and how common their trade. Warning Falstaff that he is only "too well acquainted with" his "manner of wrenching the true cause the false way," the Chief Justice advises him to settle his debt and to make amends for the slander of immorality which he has made against his debtor. Falstaff takes the hint, and the Hostess is sweet-talked into inviting him to "supper" in the hope that he might at least then settle some of the debt (2.1.157).

The final two occasions when the Lord Chief Justice appears, both in Act 5, are rather different in tenor, and assume an altogether greater constitutional import. The first of these, in the second Scene of Act 5, opens with the Lord Chief Justice troubled by news of the King's death, and with good reason. Following the Gad's Hill escapade, related in *Henry IV part 1*, the Lord Chief Justice had imprisoned the Prince for violent assault. The Lord Chief Justice puts his faith in "truth and innocency," in the prosaic fact that he was simply doing his duty (5.2.39). But he fears the worse. At first these fears seem to be justified. On encountering the newly crowned Henry, the Chief Justice is reminded of the "indignities" which he "laid upon" the Prince's person (5.2.69). The following seventy-two lines then assume the shape of a poetic paean to the common law doctrine of constitutional sovereignty in early fifteenth century England, and, indeed, in late sixteenth century England.

It is the Lord Chief Justice who speaks first, defending his prior conduct in terms which would have resonated with those in the audience who read their Plowden and who appreciated the critical distinction between the king's "two bodies." According to Plowden:

> [t]he King has in him two Bodies viz., a Body Natural, and a Body Politic. His Body natural… is a Body mortal, subject to all Infirmities that come by Nature or Accident […] But his body politic is a Body that cannot be seen or handled, consisting of Policy and Government, and constituted for the Direction of the People, and the Management of the public

> weal, and this Body is utterly void of Infancy, and old Age, and other natural Defects and Imbecilities, which the Body natural is subject to[...][4]

In truth it is unlikely that many of Shakespeare's audience would have been overly familiar with Plowden, though any members of the Inns of Court might have been.[5] But there was anyway no need. The broader thesis, that the king had a public and a private body was familiar. It was a central precept of medieval constitutional jurisprudence, and the Lord Chief Justice's defence was to be read in these terms:

> I then did use the person of your father;
> The image of his power lay then in me;
> And in th'administration of his law (5.2.73–75)

Accordingly when the young Prince had "struck me in my very seat of judgment," he had struck not merely a fellow subject, but the representative of the King's public person.[6] If Hal now seeks vengeance, the Lord Chief Justice continues, he will be undermining the very law upon which his own authority ultimately lies. Be careful, he advises:

> Whiles I was busy for the commonwealth,
> Your highness pleased to forget my place,
> The majesty and power of law and justice,
> The image of the King whom I presented,
> And struck me in my very seat of judgment;
> Whereon as an offender to your father,
> I gave bold way to my authority
> And did commit you. If the deed were ill,
> Be you contented, wearing now the garland,
> To have a son set your decrees at naught?
> To pluck down justice from your awful bench?

---

4 Edmund Plowden, *Commentaries on Reports*, (1816), 212a.

5 Kornstein notes the relative prevalence of allusions to particular Inns in *Henry IV part 2*, with explicit mention of both Gray's Inn and Clement's Inn in Justice Shallow's gentle reminiscences. There is only one further such reference in any other Shakespearean play, to the Middle Temple in *Henry VI part 2*. This might suggest a particular affinity between Shakespeare and the Inns at this early stage in his career. It was of course Gray's Inn which had a few years earlier invited him to put on a performance of his *Comedy of Errors*. There again it might be simple coincidence. See Kornstein, *Lawyers*, 139–140.

6 The authoritative commentary on the medieval theory of the sovereign's "two bodies" is of course Ernst H. Kantorowicz, *The King's Two Bodies: A Study in Medieval Political Theology* (New Jersey: Princeton UP, 1957).

To trip the course of law, and blunt the sword
That guards the peace and safety of your person?
Nay more, to spurn at your most royal image,
And mock your workings in a second body? (5.2.76–90)

The young King, newly sensitized to his rhetorical and ritual responsibilities, and to the symbolic import of their respective offices, responds in kind:

You are right, Justice, and you weigh this well.
Therefore still bear the balance and the sword;
And I do wish that your honours may increase [...]
[...] You did commit me:
For which I do commit into your hand
Th'unstained sword that you have us to bear,
With this remembrance – that you use the same
With the like bold, just, and impartial spirit
As you have done against me. (5.2.102–105, 112–117)

He will "henceforth" proceed "in formal majesty," summon "our high court of parliament" and "choose such limbs of noble counsel / That the great body of our state may go / In equal rank with the best-govern'd nation" (5.2.133–135). There is a sense of rhetorical ceremony here. It is possible to imagine the reciprocal acts of fealty and investiture, of performance within performance. "There is my hand," Henry obliges, and it is reasonable to assume that it is taken (5.2.117).

In the wake of this magisterial jurisprudential exchange it would be easy to assume that the Lord Chief Justice's final appearance, in Act 5 Scene 5, is rather more incidental; perhaps no more than a mere formality. It is certainly succinct. The Scene is, of course, renowned for its treatment of Falstaff, cast aside by his beloved Hal in the coldest of terms: "I know thee not old man. Fall to thy prayers" (5.5.47). The poignancy is undoubted. But so too is the dramatic significance. It is in the Lord Chief Justice that Hal invests a responsibility to bring Falstaff to justice, in more immediate terms to have him taken to the Fleet. It is often suggested that here the new king also replaces one surrogate father with another, more estimable, alternative.[7] Having re-invested the Lord Chief Justice, Hal observes:

You shall be as a father to my youth,
My voice shall sound as you do prompt mine ear,
And I will stoop and humble my intents
To your well-practis'd wise directions. (5.2.118–121)

7 Yoshino, "Choice," 427–431.

At the same time it can be just as readily argued that he also confirms his affinity with one form of constitutional jurisprudence over another, that of *dominium politicum et regale* as opposed to *dominium regale*; a distinction to which we will shortly turn.[8] The intent of Act 5 Scene 2 is translated into action, with the King instructing his Lord Chief Justice to administer justice according to the law: "Be / it your charge, my Lord, / To see perform'd the tenor of my word" (5.5.69–71). It must be remembered that, although entrusted to preserve the integrity of the common law, the medieval Lord Chief Justice was still the representative of the king, the guardian of his laws.[9] It is after all the King's Bench. The new King then passes on, as in their different ways do Falstaff and the Lord Chief Justice. After his death, reported in the later play *Henry V*, Falstaff was to be resurrected in *The Merry Wives of Windsor*, at the apparent insistence of Elizabeth I. The Lord Chief Justice was not. He and England are left behind, as attention turns towards grander visions in the final instalment of the Henriad; of God's chosen people on crusade.

It is tempting to try to identify Shakespeare's Lord Chief Justice. An immediate candidate is of course Sir William Gascoyne Lord Chief Justice between 1400 and 1413. It was against Gascoyne, the sources recorded, that the young Prince Henry had indeed committed an assault. In his *Chronicles*, Holinshed recorded an incident in which the Prince "had with his fist striken the cheefe justice for sending one of his minions (upon desert) to prison."[10] The same episode could be found in Sir Thomas Elyot's renowned *Book Named the Governor.* Whilst there is no reference to actual violence in the *Governor*, merely the observation that the young Henry "all in fury, all chafed, and in terrible manner, came up to the place of judgment," the resilience of the Lord Chief Justice, and the ultimate submission of the duly chastised prince is described at length:

> Sir, remember yourself; I keep here the place of the King, your sovereign lord and father. To whom ye owe double obedience, wherefore eftsoons in his name I charge you to desist of your wilfulness and unlawful enterprise, and from henceforth give good example to those hereafter shall be your proper subjects. And now for your contempt and disobedience, go you to the prison of the King's Bench, whereunto I commit you.[11]

Sir John Stow, following Elyot, likewise made much of the Prince's ensuing penitence, laying down his arms, doing public "reverence" to the "valiant" Lord

---

8 For this supposition, see Kornstein, *Lawyers*, 138.
9 See here Yoshino, "Choice," 432.
10 Quoted in Raffield, *Imaginary Constitution*, 175.
11 Thomas Elyot, *The Book Named the Governor*, (Dent, 1962), 114–115.

Chief Justice and allowing himself to be incarcerated in the King's Bench prison.[12] Whether or not the accounts were authentic is of course less important than the fact that they were present in the sources upon which Shakespeare so obviously relied, as well as being replicated in dramatic form in the popular anonymous *The Famous Victories of Henry the Fifth*, entered in the Stationer's Register in 1594 and performed by the Queen's Men in the mid-1580s.[13]

An intriguing alternative is the much-admired Sir John Popham, Lord Chief Justice at the time *Henry IV part 2* was written. The Gads Hill robbery scene in *Henry IV part 1* was clearly intended to allude to anecdotal reports of Popham's alleged similar misdemeanours as a young man. The much vaunted transformation of Popham, from troubled youth to staunch adult defender of the common law, led George Keeton, writing a century ago, to presume that it was this Lord Chief Justice who "must have been in Shakespeare's mind during the composition" of both parts of *Henry IV*, not just in the character of the Lord Chief Justice, but of Hal too.[14]

At the same time, it is reasonable to suppose that Shakespeare's decision not to name the Lord Chief Justice is deliberate. His primary purpose is dramatic, his principal responsibility being to embody the sovereign authority of the English common law.[15] The naming of the Lord Chief Justice would have added little, and very possibly have served only to distract. Rather obviously it would have left scholars of constitutional history musing over the rather discomforting fact that the real Henry V might have been rather less forgiving than his dramatic counterpart. For reasons which remain unknown, Lord Chief Justice Gascoyne had resigned his office within months of Henry coming to the throne in late 1413. The alternative is to think instead in terms of representation and embodiment; of a Lord Chief Justice who constantly chooses to speak plainly, who appears to cherish reason and balance, and who dispenses justice in terms of "measure for measure," and who is determined that the common law will retain its sovereignty no matter how dislocated the commonwealth might be.[16] It is certainly the alternative which Shakespeare prefers to insinuate. After all, as the Lord Chief Justice reminded the young King, "I then did use the person of your father" (5.2.73).

---

12 Sir John Stow, *The Annales of England*, (1592), quoted in an appendix to *Henry IV part 2*, (Arden, 1991), at 218–219.

13 For a detailed commentary here see Raffield's *Imaginary Constitution*, 176–177.

14 George William Keeton, *Shakespeare's Legal and Political Background* (London: Pitman and Sons, 1917), 7.

15 Thus rendering him, according to Kenji Yoshino, "hardly human." See his "Choice," at 439.

16 See Yoshino, "Choice," 428–430.

In this context there is a third candidate, historically more tangential perhaps, but intellectually of more immediate consonance; Sir John Fortescue, fifteenth century Lancastrian Lord Chief Justice during the troubled reign of Henry VI. Two of Fortescue's treatises in particular, his *The Governance of England*, a paean to the principles of the Ancient Constitution and the rule of the English common law, and *In Praise of the Laws of England*, a classic example of magisterial "mirror" literature, retained considerable influence in Tudor England.[17] At the heart of both texts was the assertion that the common law of England, which framed its political constitution, was an expression of Aristotelian reason and balance, a constitutional jurisprudence that had indeed evolved "measure for measure." Such governance, Fortescue determined, was *dominium et regale*, royal and political, rather than merely *regale*; an expression of law rather than the mere whim of a particular king.[18] In time common lawyers would prefer the term "ancient" constitution, in the hope that it might thereby enjoy a still greater authenticity.[19]

Governance *dominium et regale* was characterised by two particular "virtues." The first is respect for the authority of the common law. The king is "bound by oath at his coronation to the observance of his law," and so cannot amend these laws without the approval of the "body politic."[20] The second, again drawn very obviously from Aristotle, is the singular 'virtue' of government balanced between sovereign and subject, or, more particularly, between sovereign and noble subject. A realm ruled by a king who appreciates both "virtues," who respected the integrity of the common law and the "ancient" constitution, was entitled to "rejoice," and its people were destined to "live more spiritually" secure in the bosom of a Christian "commonwealth."[21] There is, as Paul Raffield has suggested, a sense of this idyll, no matter how precarious, in the depiction of Justice Shallow's Gloucestershire orchard; just as, rather obviously, it is absent from the taverns and alleyways of Eastcheap.[22]

---

17 Both written whilst Fortescue was in exile in Scotland, following the cataclysmic defeat of the Lancastrian forces at Towton in 1461.

18 John Fortescue, "Governance," in *On the Laws and Governance of England* (Cambridge: Cambridge UP, 1997): 85–90.

19 For a definitive discussion of the 'ancient' constitution, see John G. A. Pocock, *Ancient Constitution and the Feudal Law: A Study of English Historical Thought in the Seventeenth Century* (Cambridge: Cambridge UP, 1957).

20 See Fortescue, *In Praise*, in *Laws*, at 17, 48, 52.

21 Fortescue, *In Praise*, 42.

22 Raffield, *Imaginary Constitution*, 165–166.

The history of Shakespeare's *Richard II* portrayed vividly the miseries which must flow from governance in *regale* alone, in disregard of the common law. The presence of the Lord Chief Justice in *Henry IV part 2*, it can be credibly suggested, was intended to reaffirm the alternative merits of governance *dominium et regale*. And when Shakespeare contemplated this presence it is reasonable to suppose that he had the author of *The Governance of England* and *In Praise of the Laws of England* in mind.[23] The rhetoric of Act 5 Scene 2 resonates; so much so that Tillyard was famously moved to suggest that it confirmed in Shakespeare a nascent Whiggish commitment to the principles of the Ancient Constitution, of sovereignty determined by the common law of England.[24] It certainly resonated with the constitutional jurisprudence articulated by contemporaries such as Richard Hooker, in whose *Laws of Ecclesiastical Polity* could be found the affirmation that "It is neither permitted unto Prelates nor Princes to judge or determine at their own discretion, but law hath described what both shall do." For "What power the King hath he hath by law, the bounds and limits of it are known."[25] The king, in sum, "doth guide the state and the law the king."[26]

Yet there is here a certain ambiguity, as Hooker well appreciated, in the carefully staged "reformation"of the "self-fashioning" Renaissance Prince.[27] Kingship, as the *Laws* confirmed, is "painted out."[28] In *Henry IV part 2* it is foretold by the Earl of Warwick, in his attempt to reassure the dying King as to his son's suitability as a prospective successor:

> My gracious lord, you look beyond him quite.
> The Prince but studies his companions
> Like a strange tongue, wherein, to gain the language,
> 'Tis needful that the most immodest word
> Be look'd upon and learnt. (4.4.67–71)

Henry is the consummate actor; a skill he has learned from both his natural and his adoptive father: from a king who by his own confession "stole all courtesy

23 An opinion shared by Paul Raffield in his *Shakespeare's Imaginary Constitution*, 162.
24 Eustace M.W. Tillyard, *Shakespeare's History Plays* (Harmonsdworth: Penguin – Peregrine Books, 1962), 270–271, 282–3.
25 Richard Hooker, *Of the Laws of Ecclesiastical Polity* (Cambridge: Cambridge UP, 1989), 217.
26 Hooker, *Laws*, 146–147.
27 Stephen Greenblatt, "Invisible Bullets: Renaissance Authority and its Subversion, *Henry IV* and *Henry V*," in *Political Shakespeare: New essays in cultural materialism*, eds. Jonathan Dollimore and Alan Sinfield (Manchester: Manchester UP, 1985), 18–47, 30. For a similar supposition, see Wolfgang Iser, *Staging Politics: The Lasting Impact of Shakespeare's Histories* (New York: Columbia UP, 1993), 162–163.
28 Hooker, *Laws*, 146–147.

from heaven" and from a drinking companion whose rule over the chaotic carnival world of Eastcheap rests on nothing more tangible than clever word-play and a "manner of wrenching the true cause the false way" (2.1.108, 3.2.94).[29] Maintaining a state of what Tillyard termed "ironic detachment" the young king displays an enviable ability to move comfortably through the various "plural worlds" that Shakespeare created for him.[30] The young King appears to have read his Elyot as well as his Machiavelli. He knows how to appear Kingly, to seem "human, but not too human."[31] The rhetoric of Act 5 Scene 2 comes naturally. But Warwick's perception remains prescient and resonant, at least to those who would subsequently become familiar with the final part of Shakespeare's Henriad. "'Presume not that I am the thing I was' the new King advises his audience as the play closes" (5.5.36).

As noted earlier, the Lord Chief Justice disappears at the end of *Henry IV part 2*. It might be supposed that he is not needed in *Henry V*, a play that is rather less about the governance of Eastcheap or Gloucestershire, and rather more about the English on crusade. Yet, given that the entire plot of *Henry V* is triggered by the Archbishop of Canterbury's eminently contestable interpretation of the Salic Law, it might equally be thought that the colder reason of the Lord Chief Justice would have been rather more useful; except of course that it might not, if he had indeed declined to support the Archbishop's rather tortuous jurisprudential reasoning.[32] The law, the politically astute Archbishop supposes, is a malleable entity, his new King a malleable prince, a sovereign who can "steal his sweet and honey'd sentences; / So that the art and the practic of life / Must be mistress to this theoric."[33] At the close of *Henry IV part 2* it is easy to suppose that Falstaff has been cast aside, his endeavour to pervert the course of good governance through the arts of linguistic evasion likewise despatched. At the be-

29 According to Stephen Greenblatt, at "such moments *2 Henry IV* seems to be testing and confirming an extremely dark and disturbing hypothesis about the nature of monarchical power in England: that its moral authority rests upon a hypocrisy so deep that the hypocrites themselves believe it." See his "Invisible Bullets," 41. In similar terms, Wolfgang Iser notes Hal's learned ability to speak in two languages, verse and prose, and concludes that he has come to an appreciation of the nature of kingship through the dramatic experience of "improvised role-play." See Iser, *Staging Politics*, 147, 159–160.

30 See Tillyard, *History Plays*, 279–280, and also Iser, *Staging Politics*, 122, referring to the "plural worlds" of the Henriad.

31 Quoted in MacEachern, *Poetics*, 87–88.

32 See here Yoshino, "Choice," 436.

33 William Shakespeare, *Henry V*, ed. John Henry Walter (Routledge, the Arden Shakespeare, 1991), 1.1.50–52.

ginning of *Henry V* it is nothing like as easy; and there is no Lord Chief Justice around to reassure the audience and settle the realm.

Finally, just as it is tempting to try to identify Shakespeare's nameless Lord Chief Justice, so too is it every bit as tempting to read forward, to project a prophetic acuity to Shakespeare's reflections on constitutional governance, not just in the earlier histories, but in the later tragedies and problem plays too. By the time that he had apparently laid down his pen for the last time, the question of England's proper governance and more particularly the place of its sovereign was once more a matter of fierce debate. A generation later, of course, it would contribute to the eruption of violent civil war. Where Queen Elizabeth, like Hal, had learned to fashion her "honey'd words" and play the role of the constitutionally sensitive Christian Prince, her successor James I quickly displayed rather more Ricardian propensities; so much so that his famed Lord Chief Justice, Sir Edward Coke, felt obliged, with ever increasing urgency, to impress the essence of a constitution determined by the extent of the common law:

> The King is under no man, but only God and the law, for the law makes the King: therefore let the King attribute that to the law, which from the law he hath received, to wit, power and dominion: for where will, and not the law doth sway, there is no King.[34]

According to Coke, the definitive account of such a constitutional jurisprudence was to be found in the writings of revered medieval jurists such as Bracton and Fortescue. James however was not persuaded, for as he informed his Parliament on more than one occasion the "state of monarchy is the supremest thing on earth; for kings are not only God's lieutenants upon earth and sit upon God's throne, but even by God himself they are called Gods."[35] Shakespeare's Richard II could not have put it better. The "breath of worldly men cannot depose" the "deputy elected by the Lord."[36] But it could; as James's son was to discover to his cost, a generation later to be so brutally and spectacularly "unking'd."[37]

The nature of monarchy would change dramatically during the century to follow, as the tensions inscribed in the idea of the king's two "bodies," the platonic and the physical, would become ever more apparent. The former could no longer guarantee the security of the latter, if indeed it ever could. There may have been a few doubters after 1649; though it is difficult to imagine there could have

---

34 Coke, 4 *Reports* (1604) 2: Preface xixa.

35 King James, *Political Writings* (Cambridge UP, 1994), 181.

36 William Shakespeare, *Richard II*, ed. Peter Ure (Routledge, the Arden Shakespeare, 1966), 3.2.54–57.

37 The reference to Richard being "unking'd" is, of course, taken from *Richard II*, at 4.1.220

been many. There would have been fewer still after the events of 1688. On this occasion Charles's second son escaped with his life, just. Parliament was displeased with James II and had him removed. Looking about for a replacement, it alighted upon the Prince of Orange and invited him over to become William III. He was of course anointed as well as crowned. The fiction of a Christian Prince would retain a place in the more fanciful reaches of English constitutional theology. The reality of being King of England would however be very different. There would be conditions, declarations of right and a Bill of Rights, in time an Act of Settlement. There may have been two royal 'bodies' still in the closing years of the 1590s, when Shakespeare cast the characters of *Henry IV part 2*. By 1688 there was only one that mattered.

Riccardo Baldissone

With Teeth and Nails: The Embodied Inservitude of Étienne de La Boétie

In his brief text *De la Servitude Volontaire*, or on voluntary servitude, Étienne de La Boétie provides us with an original and radical construction of the relation between nature, body and power. As a humanist scholar, La Boétie grounds his readings of classical texts in his construction of the human aspiration to freedom, which he conceives of as a natural expression of a more general animal desire for liberty. The practical gap between such a supposed natural inclination and actual human practices prompts La Boétie to search for the motivation of the forgetting of freedom. His explanation for the general human condition of voluntary servitude, which takes further a suggestion by Plutarch, is brutally simple: most humans freely opt for serfdom because they are born and raised as serfs. They continue to offer their bodies and the products of their bodily activities out of habit, as if their servitude were a natural human condition. According to La Boétie, power is the provisional result of this practice of gift-giving that makes the donors subjects. Their offer must be repeated in order to continue to be effective, because their gift is not an abstract entity (such as the modern concept of sovereignty, which is a recasting of a theological concept), but it is the offer of their bodies as bodies-for-another. Such a reiterated offer of bodies and products of bodily practices reproduces the identities of subjects as subjects. And yet, as the notion of voluntary servitude attributes to the multitude of subjects the main role (albeit negative and self-defeating) in the history of human subjugation, it also rescues all these subjects from their subaltern representation without having to appeal to any general plan, be it of providence or progress. La Boétie's conception of servitude and domination as relations that are constantly reproduced represents an alternative not only to the notion of the substantial continuity of political power, but also to the more general logic of identity on which it is predicated. Instead of recasting the metaphysical gesture as the revolutionary rupture that brings change from the outside, we may well consider following La Boétie's invitation to defuse the dynamic of power from the inside, by ceasing to offer up our bodies.

The origin, the composition and even the date of the first publication of the brief essay *De la Servitude Volontaire*,[1] or on voluntary servitude by Étienne de La Boé-

---

1 Étienne de La Boétie, *De la servitude volontaire ou Contr'un*, ed. Malcolm Smith (Genève:

tie are conjectural. The armed revolt of the population of the Guyenne and Bordeaux against the fiscal impositions of the French king Henri II and the harsh repression that followed in 1548 are the likely trigger for the composition of La Boétie's brilliant pamphlet. However, the text's only references to contemporary issues are the approving mentions of newly emerging poets such as Ronsard, Baïf and Du Bellay.

Whist these references help us to set the year 1549 as the earliest possible date for the last revision of the essay, they could also appear to confirm Montaigne's suggestion of a literary "matter and occasion"[2] for La Boétie's endeavour. Actually, Montaigne pointed out to a hint apparently far more remote, namely a political remark by Plutarch, who attributed the responsibility of Asiatic despotism to the inability of Asian inhabitants to say 'no' to their despots.[3]

And yet, we may legitimately suspect that with his suggestion Montaigne discreetly manoeuvred to avoid political trouble to the memory of his former fellow magistrate, older friend, and mentor. By the time Montaigne had nonchalantly dropped his remark in his essay on the education of children, many things had changed since the 1548 Bordeaux rebellion. In a short span of years, he had to witness the early death of his dearest friend in 1563, the death of his father in 1568, and the transformation of the French political horizon, which was bluntly redefined by the religious clash between the Catholic crown and the Huguenots, who were the French followers of Calvin.

The popular resistance to royal taxation had given way to a totalizing struggle[4] that also redefined the previous conflicts and their combatants. Also

---

Librairie Droz, 1987): further references in the text, abbreviated as SV. The English translations of the quotations from the original text are loosely based on the version in Harry Kurz, *Anti-Dictator: The Discours sur la servitude volontaire of Étienne de La Boétie* (New York: Columbia University Press, 1942).

2 "Comme se sien mot, que les abitant d'Asie seruoient à un seul, pour ne sçavoir prononcer une seule sillabe, qui est Non, donna peut-estre la matiere et l'occasion à la Boitie de sa Servitude Volontaire." ["As his [Plutarch's] saying, that the inhabitants of Asia came to be slaves to one only, for not having been able to pronounce one syllable, which is No, gave perhaps matter and occasion to La Boétie to write his Voluntary Servitude."] (Michel de Montaigne, *Essais* (Paris: Garnier-Flammarion, 1969), I.XXVI "*De L'Institution des Enfants*," 204). [All the translations in brackets are by the author.]

3 Actually, the sense of the text by Plutarch is somewhat different: "He who said a long time ago that the inhabitants of Asia were slave to a single man because they could not pronounce a single syllable, which is 'no,' didn't know what he was talking about, or else he was joking." In Plutarch, *Moralia* 987d–e.

4 "Nulle dissention n'est si grande ny si dangereuse que celle que vient pour la religion. Elle separe les cytoiens, les voisins, les amis, les parens, les freres, le père et les enfans, le mary et la femme ; elle rompt les aliances, les parantés, les mariages, les droitz inviolables de nature,

the wit of La Boétie was enrolled post mortem under the Protestant banner, since after the Saint Bartholomew's day massacre substantial excerpts of his *Voluntary Servitude* were published to attack the king Charles IX, who was the champion of Catholicism. In such changed circumstances, Montaigne opted to avoid the posthumous publication of both the essay on voluntary servitude, and La Boétie's *Memoire sur la Pacification des Troubles*[5] (On the Pacification of the Civil Wars).

The latter work's proposal of a liturgico-theological compromise between Catholics and Protestants lost its *raison d'être* with the opening of Council of Trento.[6] However, the uncompromising rebuttal of monarchic power had, if anything, made the earlier essay gain in virulence inasmuch as the circumstances of its composition faded away. This trend was to characterize the future trajectory of the text.

However, Montaigne's decision was undoubtedly difficult and painful, as it appeared to deny his friend a well-deserved readership. The same Montaigne bore witness to an uneasiness, which reached the highest point of discomfort in the prescient words of the dying La Boétie: "*mon frère, mon frère, me refusez vous doncques une place?*"[7] [my brother, my brother, do you deny me a place?].

But what was La Boétie's place? Borges tells us that Ariosto "*iba por los caminos de Ferrara / y al mismo tiempo andaba por la luna*"[8] [he travelled the roads of Ferrara and, at the same time, walked the moon]. Whilst La Boétie walked the streets of his native city Sarlat or those of Bordeaux, at the same time he strolled elsewhere too. He may have wandered along the *calli* of Venice, as Montaigne

et penetre jusques au fondz des cœurs pour extirper les amitiés et enraciner des haynes irreconsiliables" ["No contrast is as vast and dangerous as that which is originated by religion. Religion splits citizens, neighbours, friends, relatives, brothers, father and children, husband and wife; it breaks alliances, kinships, marriages, inviolable natural rights, and it penetrates into the very deep of hearts to extirpate friendship and implant irreconcilable hate."] (Étienne de La Boétie, *Memoire sur la Pacification des Troubles* (Genève: Droz, 1983), 49).

5 In his 1570 preface to the printed edition of the collected work of La Boétie, Montaigne writes in regard of the two missing works: "Mais quant à ces deux dernieres pieces, ie leur trouve la façon trop delicate & mignarde pour les abandonner au grossier & pesant air d'une si mal plaisante saison" ["But as to these two latter works, I find that the issue is too much delicate and subtle to abandon them to the rough and heavy air of such an unpleasant season"]. (*Œuvres Complètes d'Éstienne de La Boétie*, ed. Paul Bonnefon (Paris: Rouam, 1892), 62).

6 Also in this case, Montaigne's cautiousness can be explained as an attempt to spare the memory of his friend criticism from the Catholic side.

7 Michel de Montaigne, "Lettre à son père sur la mort d'Étienne de La Boétie," in *Œuvres Complètes d'Éstienne de La Boétie*, 321.

8 Jorge Luis Borges, "Ariosto y los árabes," in *Sur*, 265 (1960): 19–21. Ariosto writes in his *Orlando Furioso*, one of La Boétie's favourite readings, of 'voluntaria eterna servitude' (Ludovico Ariosto, *Orlando Furioso* XVL.46).

suggests.[9] Certainly, just like his lifelong friend, he kept wearing out the stones and the polished marbles of the streets of ancient Rome and Athens. There he lived together with his fellow humanist scholars, sharing with them the languages and thoughts of long dead authors.

However, together with Montaigne, La Boétie did not embrace the *humanae litterae* in opposition to the *divinae litterae*,[10] as he and his friend were and remained devout Catholics.[11] They rather revived the values of classical authors as a kind of *philosophia perennis*,[12] a perpetual wisdom that could then be put to work regardless of historical and geographical differences. And yet, La Boétie did not subject this recovery to the quietist logic of *nihil sub sole novum.*[13] On the contrary, his rediscovery of nature and of natural qualities nurtured his unforeseen view of the present, which he thus saw anew and with wonder.

La Boétie's wonder about the political condition of France was a powerful rhetorical tool, which predisposed the reader to the resulting series of extraordinary reversals of political common sense. Of course, the contrivance of turning that which is current and usual into something unusual and astounding was not new. Moreover, also his appeal to the natural order of things was a well-trodden *topos:* it was not only widely represented in classical texts, but it had been also deployed in medieval times as a major theoretical weapon to justify the new centralized power of the Church.

Since the eleventh century the Popes and their Canonists urged the earthly powers to submit to papal authority as god's representative.[14] They presented the new arrangement as a due restoration of the natural order of things, which they

9 "Et sçay davantage que, s'il eut eu à choisir, il eut mieux aimé estre nay à Venise qu'à Sarlac: et avec raison" ["And I moreover know, that could it have been in his own choice, he would have preferred to have been born in Venice, rather than in Sarlac: and with reason"] (Montaigne, *Essais* I.28 "*De l'Amitié*," 242).

10 The opposition between human and divine texts is probably the result of the efforts of Florentine scholars such as Bruni to produce a concept of literature as different from theological writings.

11 "Je suis chrestien, je suis catholique: tel ay vescu, tel suis je deliberé de clorre ma vie" [I am Christian, I am Catholic: in this way I lived, in this way I decided to conclude my life], says La Boétie to Montaigne short before dying. *Œuvres Complètes d'Éstienne de La Boétie*, 313.

12 The term *philosophia perennis* first appeared in the title of the treatise by Agostino Steuco *De Perenni Philosophia Libri X*, published in 1540. In the treatise, Steuco argued for the substantial convergence of ethical and philosophical doctrines towards Catholicism.

13 This is the sentence in the *Vulgata* with which Jerome rendered in Latin the Hebrew phrase אֵין כָּל חָדָשׁ תַּחַת הַשָּׁמֶשׁ (en kol chadásh táchat hashámesh), 'nothing new under the sun,' in *Qohelet* (Ecclesiastes) 1.10.

14 See Brian Tierney, *The Crisis of Church and State, 1050–1300* (Englewood Cliffs: Prentice-Hall, 1964).

claimed had since been obstructed and perverted by the incrustation of (bad) custom.[15] By dressing innovation in the clothing of restoration they set an ideological pattern that was to inspire the major political revolutions to come,[16] and which continues to reemerge through our ecological concerns.

La Boétie, just like Rousseau was to do two centuries later, restated the pattern of a perverted nature. His appeal to nature went even beyond the human sphere, as he recalled animal behaviour as a reminder of the temporarily lost human aspiration to freedom. Moreover, in order to explain this loss La Boétie had to go also beyond the boundaries of nature and take into account the weight of custom.

As a Renaissance scholar, La Boétie was indeed conjugating the present with a past whose rebirth he urged.[17] In turn, this very operation produced a further entanglement with time, as it opened towards a series of future rediscoveries.[18] All these resumptions enriched the text, so to speak, with further hermeneutic layers, which bore the perspective of each interpreter. La Boétie thus came to wear from time to time the clothes of a Huguenot, an illuminist, a republican and an anarchist.

Whilst the present reading would take responsibility for its inevitably projective construction of the *Voluntary Servitude*, it would also attempt to put to use the rich textual network that surrounds and substantiates it. Hence, the text and the textual network that complement the *Voluntary Servitude* will be used more as a catalyst for producing further reactions than as an excavation site to be explained through conjectural reconstructions.

By using the text-plus-network of the *Voluntary Servitude* as a visible theoretical tool (if not a weapon), rather than an invisible window onto the landscape of its political contents, the present text would propose an alternative to the im-

---

15 As Berman recalls, "faced with an obnoxious custom, the Gregorian reformers would appeal over it to truth, quoting the aphorism of Tertullian and St. Ciprian, 'Christ said, I am the truth.' He did not say 'I am the custom.'" In Harold J. Berman, *Law and Revolution: The Formation of the Western Legal Tradition* (Cambridge, MA: Harvard University Press, 1983), 112.

16 See Eugen Rosenstock-Huessy, *Out of Revolution: Autobiography of Western Man* (Oxford: Berg, 1993).

17 'Rebirth' is the literal English translation of the French word Renaissance, which was coined by the French historian Jules Michelet in his 1855 *Histoire de France*, on the model of the Italian word *rinascita*, as used by Giorgio Vasari in his 1550 art treatise *Le vite de' più eccellenti pittori, scultori, e architettori.*

18 It would be too long to list all the rediscoveries of the *Voluntary Servitude*. However, the fact that they generally happened in moments of cultural and political opening witnesses the ability of the text to conjugate past, present and future.

mediately political use of the *Voluntary Servitude*, which was the task of most of its previous recoveries.[19]

Instead of constructing the pamphlet as offering just another description, albeit unusually radical, of the political horizon, this reading aims to follow La Boétie's formulations in both directions of their textual predecessors and their future uses. Whilst following Deleuze's invitation to experiment instead of interpreting,[20] this approach also expresses a more general shift of focus, from the metaphysical question about how thing stand to the genealogical concern about how we put them.[21]

La Boétie's own reconfiguration of things began from the very title of his best known work. The felicitous phrase 'voluntary servitude' not only immediately captured the attention of his readers with its oxymoronic effect, but it also expressed from the outset the contradiction that triggered La Boétie's wondering question:

> *quel mal encontre a esté cela, qui a peu tant denaturer l'homme, seul né de vrai pour vivre franchement; et lui faire perdre la souvenance de son premier estre, et le desir de le reprendre* [what wicked encounter is that which could so denature man, who was born only to live free; and which made him lose the memory of his first condition, and the desire to regain it] (SV, 44). [22]

The title phrase 'voluntary servitude,' as the description of the human desire to be subjected, is also a synthesis of the argument mounted by La Boétie. It is not

---

19 There are notable exceptions. In 1976, Abensour and Gauchet insisted on keeping the text of the *Voluntary Servitude* open. See Miguel Abensour and Marcel Gauchet, "Présentation: Les leçons de la servitude et leur destin," in Étienne de La Boétie, *Le discours de la servitude volontaire* (Paris: Payot, 1976), VII–XXIX. More recent exceptions are Nicola Panichi, *Plutarchus redivivus? La Boétie et sa réception en Europe* (Paris: Honoré Champion, 2008); Marc Schachter, *Voluntary Servitude and the Erotics of Friendship* (Burlington: Ashgate, 2008).

20 "Expérimentez, n'interprétez jamais" in Gilles Deleuze and Claire Parnet, *Dialogues* (Paris: Flammarion, 1977), 60.

21 At the risk of oversimplifying matters (or awkwardly paraphrasing Derrida), we may say that the first approach follows the royal road of Western metaphysics and it inevitably reifies texts and authors, in the attempt at producing them as objectively as possible. On the contrary, the second perspective claims as constructive practices both the work displayed in the text and the operation of its reconsideration.

22 In 1974, Clastres reformulated the question from within an anthropological perspective: "Why did some people cease to be primitives? What tremendous event, what revolution allowed the figure of the Despot, of he who gives orders to those who obey, to emerge?" In Pierre Clastres, *Society Against the State: Essays in Political Anthropology*, trans. Robert Hurley and Abe Stein (Oxford: Blackwell, 1977), 173.

surprising, therefore, to find that several commentators endeavoured to trace the sources that inspired this definition.

In 1923, Barrère[23] went so far as to identify the ancestor of the notion of voluntary servitude in the Greek term ἐθελοδουλεία (ethelodouléia), which first appeared in the text of the platonic dialogue *Symposion.*[24] Actually, the servitude favourably depicted in the dialogue by the character Pausania was an element of an erotic homosexual friendship.

According to Barrère, La Boétie was politically inspired by Thucydides, who contended that the responsibility for subjugation should be attributed less to the subjugator (δουλωσάμενος, *doulōsámenos*) than to the subjugated who accepts servitude though having the power to prevent it.[25]

A third possible source could be found in Xenophon's dialogue *Œconomicus*, which La Boétie himself translated into French as *La Mesnagerie.*[26] Though Xenophon did not mention voluntary servitude, his character Socrates dealt at length with the metaphor of the slavery to the passions, which was to exert a wide influence on Western thought especially through later religious recastings.

However, the immediate morphological antecedent to the French phrase *servitude volontaire* is first documented in the well-known first Philippic oration pronounced in 44 B.C.E. by Cicero against Marcus Antonius. Cicero accused his fellow senators of *voluntaria servitus*, or voluntary servitude in regard to both the memory of the dead Caesar and Antonius.[27]

During the course of the next decades, the word *ethelodouléia* entered the religious sphere in Philo's short treatise *On Drunkenness*,[28] where it stigmatized

---

23 Joseph Barrère, *L'Humanisme et la politique dans le Discours de la servitude volontaire: étude sur les origines du texte et l'objet du Discours d' Estienne de La Boétie* (Paris: Champion, 1923).

24 "ἡ ἐθελοδουλεία οὐκ αἰσχρὰ εἶναι οὐδὲ κολακεία" (ē ethelodouléia ouk aiskhrá éinai oudé kolakéia) [voluntary servitude is neither shameful nor a flattery], in Plato, *Symposion*, 184c.

25 Thucydides I.69.1.

26 See *La Mesnagerie de Xenophon. Les Règles de mariage de Plutarque. Lettres de consolation de Plutarque à sa femme, le tout traduict de grec en françois par Feu Monsieur Estienne de La Boëtie. Ensemble quelques vers latins et françois de son invention. Item, un Discours sur la mort dudit Seigneur de La Boëtie, par M. de Montaigne* (Paris: Imprimerie de Fédéric Morel, 1571).

27 "Quae, malum, est ista voluntaria servitus?" [what, alas, is this voluntary servitude?] In Cicero *Philippicae* 1.6. The expression was later given a moral overtone by Seneca: "*Nulla servitus turpior est quam voluntaria*" [No servitude is more shameful than a voluntary one]. In Sen., *Ad Luc.* 17.

28 "ἀλλὰ μιμησάμενοι τοὺς ἐθελοδούλους ἑκόντες ἑαυτοὺς πικροῖς δεσπόταις ὑπέρριψαν γένος ὄντες ἐλεύθεροι" (allà mimesámenoi toùs ethelodoúlous hekóntes heautoùs pikróis despótais hypérripsan génos óntes eléutheroi) ["but because imitating those who hug their chains, they

the voluntary slavery to the passions. Moreover, only few years later Paul defined the human condition through the metaphor of the δοῦλοι τῆς ἁμαρτίας (*doũloi tēs hamartías*), slaves to sin.[29]

However, regardless of these illustrious predecessors, it is arguable that La Boétie drew direct inspiration for his pamphlet from the very author whose identity was hinted at by his friend Montaigne, namely Plutarch. Most probably, this inspiration did not come from the passage referred to by Montaigne.[30] It would be better to consider a sentence in the life of Aratus, "τῶν δὲ πολλῶν ἤδη διὰ συνήθειαν ἐθελοδούλως ἐχόντων" (*tōn de pollṓn ḗdē dià synḗtheian ethelodoúlōs ekhóntōn*), which, in the light of its future effect on La Boétie, may be well translated as 'by this time many [citizens] were enduring by habit in voluntary servitude.'[31]

In this sentence, the adverb *ethelodoúlōs* illustrates a mode of behaviour, serving voluntarily, which is maintained because of habit. Moreover, the sentence describes the relation of voluntary political servitude of subjects to their despots. Hence, it sketches precisely the political conundrum addressed by La Boétie. In case this may still appear too weak a clue, we may appeal to Montaigne's judgement on Plutarch, who "*guigne seulement du doigt par où nous irons*,"[32] that is, who merely points out his finger where we are to go.

As it is likely that La Boétie shared Montaigne's way of putting Plutarch to work, it is also arguable that he followed the direction indicated by Plutarch. However, before showing how La Boétie's developed Plutarch's suggestions, it would be worth exploring a parallel transformation of the notion of voluntary servitude, which was later to surface with devastating effect during La Boétie's lifetime.

After Paul, the Gospel of John reiterated (in the singular) the metaphor of the slave to sin.[33] From then on, the topos of the servitude to sin travelled from text to text: it moved from Origen to John Chrysostom, and from Augustine to John of Damascus.[34] However, Philo's religious recasting of the platonic *ethelodouléia* had to wait for its Latin version *voluntaria servitus* until the twelfth century,

---

have voluntarily laid themselves at the feet of cruel masters, though they were born to freedom"], in Philo, *De Ebrietate*, 122.

29 Romans 6.17.

30 Schachter, *Voluntary Servitude and the Erotics of Friendship*, 188 on.

31 Plutarch, *Vitae*, Aratus 25.5.

32 Montaigne, *Essais* I.XXVI.115.

33 "δοῦλος ἐστιν τῆς ἁμαρτίας" (doũlos estin tēs hamartías) [he is a slave of sin], in John 8.34.

34 Origen, Homilies on Joshua 10.3; John Chrysostom, Homily 29.22; Augustine, *Tractatus in Johannis* 41.7; John of Damascus, Orthodox faith 4.23.

when Bernard of Clairvaux recovered it, together with the image of the yoke already evoked by Xenophon's Socrates.

In the text of Bernard's eighty-first Sermon on the Songs of Songs, Calvin found the expression *voluntaria servitus*, which described the yoke that weighs down the human soul. According to Bernard as quoted by Calvin, because of this yoke, the soul is "enslaved by necessity, free by its will; and, what is more wonderful and more miserable, it is guilty, because free; and enslaved wherein it is guilty; and so therein enslaved wherein it is free."[35]

Though in the previous sentences language may seem to go on holiday, to quote Wittgenstein,[36] Calvin's following comment on Peter Lombard duly clarifies the issue at stake behind the series of aporias offered by Bernard. Calvin locates in Lombard the pestilential belief that man (sic) can avoid sin because he sins freely.[37]

As Nietzsche would have it, human freedom and will are theologically necessary to grant human punishability. And yet, from a theological perspective neither human will nor freedom can be autonomous and independent from god's providential plan. Bernard tackles the resulting double bind by eroding, as it were, the logical absoluteness of both bondage and freedom, which have to be understood in regard to necessity and will respectively.[38]

Hence, Bernard can affirm that "we are under a yoke, but no other yoke than that of voluntary servitude; therefore, in respect of servitude, we are miserable,

35 "Ancilla, propter necessitate: libera propter voluntatem: et, quod magis mirum magisque miserum est, ideo rea, quod libera: eoque ancilla, quo rea: ac per hoc, eo ancilla, quo libera." Bernard de Clairvaux, *In Canticum Sermones* 81.9, quoted in Jean Calvin, *Institutio Christianae Religionis* II.3.5, trans. John Allen.

36 "For philosophical problems arise when language goes on holiday," in Ludwig Wittgenstein, *Philosophical Investigations*, trans. Gertrude Elizabeth Margaret Anscombe (New York: Macmillan, 1953), par. 38.

37 "Or le maistre des Sentences, pour n'avoir seu distinguer entre Contrainte et Necessité a ouvert la porte à cest erreur, qui a esté une peste mortelle à l'Eglise, d'estimer que l'homme pouvoit eviter le peché, pource qu'il peche franchement" [the master of the Sentences [Lombard], by not knowing how to distinguish between necessity and compulsion, gave occasion to a pernicious error, which was a mortal plague for the Church, of reputing that man can avoid sin, because he sins freely]. In Calvin *Inst.* II.3.5 (French version, in which Calvin adds the sentence on the mortal plague).

38 "Ita nescio quo pravo et miro modo ipsa sibi voluntas peccato quidem in deterius mutate, necessitate facit, ut nec necessitas (quum voluntaria sit) excusare valeat voluntatem, nec voluntas (quum sit illecta) excludere necessitate" [Thus, by some means strange and wicked, the will itself, being deteriorated by sin, makes a necessity; but so that the necessity, inasmuch as it is voluntary, cannot excuse the will, and the will, inasmuch as it is enticed, cannot exclude the necessity]. In Bernard, SC 81.7, as quot. in Calvin, *Inst.* II.3.5.

and in respect of will, inexcusable, because the will, when it was free, made itself the slave of sin."[39] Calvin thus concludes that "everything good in the will is only the work of grace."[40]

When, in 1536 Calvin published the first edition of his magnum opus *Institutio Christianae Religionis* (Institutes of the Christian Religion), the book only included six sections, and it did not contain any mention of Bernard of Clairvaux. In the course of a long re-editing process that produced four further editions, the treatise swelled to include seventy-nine chapters and fifteen quotations from Bernard's work.[41] The passage on voluntary servitude only appeared in print in the last and definitive 1559 edition of the book.

There is no apparent link between Calvin's decision to recover Bernard's expression 'voluntary servitude' and La Boétie's homonymous pamphlet. And yet, this very phrase is likely to have sounded familiar to both the Calvinist editors of La Boétie's unauthorized publications and their Calvinist readers. Moreover, the strongly negative connotation of the theological notion of voluntary servitude should have reinforced the stigma that the political notion of voluntary servitude attached to the operation of monarchic power.

Nevertheless, considering the text of the 1561 *Memoire*, in which La Boétie outlined a positive intervention in the religious clash designed to strengthen French religious and political unity, Montaigne's later scruples appear to be more than justified. The political task of the author of the *Memoire* was anything but the undermining of monarchy.

The changed circumstances between 1548 and 1561 played an important role in reorienting La Boétie's political priorities.[42] Moreover, whilst the *Memoire* was intended as a proposal to be implemented in the specific conditions of the French religious conflict, the text of the *Voluntary Servitude* transcended its context and attained a level of generalisation that secured it a well-deserved posthumous fame.

At any rate, the decontextualized and detemporalized approach that favoured the subsequent hermeneutic recoveries of the *Voluntary Servitude* was also a manifestation of the peculiar relation of humanist culture to the process

---

39 "Postea dicit nos premi iugo, non alio tamen quam voluntariae cuiusdam servitutis: ideo pro servitute esse miserabiles, pro voluntate inexcusabiles: quia voluntas, quum libera esset, servam se peccati fecit." In Bernard, SC 81.7, as quot. in Calvin, *Inst.* II.3.5.

40 "quicquid boni est in voluntate, esse unius gratiae opus." In Calvin, *Inst.* II.3.6.

41 See Anthony N. S. Lane, *John Calvin Student of Church Fathers* (Edinburgh: T. & T. Clark, 1999).

42 However, we may note that in the *Memoire* La Boétie focuses on reducing divergences in the liturgy rather than in the doctrine, thus confirming his interest in practices.

of temporalization. Of course, a re-enacting of such a particular relation with time has now become impossible, because of the distancing from the past associated with modern historicisms. And yet, also the historicist pretensions to offer an objective reconstruction (even asymptotic) of the past seem no longer able to stand their ground. Whilst during the nineteenth century Stirner's rejection of objectivity and Nietzsche's claim of our inevitably perspectival reading of the past could not yet theoretically undermine historicism, in the late 1900s Lyotard's scepticism toward grand narratives at last opened the way to the dismissal of the notion of historical progress. We may now build on the acknowledgement of the inevitability of our historical projections a productive relation to the past, which would be neither accessed through its humanist immediate re-enactment nor its historicist objective reconstruction.

However, before engaging with a deliberately projective reading of the text of *Voluntary Servitude*, it would be worth cautioning against the use of the very term 'humanism,' which is problematic inasmuch it hides local and temporal specificities.[43] For example, the label of humanist scholar may be too summarily conflated into one definition that might cover a fourteenth-century Italian writer such as Dante, a fifteenth-century German thinker such as Cusanus, and a sixteenth-century French author such as La Boétie.

The issue is not new, as it was raised in the debate between Burckhardt and Burdach over the continuity (or the discontinuity) of the Renaissance with regard to the Middle Ages.[44] On that occasion, the controversy was framed by the historicist presupposition of the possibility of an objective historical periodization. On the contrary, the reconsideration of grand narratives, including the historicist one, allowed the construction of such objective periodization as the effect of an objective historical gaze, which in turn iterated (albeit unwillingly) the performance of the eye of god.

Hence, the topos of discontinuity may also not be explored as a feature of the supposedly objective chronological context, but rather as construed from within the perspective of each author. In this case, the similarity between the

---

43 *Pace* Benjamin, and his remark: "a science in conflict with the language of its own investigations is an absurdity," in Walter Benjamin, *The Origin of German Tragic Drama*, trans. John Osborne (London: Verso, 2003), 42. A knowing path that does not question its own language at best is self-referential and at worst is a legitimating tool for some kind of status quo.

44 See Jacob Burckhardt [1860], *The Civilization of the Renaissance in Italy*, trans. S. G. C. Middlemore (London: Harper, 1878); Konrad Burdach, *Reformation, Renaissance, Humanismus. Zwei Abhandlungen über die Grundlage moderner Bildung und Sprachkunst* (Berlin: Gebrüder Paetel, 1918).

patterns at work in the texts of sixteenth-century French Renaissance authors such as Calvin and La Boétie is striking, regardless of their field of application.

On the one hand, for Calvin the historical discontinuity to be overtaken is not characterised by a complete absence, but it is the effect of a confinement: the doctrine delivered by Augustine "was afterwards shut up in the cloisters of monks for almost a thousand years."[45] On the other hand, according to La Boétie, the natural human aspiration to freedom had not completely disappeared, since only its conscious memory has been driven into oblivion by the habit of servitude.

However, whilst Calvin hints at a particular historical gap, which justifies his supposed recovery of the previously hidden Christian wisdom, La Boétie's exploration of the denaturation of man (sic) brings forth a hermeneutic paradigm that follows the model of his Greek mentors, from Thucydides to Plutarch. The theoretical ambition of the young La Boétie is nothing less than the outlining of the general dynamic of the forgetting of freedom, to paraphrase Heidegger.

The rhetorical strategy of the *Voluntary Servitude* is deceptively simple: once the current renunciation of freedom is acknowledged as an unnatural condition, the understanding of this condition would also provide the key to its overcoming. In the course of the argument the path bifurcates into a phenomenology of power relations and an ontology of freedom. These two components intersect with a contrapuntal effect, until they converge towards the conclusion, which is followed by a series of considerations on power and those who hold it.

A tyrant has only the power that others give him:[46] this is the first and fundamental statement in the pamphlet. The assertion constructs the power (*puissance*) of the despot as the paradoxical effect of the will of his subjects. La Boétie emphatically underlines the monstrosity of such a seemingly self-harming behaviour:

> *quel monstre de vice est cecy, qui ne merite pas encore le tiltre de couardise, qui ne trouve point de non assés vilain, que la nature desadvoue avoir fait et la langue refuse de nommer* ? [what monstrous vice, then, is this which does not even deserve to be called cowardice, a vice for which no term can be found vile enough, which nature herself disavows and our tongues refuse to name?] (SV, 36).

The absence of a notion and a word that stigmatizes the will to serve is here subtly turned into evidence of the unnatural character of such a will. This reversal at once explains the conceptual void and it justifies La Boétie's endeavour to fill it.

45 "mille fere annis postea in claustris monachorum retentum fuit," in Calvin, *Inst.* II.3.6.
46 "un tyran […] n'a puissance que celle qu'ils luy donnent" (SV, 34).

However, the appeal to nature also opens a gap between the supposed natural human inclination and the actual practice of millions of men carrying the burden of subjection not by force, but under the spell, as it were, of the name of just one man.[47] More important for La Boétie, this divergence is not so much a theoretical gap but a practical one.

The priority accorded to practice by La Boétie explains another reversal that takes place in his pamphlet, where action is followed, rather than preceded, by its theoretical justifications. This reversal immediately derives from La Boétie's construction of power as the gift of the multitude to the sovereign (to put it in anachronistic modern terms), so that the sovereign "is automatically defeated if the country refuses consent to its own enslavement. It is not necessary to deprive him of anything, but simply to give him nothing."[48]

La Boétie also rephrases the consideration in the form of a direct request: "Resolve to serve no more, and you are at once freed! I do not ask that you place hands upon the tyrant to topple him over, but simply that you support him no longer."[49] The direct demand clarifies at once the aim of the text and the scope of La Boétie's erudite elaborations, which are not intended to explore the possibility of getting rid of the yoke of servitude (a possibility which he does not doubt at all), but rather to explain why this liberation has not yet happened.

The delay is less the effect of a historical contingency than a more general feature of a transhistorical dynamic, which according to La Boétie produces the iteration of the forgetting of freedom. If compared with Calvin's delayed recovery of the pristine Christian message as mediated by Augustine, La Boétie's construction expresses an aspect of Renaissance thought that later succumbed to the linearity of the narrative of progress.

---

47 "Grandes chose certes, et toutesfois si commune, [...] voir un million d'hommes servir miserablement, aiant le col sous le joug, non pas contrains par une plus grande force mais aucunement (ce semble) enchentés et charmés par le nom seul d'un" (SV, 34). As an alternative to the absolute singularization of the despot, La Boétie offers a plural collective subject, which he describes with his astounding neologism *tous uns* [all ones] (SV, 42). This grammatical pluralisation of the One produces a different subjectivation path, which is immune to the spell of the Western *reductio ad unum*, both in its monarchical and democratic versions. We will have to wait until William James' pluriverse, and later on, Simondon's transindividual, Deleuze's multiplicities, Jean-Luc Nancy's being singular plural and Stiegler's transindividuation to be able to appreciate La Boétie's poietic gesture.

48 "Il est de soymesme defait, mais que le païs ne consente pas à sa servitude. Il ne faut pas luy oster rien, mais ne lui donner rien" (SV, 37–38).

49 "Soiés resolus de ne servir plus, et vous voilà libres! Je ne veux pas que vous le poussiés ou l'esbransliés, mais seulement ne le soustenés plus" (SV, 40).

Calvin's revival of Augustine may be understood as a variation on the humanist theme of the rediscovery of classical culture as a historical model (albeit somewhat unattainable), which hence betrays these very classics by subjecting them to the perverting linear dimension of Christian history. La Boétie, just like Machiavelli shortly before him, derives instead by analogy from the classics a series of theoretical tools, whose hermeneutic practice is oriented by the task of political intervention.

Such is the notion of voluntary servitude, which attributes to the multitude of subjects the main role (albeit negative and self-defeating) in the history of human subjugation. This extraordinary move rescues all these subjects from their subaltern representation without having to appeal to any general plan, be it of providence or progress.

Though La Boétie presents nature as the minister of god and the governess of men,[50] she is devoid of any finality, apart from casting humans from the same mould so that we could *"entreconnoistre tous pour compaignons ou plutost pour frères"* [acknowledge each other as comrades or better as brothers] (SV, 41). Moreover, La Boétie insists on human similarity rather than sameness, as he remarks that we *almost* recognise ourselves in others.[51]

As La Boétie is fully aware that his irenic statements do not exactly correspond to actual human experience, he turns this discrepancy into evidence that "we are so bastardized that we are unable to recognise our inborn goods and affections."[52] As a support to his argument he then submits the evidence of natural animal behaviour that it is not corrupted by human custom:

> The very beasts, God help me, if men are not too deaf, cry out to them, 'Long live Liberty!' Many among them die as soon as captured [...]. Others, from the largest to the smallest, when captured put up such a strong resistance by means of claws, horns, beak, and paws, that they show clearly enough how they cling to what they are losing.[53]

In order to be sure that these frenzied reactions would have been understood as examples of meaningful responses, La Boétie offers an example whose esoteric

50 "la ministre de dieu, la gouvernante des hommes" (SV, 41).
51 "quasi reconnoistre l'un dans l'autre" (SV, 42).
52 "sommes tant abastardis que nous ne puissions reconnoistre nos biens ni sembleblement nos naifves affections" (SV, 42).
53 "Les Bestes, ce m'aid Dieu, si les hommes ne font trop les sourds, leur crient, " Vive liberté ! " Plusieurs en y a d'entre elles qui meurent aussy tost qu'elles sont prises [...]. Les autres, des plus grandes jusques aus plus petites, lors qu'on les prend, font si grand' resistence d'ongles, de cornes, de bec et de pieds, qu'elles declarent assés combien elles tiennent cher ce qu'elles perdent" (SV, 42).

(in sixteenth-century France) narrative would have attracted an aura of veritable parable:

> What else can explain the behaviour of the elephant who, after defending himself to the last ounce of his strength and knowing himself on the point of being taken, dashes his jaws against the trees and breaks his tusks, thus manifesting his longing to remain free as he has been and proving his wit and ability to buy off the huntsmen in the hope that through the sacrifice of his tusks he will be permitted to offer his ivory as a ransom for his liberty?[54]

It would be difficult to underrate the radical boldness of La Boétie's reference to beasts as sharers of a common nature with humans. Christian tradition always insisted on the superior position of human beings within the creation, with Francis' affectionate manner towards animals as an outstanding exception. However, La Boétie's familiarity with the classics offered him another perspective. In particular, given his legal studies, he was possibly familiar with the definition of natural law in the Justinianic Code:

> *Jus naturale est quod omnia animalia docuit: nam jus istud non humani generis proprium est sed omnium animalium quae in coelo, quae in terra, quae in mari nascuntur* [natural law is that which she has taught all animals: this law is not characteristic of human beings but of all animals that were born in the sky, on earth and in the sea].[55]

We owe the theorization of the *ius naturale*, or natural law, to the third-century Tyrian jurist Ulpian, who added it to the previous domains of the *ius civile*, the civil law that applied to Roman citizens, and the *ius gentium*, the law of nations that regulated the dealings with non-Roman subjects. In 212 the *Constitutio Antoniniana* had granted Roman citizenship to all free subjects of the Empire, so that Roman law had in fact become the *ius gentium*.[56] The newly devised natural law then opened a wider legal sphere, in which the intervention of the *ius gen-*

---

54 "Que veut dire autre chose l'elephant, qui s'estant defendu jusques a n'en pouvoir plus, n'i voiant plus d'ordre, estant sur le point destre pris, il enfonce ses machoires, et casse ses dents contre les arbres, sinon que le grand desir qu'il a de demourer libre ainsi qu'il est, lui fait de l'esprit et l'advise de marchander avec les chasseurs si pour le pris de ses dens il en sera quitte, et s'il sera receu a bailler son ivoire, et paier ceste rançon pour sa libreté?" (SV, 43).

55 The Justinian compilations of Roman law, which are known as *Corpus Juris Civilis* [Body of Civil Law], were commissioned in the sixth century by the emperor Justinian to Byzantine jurists. They especially drew on previous works by second- and third-century jurists Gaius, Paulus, Ulpian, Modestinus and Papinianus. The quotation is from one of these compilations, the *Institutiones* [Institutes] (hereinafter *Instit.*), I.2.

56 See Tony Honoré, *Ulpian: Pioneer of Human Rights* (Oxford: Oxford University Press, 2002).

tium could be construed as a later encroachment (*invasio*).[57] Slavery is a clear example of an institution recognized by the *ius gentium*, though being contrary to nature:

> *Et libertas quidem* [...] *est naturalis facultas ejus, quod cuique facere libet, nisi si quid vi aut jure prohibetur. Servitus autem est constitutio juris gentium qua quis dominio alieno contra naturam subjicitur* [Freedom [...] is a man's natural power of doing what he pleases, so far as he is not prevented by force or law. Slavery is an institution of the law of nations, against nature subjecting one man to the dominion of another].[58]

The appeal to natural law allowed Ulpian and likeminded jurists to give legal expression to the claim of slaves, whose legitimacy would have been otherwise denied according to both civil law and the law of nations.[59] Moreover, animals were, according to Ulpian, endowed with a certain degree of acquired ability (*peritia*), which also determined the eventual liability of the owner for his animal's behaviour.[60]

Despite the eleventh-century recovery of the Justinian Code, the theological understanding of natural law as expressed by Aquinas only included animals by means of similitude.[61] Hence, La Boétie's use of animal behaviour as an example to be followed by humans could only be related to classical sources. It is not surprising that the praise of animals as compared to humans is also to be found in a work by Plutarch, namely the short dialogue *That brute beasts make use of reason*, or *Gryllus*. The main character of the dialogue, a former man who has been magically turned into a hog,[62] vehemently argues for the animals' superior love of liberty: "nor will the lion be a slave [δουλεύει, *douléuei*] to the lion, nor the horse to the horse, as one man is a slave to another, willingly and patiently embracing slavery, which derives its name from that of cowardice [δειλίας, *deilías*]."[63]

---

57 "Utpote cum jure naturali omnes liberi nascerentur [...] sed postquam jure gentium servitus invasit" [for by natural law all men were born free [...] but afterwards slavery encroached on by the law of nations], in *Instit.* I.5.

58 *Instit.* I.3.

59 See Honoré, *Ulpian*, 86 on.

60 The quotation is from another Justinian compilation, the *Digestum* [Digest], at 9.1.1.7.

61 Aquinas, *Summa Theologiae*, I-II.91.2.3. Just few years after La Boétie's death, the last great schoolman Suarez was to exclude even this analogical participation.

62 The name of the main character, Γρύλλος (*Grýllos*), that is grunter, is a variant of the noun γρῦλος (*grŷlos*) which is in turn an onomatopoetic representation of the sound produced by the pig.

63 Plutarch, *Moralia* 532e.

In general, La Boétie seems to have metabolized a series of references from classical philosophical, literary and legal texts to the well-defined condition of slavery, which he transformed within his text into the generic notion of servitude. This shift allowed him not only to conflate past and present but also, and more important, to open the way for an extension of his considerations on tyranny to every kind of domination.

This extension springs precisely from La Boétie's description of servitude as a series of practices in which one's body is put at the service of someone else. "You do not refuse to offer your own bodies unto death,"[64] recalls La Boétie to the subjects turned soldiers. And when the same despot turns against his own subjects, La Boétie continues, "how can he have so many arms to beat you with, if he does not borrow them from you?"[65] And also "the feet that trample down your cities, where does he get them if they are not your own?"[66]

Even during times of peace, La Boétie relentlessly insists, "you yield your bodies unto hard labor in order that he may indulge in his delights and wallow in his filthy pleasures."[67] In the topsy-turvy world of servitude, La Boétie asks, is there anything worse than the life of a tyrant's courtier, "who has nothing to call one's own, receiving from someone else one's sustenance, one's power to act, one's body, one's very life?"[68]

And yet, it is precisely one's body that can act as a general term of comparison, as embodiment is a condition shared by the tyrant, by one's fellow humans and by animals. It is because the tyrant has only one body that he needs to appropriate the bodies of the others in order to exercise his power. And this is why, inasmuch as anyone has power upon her own body, "all that is required to have liberty is the desire for it."[69]

Moreover, though the body is the *locus* of an uneven distribution of natural capacities, La Boétie is convinced that nature "has not put in the world the stronger or the cleverer so that that they may act like armed brigands in a forest and attack the weaker."[70] On the contrary, the body is the witness of human likeness.

---

64 "vous ne refuses point de presenter a la mort vos personnes" (SV, 39).
65 "comment a il tant de mains pour vous fraper, s'il ne les prend de vous?" (SV, 40).
66 "Les pieds dont il foule vos cités, d'ou les a il s'ils ne sont des vostres?" (SV, 40).
67 "vous rompes a la peine vos personnes, afin qu'il se puisse mignarder en ses delices et se veautrer dans les sales et vilains plaisirs" (SV, 40).
68 "qu'on n'aie a soy tenant dautrui son aise, sa liberté, son corps et sa vie ?" (SV, 70).
69 "pour avoir liberté il ne faut que la desirer" (SV, 38).
70 "n'a pas envoié icy bas les plus forts ny les plus avisez comme les brigans armez dans une forest pour y gourmander les plus foibles" (SV, 41).

The body is also a common element to humans and animals. And as previously recalled, the animals' clinging to freedom is expressed by their use of claws, horns, beak, paws and any other bodily part as weapons to defend this very freedom. Hence, there could not be a clearer expression of the equally natural clinging to freedom than a similar human use of the body, as claimed in the address of the two Spartan voluntary hostages to Xerxes' lieutenant Hydarnes: "if you had any knowledge of it [liberty], you yourself would advise us to defend it, not with lance and shield, but with our very teeth and nails."[71]

Whilst, for La Boétie, nature can inspire the rejection of voluntary servitude, according to Calvin this very nature produces, since the Fall, the condition of voluntary servitude to sin. This production is indeed continuous, "for our nature is not only utterly devoid of goodness, but so prolific in all kinds of evil, that it can never be idle."[72] Moreover, Calvin's condemnation does not only target the body, since he maintains that everything humans receive from nature is flesh, so that "the whole man (sic) is in himself nothing else than concupiscence."[73] The only escape from the voluntary servitude to the flesh is the result of the external intervention of divine grace.

La Boétie champions instead the rejection of voluntary servitude as a mere act of will. However, he is aware that his disclosure of the mechanisms of power could not suffice to motivate his readers. Though the simple practice of refusing to renew one's obedience has always been within anyone's reach, it was not put in place very often in the course of history.

In other words, even if La Boétie is persuaded that the aspiration to freedom is a natural human endowment, he cannot dismiss the evidence of the practice of human servitude:

> Let us therefore admit that all those things to which he is trained and accustomed seem natural to man and that only that is truly native to him which he receives with his primitive, untrained individuality. Thus custom becomes the first reason for voluntary servitude.[74]

As a result, La Boétie can summarize his explanation of the general forgetting of freedom in just one line, which predates (with a twist) the famous opening of

---

71 "si tu en avois tasté, toymesme nous conseillerois de la deffendre, non pas avec la lance et l'escu, mais avec les dens et les ongles" (SV, 49).

72 "Non enim natura nostra bonitatum inops & vacua est: sed malorum omnium adeo fertilis & ferax, ut otiosa esse non possit," in Calvin, *Inst.* II.1.8.

73 "totum hominem non aliud ex seipso esse quam concupiscentiam," in Calvin, *Inst.* II.1.8.

74 "Disons donc ainsi, qu'a l'homme toutes choses lui sont comme naturelles, a quoy il se nourrit et accoustume; mais cela seulement lui est naïf, a quoi sa nature simple et non altérée l'appelle; ainsi la premiere raison de la servitude volontaire c'est la coustume" (SV, 51).

Rousseau's *Du Contrat Social*:[75] "the essential reason why men take orders willingly is that they are born and raised as serfs."[76]

La Boétie has neither a static understanding of human beings nor of their relations. Nevertheless, when he compares humans to plants, whilst he shows by analogy the plasticity of all living beings, and their high sensitivity to the conditions in which they are raised, he also underlines in a quasi-Aristotelian fashion the fragility of their natural potential:

> The good seed that nature plants in us is so slight and so slippery that it cannot withstand the least harm from wrong nourishment; it flourishes less easily, becomes spoiled, withers, and comes to nothing. Fruit trees retain their own particular quality if permitted to grow undisturbed, but lose it promptly and bear strange fruit not their own when grafted.[77]

La Boétie has recourse to the powerful metaphor of grafting only to underscore the somewhat alien nature of the products of this operation, and he does not consider it as an opening of new perspectives. In truly classical style, for La Boétie the conquest of freedom is less an invention than a recovery of a lost condition.

However, in his remarkable appeal to cease to obey there is an even more subversive indication than the explicit refusal of authority in the name of nature. As previously recalled, La Boétie shifts the seat of power from the powerful to the seemingly powerless. This radical (at that moment) shift of the source of political authority – or, in modern parlance, sovereignty – was clearly an effect of his classical reading.

Such classical reading supported La Boétie's bold decision to plainly disregard the notion of the divine derivation of sovereignty, which in his time was used to justify political power. This Judaeo-Christian notion ended up setting its mark also upon the classical world, but only at a later stage. For example,

---

75 "L'homme est né libre, et partout il est dans les fers" [man (sic) was born free, and he is everywhere in chain], in Jean-Jacques Rousseau [1762], *Du Contrat Social ou Principes du Droit Politique*, 1.1.

76 "la premiere raison pourquoy les hommes servent volontiers, est pource qu'ils naissent serfs et sont nourris tels" (SV, 54–55).

77 "Les semences de bien que la nature met en nous sont si frêles et si minces, qu'elles ne peuvent résister au moindre choc des passions ni à l'influence d'une éducation qui les contrarie. Elles ne se conservent pas mieux, s'abâtardissent aussi facilement et même dégénèrent; comme il arrive à ces arbres fruitiers qui ayant tous leur propre, la conservent tant qu'on les laisse venir naturellement; mais la perdent, pour porter des fruits tout à fait différents, dès qu'on les a greffés" (SV, 47).

still in 70 C.E., the emperor Vespasian had his jurists invent a fictional transfer of power from the Roman citizens, in order to legally justify his authority.[78]

The courageous recovery of pre-Christian modes of political subjectivation[79] by La Boétie (and Machiavelli, as previously recalled) may be compared to an autologous blood transfusion in the body of Western political texts. Moreover, La Boétie's outstanding intellectual contributions are not limited to political thought, as he raises a theoretical challenge that may be generalised beyond the political sphere.

Of course, La Boétie astonishing feat is the reclamation of long forgotten theoretical tools and their application within the horizon defined by political theology. And the fact that the *Voluntary Servitude* did not lose its disruptive force, even down to modern times, is a confirmation that "all significant concepts of the modern theory of the state are secularized theological concepts,"[80] as Schmitt would argue.

However, La Boétie has not only provided us with a non-theological construction of political power. His invitation to stop obeying also constructed power as the effect of a practice of gift-giving that makes the donors subjects. This very act of giving must be repeated in order to continue to be effective, because the gift is not an abstract entity (such as the modern concept of sovereignty, which is a recasting of a theological concept), but the offer of the body as a body-for-another.[81]

Of course, La Boétie does not forget the metonymic substitution of the body for the products of bodily activities:

> You sow your crops in order that he may ravage them, you install and furnish your homes to give him goods to pillage; you rear your daughters that he may gratify his lust; you bring up your children in order that he may confer upon them the greatest privilege he knows – to be

---

78 *Lex de Imperio Vespasiani*, in Johnson, Coleman-Norton & Bourne, *Ancient Roman Statutes* (Austin: University of Texas Press, 1961), 149.

79 This anachronistic definition clashes with the Hegelian dogma of the modern invention of subjective freedom, which rationalizes the Lutheran subordination of all social relations to the dyadic rapport between the individual and god.

80 Carl Schmitt, *Political Theology: Four Chapters on the Concept of Sovereignty*, trans. George Schwab (Cambridge, Mass.: MIT Press, 1985), 36.

81 La Boétie's insight could be easily extended to the relations in the economic sphere. For example, Pateman underlines the fiction behind the selling of labour or labour-force on the labour market: that which is actually sold is the whole person, as a part-time slave. We may add that the legal arena is nowadays endowed with the legitimation to set the limits for the use of the body of the part-time slave, just like at the time of Ulpian with the full-time slave. See Carol Pateman, *The Sexual Contract* (Stanford: Stanford University Press, 1988).

led into his battles, to be delivered to butchery, to be made the servants of his greed and the instruments of his vengeance.[82]

The reiterated offer of bodies and products of bodily practices is the habit that produces the identities of subjects as subjects. Hence, "it is not a human being that is 'pursuing' servitude, but human beings in specific patterns."[83] Whilst the repetition of these behavioural patterns continues to produce a definite power, its interruption would provoke the sudden disappearance, so to speak, of that power. In other words, La Boétie does not conceive of servitude and domination as enduring entities or permanent conditions, but as relations that have to be constantly reconfirmed, because they are the effect of iterated practices.

On the contrary, Christian thinkers considered the notions of *potentia* and *potestas* – which are both translated into English as power – firstly as divine attributions. In the transference to earthly authorities, the concept of *potestas* maintained its transcendental link, and in the case of the Pope, also the *plenitudo*, or fullness of power of the original holder.[84]

Within this theoretical framework, it was not the continuity of power that had to be explained, but rather its interruption. As previously recalled, in the narrative of medieval canonists the deviation of power from its natural course was attributed to custom.

Another support for the notion of the continuity of power came from an unlikely source, namely the supposed tendency to self-preservation of living beings. Whilst this notion was somewhat prefigured by Aristotle,[85] it was motivated

82 "Vous demés vos fruicts, afin qu'il en face le degast; vous meublés et remplissés vos maisons, afin de fournir a ses pilleries; vous nourrissés vos filles afin qu'il ait dequoy saouler sa luxure; vous nourrissez vos enfans, afin que pour le mieulx qu'il sçauroit faire, il les mene en ses guerres, qu'il les conduise a la boucherie, qu'il les face les ministres de ses convoitises, et les executeurs de ses vengeances" (SV, 40).

83 Miguel Abensour, "Is there a proper way to use the voluntary servitude hypothesis?," *Journal of Political Ideologies* 16.3 (2011): 329–348, 337.

84 Though the phrase *plenitudo potestatis* is first documented at the time of Pope Leo I (440–461), only with Pope Innocent III (1198–1216) it became a theologico-political claim. In the sixteenth century, theorists such as Jean Bodin and Alberico Gentili defined sovereign power (*maiestas*) in terms of a "*summa* [...] *legibusque soluta potestas*" [highest [...] power and not subject to any law] or "*plenitudo potestatis vel potestas extraordinaria*" [fullness of power or extraordinary authority] respectively. In Jean Bodin, *De Republica Libri Sex* (Parisiis: Apud Iacobum Du-Puys sub signo Samaritanae, 1586), 78; Alberico Gentili, "De Potestate Regis Absoluta," in *Regales Disputationes Tres: I, De potestate regis absoluta; II, De unione Regnorum Britanniae; III, De vi Civium in regem semper iniusta* (Londini: Apud Thomam Vautrollerium, 1605), 10.

85 *De Anima*, 416b 16–17.

by the Stoic notion of οἰκείωσις (*oikeíōsis*), which may be translated as 'appropriation,' 'familiarisation,' or 'endearment.'

According to Diogenes Laërtius "[the Stoics] say that an animal has the primary tendency [ὁρμή, *hormḗ*] to preserve itself, because nature from the outset endears [*oikeioúsēs*] it to itself."[86] Cicero translated *hormḗ* into Latin as *appetitus* and *appetitio*, appetite or desire.[87] Aquinas then transformed it into a general tendency, which does not necessarily involve consciousness and which he attributed to every substance.[88]

Generally speaking, in Thomist metaphysics, change is either produced as a change of one substance into another substance, or as a modification of an already existing substance. In any case, change requires an external cause. The continuity of a substance hence precedes change or, in broader philosophical terms, being is prior to becoming.[89]

On the contrary, according to La Boétie, the power of a ruler owes its continuity to the repetition of the practices of submission of his subjects. Such a non-substantial conception of power represents an alternative not only to the constructions of the substantial continuity of political power, but also to the more general logic of identity on which it is predicated.

The extent of La Boétie's theoretical challenge was not fully appreciated by his contemporaries, who mostly put to work his argumentative sharpness as a partisan tool: nor could it be grasped by the devisers of modernities, who took the conceptual straitjacket of the Schoolmen to the extreme of championing a purely factual scientific machinery. A paradigm that could accommodate La Bo-

---

86 "Τὴν δὲ πρώτην ὁρμήν φασι τὸ ζῷον ἴσχειν ἐπὶ τὸ τηρεῖν ἑαυτό, οἰκειούσης αὐτῷ τῆς φύσεως ἀπ' ἀρχῆς" (Tḕn dè prṓtēn hormḗn phasi tò zṓon ískhein epì tò tēréin heautó, oikeioúsēs hautṓ tḗs phýseōs ap'arkhḗs), Diogenes Laertius on Chrysippus, in *Vitae Philosophorum* VII.85.

87 "Omne animal se ipsum diligit ac, simul et ortum est, id agit, se ut conservet, quod hic ei primus ad omnem vitam tuendam appetitus a natura datur, se ut conservet atque ita sit affectum" [Every living creature loves itself, and from the moment of birth strives to secure its own preservation, because the earliest impulse bestowed on it by nature for its life-long protection is the instinct for self-preservation and for the maintenance of itself in the best condition possible to it in accordance with its nature], in Cicero, *De Finibus* 5.24. Cicero renders *hormē* as *appetitio* in *De Officiis* 2.5.

88 "quaelibet substantia appetit conservationem sui esse secundum suam naturam" [any substance desires the conservation of its own being according to its nature], in Aquinas, *Summa Theologiae* I–II.94.2.

89 The metaphysical priority of continuity over change was to survive the invention of modernities, and it was even to become the cornerstone of the new sciences in the shape of the physical principle of inertia.

étie's understanding of practices only began to emerge from Nietzsche's indictment of the logic of being and identity.

However, only during the long sixties such a slowly emerging paradigm was brought closer to the political concerns of La Boétie by Foucault. The present work may be considered as a contribution to the construction of this practices-centred paradigm, whose perspective in turn oriented the inevitably projective reading of La Boétie's work proposed here.

Whilst this perspective endowed the present reading with undoubtedly anachronistic accents and expectations,[90] it may hopefully also help to convey La Boétie's still radical message. Instead of recasting the metaphysical gesture as the revolutionary rupture that brings change from the outside, we may well consider following La Boétie's invitation to defuse the dynamic of power from the inside, by ceasing the offering of our bodies.

90 Nietzsche's perspectival view opened the way to the reconsideration of anachronism. For example, Clio, the muse of history, claims on behalf of Péguy that past occurrences repeat subsequent ones. Clio repeats in advance Borges' rephrasing of Eliot: a writer creates her own predecessors. For a generalised application of anachronistic repetition, see Riccardo Baldissone, "The Multiplicity of Nothingness: A Contribution to a Non-Reductionist Reading of Stirner," in *Max Stirner*, ed. Saul Newman (London: Palgrave Macmillan, 2011). On the Nietzschean constellation of authors with a perspectival understanding of the past, see Riccardo Baldissone and Marc De Wilde, "Modifying the Past: Nietzschean Approaches to History," *Pólemos*, 7.2 (2013), 175–205.

III Liminal Bodies: The Life/Death Edge on Stage and in the Body Politic

Daniela Carpi

The Funeral Oration over Caesar's Body: Techniques of Mass Communication

I come to bury Caesar, not to praise him
(W. Shakespeare, *Julius Caesar*, 3.2.75)

Shakespeare's tragedy *Julius Caesar* is focused entirely on the concept of power, on the problem of legality/legitimacy, and on the threat of tyranny. The theme of rejection and rebellion against established power is interwoven with the problem of sedition and consent: the Roman mob is directly involved in the approval of the action of the conspirators, since it is illegitimate power that demands the consent of the subjects. The theme of the possibility of a republican form of government,[1] extremely forward looking in Shakespeare's time, is connected with a very contemporary theme, namely the manipulation of the masses, as it appears in the astute funeral orations before Caesar's body delivered both by Brutus and by Antony. A close reading of these orations from the standpoint of mass communication opens new interpretative insights which permit us to recognize the extraordinary modernity of Shakespeare's text.

Paradoxically, the tragedy's true protagonist is not Caesar, but Brutus: Caesar appears mostly as the "guest of stone" and as the "sacred corpse." However, as Horst Zander observes, even if Brutus affirms that he wants to kill Caesar's spirit and not his body,

> Brutus merely kills the man, whereas the spirit of Caesar ironically derives more power than ever before from this very murder. The disembodied Caesar is mightier than the living one; in fact, even his corpse – to which Antony gives a voice – is more eloquent than the living Caesar ever was.[2]

In Antony's case as well, his presence is concentrated in the third act at the very heart of the tragedy, only to disappear, giving way to Octavius in the last two acts. But how is the surprising power of Antony's speech to be explained, a power that leads the reader to consider him as a central character in the play? The answer to this question must be sought in the profound logic out of

1 See Daniela Carpi, "Law and Sedition in *Julius Caesar*," in *Shakespeare and the Law*, ed. Daniela Carpi (Ravenna: Longo, 2003): 103–115.

2 Horst Zander, "Julius Caesar and the Critical Legacy," in *Julius Caesar: New Critical Essays*, ed. Horst Zander (London: Routledge, 2005): 3–56, 6.

which the tragedy grows. Such logic establishes the close connection between Shakespeare's interest in Roman history as understood by his Elizabethan audience and his interest in the dynamics through which power is enabled to legitimize itself. The iconology of power is in itself a manifestation of power. Mark Antony's verse speech succeeds in demonstrating the illegitimacy of "tyrannicide" by using clever manipulative techniques that address a plurality of voices – verbal utterance and body language – which serve as the foundation of the whole tragedy.

> The liminal position of the theatre, which it shared with other forms of festivity, far from simply ventriloquizing the discourses of political domination, engaged in forms of representation through which other, potentially subversive voices could be heard.[3]

In order to analyze the words and gestures used by Antony in his oration as a means of manipulating the crowd, it is necessary to begin with a general analysis of terms such as "communication," "masses," "power" and by giving special attention to that type of communication that binds the masses to an individual invested with authority. As Zander observes, "In this drama language is designed to make things happen, to influence, to persuade, to seduce and to manipulate others."[4]

1 Communication

Scholars who conduct research in the field of the sciences of communication encounter the problem of having "to circumscribe" and "to concentrate upon" one object of study – communication – which expands into multiple levels of meaning, but is also constantly changing.[5]

To begin with a semantic-etymological analysis, the verb "to communicate" comes from the Latin *communicare*, derived from *communis*, and pertains directly to verbal exchange between persons.[6] The Latin root contains in itself the idea of sharing, as well as the idea of a community constituted by a number of indi-

3 See John Drakakis, "'Fashion it thus'; *Julius Caesar* and the Politics of Theatrical Representation," in *Materialist Shakespeare: a History*, ed. Ivo Kamps (London, New York: Verso: 1995): 280–291, 282.
4 Zander, "Julius Caesar and the Critical legacy," 9.
5 See Terence P. Moran, *Introduction to the History of Communication: Evolutions and Revolutions* (New York: Peter Lang, 2010).
6 Kal Erik Rosengren, *Communication: An Introduction* (London: Sage, 2000), 1.

viduals; consequently, this implies the concept of mutual relationship, of exchanging and spreading knowledge through language. It is obvious that "to communicate" means to make information available, to share, to participate, to be in relationship with, to debate together: the recurring assumption is always the relationship with others, sharing life experiences as well as material and cultural objects.[7]

If the term is examined from a philosophical standpoint, communication is a "synonym of coexistence or of life with others"; therefore "communication" indicates the totality of the specific ways in which we may express ourselves, provided that such communication deals with human acts, namely, those in which a certain possibility of participation and understanding can be safeguarded.[8]

The third aspect of communication involves the sociological sphere. According to Harold Lasswell, the study of communication is concerned with the speaker of the message, to whom the message is addressed, what is transmitted, and with what results.[9] Therefore the act of communication has as its center a subject understood as a social actor belonging to a particular system. This human subject interacts with an audience in order to transmit a message which is perceived by other subjects who are not mere passive recipients of the communication: they perform an active role in converting the received message into meaning.

Considering the diverse aspects of the term, human communication can be defined as an intersubjective interaction endowed with reciprocal deliberateness and with a certain degree of awareness that makes specific meaning possible through a shared system of signs. The symbolic and conventional systems of meaning and signs are shaped by culture which also plays a fundamental role in the characterization of human language. [10]

It is evident that communication operates at different levels and with a remarkable degree of complexity. In particular, speech plays a central role in the exercise of power, since it is the principal means through which power manifests itself and is secured. In particular, public oratory is a crucial part of the process of securing political consensus. Indeed, the process allows us to glimpse the rhetorical means by which political discourse exerts its linguistic power over an audience. As Van Dijk observes: "Politicians can [...] exercise their political

7 See Rosengren, *Communication*, 12.

8 Nicola Abbagnano, *Dizionario di filosofia* (Torino: Utet, 1971), 143.

9 See Harold Lasswell, *Power and Personality* [1948] (New Brunswick, New Jersey: Transaction Publishers, 2009).

10 See Rosengren, *Communication*, 31.

power through public discourse and through such public discourse they confirm and reproduce, at the same time, their political power.[11]

2 The Concept of the Masses

The primary meaning of mass certainly defines "a fundamentally unlimited plurality, a complex of unities forming a homogeneous whole which, precisely because of its own homogeneity, cannot be subdivided into single components."[12] Communication addressed to the masses needs special attention, since it implies the masses on the one side and, on the other, an agency invested with particular authority. In this instance the fundamental characteristic of the masses is their malleability; the importance of the particular authority of the communicator is equal to the message to be communicated. In order to reach a successful mass communication, the subject in authority must have competence (or expertise) and credibility (or believability). Both these elements depend on a series of assumptions on the part of the addressee; indeed, such assumptions are present even before the communication occurs and are essential aspects of the predisposition of the recipient toward the speaker: for example his/her sex, social status, age, cultural affiliations etc.

In relation to the first element, competence, expressive or contextual factors come into play and they may influence the impression formed by the addressee of the speaker's expertise in matters such as: non-verbal aspects of communication, the way in which the speaker is introduced to other persons and the citation of authoritative persons. In relation to the second element, 'believability', in order to appear credible a speaker must show (or simulate) human warmth, conviction, sincerity, and intelligence.[13]

---

11 Teun A.Van Dijk, "Discourse and Manipulation," *Discourse & Society*, 17.2 (2006): 359–383, 362.

12 Egeria Di Nallo, *Per una teoria della comunicazione di massa* (Milano: Franco Angeli, 1977), 35.

13 Paolo Mancini and Rolando Marini, *Le comunicazioni di massa* (Roma: Carocci, 2006), 79–80.

3 Manipulation

The term "manipulation" is understood as

> a communicative and interactional practice in which a manipulator exercises control over other people, usually against their will or against their best interests. [...] manipulation not only involves power, but specifically abuse of power, that is domination. That is, manipulation implies the exercise of a form of illegitimate influence by means of discourse: manipulators make others believe or do things that are in the interest of the manipulator, and against the best interests of the manipulated.[14]

Manipulation implies an abuse of power obtained through the exercise of a form of illegitimate influence which takes advantage of the lack of awareness of those who are being manipulated. Consequently this term takes on a negative connotation in as much as it points to all attempts used to induce a person to do something that he/she has not willed, while having them believe that they are acting in the full freedom of their own choice. It is precisely in this manner that manipulation differs negatively from persuasion:

> in persuasion the interlocutors are free to believe or act as they please, depending on whether or not they accept the arguments of the persuader, whereas in manipulation recipients are typically assigned a more passive role: they are victims of manipulation. This negative consequence of manipulative discourse typically occurs when the recipients are unable to understand the real intentions or to see the full consequences of the beliefs or actions advocated by the manipulator.[15]

4 The Oration of Brutus

In *Julius Caesar* after the murder of Caesar has taken place, the conspirators are concerned about the reaction of the crowd, should they present themselves as the new rulers. Thus, they attempt to orchestrate their first public appearance and Brutus decides to permit Mark Antony, Caesar's friend, to speak at Caesar's funeral but only after he, Brutus, has provided a context for the judgment of the masses. From a stylistic viewpoint, it is worth noting that Mark Antony's speech is in verse, whereas Brutus' is in prose; Brutus's speech is rhetorically constructed to appear rational, but it is lacking in the affective power of Antony's poetic oration. Indeed, throughout the play Brutus's "reason" is shown to be deficient

---

14 Van Dijk, "Discourse and manipulation," 360.
15 Van Dijk, "Discourse and manipulation," 361.

in that he, himself, can be manipulated by Cassius and others to come to conclusions that are 'unreasonable'

From a linguistic point of view, Brutus introduces a form of address which Antony will paraphrase and re-order later: "Romans, countrymen and lovers" (3.2.13).[16] The apostrophe is used to establish a precise social order which corresponds to a personal hierarchy of values. By placing "Romans" first, Brutus underscores that being Roman is an indispensable feature of a shared identity. But the Romans he addresses are also "countrymen," namely co-citizens, who are bound by civic sentiment to their own city. Lastly, they are "lovers," friends who share an affective bond particularly at times of social and political change. In essence, the concepts articulated in Brutus' speech are four: honour, love, freedom and ambition. His primary intent is to present the conspirators as honourable men and therefore worthy of respect and trust: "Believe me for mine honour and have respect to mine honour, that you may believe" (3.2.14–15).

The second forceful element of his argument is love. It is not only the love that he himself feels towards Caesar ("If there be any in this assembly, any dear friend of Caesar's, to him I say that Brutus' love to Caesar was no less than his"), but also, and above all, the love he bears to Rome and its citizens. What returns here is the theme of "countrymen," a category deliberately placed second in order of priority in his speech, as well as in the initial apostrophe. This allows Brutus to link the conspirators' actions with the concept of 'freedom':

> Had you rather Caesar were living, and die all slaves, than
> that Caesar were dead, to live all free men? (3.2.22–23)

By posing this rhetorical question Brutus connects the issue of love to liberty: it is for the sake of the Roman people and for their freedom that he has decided to kill Caesar, and not for his own personal interest. Caesar was, he claims, guilty of ambition, in that he was willing to see Rome transformed into a monarchy.

By emphasizing these four concepts Brutus obtains the initial consensus of the crowd which appears ready to acknowledge the need for the assassination, although by proclaiming Brutus as 'king,' they show that they have not fully understood the political implications of Brutus's rhetorical question. Obviously the conspirators seem, at this point, to have reached their goal: the consensus of the masses and the transformation of a revolutionary government into a legitimate one, albeit that they have no clear conception of what that change involves.

16 William Shakespeare, *Julius Caesar*, ed. John Dover Wilson (Cambridge: Cambridge University Press, 1971). All references in the text will be taken from this edition.

However, Brutus is aware of the volatility of the crowd and that it can be easily manipulated. He is also aware (because of the numerous warnings of the more politically sceptical Cassius) that Antony, although apparently favourably disposed to the conspirators, could reverse the situation if he is left free to speak. Therefore Brutus agrees to allow Antony to speak, but not before he has provided a full context that takes the form of seeking the permission of the crowd as party to his strategy.

> Good countrymen, let me depart alone,
> And for my sake, stay here with Antony.
> Do grace to Caesar's corpse, and grace his speech
> Tending to Caesar's glories, which Mark Antony,
> By our permission, is allowed to make. (3.2.58–63)

The clause "let me depart alone" cedes temporary power to his audience, while the phrase "our permission" enlists the support of the audience in the decision to allow Antony to speak. Before departing Brutus informs the people that Antony will have some advantage from Caesar's death, namely "a place in the commonwealth," thus implying that Antony himself has a share in the benefits derived from Caesar's death. The fact that Brutus emphasizes that Antony can speak only with the conspirators' (and by implication, with the crowd's) permission establishes a hierarchical order, thus strengthening and reaffirming that power of the word that the audience has just conferred upon him.

These considerations are fundamental to the analysis of Antony's speech: they help us to understand the subtle and dangerous context into which Antony comes, as well as the conceptual and linguistic choices he must make as he delivers his funeral oration.

5 Antony's Oration

> Friends, Romans, countrymen, lend me your ears
> I come to bury Caesar, not to praise him
> (3.2.76–78)

Antony's exordium is direct in that it addresses the audience immediately and as equals, without any need for introduction or periphrasis. His entry upon the stage is not dramatic, but it does build on the situation and the atmosphere set up by Brutus: his opening recalls Brutus' words, but in a different order, thus underscoring an alternative hierarchy of values. His initial 'Friends' immediately establishes a common bond with the crowd that is affective rather than rational, emotional rather than analytical. Antony goes on to claim that he has no desire to contradict Brutus, and that he comes to 'bury' Caesar and not to 'praise him'. This clarification, that appears to be connected with Brutus' words, however, insinuates an antiphrastic suspicion by its redundancy. Perhaps someone (not Brutus, not Antony) may consider Caesar as a man worthy of praise. When a concept is expressed, even with a negative valence, it takes on weight: "not to praise him" in a covert way actually implies praise, and as the speech develops, Antony begins to undermine the conspirators' claim of Caesar's perfidy and thereby to demolish Brutus' credibility. However, at this early point the crowd has yet to respond to his subtle provocation.

> The evil that men do lives after them,
> The good is oft interred with their bones –
> So let it be with Caesar. (3.2.78–80)

Antony's remark is proverbial, and it seeks a direct agreement from his audience. At the same time an emotional component begins to emerge: the theme of injustice arouses emotional reactions in the orator and his audience. Truly, it is unfair that only the evil done should survive the man and be remembered, whereas the good that he has accomplished is buried with his body. Mark Antony states that the same will happen to Caesar; but the question arises of whether the neutral pronoun "it" refers to the evil that will be remembered or to the good that will be forgotten. Furthermore, what good was Caesar supposed to have accomplished since Brutus' description is so negative? Even the fact of speaking about injustice raises suspicion: what kind of injustice is here in question if the murder was executed for the good of the Roman people and thus for a just cause? Antony undermines Brutus' oration by setting one word against the other: one meaning clashes against the other and is subverted.

Rhetoric was ubiquitous in the English Renaissance with the consequence that *ars poetica* and *ars rhetorica* cannot be distinguished during the period. Brian Vickers notes that "the period roughly between Sidney and George Herbert sees the flowering of rhetoric in English literature."[17] By extension, as Gary Wills observes, "Oratory in *Julius Caesar* has serious political import – it can make or unmake the state. The *suasoria*, an exercise in persuasive declamation, drives the

17 Brian Vickers, *Classical Rhetoric in English Poetry* (Carbondale: Southern Illinois University Press, 1970), 44.

action"[18] and such oratorical skill is clearly visible in both Brutus' and Antony's funeral orations.

In this passage in particular Antony balances evil with good and combines two rhetorical devices: personification, attribution of personality to an impersonal thing, and tautology which is the repetition of an idea in a different word, phrase, or sentence. He is essentially repeating the same sentiments although he uses different words to do so:

> The noble Brutus
> Hath told you that Caesar was ambitious:
> If it were so, it was a grievous fault,
> And grievously hath Caesar answered it. (3.2.78–79)

In this original statement of grievance, Antony uses a *syllepsis,* but also present is the device of *chiasm*, which contribute to increasing the effects upon the crowd of Antony's artful contrivances. His intention of criticizing the conspirators gradually emerges through the euphuistic artificiality of his language.

For the first time Antony names Brutus and he re-iterates the claim that he and the conspirators are 'noble'. In an astute rhetorical manoeuvre Antony then proceeds to link Brutus' nobility with Caesar's ambition thus inaugurating a strategy designed to undermine Brutus' integrity by the conditional "if it were so," a hypothetical phrase that casts a doubt on what Brutus has affirmed, without, however, diminishing the gravity of the accusation levelled against Caesar. From a rhetorical standpoint, the last sentence in the above quotation contains a *polyptoton:* the word "grievous" is repeated twice in quick succession, but on the second occasion with a different syntactical function.

> Here under leave of Brutus and the rest –
> For Brutus is an honourable man,
> So they are all, all honourable men –
> Come I to speak in Caesar's funeral. (3.2.82–85)

The most common rhetorical device used by Antony is irony. This is an expression of something which is contrary to the intended meaning; the words say one thing but mean another. Shakespeare uses this line as an *antistrophe* throughout the speech, a repetition of the same word or phrase at the end of successive

---

18 Garry Wills, *Rome and Rhetoric: Shakespeare's Julius Caesar* (New Haven and London: Yale University Press, 2011), 34.

clauses or stanzas. Antony's strategy is not to refute openly what Brutus stated, but to begin to instill doubts among his audience.

If earlier Antony has insinuated suspicions about Brutus' claims, he now confirms that he is speaking with the permission of the conspirators, almost as if he wants to excuse his own insinuations. However, he makes one digression that almost has the tone of an aside: throughout his speech he repeats with hammering insistence the word "honourable," until it is, by an incremental irony, reduced to the level of an empty slogan, deprived of all meaning. The main attribute of the conspirators, their 'honour' is thereby gradually eroded and nullified.

> He was my friend, faithful and just to me;
> But Brutus says he was ambitious,
> And Brutus is an honourable man. (3.2.86–88)

Only then does Antony proceed to offer his own personal experience of Caesar. For him, the so-called tyrant was above all a loyal and just friend, and it should not be forgotten that friendship was the first element Antony mentioned at the beginning of his oration, reversing the order of the categories at the beginning of Brutus' eulogy. He does not make categorical statements, rather, he claims to be offering a perspective that will withstand immediate comparison with that of Brutus; but the repetition of the refrain "Brutus is an honourable man," turns gradually into a mocking accusation of dishonour. As Francesco Muzzioli observes, "[t]he repetition of the appreciation in the style of a refrain is sufficient to make it sound empty (would he repeat it so many times if he were convinced?) and to underscore its irony."[19]

At this point Antony embarks on his own celebration of Caesar:

> He hath brought many captives home to Rome
> Whose ransoms did the general coffers fill.
> Did this in Caesar seem ambitious?
> When that the poor have cried, Caesar hath wept:
> Ambition should be made of sterner stuff;
> Yet Brutus says he was ambitious,
> And Brutus is an honourable man.
> You all did see that on the Lupercal
> I thrice presented him a kingly crown,
> Which he did thrice refuse. Was this ambition? (3.2.89–99)

19 Francesco Muzzioli, *Le strategie del testo. Introduzione all'analisi retorica della letteratura* (Roma: Meltemi editore, 2004), 15 (my translation).

This is not a matter of personal perspective, the opinion of a single individual, but a statement of irrefutable fact, of public knowledge, used to demonstrate the error of judgment into which the crowd has been persuaded by Brutus to fall. This is an effective and convincing strategy, since Brutus had refrained from deploying concrete evidence, relying instead on a narrative of certain posturings on Caesar's part and suspicions about his possible future actions if he were not constrained, but that were not clearly evident at the time.

Antony's strategy is based upon three points and he chooses arguments of strong emotional impact precisely because he knows that his audience already knows them. The first "fact" concerns economics: Caesar filled the state's coffers by generating income from the ransom of prisoners. How can a man who provides for the needs of the populace be considered ambitious? The second "fact" deals with Caesar's compassion for the poor: ambition is incompatible with such philanthropic sentiments. Once more Antony undermines ironically the words of Brutus by repeating the claim that he is "an honourable man," but by now the claim is shown to be deficient, and almost empty of meaning. The third claim is political in that it recalls an episode that took place during the Lupercalia. On that occasion Antony offered the laurel wreath, the symbol of kingly power, to Caesar not once but three times, and three times it was rejected. No doubt this is the most convincing argument because the people had witnessed it – indeed, if Casca's narrative is to be believed, the people *insisted* upon it. The episode constitutes a crushing rebuttal of what Brutus had asserted, namely that Caesar was ambitious.

> Yet Brutus says he was ambitious,
> And sure he is an honourable man. [...]
> I speak not to disprove what Brutus spoke,
> But here I am to speak what I do know. (3.2.94–95, 101–102)

After successfully undermining Brutus's rational arguments Antony repeats that he does not want to contradict him: he is quite aware that the conspirators may silence him at any moment, and so he tries to reassure them. However, he still insists upon offering a personal testimonial that allows him to identify with every member of his audience. Moreover, his questioning of "judgement," and his claim that "men have lost their reason" is designed to subtly undermine the 'reason' that Brutus had relied upon in his oration.

> You all did love him once, not without cause;
> What cause withholds you then to mourn for him?
> O judgment, thou art fled to brutish beasts,
> And men have lost their reason! Bear with me;

> My heart is in the coffin there with Caesar,
> And I must pause till it come back to me. (3.2.103–108)

This is the culmination of Antony's argument in which he explicitly accuses his audience of being unstable and inconsistent in their love for Caesar. Marullus had already mentioned the volatility of the populace at the beginning of the play when he observed that the triumph of Caesar and Pompey's death in battle earlier had been preceded by the triumph of Pompey as the champion against the enemies of Rome. On that occasion Marullus had openly accused the Roman people of ingratitude (1.1. 40–60), since their lauding of Pompey as the protector of the Roman state was succeeded by the hailing of his adversary Caesar. Thus the masses are described from the very beginning as dangerous and easily manipulated, blinded by ceremonial pomp, and prey to the ablest orator.

The communicative function set in motion by Antony is rich in rhetorical/ poetic devices: *litotes* (stating a concept by negating its opposite), the use of rhetorical questions or *anadiplosis* (repetition of one or more terminal elements in a speech segment at the beginning of the following segment). The bewilderment of Antony before the reaction of the crowd is such that he finds it necessary to insert a direct apostrophe to a personified Judgment resulting from a loss of "reason." This decline in status from the "human" to the "bestial" is alleged to be a direct consequence of the gullibility of the populace, as political carnival is used by those in power to eradicate the past. The assonance between Brutus and "brutish beasts" skilfully and astutely plays with the hidden accusation against Brutus of being "brutish" himself, while the populace is diminished since they believe in Brutus' "brutishness."

The whole theatrical posture of Antony is now focused on emotions. He makes use of metonymy: the emotion he feels is represented materially by reference to an actual bodily organ, his heart, which now lies in the coffin with Caesar. As a consummate orator, Antony makes use of every available theatrical device: at this point he actually feigns being overcome by emotion and interrupts his oration. *Aposiopesis* rounds off this part of the speech, a rhetorical device that is a form of ellipsis by which a speaker comes to an abrupt halt, seemingly overcome by emotion.

This *aposiopesis* has the function both of having his words penetrate into the soul of his listeners, as well as verifying the impact his words have upon his audience both by speaking *for* them and by placing words in their mouths. The response of the crowd is immediate, and the effect is to misrecognise emotion as 'reason' at the same time as it provokes alternative forms of reasoning:

I Plebeian: Methinks there is much reason in his sayings
4 Plebeian: He would not take the crown;
Therefore 'tis certain he was not ambitious. (3.2.108–111)

At this point in the scene the audience is relatively passive: the crowd is obviously involved emotionally, but it is slow to take any active role in the interaction, it is subjugated by the orator's words. It is almost hypnotized into an acceptance of Antony's narrative, and it answers Antony's rhetorical questions in a prescribed manner. Thus Antony appears as the master puppeteer who manipulates the reaction of the crowd. His verbal manipulation has almost hypnotised his listeners (notice the lack of nouns denoting specificity, and their replacement by generalities that deprive the audience of individual identity): the crowd reacts just as the orchestrator of their emotions has conditioned them to act.

An initial climax of the speech (the first of many) concludes with Antony's pause in silence, that allows his audience to reflect, under controlled conditions, on their allegiances. The fact that the entire scene is based on the power of the word is emphasized by the knowledge that Caesar too had the capacity to dominate the world through the strength of the word: "But yesterday the word of Caesar might / Have stood against the world." Once more the force of authority is centered on a careful deployment of persuasive rhetoric: he who uses linguistic manipulation, rather than violent repression, is invested with an authority in which subjects willingly acquiesce. Violent repression, according to this strategy, suggests a certain weakness on the part of the holder of power and the resort to force is considered a failure of government, while the aim of manipulation is to persuade subjects to adhere "voluntarily" to the will of the ruler. Antony does not act in the people's interest (no one does in the play, except perhaps Brutus at his most idealistic and politically naive), but pursues his own partisan objective without the listeners becoming aware of it:

O Masters, if I were disposed to stir
Your hearts and minds to mutiny and rage,
I should do Brutus wrong and Cassius wrong,
Who, you all know, are honourable men. (3.2.121–125)

The emotional function of these words is accompanied by a much more sinister, and suggestive conative function. Antony begins with a conditional sentence claiming ostensibly to weaken the violence of "mutiny" and "rage," and neutralizing the notion of a true provocation, while at the same time encouraging "mutiny" and "rage." For the first time since Antony has begun to speak, the word "mutiny" appears: for the first time the possibility of actively resisting the action of the conspirators is put forward. Their allegedly "democratic" action in assassinating Caesar now begins to be interpreted as a sordid political murder, requiring a violent response directed against the action of the conspirators. Antony's subtle provocation of his audience is underpinned by the claim that Caesar was *more* democratic in the provision that his will makes for the citizens of Rome. Caesar's "will" – a pejorative term as it appears in the play – is converted into a stage property designed to sway a volatile audience by suggesting that it now has its own vested interest in challenging the conspirators:

> But here's a parchment, with the seal of Caesar;
> I found it in his closet –'tis his will.
> Let by the commons hear his testament –
> Which, pardon me, I do not mean to read –
> And they would go and kiss dead Caesar's wounds,
> And dip their napkins in his sacred blood. (3.2.129–135)

The preposition "but" that opens the adversative sentence is significant: up to that moment Antony has relied on emotions, personal memories, or facts of common knowledge as evidence, but he now resorts to an actual physical legal document: the will. Law itself will be able to demonstrate Caesar's generosity. The legal terms used here – "seal," "testament," "legacy," "bequeath" – invoke the juridical system of the time. Notice how the noun "will" means both the object itself, the will, *and* the testator's intention, almost to endow the impersonal juridical document with an emotional connotation that affectively links Caesar's own intentions with the 'will' of the people. It is a type of tangible juridical proof, whose details Antony cleverly pretends not to want to disclose, in order to stimulate the desire of his audience. In this way he displaces his intended violation of the promise he made to the conspirators, onto the "will" of the people. In this way Roman "democracy" is shown to be a Machiavellian ruse of the powerful to secure and maintain power.

6 "Then make a ring about the corpse of Caesar"

The reference to juridically irrefutable facts is not the only fundamental change in the trajectory of the speech; it is now augmented with the sanctification of Caesar's body. As Luciano Cavalli observes, "[t]he bequest to the Roman people is such that if the citizens knew it, to keep it in eternal memory, they would rush to kiss the leader's wounds, they would dampen their handkerchiefs 'in his sacred blood.'"[20] In what is effectively a strong Christological allusion, Mark Antony consecrates Caesar's blood as a source of salvation for the people.

The fall of Caesar is made to recall the Fall from Eden: the assassination has violated a sanctified order. In this context, Caesar's drama is no longer the drama of a single person, but is universal; as Adam's betrayal is followed by eternal misery, so Brutus' betrayal will bring death and devastation in a civil war. "Then I, and you, and all of us fell down."

Mark Antony's next move is highly significant: after ordering the people to gather around Caesar's corpse, he asks permission to come down from the podium and he mingles with the crowd. In this way, Antony seeks to minimise the social, cultural, and economic differences that exist between himself and the populace, while he awaits its response. Such a move does not leave the crowd indifferent: the people grant Antony's request with the call for "Room for Antony, most noble Antony." Now the epithet "noble" in its original substantive meaning is transferred to Antony, who is the agent of its refurbishment following his negative and ironical application of the term to the conspirators.

This new phase of the oration is the strongest one from an emotional standpoint, and it is Antony himself who alerts the populace to it: "If you have tears prepare to shed them now" (3.2.170). The tears not shed earlier, are now encouraged as the stage audience confronts a tangible body that can be touched, and that is an unmediated testimony to the savage violence of the conspirators. Antony begins by displaying Caesar's toga to which he attaches a symbolic meaning: it is the garment that Caesar wore when he defeated the Nervii, a crucial episode in the Gallic wars, and capable of being commonly recognized. Now the cloak is pierced with stabwounds and covered with blood, symbolizing that the fall of Caesar and the fall of Rome are one and the same thing. The powerful effect of naming every wound as if each conspirator had put his signature is a testimony to Antony's consummate theatricality, and underscores his skill in public oratory.

Another important element in this speech is its progressive disassemblement of Caesar's body. Caesar is no longer referred to as a whole but instead single details are emphasized, first his cloak, then his wounds and then the flowing blood, all of which contribute incrementally to the image of an unjust assassination. This transition favours the process of sacralization of Caesar's body; it shows the sacral and propitiatory valence of what happened, as if Caesar him-

20 Luciano Cavalli, *Giulio Cesare, Coriolano e il teatro della repubblica. Una lettura politica di Shakespeare* (Soveria Mannelli: Rubettino editore, 2006), 68 (my translation).

self, as a Christological figure, had heroically accepted his own death in order to save the people and give it a new prosperity.

Crying is not a simple consequence of the emotions aroused by Antony, it is another reference to original sin: the "gracious drops" represent the baptismal water bringing redemption from ancestral guilt. This growing piety authorizes Antony to make his most theatrical gesture: to lift the torn cape in order to show Caesar's corpse.

> That cruel exhibit produces the emotional shock necessary so that a new definition of the event may irreversibly prevail among the masses – whose original propensity towards violence has now been awakened and steered towards a specific target. [21]

Linguistically, with reference to Caesar's body, Antony uses the verb "to mar." As one editor has observed:

> Shakespeare uses this verb only as a past participle and in reference to signifying objects: speech, writing, a dramatic piece [...] In this light the verb acquires a particular significance, since it comes with the preposition "with" and not with the more appropriate preposition "by": Caesar's body, the very sign of the symbolic Cosmos, has been disfigured by the traitors, it has also been scrawled upon with the traits (a word that surfaces in traitors) of profane writing, of anti-symbolic writing.[22]

It is the peculiarity of the prepositional construction that makes this predicate so incisive.

The special emphasis placed on Caesar's body can once more be seen as an anticipation of the great awareness of the body in contemporary society. It is sufficient to think of the overwhelming presence of the body in media and in mass communication, and of the way in which it is considered sometimes as an absolute idol, at other times an insignificant and despised object, a product, like many others, of consumerism. In this very contemporary Shakespearian awareness of the relationship between the masses and the orator, in sacralizing Caesar's body, Antony produces a last, definitive *coup de théâtre* that is the culmination of his manipulation of the crowd. Caesar's body, in its extreme humiliation as a violated and mutilated corpse, does appear *in primis* as decaying and transient matter, but it is also elevated as a symbol of a higher quasi-religious reality, as the union of the faithful in a sacred conjugal community and union (symbolized by the immersion of the handkerchiefs in the blood). As a

21 Cavalli, *Giulio Cesare, Coriolano e il teatro della repubblica*, 70.

22 Notes to Act 3 in William Shakespeare, *Giulio Cesare*, eds. Nemi D'Agostino and Alessandro Serpieri (Milano: Garzanti, 1998), 216 (my translation).

matter of fact, in the body the relationship between the sacred and the profane, between life and death, is consummated. According to James Frazer in *The Golden Bough*, the bloody sacrifice of the body followed by a sacrificial banquet has always played a central role in all religions. As Ferrarotti also asserts, "[t]he flesh, the body, and the sacrificial rites which concern them take up a considerable space both in eastern religions and in biblical myths."[23]

In this scene around Caesar's corpse the Christian ambiguity towards the body emerges: though the body is sinful and therefore "inauspicious" because Caesar as a man should perhaps have been punished, it is also, especially here, a body purified by death, sanctified by intentions, salvific in its outcome of sacrifice for the common good. Here the contradictory character of the sacred and of its double nature appears. Caesar has become the totem, the taboo which cannot be approached since it is intangible in its sacrality, but to which one must accede in order to acquire salvation (salvific blood). This is the transcendence implicit in the dead body itself of the "king."

The more Antony steers the attention of the populace towards Caesar's humiliated corpse, the more it appears as a sublimated and sacralized body. In its suggested identification with the tortured body of Christ, it has become a transcendent body. In the words of Antony, the Word and the Body coincide again, since it is precisely through Antony's words that the body takes on a sacral identity. Just as in contemporary society image and gaze prevail (we live within a visual civilization), in the same way this scene at its climax is built on sight, gaze, and color (blood red). At this point the oration becomes visual, centered on the reading of signs (Antony's performance) and on image (the dead body). This is about actual human experience in the making, the dialectics between life and death, body and signified.

In order to make Caesar's body into an authentic sacral object it is necessary to render it alien: hence its dismemberment, the reduction of its various parts into relics, with the possibility of the people taking possession of shreds, pieces, blood drops, so that the body becomes sublimated. What takes place is the separation between a phenomenological manifestation and a signifying manifestation: the signifying logos is disembodied, made alien and the body itself is disembodied in such a way that it loses its own materiality and becomes symbolic. The use of the senses (seeing, touching), aroused in the crowd, becomes a mediation between spirit and matter: by means of seeing up close and touching, the

23 Franco Ferrarotti, "Corpo, sensi e religioni," in *Corpo e religione*, eds. Roberto Cipriani, Gaspare Mura (Firenze: Città Nuova, 2009), 20 (my translation).

populace almost contributes to a transubstantiation of Caesar's corpse into mystical body. In the words of Ignazio Sanna,

> [t]he importance given to the body is due above all to the fact that the salvation announced by the Christian message is an "incarnated" salvation. It is manifested specifically as salvation which is actuated by means of the body.[24]

Caesar's name, that is to say what defines his identity and uniqueness, acquires a wider significance: Caesar becomes a symbol of the ideal "monarch," both respectful of his people and their friend. In the words of one member of the stage audience: "3 Plebeian: O royal Caesar!" (3.2.245).

The forms of verbal communication, which we have examined in the course of the analysis of Mark Antony's oration, are strengthened and underscored by non-verbal means of communication, such as gestures both of an emotive, and a deictic kind: these communicative typologies make visible what is expressed by words. The particular posture held by Brutus and by Antony towards the listening masses lends itself also to an analysis that makes reference to proxemics, that is, to that "part of semiology that studies physical space, and especially the tendency to interpose a larger or smaller space between oneself and others as an element of communication."[25] The anthropologist Edward T. Hall has observed that there is a close correlation between human relationships and the physical distance they place between themselves. In particular he has singled out four different inter-personal zones: 1) intimate distance, for interaction of conjugal, parental, or acquired family members; 2) personal distance, for interaction between friends; 3) social distance, for communication between acquaintances; 4) public distance, for relations in the public sphere.[26] As mentioned above, the different emphases placed on their speeches by Brutus and Antony can be observed also in their respective behaviours toward the audience. Even before beginning to speak, Brutus takes some precautionary measures: aware that the crowd may be dangerous, he orders to have it partially dispersed: "Cassius, go you into the other street / And part the numbers" (3.2.12–14). In addition, Brutus' oration begins with a call to silence which must last until the conclusion of his speech. By imposing silence upon the masses, Brutus asserts his superiority and in so doing he establishes a public distance between himself and the masses.

---

24 Ignazio Sanna, "Corpo e religione. Il corpo umano e la salvezza cristiana," in *Corpo e religione*, eds. Cipriani, Mura: 71–81, 71 (my translation).
25 Edward T. Hall, "Proxemics," *Current Anthropology* 9.2–3 (1968): 83–100, 83.
26 Edward T. Hall, *The Hidden Dimension* (New York: Doubleday & Co. Inc., 1966).

By contrast, Antony does not restrain the audience from speaking; on the contrary, he astutely gives it permission to intervene whenever he deems it appropriate. In this way he solicits the emotional participation of the masses in what he has to say. Secondly, he steps down from the orator's podium in order to mix physically with the crowd. This action has a symbolic significance, as we saw earlier: in this way, the distance is no longer objective, rather, it becomes the distance of personal relationships, of a shared communication, even though its purpose is clearly political.

Antony's words are clothed in ritual. In sociological and anthropological terms, a rite is a body of practices and beliefs which constitutes the cultural models of a society; they carry out the function of transmitting values and norms; they establish the institution of roles, identity recognition, and social cohesion. As Edoardo Scognamiglio observes,

> [a]s for society, so for religion, the exterior form is the condition of its existence. In this perspective the spiritual body also stands for the social and liturgical body, official as well as cultural, which is marked by a particular form of participation in the divine mystery. The body is then recognized in its symbolic dimension, that is: distinction, participation, and union with the divine.[27]

Caesar's assassination itself has ritualistic connotations: the homicide is not a mere act of violence, but is invested with dignity "lifting it to a level of rite and ceremony"[28]; in fact, Brutus affirms "Let us be sacrificers but not butchers." Caesar is killed on the threshold of the Curia, the symbolic space of the senatorial institution; participation in the Senate is possible only through a pre-established ritual, ruled by precise and ancient norms. The very occasion for which the oration is delivered is precisely the celebration of a funeral rite in Caesar's honour, as Regina Schwarz observes in relation to another Shakespeare play:

> [r]itual summons the holy, mysterium tremendum, and its acts are neither imitation of life or imitation of imitations, but acts that enable the sacred to be manifest and transcendence to erupt into immanence. The effect of such acts on the audience – and they are not an audience, but participants – is to be conclusively altered.[29]

27 Edoardo Scognamiglio, "Immagini del corpo nell'Islam," in *Corpo e religione*, eds. Cipriani, Mura: 98–125, 118 (my translation).

28 Brents Stirling, "Ritual in *Julius Caesar*," in *Shakespeare, Julius Caesar. A Casebook*, ed. Peter Ure (Bristol: A. E. Dyson, 1969): 160–171, 160.

29 Regina Schwarz, "The Mass and the Theatre: Othello and Sacrifice," *Pólemos*, 1 (2009): 87–108, 92.

Indeed, the particular ritual of this scene recalls the celebration of the Mass, with the officiant first in front of, then among the faithful, with the crowd being an integral part of the ritual, and with Caesar's body at the center as the spiritual body of Christ. As Bernard Beckerman has demonstrated,

> [p]laygoing is a little like churchgoing. It is a public act for private ends. It is a private act performed publicly. It is intimate and individual. It is impersonal and communal. It brings us nearer to the apprehension of our own godhood while at the same time it reinforces awareness of the transitory properties of our flesh. Yet likeness is not identity. Playgoing is a surrender to illusion while churchgoing is a ritual embodiment of a higher truth. Through churchgoing we hope to step from one truth to the truth. Playgoing holds out the possibility that we can slip through fancy to a lookout upon truth.[30]

Brutus's interpretation of the scene, however, is seriously undercut by the barbaric violent gestures that link the opposites of bloody slaughter with the concept of "freedom." Antony's strategy, however, restores the unity of concept and image by endowing the body of Caesar with a religious signification. The juxtaposition of the scene around Caesar's body and the Catholic Mass underscores a peculiar hieratic ritual, because although Antony's motives are accessible to the theatre audience, the scene is endowed with a degree of irony. Rite demands a profound emotional preparation: going back to the different parts of the speech analyzed above, it is clear that ritual works as an emotional preparation, so much so that the audience comes into that state of mind which enables it to understand and participate in the acts that will be performed. This predisposition happens by means of the description of Caesar's actions; evident in descriptions such as: "He hath brought many captives home to Rome"; "When the poor have cried, Caesar hath wept"; and a previous ritual had shown Mark Antony attired as an officiant: the attempt at crowning the "dictator" during the Lupercalia festivities. Such gestures are highly symbolic because they comprise a series of codified actions through which kingly power articulates itself. The signs set in motion by Antony are characterized by a strong visual component and they take on the appearance of a real ceremony.

Such ritualistic aspects run through Antony's entire speech as when, for example, he points out to the populace that on the very day of Caesar's funeral no one deigns to pay homage to him: "And none so poor to do him reverence." To pay respect to the deceased is a social convention, a popular ritual embedded

30 See Bernard Beckerman, "Shakespearean Playgoing Then and Now," in *Shakespeare's More Than Words Can Witness: Essays on Visual and Nonverbal Enactment in the Plays*, ed. Sidney Homan (Lewsbergu, PA: Bucknell University Press, 1986): 142–159, 142.

within a hierarchical society. Thus, the allusion to an absence of ritual in this case becomes significant.

What is also ritualistic is the moment when the parchment with Caesar's seal (the will) is exhibited to the people: here, as one critic has argued, the lexicon belongs to the juridical subcode, just as Antony's gestures recall those of trial ritual:

> conceived, according to its genealogy as a ritual, a trial has a protective function with respect to "violence without reason" (Girard); it serves to channel it, to expel from society what is foul in order to restore purity and cohesion and thus to remove the specter of a sacrificial crisis: society evokes crime in as much as it is a founding element which must be celebrated and exorcized at the same time.[31]

The elements of 'celebration' and 'exorcism' come together in the body of Caesar and underscore the ritualistic connotations of Antony's speech. However, the actual rite, perverted by the gestures of the conspirators, is enacted when the crowd gathers in a circle around Caesar's corpse. The circular positioning is imbued with a symbolic-religious value. Indeed, the circle is the symbol of fullness and harmony, as well as being the representation of a spiritual altar on which to perform rituals, such as meditation and spiritual practices. Each of Caesar's wounds is described, each is assigned an aggressor, as if the killing itself had followed a pre-established, if perverse, ritual. The reaction of the crowd is first orchestrated by Antony, but it gradually becomes a spontaneous reaction: tears (recalling the baptismal water). The people unleash their grief by crying; this marks the beginning of a cathartic process that will culminate in the sacralization of Caesar's body, and its transformation into the status of a relic. The relic makes it possible to perceive the body of the saint as an eternal body. Except of course, that Caesar's Rome is mortal and will ultimately decay. Here the anachronism of Christian ritual grafted onto the beginnings of imperial Rome serves to promote in the theatre audience a gentle irony whose roots lie in Elizabethan political theology.

Caesar goes from being an ethical body (his human traits of generosity and understanding of his people, the imprint of the Creator found in the materiality of his earthly actions) to a metaphysical/mystic body (the sacralized body, transcendental, which gives eternal life). The display of a saint's body, of his relics, of his remains, represents a ritual act addressed to the collectivity of the faithful: an

---

31 Eleonora De Conciliis, review of Antoine Garapon, *Del giudicare. Saggio sul rituale giudiziario* (Milano: Raffaello Cortina, 2007), *Kainos*, 9 (2009), (my translation), available at http://www.kainos.it/numero9/sommario9.html (last accessed, January 2015).

act capable of transfiguring its finite corporeality, thus turning it into a vehicle of infinity and transcendence. This collective ritualistic performance therefore attributes to the body a particular status, a privileged symbolic meaning: a bridge between the contingent and the absolute, between man and his God. Caesar becomes, by an odd anachronism, the Lord's anointed, the salvific saint in a collective ritual which merges the orator with the crowd.

However, it should be kept in mind that Antony's resort to religious ritual has a primarily political motive: his intention is to vindicate Caesar's death by unleashing the populace against the conspirators. Thus, it has the practical function of inciting rebellion and eliminating the power won by the conspirators, utilizing the very materials of monarchy against which the conspirators' plotting has been directed The collective cry of "mutiny" and "revenge" seals the success of Antony's rhetorical strategy, but it also reveals his commitment to a Machiavellian form of scheming that would not have been lost on an Elizabethan audience.

7 Conclusions

The foregoing analysis has attempted to show that at the base of the speeches of both Antony and Brutus, – that proceed by contrasts: brevity vs. expansiveness, prose vs. verse, self-involvement vs. outreach, quick but shallow acceptance vs. emotional upheaval[32] – there is an urgent necessity to consolidate illegally won power (the conspirators) by obtaining the consensus of the crowd as guarantor of a new legitimacy. Similarly, but using more effective rhetorical means, Antony enlists the support of the people in order to subvert the conspirators' coup. Each displays the operation of power through language and gesture, and each enlists theatrical means of representation with varying success. Laura di Michele has shown how power is committed to theatricalizing itself through mimesis as a means of securing agreement:

> On the stage [...] the story of authority and of the subjects is outlined; the unfolding of their power relationships and their tensions, of their mutual rites of glorification and violence is played out [...]; it is in the incessant interchange between the real and its mimetic representations that theatre and the spectacle of power [...] appear as a symbolic space for the construction of meaning.[33]

---

32 Wills, *Rome and Rhetoric*, 54.

33 Laura Di Michele, *La scena dei potenti. Teatro, politica, spettacolo nell'età di W. Shakespeare* (Napoli: Istituto Orientale Universitario, 1988), 7 (my translation).

In *The Human Condition* Hannah Arendt[34] states that power depends on a temporary and unstable pact among various wills that hold a group together. Arendt underscores the idea that power is based on the consensus of the people, although she is a little vague on precisely how that consensus is secured. Such an appeal to consensus, however, and the means by which it is secured, is particularly visible in *Julius Caesar*, where the conspirators stand before the people in an attempt to legitimize the murder of Caesar, the presumed tyrant. Mark Antony, in turn, uses his rhetorical skills to refute the conspirators' actions and he appeals to the emotions rather than to the capacity for reason of the Roman populace.[35] In both cases the manipulation of the crowd is essential for success. As Van Dijk observes,

> [a]n analysis of this power dimension involves an account of the kind of control that some social actors or groups exercise over others. We also have assumed that such control is first of all a control of the mind, that is, of the beliefs of recipients, and indirectly a control of the actions of recipients based on such manipulated beliefs.[36]

The type of manipulation that has been exposed in this essay is inherent in social domination and in its use in the practices of discourse. The extraordinary modernity of Shakespeare, who as always foreshadows contemporary times,[37] is shown by his awareness of the means appropriate to control the collective mind of the masses. He anticipates the use of the typical stylistic elements of political control, such as resorting to slogans, designed to instill in people's minds particular ideas. The repetition of "Brutus is an honourable man" in all its variations recalls precisely the political stratagem of using slogans to secure political domination: their meaning is gradually emptied of the original significance and in a context transformed by the orator. Politicians are in a position to be able to exercise their power by means of oratorical ability, which in its turn has the function of strengthening power itself.

Moreover we must call to mind the persistent anti-theatrical sentiments at work throughout this period. The two orations we have examined are theatrical

---

34 Hannah Arendt, *The Human Condition* [1958] (Chicago: University of Chicago Press, 1998).
35 See Daniela Carpi, "Potere e legittimità in *King Lear, King John, Julius Caesar*," in *Iconologia del potere. Rappresentazione della sovranità nel Rinascimento*, eds. Daniela Carpi, Sidia Fiorato (Verona: Ombre Corte, 2011): 106–118.
36 Van Dijk, "Discourse and manipulation," 362.
37 See Daniela Carpi, "From Renaissance to Postmodernism: Anticipations of Legal Unrest," in *Liminal Discourses of Law*, eds. Daniela Carpi, Jeanne Gaakeer (Berlin, Boston: De Gruyter, 2013): 177–189.

performances, and in a newly opened theatre, The Globe: "In the light of a persistent outpouring of anti-theatrical sentiments throughout this period, combined with what James Barish identified as a 'deep suspicion' towards theatricality as a form of behavior in the world"[38] Brutus' and Antony's gestures are acts of political defiance in themselves. The characters seem to stage their own play within the play: "they are self-conscious actors fully aware of their historical roles."[39] The political and theatrical events are intertwined. Moreover, very often a visual as well as a verbal rhetoric is constructed, as when Brutus suggests that the conspirators should hide their intentions in smiles and affability, which reminds us of Lady Macbeth's instructions to her husband. Thus the presenting of 'a false face' emphasises the play-within-the-play perspective, that serves to align rhetoric, physical gesture and image as the materials endemic to theatre and politics alike.

Julius Caesar is not so much a celebration of theatre as an unmasking of the politics of representation *per se*, and the mimetic representation of politics. The play does not *express* meaning; rather, in its readings of Roman history it *produces* meanings.[40]

38 Drakakis, "'Fashion it thus'; *Julius Caesar* and the Politics of Theatrical Representation," 282.

39 Zander, "Julius Caesar and the Critical Legacy," 10.

40 Drakakis, "'Fashion it thus'; *Julius Caesar* and the Politics of Theatrical Representation," 289.

Raffaele Cutolo

Motionless Bodies: Shakespeare's Songs for Sleep and Death

1 The Phenomenology of the Motionless Body in Sleep and Death

To be, or not to be: that is the question:
Whether 'tis nobler in the mind to suffer
The slings and arrows of outrageous fortune,
Or to take arms against a sea of troubles,
And by opposing end them? To die: to sleep;
No more
(W. Shakespeare, *Hamlet*, 3.1.55–60)

Hamlet's emblematic question puts Shakespeare in the uncomfortable position of reflecting on the unstable edge of the life/death border. The answer to *the question* – suppose there is one – is to be looked for in the philosophical contradiction created by an apparently insignificant word such as the preposition that binds the two extremes of this hamletic ontological dichotomy. If to be *or* not to be is the question, Shakespeare's following lines seem to indicate that to be *and* not to be might be the possible answer. Formally, it could be argued that two opposite propositions are unable to exist in a relation of conjunction without mutual contradiction, which remains true within the framing of conceptual dualism, where A cannot simultaneously be non-A. However, a shift from reductionist particularism into a more holistic paradigm fosters the conceiving of a variety of experiences that jeopardise the stability of the dualism that regulates the Self's conception and perception of reality. Bodily states like sleep, coma, or death are connected to alterations of sensory experience, which is diminished or completely nullified.

The still body, intended as dead or apparently dead, challenges the *cogito* because of the impossibility for the *res cogitans* to reveal itself. The fulcrum of Hamlet's soliloquy lies in a subversion of the *cogito*, for it is through "opposing" (3.1.59) that the Self is identified; by ending its existence, or at least by contemplating the finiteness of it, the self actually reaffirms itself. Hamlet's projection, by the contemplation of not-being-there attempts to satisfy an ontological need of the I, that is the awareness of being there or, in Heideggerian terms, being (Dasein), because "[o]nly in running ahead and bringing the possibility of death understandingly close does Dasein become itself. The most essential potentiality of

Being-There is non-Being."[1] Death, as Dasein's only certainty, is the key to reuniting Hamlet's "to be" and "not to be," because it is only in death, or apparent death, that the I *is* and *is not* at the same time.

The soliloquy does not represent a total refutation of Cartesianism, which sees man as a temporary union of body and mind, and in fact, for Shakespeare, the body is the "mortal coil" (3.1.66) to be abandoned at the moment of death, when such a union breaks.[2] What is in contrast with Cartesian theories is what happens, at least according to the soliloquy, at the moment of death. On Cartesian grounds

> [t]he particularities of the body's experience, the sensations and thoughts generated in this union, are what individuate one man from another. After death, without a body, the mind or soul is shorn of all sensory memory and imagination, for these depend on the bodily union.[3]

Descartes's *res cogitans* ceases to be at death; Shakespeare's does not, since he contemplates the possibility that "in that sleep of death [...] dreams may come" (3.1.65), thus implying a continuity of the bond between the two entities. These hypothetical dreams of the eternal slumber, as products of thought, stand in opposition to the *cogito*, because they indicate a persisting connection of the *res cogitans* to the dead body; hence the ontological question is taken a step further: when we die, are we or are we not? This question could find a possible answer in the creation of Purgatory, a Catholic invention that Shakespeare utilises as the realm of the Ghost: an atopy that is inhabited by what is simultaneously dead and not dead. This is a dimension that enables the possibility of the existence of an in-between state, that of the *un*dead, where the possibility of being and not-being seems more plausible.[4]

The adjacency between sleep and death is fostered by a phenomenological analogy brought forth by the motionless body, suggested also by the proverb *son-*

1 Lawrence Cahoone, *The Dilemma of Modernity: Philosophy, Culture, and Anti-Culture* (Albany: State University of New York, 1988), 152.

2 The Elizabethan tragedy deploys those cultural tendencies of fear of total nihilation, identifying a fascination of the Renaissance audience with the themes of death and resurrection. See Daniela Carpi, "Il paesaggio di morte nel teatro elisabettiano-giacobiano," *Il lettore di provincia*, 33.15 (2002): 41–49, 43.

3 Richard A. Watson, "Transubstantiation among the Cartesians," in *Problems of Cartesianism*, eds. Thomas Lennon, John Nicholas and John Witney Davis (Montreal: Mc Gill-Queen's University Press, 1982): 127 – 148, 148.

4 See Maurice A. Hunt, *Shakespeare's Speculative Art* (New York: Palgrave Macmillan, 2011); Stephen Greenblatt, *Hamlet in Purgatory* (Princeton: Princeton University Press, 2001).

num imago mortis, which was taught during the Renaissance in order to accustom man to the idea of death.[5] This analogy stems from the body's orientation in relation to the world that the two share: in sleep and in death the body is deprived of its verticality, which is associated with life and vitality. The resemblance of the two led to their mythical representation as twin brothers: Hypnos and Thanatos, respectively the god of sleep and the god of death, are both children of the night, Nyx and this familial bond links them to all other elements of such imagery, especially to dreams.[6] "The equivalence of sleep and death, and near-equivalence of both with dreams in the sense of an existential after-life, are prompted by – and lead to – an equivalence between being and doing, between the existential and the active."[7] Considering "being" as existence itself, and "doing" as its activity, performing can be described as "showing doing,"[8] which implies the simultaneous existence of an addresser and an addressee, where the former is aware of the presence of the latter. In the case of death and sleep, the correspondence between being and doing impedes the occurrence of showing doing. In other words, it is impossible to show sleep or death to someone else, without being actually asleep or dead, therefore if I perform sleep/death I cannot be asleep/dead, and if I am asleep/dead I cannot be performing. Performance resolves the disequilibrium between sleep and death on two different levels: firstly, because of the impossibility of co-existence of being, and doing – thus of showing doing – and secondly, because in performance death and sleep *are* actually the same. The impossibility of showing death or sleep to the Other reasserts their belonging to the Self: they both imply what Heidegger calls *Jemeinigkeit* of Dasein: a sense of "mineness" that characterises existence, and thus death. By stating that "[b]y its very essence, death is in every case mine,"[9] Heidegger forges a relation between the Self's being and death, eliminating – as

---

5 See Rolf Schneller, *Shakespeare's Patterns of Self-Knowledge* (Columbus: Ohio State University Press, 1972), 378.

6 In Greek mythology, Hypnos's sons (or brothers in other versions) are the Oneiroi, from the Greek *oneiros*, meaning dream. There are three Oneiroi: "Morpheus, the god associated with the human element in dreams, his brother Phobetor, associated with animal forms, and his brother Phantasos, associated with inanimate objects." Jan Dirk Blom, *A Dictionary of Hallucinations* (New York: Springer, 2010), 373.

7 S. Viswanthan, *Exploring Shakespeare: The Dynamics of Playmaking* (New Delhi: Orient Longman, 2005), 35.

8 See Richard Schechner, *Performance Studies: An Introduction* (New York: Routledge, 2013 [2002]), 28.

9 Martin Heidegger, *Being and Time* (Oxford: Blackwell, 1962), 284.

Levinas would later denounce[10] – the possibility of a dying of the other or a dying for the other. Shakespeare's projection towards death as a liberating moment for the Self traces the climax of an aesthetic solipsism whose natural culmination, although maybe premature for the Renaissance, is suicide.[11] Suicide in Shakespeare is not the affirmation of being through death, which justifies Hamlet's disjunctive *aut* in the enunciation of "the question," yet it is contemplated as a possibility in order to achieve self liberation on a twofold scale: for the Self, and from the Self. Man, in Hamlet's words, "might his quietus make / With a bare bodkin" (3.1.83–84), a concept that is reprised in *Julius Caesar*, when Cassius affirms that "life, being weary of these worldly bars, / Never lacks power to dismiss itself." (1.3.99–100)[12] By dying, man frees the Self from the suffering of life, which is perceived through the body, the mortal constituent of the Self, and that is dismissed at the moment of death. Again, there is a conception of life in relation to death, of being-towards-death, which delineates an actuality of life determined by the potentiality of death.

As it has been noted, Cartesianism's body-mind separation led to an understanding of the body as the boundary[13] between the Self and the world: the body separates us from the world, but at the same time it puts us in contact with the world. In Merleau-Ponty's words, "[t]he body is the vehicle of being in the world, [...] I am conscious of my body via the world, [...] I am conscious of the world through the medium of my body."[14] The correlation of the body to the earthly dimension of the world is significant especially at the moment of death, when the

10 See François Raffoul, *The Origins of Responsibility* (Bloomington: Indiana University Press, 2010).

11 The solipsistic experience will reach its aesthetic peak in the nineteenth century. An example of this is Walter Pater's Sebastian Van Storck, the third *Imaginary Portrait*, where the protagonist's killing disguises a Self-liberating experience. Sebastian drowns in the attempt to save a child, who, Pater writes, "lay asleep swaddled warmly in his [Sebastian's] heavy furs." The images of sleep and death are again compared, in a juxtaposition that affirms their iconological adjacency. Walter Pater, *Imaginary Portraits* (Rockville: Arc Manor, 2008 [1887]), 71.

12 On the topic of suicide in Shakespeare see Larry R. Kirkland, "To End Itself By Death: Suicide in Shakespeare's Tragedies," *Southern Medical Journal*, 92.7 (1997): 660–666; Richard Courtney, *Shakespeare's World of Death: The Early Tragedies* (Toronto: Dundurn, 1995); Eric Langley, *Narcissism and Suicide in Shakespeare and His Contemporaries* (Oxford: Oxford University Press, 2009).

13 See Norbert Elias, *Society of Individuals* (London: Continuum, 2010 [1991]), 117.

14 Maurice Merleau-Ponty, *Phenomenology of Perception* (London: Routledge, 2002 [1945]), 94–95.

burial of the prostrate body, now a corpse, reaffirms "a mutual and reciprocal identity with its environment."[15]

The concept expressed by *somnum imago mortis* brings to the forefront the question of the image and the relation between appearance and reality that images imply. Appearance and reality have long stood in a dichotomous position that mirrors the philosophical antinomy between immanence and transcendence. In his rereading of Plato's *Dialogues*, however, Eric Perl argues that "immanence and transcendence are not opposed but that, on the contrary, the former implies the latter."[16] Such an implication paves the way to a new conception of the relationship between reality and appearance, because it shapes the realm of the in-between, conferring existence, which is being, to that which appears. In other – Kantian – words, the phenomenon becomes noumenon. Images themselves challenge ontology, in that their being representations of reality does not create another reality.

> [T]he reality is in the image, in that it is cognitively presented by it. [...] [B]y understanding Plato's metaphysics of images in intentional terms we can see how the paradigm is in the image. An image presents, or, better, is a presentation of, the reality. "Image," then, means precisely the presence of the other, the presence of that which the image itself is not.[17]

The core of the analogy between sleep and death relies on both physical and metaphysical aspects: sleep and death share an outer appearance of the body, which lies horizontal and motionless, and an inner abandonment that is understood as a journey beyond. The motionless body challenges the illusion of the "permanent present," which fosters the conception of the present as indefinitely durable, by reinforcing the idea that "a body in motion (i.e., that is alive) tends to stay in motion (i.e., stay alive) unless halted by an irresistible force."[18] A still body is perceived negatively because it counters the illusion of the permanent present on two levels: it is not vertical, and it does not move. For these reasons, still bodies are approached with caution, unless they are evidently asleep, therefore not completely motionless; we question them to make sure that their horizontality and stillness do not represent a real threat to their vitality.

---

15 Karen Raber, "The Common Body: Renaissance Popular Beliefs," in *A Cultural History of Human Body in the Renaissance*, eds. Linda Kalof and William Bynum (Oxford: Berg, 2010): 99–124, 123.

16 Eric Perl, "The Presence of the Paradigm: Immanence and Transcendence in Plato's Theory of Forms," *The Review of Metaphysics*, 53.2 (1999): 339–362, 340.

17 Perl, "The Presence of the Paradigm," 356.

18 David P. Ausubel, *Death and the Human Condition* (Lincoln: iUniverse, 2002), 18.

2 Apparent Deaths in Shakespeare

Besides the biological aspects dealing with breathing and heart-beating, it is waking that determines the most evident difference between sleep and death, which explains why, in the case of comatose states, it is only by the process of waking that it is possible to assert a complete and mutual rejoining of the Self and the body. Waking also enacts the possibility to restore the verticality of the body, allowing an orthogonal rotation that confirms the completion of the journey back from the other dimension. From a merely corporeal point of view, the alternation between sleep and waking has a fundamental role and grants the optimal functionality of the body, including the brain.

Shakespeare assiduously goes back to the theme of sleep, and to issues that are related to sleep, or lack thereof. It is in fact "lack of sleep [that] drives Macbeth and Lady Macbeth to their respective madness and suicide,"[19] thus depicting an extreme outcome which confirms that the irregularities in the sleep/wake rhythm can have catastrophic, even fatal, effects. After committing regicide, Macbeth pronounces a speech of self-condemnation for himself and his wife, predicting that their lives will be marked by terror, and their sleep tormented by the nightmares of guilt and regret.

> Ere we will eat our meal in fear and sleep
> In the affliction of these terrible dreams
> That shake us nightly: better be with the dead,
> Whom we, to gain our peace, have sent to peace,
> Than on the torture of the mind to lie
> In restless ecstasy. Duncan is in his grave.
> After life's fitful fever he sleeps well.
> (3.2.17–23)

There will be no rest for Macbeth, whose existence is destined to be haunted by the memory of his deed. A restful and peaceful sleep is considered as the consequence or reward for the fair conduct of one's life, which is why the punishment for Macbeth's crime is his condemnation to "sleep no more" (2.2.35; 2.2.41; 2.2.43).[20] Waking, as part of sleeping, is necessary for the human brain to gather appreciation and awareness of the two states as distinctive: moreover,

19 Ben Crystal, *Springboard Shakespeare: A Midsummer Night's Dream* (London: Bloomsbury Arden Shakepseare, 2013), 87.

20 See Brayton Polka, *Shakespeare and Interpretation, or What You Will* (Lanham, University of Delaware Press, 2011), 56–57; Harold Bloom, *Bloom's Major Literary Characters: Macbeth* (New York: Chelsea House Publishers, 2005), 14, 44, 45.

it determines the possibility-necessity to come back from the trans-dimensional journey that sleep forces us to.

Sleep and death lend themselves to a poetic of counterfeiting because of the imagery that they evoke: Shakespeare's use of the sleep/death resemblance serves the purposes of plot intricacy, and it allows him to create misunderstandings fostered by the motionless bodies on stage. Sleep is the vulnerable state during which mischief can be accomplished, whether delightfully comic, as in the case of *A Midsummer Night's Dream*, or with more murderous attempts, as in *Hamlet* or *Macbeth*. The common feature of Shakespearean slumber is the fact that once waking from sleep, all characters encounter changes and surprises, most of which are unpleasant or somehow traumatic. In *Romeo and Juliet*, in the monologue that precedes her drinking Friar Laurence's vial, Juliet foresees a dreadful awakening. She fears waking up among the dead, in a dark and haunted place, where the lack of air will suffocate her to death.

> How if, when I am laid into the tomb,
> I wake before the time that Romeo
> Come to redeem me? There's a fearful point!
> Shall I not, then, be stifled in the vault,
> To whose foul mouth no healthsome air breathes in,
> And there die strangled ere my Romeo comes?
> Or, if I live, is it not very like,
> The horrible conceit of death and night,
> Together with the terror of the place, –
> As in a vault, an ancient receptacle,
> Where, for these many hundred years, the bones
> Of all my buried ancestors are packed:
> Where bloody Tybalt, yet but green in earth,
> Lies festering in his shroud; where, as they say,
> At some hours in the night spirits resort; (4.3.30 – 44)

The proximity between sleep and death is accentuated in Shakespeare by a fictional type of sleep that collocates itself closer to death: it is phenomenological death, or temporary apparent death; yet it differentiates itself from death because the body experiences eventual awakening. Friar Laurence explains almost clinically to Juliet that the vial will cause her heart to stop beating.

> Take thou this vial, being then in bed,
> And this distilled liquor drink thou off;
> When presently through all thy veins shall run
> A cold and drowsy humour, for no pulse
> Shall keep his native progress, but surcease:
> No warmth, no breath, shall testify thou livest;

> The roses in thy lips and cheeks shall fade
> To paly ashes, thy eyes' windows fall,
> Like death, when he shuts up the day of life;
> Each part, deprived of supple government,
> Shall, stiff and stark and cold, appear like death:
> And in this borrow'd likeness of shrunk death
> Thou shalt continue two and forty hours,
> And then awake as from a pleasant sleep.
> (4.1.93–106)

The "borrow'd likeness" is not innocuous, and it is in fact before the motionless dead-like body of Juliet that Romeo, unaware of the effect that the potion has had on her, kills himself, and that her father orders that the "all things that we ordained festival / turn from their office to black funeral" (4.5.85–86). Juliet's apparent death enacts an iconological parallelism between the bed and the grave, which is anticipated by the Nurse through the rhyme bed/dead – Ay, let the county take you in your bed. / […] / Alas, alas! Help, help! My lady's dead! (4.5.11,15) – the chamber and the tomb, sleep and death, all sharing a common feature, which is her motionless body that lies horizontally.

Friar Laurence does not describe a sleep from which Juliet cannot be woken, but he provides us with a detailed description of a state that "appear[s] like death," but that cannot be considered death, because it is not permanent. Kara Peterson's analysis of Shakespearean revivifications is based on the Early Modern belief that "wombs can move about the female body, oppress the breathing, and produce the symptoms of a moribund appearance such that a woman suffering from suffocation of the womb is believed dead."[21] Peterson does not argue that Juliet had experienced such suffocation, but that the symptoms caused by the Friar's vial were the same. Since Juliet's *postmortem* is briefly conducted by her father, whose medical knowledge does not enable him to recognise what Peterson refers to as hysterical suffocation, she is quickly declared dead.

> Ha! let me see her. Out alas! She's cold.
> Her blood is settled, and her joints are stiff;
> Life and these lips have long been separated.
> Death lies on her like an ultimately frost.
> (4.5.25–28)

---

21 Kaara L. Peterson, "Shakespearean Revivifications: Early Modern Undead," *Shakespeare Studies*, 32 (2004): 240–266, 243.

Capulet's diagnosis is based on the first and most evident signs gathered from sensible observation: Juliet's still body is cold and does not respond to external stimuli. However, a temperature drop normally occurs during the night.[22] "Juliet's faked symptomology acts as a sort of red herring, and the play works to show how the projection of symptoms or diagnoses of the female body are fraught with error or mediated by deceitful performances."[23] It is in the name of such performances that Shakespeare can move along the intertwining realms of existence and appearance, between ontology and phenomenology, thus eliminating the differentiating boundaries between the two experiences of real death and apparent death. His fictional invention places the Self in some sort of in-between state, where the simultaneous deployment of to be and not to be is made possible.

Imogen in *Cymbeline* is another female character who experiences fake death, after drinking a poison that she thinks is in fact a cordial that would restore her health. According to the stage direction in Act 2 scene 4, "Imogen goes into the cave," therefore, the moment of her death is not performed before the audience, who, however, is aware of what the vial contains.[24] Once found, Imogen's "dead" body disguised in men's clothing is carried back onto the stage by Arviragus, whom Belarius questions over the corpse:

Belarius: How found you him?
Arviragus: Stark, as you see:
Thus smiling, as some fly had tickled slumber,
Not as death's dart, being laughed at; his right cheek
Reposing on a cushion.
Guiderius: Where?
Arviragus: O' the floor;
His arms thus leagued: I thought he slept, and put
My clouted brogues from off my feet, whose rudeness
Answered my steps too loud.
(4.9.209–15)

22 Such drop is "due to both a circadian body temperature fluctuation plus reduced heat producing muscle movement." See William H. Moorcroft, *Understanding Sleep and Dreaming* (Boston: Springer, 2013), 121.

23 Peterson, "Shakespearean Revivifications," 249.

24 The Queen plots to kill both Cymbeline and Imogen, so that her son, Cloten, will be crowned king. She therefore takes from Cornelius, the court doctor, what she believes to be deadly poison. Cornelius, however, suspecting the Queen's plan, substitutes the poison with a liquid which will make the imbiber's body apparently dead.

Through Arviragus's description of how he found Fidele/Imogen, Shakespeare, once again, draws the images of death and sleep together. Her "smiling," her "right cheek reposing on a cushion," and her "arms [...] leagued," indicate that Imogen had laid her body in a comfortable position in an attempt to find relief from her sickness (4.2.1–46). Moreover, since her illness[25] depends more on an inner malaise, it is sensible to think that she purposely lay down to sleep, combining her longing for some peace of mind with the effects of Cornelius's drug. Arviragus's description, in fact, does not prove that Imogen is actually dead, but does quite the opposite, asserting that she is in a profound sleep from which she cannot be woken. The Nurse, Capulet, Romeo in the case of Juliet, and Arviragus in the case of Imogen, jump to the conclusion that they are looking at a dead body, because Juliet and Imogen do not wake up.

Shakespeare draws from sleep and death by simultaneously using the similarity of the horizontal motionless body, common to both, and their contrastive element, waking, in order to create a third state that shares all of them, and that lies, to go back to *the* question, between what is and what is not. As Plato observed, "'[I]f something should appear such as at once to be and not to be, this will lie in between that which purely is and that which wholly is not, and neither knowledge nor ignorance will be about it, but again what appears between ignorance and knowledge,' that is, opinion."[26] Although for different reasons and with different awareness before waking, Juliet and Imogen are and are not dead/alive at the same time, achieving unity of to be *and* not to be through their motionless body. Even more so than slumber, Shakespeare's apparent death creates a new in-between state that is immanent and transcendent at the same time.

3 The 'Going-Beyond' and Shakespeare's Songs

Not only do sleep and death share a physical similarity dictated by the horizontal motionless body that is common to both, but as moments of abandonment of the sensory and conscious body, they acquire a metaphysical significance in the etymological sense of *μετὰ τὰ φυσικὰ:* that which is beyond the natural. This *beyond* constitutes the core of the sleep/death juxtaposition, because it characterises

25 "Imogen sinks into a 'passive heart-sick' melancholy, with 'grief and patience' mingled (4.2.37,57–58). Feeling 'very sick' and 'distressed' (4.2.5,47), Imogen drinks [...] a cordial that might restore her health." Warren Chernalk, *The Myth of Rome in Shakespeare and His Contemporaries* (Cambridge: Cambridge University Press, 2011), 239–240.
26 Plato, *Republic*, 478d5–11.

both states as moments of transcendence to a dimension that can be entered only through disembodiment. Thanks to an abandonment of its corporeal component, the Self is able to enter a new dimension, where the distinction between what *is* and what *appears* gradually fades into the blurred merging of that which is known and that which is not knowable.

In *A Midsummer Night's Dream* Theseus affirms that "Lovers and madmen have such seething brains, / Such shaping fantasies, that apprehend / More than cool reason ever comprehends. / The lunatic, the lover, and the poet / Are of imagination all compact." (5.1.4–8). Shakespeare draws madmen, lovers, and poets together according to the parameter of imagination, thus implying that in madness, love, and poetry the individual perceives another reality, and is able to do so not through his/her senses. In such states, man goes *beyond* "cool reason" and achieves a metaphysical understanding of another world.[27] The body is unnecessary for this trans-dimensional journey, and peculiarly, Shakespeare's affiliation of madness, love, and poetry as the means to "apprehend more than cool reason [...] comprehends" appears in *A Midsummer Night's Dream*, whose entire narrative is based on the alternation of sleep and waking.

The border between reality and imagination fades in favour of a confused in-between where images acquire new existential meaning: during slumber, in the dream, in the woods, in the realm of the unconscious, another dimension becomes real, "And as imagination bodies forth / The forms of things unknown the poet's pen / Turns them to shapes, and gives to airy nothing / A local habitation and a name. (5.1.14–17). The unknown becomes knowable, hence poetry is to be seen as the vessel that carries the disembodied self to an appreciation and understanding of the imaginable. It seems that Shakespeare, like both Plato and Aristotle, maintains that "in art, we touch hidden truth,"[28] and that this anagnoretic (or anamnestic) process, very much like death and slumber, has a kairological nature determined by its timelessness.

It is in fact thanks to the trans-dimensional journey of the poet that man acquires knowledge from the all-knowing, divine Muses. Homer invokes the Muses,

---

27 The association of madness to poetry and love also appears in Plato's *Phaedrus*, where Socrates defines four different kinds of madnesses. "The divine madness was subdivided into four kinds, prophetic, initiatory, poetic, erotic, having four gods presiding over them; the first was the inspiration of Apollo, the second that of Dionysus, the third that of the Muses, the fourth that of Aphrodite and Eros." The irrational element, as well as the transcending nature of these states is also asserted by the presence of the divine, to whom the madman aspires in the achievement of such state. See Plato, *Phaedrus*, 244a.

28 Eric S. Rabkin, "Loss and Recuperation," in *Why Plato? Platonism in Twentieth Century English Literature*, ed. Daniela Carpi (Heidelberg: Winter, 2005): 19–42, 23.

so that they can *sing* the truth to him: "Sing to me now, you Muses who hold the halls of Olympus! / You are goddesses, you are everywhere, you know all things- / all we hear is the distant ring of glory, we know nothing-"[29] In her phenomenological analysis of the voice, Adriana Cavarero draws a parallelism between the singing of the Muses and that of the Sirens, identifying a substantial difference in the addressee of the sung message. Whilst the "Sirens' song can be heard by all mortals, [...] [t]he Muse's song is only heard by the poet, who is privileged among mortals and does not die from having heard it."[30] This highlights the claim that poetry stems from a journey towards the divine, and it is by returning from such journey that the poet is raised to a status that Cavarero defines as privileged. Poetry, songs, and the truth, seem thus all connected to a journey of the bodiless self, that achieves the ability to transcend to another dimension, and to return with a new capability to produce art. Among all arts, music has a "capacity to foster transcendence, [...] activates the brain and possesses the potential to give the hearer sense of being transported 'out of this world' into a state of timelessness,"[31] which explains why rites, and especially rites of passage, have a musical accompaniment. Sorrow stemming from death generates tears and laments, which, from a musicological point of view, feature characteristics of the recitative: they have a melody, although monotone and repeated, and they present a rhythmic structure, thus representing a "connection between sung recitation and weeping."[32]

Poetry and music in the songs convey a message of change, a passage to another dimension that is the result of the association of poetic language with music, which has the power to distort the human perception of space and time. If music initially acts on a sensory level, and is thus physical, it also proves able to act on an emotional level, and is thus metaphysical. Through the alteration of the *hic et nunc*, music carries the self from one level to the other; it "induces a state of "trancing" [...] a transient state of being dissociated from everyday life, a feeling of being temporarily "out of time" [...] [I]t acts as a trigger that stirs memories and emotions, enticing the brain to create manifold associations, resulting in an "inner view."[33]

---

29 Homer, *Iliad*, 2.484–486.

30 Adriana Cavarero, *For More Than One Voice* (Stanford: Stanford University Press, 1995), 106.

31 Douglas Davies, *A Brief History of Death* (Oxford: Blackwell, 2005), 106.

32 Selawomira Zeranska-Kominek, "Death as the Beginning of Life. Weeping as the Beginning of Music," in *Traditional Musical Cultures in Central-Eastern Europe: Ecclesiastical and Folk Transmission*, ed. Piotr Dahlig (Warsaw: University of Warsaw, 2009): 67–80, 76.

33 Thomas Schäfer, Jörg Fachner, Mario Smukalla, "Changes in the Representation of Space and Time while Listening to Music," *Frontiers in Psychology* 4.508 (2013): 1–15, 6. See also

This inner view discards the chronological conception of time, which passes independently from the self, and generates a kairological experience for the self, whose new perception of the passing of time is internalised. In a way, the musical experience features the same "mineness" of death and slumber, because of its impossibility to exceed the I. Therefore, if our being-in-the-world and our not-being-in-the-world share the same *Jemeinigkeit*, our being-in-another-world through the musical experience must maintain a similar condition.

The content of the songs itself reasserts the concept of the transient self. Shakespeare's songs are "aubades, Bacchic songs, ballads, carols, dirges, hymns, reverdies (nature songs celebrating the coming of spring), sea chanties, serenades, songs of the greenwood, and wedding songs,"[34] and therefore mainly deal with the themes of travelling, love, drunkenness, divinity, and death. Such situations and events all express an alteration of the self: a journey – either physical or metaphysical – in which the Self abandons the deictic constraints of the present time and space, in order to embrace a timeless and spaceless dimension, characterised by a self-evident superfluousness of the body, which is relegated to mere bearer of the hamletic mortal coil.

Shakespeare's acknowledgment of the effects of music on the soul is evident in the significant song that opens the third act of *King Henry VIII* and which celebrates music's power to dismiss human grief,[35] in an allegory that reasserts the adjacency of sleep and death.

> Orpheus with his lute made trees,
> And the mountain tops that freeze,
> Bow themselves when he did sing:
> To his music plants and flowers
> Ever sprung; as sun and showers
> There had made a lasting spring.
> Every thing that heard him play,

Jörg Fachner, "Time is the Key: Music and Altered States of Consciousness," in *Altering Consciousness: Multidisciplinary Perspectives, Volume 1*, eds. Etzel Cardeña, Michael Winkelman and Santa Barbara: ABC-CLIO, 2011): 355–376.

34 Edward Hubler, *Shakespeare's Songs and Poems* (New York: McGraw-Hill, 1959), lv.

35 See also *The Merchant of Venice*, 5.1.70–88. Lorenzo asserts here that music has the power to change the nature of living beings, it can turn wild animals into docile creatures (5.1.78). According to Lorenzo, "the poet/ did feign that Orpheus drew trees, stones and floods,/ since naught so stockish, hard and full of rage,/ but music for the time doth change his nature (5.1.79–82). In Lorenzo's view, not only is music connected to the nature of living beings for its power to affect it, he also affirms that the man who lacks the sensitiveness to react to the sound of music is not to be trusted, for he is "fit for treasons, stratagems, and spoils./ The motions of his spirit are dull as night,/ And his affections dark as Erebus (5.1.85–87).

Even the billows of the sea,
Hung their heads, and then lay by.
In sweet music is such art,
Killing care and grief of heart
Fall asleep, or hearing, die. (3.1.3–14)

Although in the first stanza of the song the god maintains its original Greek Mythological matrix, in the second stanza the song conveys a more soporific mood that fosters a juxtaposition of Orpheus with Morpheus.[36] The last three verses of the song create an ambiguity that is generated by the grammatical function of "killing" in line 13. By considering "killing" as a verb, line 13 becomes an explanation of music's capability, which is to kill "care and grief of heart"; subsequently, "fall" in line 14 is an imperative addressed to the listener, therefore deprived of the implicit subject "you." However, if "killing" in verse 13 is considered as an adjective, the noun phrase "killing care and grief of heart," becomes the subject of "fall asleep, or hearing, die."[37]

At the core of these two possible readings there lies a belief in the healing power of music, as well as a reassertion of a similar nature that creates a bond between music, sleep, and death: this is their capacity to "reveal[-] to man an unknown world, a world quite separate from the outer sensual world surrounding him, a world in which he leaves behind all precise feelings in order to embrace inexpressible longing."[38]

4 Songs for the Dead: "Fear No More" Between Dirge and Lullaby

"Like other writers of his time, Shakespeare relied on the sensual properties of music to sophisticate and even reinterpret his lyrics."[39] By transcending the

36 "In 3–8, Orpheus's song seems productive and renewing; in 9–14, it is more soporific and enervating. [...] In fact, the mood of the second stanza would more appropriately evoke Morpheus (god of sleep) than Orpheus." See William Shakespeare, *King Henry VIII*, ed. Gordon McMullan, (London: The Arden Shakespeare, 2000), 317.

37 See Valerie Langfield, *Roger Quilter: His Life And Music*, (Woodbridge: The Boydell Press, 2002), 131.

38 *E. T. A. Hoffmann's Musical Writings: Kreisleriana, The Poet and the Composer, Music Criticism*, ed. David Charlton (Cambridge: Cambridge University Press, 2003), 94.

39 Tiffany Stern, "'I Have Both the Note and Dittie About Me': Songs on the Early Modern Page and Stage," *Common Knowledge*, 17.2 (2011): 306–320, 320.

order of time, the songs in a play can accompany the audience on a journey to an inner level of narration, utilising the combination of words and music to foster a new reading of the text. In the light of the adjacency between sleep and death – especially within performance – and the transcending power of music, two types of song, the dirge and the lullaby, acquire new referential meaning within the context of apparent death. With the introduction of this non-death, in fact, the role of the dirge changes significantly, for it no longer serves the purpose of accompanying the soul's transcendence to the afterlife. Since waking determines the fundamental differentiation between real and apparent death, the relation between the *signifiant* (the song) and the *signifié* (carrying the bodiless soul beyond) is altered by the absence of real death, which is replaced by a state that is closer to slumber.

The dirge "Fear No More" in *Cymbeline* (4.2.258–281) lends itself to this literary-musical analysis because, from a situational point of view, it stands in an ambiguous position. This is due to the co-textual and contextual incongruences created in the play by the dialogue preceding the song, the consequent absence of music, and Imogen/Fidele's apparent death. After Fidele is believed to be dead, Arviragus and Guiderius agree to give the boy a funeral rite, and proper burial; thus the former exhorts the latter to "sing him to the ground" (4.2.236). Guiderius, however, claims that he "cannot sing" (4.2.240) and states that it would be inappropriate to sing the dirge "for notes of sorrow out of tune are worse / than priests and fanes that lie (4.2.241–242). Either because their "voices / have got the mannish crack" (4.2.235–236), or because they do not feel up to the performative task required by the moment, the dirge is recited and not sung. This creates an incongruence on two levels: on the one hand, the indication "Song" before the dirge is meaningless, because there is no song to be sung, and on the other, the recited dirge deprives the ritual performance of the solemnity fostered by music.

The reasons that led Shakespeare to decide that "Fear No More" was to be spoken rather than sung may deal with the lack of boy soprano voices in the theatre company when *Cymbeline* was produced, or with the characters' inability to sing competently the dirge because of their profound grieving.[40] What remains is that "Fear No More" was never intended to be sung, which creates a contradiction in logical and ontological terms, because a song that is not sung cannot be defined as a song. Among Shakespeare's songs, "Fear No More" enjoys a great variety and frequency of musical adaptation, and since the eighteenth century

---

40 See Peggy Muñoz Simonds, *Myth, Emblem, and Music in Shakespeare's Cymbeline: An Iconographic Reconstruction* (Cranbury: Associated University Press, 1992), 357.

several composers have created musical accompaniments for this dirge: William Boyce (1746), Thomas Arne (1759), Ralph Vaughn Williams (1945), Hubert Parry (1906), Roger Quilter (1921), Gerald Finzi (1929), Constant Lambert (1942), John Dankworth (1964),[41] Stephen Sondheim (1974), and Loreena McKennitt (1998) among others. What is noteworthy is that most of these transpositions highlight, or rather reassert, the sleep/death adjacency, through a musical accompaniment that does not express the sadness and mourning conveyed by the death march, but which features some of the typical characteristics of a lullaby. Lullabies could be defined as songs for soothing infants and promoting sleep and from a musical point of view, it is possible to identify common musical features that are cross-culturally present in most lullabies. Generally, "[l]ullabies are highly repetitive in terms of their individual sounds, words, verbal and melodic phrases, and rhythms."[42]

In most of the above-mentioned adaptations, it is interesting to notice how the composers abandoned some of the features of the lullaby, especially those typical of infant-directed speech, but retained others, such as the contained dynamic and slow tempo. The musicalisations of "Fear No More" maintain a calmness that is intended to soothe the listener and convey a feeling of rest, yet they do not transmit an idea of lament, mourning, or grieving, and are not marked by the sombre gravity of the death-march percussions. If such adaptations were intended as songs of death, they seem to portray the serenity of eternal rest, rather than the sorrowful melancholy that devastates the living. Fidele's apparent death is neither death, nor sleep, and similarly, the musical rewritings of "Fear No More" are neither dirges, nor lullabies.

Gerald Finzi, for example, "treats the poem as a stately sarabande, which gives the setting a powerful ritualistic quality;"[43] the song, however, especially in the piano-voice version, features a "monotonous plod,"[44] which contributes to conveying to the listener a sense of calmness and repetitiveness. This is expressed by the dynamics of the musical piece which are constantly under control

---

41 See *Music in Shakespeare: A Dictionary,* eds. Christopher R. Wilson and Michela Calore, (London: Thoemmes Continuum, 2005), 135.

42 Sandra E. Trehub and Laurel Traior, "Singing to Infants: Lullabies and Play Songs," in *Advances in Infancy Research. Volume 2,* eds. Carolyn Rovee-Collier, Lewis P. Lipsitt and Harlene Hayne, (Stamford: Ablex Publishing, 1998): 43–77, 50. See also Anna M. Unyk, Sandra E. Trehub, Laurel Traior and Glenn E. Schellenberg, "Lullabies and Simplicity: A Cross-Cultural Perspective," *Psychology of Music* 20 (1992): 15–28.

43 Trevor Hold, *Parry to Finzi: Twenty English Song-Composers* (Woodbridge: The Boydell Press, 2002), 418.

44 Hold, *Parry to Frinzi*, 418.

Exc. 1

and generally remain in the range between *mezzopiano* (*mp*) and *mezzoforte* (*mf*), almost indicating that the singing and its accompaniment should never be too soft or too loud. The piece features a *fortissimo* (*ff*) that is immediately decreased to a *mf* within the same measure, and through a *diminuendo* in the next measure becomes again a *mp* in the following (Exc. 1). This occurs in a peculiar moment in the song: the music is the only protagonist of this moment, since the singer is not singing, and the *ff* in the accompaniment cannot interfere with the lyrics; it asserts its transcending power and uses its abilities to convey a sense of change. Such transformation occurs at two levels: textual and musical.

As far as the former is concerned, there is a metric change from the trochaic tetrameter of verses 258–275 to trochaic trimeter of verses 276–279 "No exorciser harm thee! / Nor no witchcraft charm thee! / Ghost unlaid forbear thee! / Nothing ill come near thee!" Arviragus and Belarius alternate in pronouncing these formulaic exclamations, no longer addressing Fidele, but respectively exorcisers, witchcraft charms, ghosts, and illness, in a chiasmus that combines the earthly (exorcisers and illness) with the unearthly (charms and ghosts), thus not eliminating completely the possibility that Fidele might wake up again.

There are also three major musical changes which concur in transmitting the modifying nature of the moment: dynamic, tempo, and key. The first features the above-described rapid *diminuendo* from *fortissimo* to *mezzopiano*, the second a change from 6/4 to 4/4, and the third a key change from B*b*maj to B*b*min. This last change stimulates particular interest in the sleep/death perspective, because it shifts the song from one key to its minor correspondent, almost indicating two opposite aspects of the same entity. This state of uncertainty continues in the following measures when the time signature goes back to the initial 6/4 (Exc. 2). Although there is no apparent key change, the song mood seems to shift again from minor to major, leaving a doubt as to whether the measures preceding the final one are meant to be B*b*min or D*b*maj. The resolution only comes on the final chord, where the sung B*b* on the word "grave" is accompanied by a B*b*maj chord, which features the natural D instead of D*b*, and which brings the song back to its original key. The sudden key change occurs between two

Exc. 2

keys which are not adjacent, thus contributing to the creation of a sense of surprise conveyed by the final chord which inspires peace, light and transcendence; this can be read as a "waking" moment either in this world, or another.

The concept of ascendance applies to the ending of Johnny Dankworth's jazz version as well, where the line "and renowned be thy grave" is repeated twice. The second time, however, the word "grave" is sung on the 7th interval, and therefore creates suspense impeding the natural conclusion of the final chord. Moreover, the accompaniment recalls the sound of a siren, conveying a somewhat alarming mood that seems to indicate a sudden change from a flat and repetitive calmness to a more cheerful vitality. Dankworth's music accompanies Cleo Laine's voice in the sinuous shifts between low and high notes. The slowness of the tempo marks the stability of the modules that repeat themselves throughout the stanzas, but it is interrupted, similarly to Finzi's rendition, by the sudden change featured for lines 275–279. These lines precede the end and, with their delicateness, seem to accompany the listener into those final measures in which no musical resolution is reached.

A third version of the song that fosters an interesting analysis is Sondheim's "Fear No More" in the musical *The Frogs*. This musical is Sondheim's adaptation of Aristophane's homonymous play, it was composed in 1974, but not performed on Broadway until thirty years later. Sondheim's revision introduces the characters of Bernard Shaw and William Shakespeare, who duel in a verbal competition on different themes: women, man, the life force, and death. This philosophical discussion about death gives Shakespeare the opportunity to sing "Fear No More."

Exc. 3

The lyrics of the song are not exactly the same as those found in *Cymbeline*; in fact, Sondheim's version presents several omissions. The song is preceded by a spoken introduction by Shakespeare, who says "Cowards die many times before their deaths; / The valiant never taste of death but once. / Of all the wonders that I have heard / It seems to me most strange that men should fear; / Seeing that death, a necessary end, / Will come when it will come."[45] In Sondheim, as well as in Finzi, we find indications such as *poco crescendo* or *diminuendo*, which indicate the soft character of the piece. The time signature 3/4 is kept throughout the whole piece, which only uses Shakespeare's tetrameters, thus eliminating the inconvenient necessity to adapt the musical metric to the poetic metric change of the play's song. The song's stability is also asserted by the unchanging key, Dmaj, which provides a supportive base for the final D on the word "dust" that concludes the song on the tonic, leaving no possibility for openness of interpretation (Exc. 3). Sondheim shows no interest in highlighting a sudden change at the end, nor in conveying a sense of ascendence, thus reasserting the concept of death as natural and necessary. The contextualisation of the song within the contest against Shaw, and as an argument on the topic of death, fosters Shakespeare's view of death as a moment to be welcomed without fear.

45 William Shakespeare, *Julius Caesar*, 2.2.32–37.

Despite their belonging to different musical genres, the adaptations of "Fear No More" generate a distance from the ritual death march by using musical features that characterise these songs as calm, soothing, and somehow transcending. If on the one hand they do not feature the same repetitiveness and monotony of the lullaby, on the other, their slow tempo and controlled dynamic change delineate a calm atmosphere that is suited for sleep. None of these adaptations sounds sad, mourning, or lamenting, therefore if they are meant to be dirges, or death songs, they definitely convey the idea that death is not only natural, but also peaceful and liberating. The very opening of the song introduces the concept of fear, and reasserts what Shakespeare recites before the number in Sondheim, that is to say that death is not to be feared, because it is "necessary" and "will come when it will come."

With the introduction of apparent death, Shakespeare provides an alternative to Hamlet's question, giving theatrical life to the parallelism that Hamlet himself introduces in the monologue, when he draws sleep and death together in the association "to die, to sleep / no more" (3.1.59–60). However, such a stratagem maintains its veridicality and valence only on the stage, in a dimension that is circumscribed by the suspension of disbelief, and which enables the overlapping of "being" and "appearing." That of the performance is a realm where space and time acquire new meaning, and it is only within this realm that actual death and actual slumber, will never be.

IV Staging the Queenly Body: The Performance of a Female Body Politic

Cristina Costantini

Katechontic Elizabeth: The Physical Repository of Sovereignty through Law, Literature and Iconography

1 Moulding Intellectual Traditions: Perceptions of Elizabethan Queenship and The Politics of the Past

In several of his remarkable and influential works on English Ancient Constitutionalism, J.G.A.Pocock[1] has vividly indicated two general sources for the edification of the *common law mind*,[2] conceived as the endemic mentality, which in several ways contrasted continental conceptions and ideologizations of European legal tradition: Humanism and English Ecclesiology. In a critical discussion on the matter, Glenn Burgess's contribution has innovated significantly upon the scientific debate for at least three important reasons.[3] First of all, he brought to light the rhetorical valence of the expression "ancient constitution" itself and its misleading extent, in order to react to a fictional and mythologised image of a fixed constitution, which existed sometime in the past.[4] In this renewed perspec-

---

1 J.G.A. Pocock, "England," in *National Consciousness, History and Political Culture in Early Modern Europe* ed. Orest Ranum (Baltimore: Johns Hopkins University Press, 1975), 105–106; J.G.A. Pocock, *Machiavellian Moment. Florentine Political Thought and the Atlantic Republican Tradition* (Princeton: Princeton University Press, 1975), 340–341; J.G.A. Pocock "The History of British Political Thought. The Creation of a Center," *Journal of British Studies*, 24.3 (1985): 283–310, 283.

2 James W. Tubbs, *The Common Law Mind: Medieval and Early Modern Conceptions* (Baltimore: Johns Hopkins University Press, 2000); Donald R. Kelley, "History, English Law and the Renaissance," *Past and Present*, 65.1 (1975): 24–51; Christopher Brooks and Kevin Sharpe, "Debate: History, England Law and the Renaissance," *Past and Present*, 72.1 (1976): 133–142.

3 Glenn Burgess, *The Politics of the Ancient Constitution. An Introduction to English Political Thought, 1603–1642* (London: Macmillan Press Ltd, 1992).

4 The phrase "the ancient constitution" is a misleading one [...] "The ancient constitution" was not a constitution of the past; it was the present constitution, the constitution of the seventeenth century [...] In short, an ancient constitution was a modern constitution that had ancient foundations. A study of the ancient constitution of England will, then, be a study of the relations between the past and the present. What sort of a process transformed the Saxon polity into that of seventeenth century England? Even more important than this was the question of why men ever

tive, what is under scrutiny is not a frozen set of practices and events, but the complex body of relations between the past and the present and its strategic administration by selected elites. Secondly, Burgess emphasized the inherent ambiguities that lay behind the formal structure of the concept of "common-law mind," the preconceptions which gave form to it and their fundamental role in the ways in which political matters were discussed. Finally, he also clarified that the study of past ideas must always involve a process of de-familiarization and, to this extent, he emphasised the need to add a supplementary item to the sources traced by Pocock, namely the intellectual tradition of common law itself. Working from this foundation, my aim is to discuss the perceptions of Elizabethan queenship and the conceptualization of Elizabethan policy-making according to the competing paradigms used to construct legal traditions. As a comparatist scholar, I think that the main issue is not, or not only, the understanding of Elizabethan public discourse and its characterization, that does not exclusively involve questions of methodology and interpretation, but rather it is a question of the relevance acquired by the skilful representation of sovereignty in the process of building an indisputable national autonomy. In order to sustain this argument, what is required is a systematic analysis of the living bodies of contending customs and memories, artfully condensed in a series of canonical texts that emphasise commemoration. The proclaimed self-sufficiency of English Law and Constitution, through the strenuous defence of the Elizabethan settlement, was at the centre of juridical and geopolitical tensions, which ultimately came to disrupt what was widely asserted to be the unity of the Western Legal Tradition.

In this regard I shall move from the reflections developed by H.J. Berman in his book *Law and Revolution*,[5] sharing with this critical account a theological approach to political and jurisprudential analysis. However, I intend to focus more on the motives of dissimilarity and divergence, rather than on the apparent similarity between the revolutions that transformed the Western Constitution: that is to say, the structural and related issues of nationhood, order, power and legitimation.

Having clarified the context for my analysis, my main concern will be to examine the governance and administration of Elizabeth's representations. In particular, I will concentrate on the following issues:

believed that the past could legitimate the present or (a more answerable question) *how* they believed it was able to do so." (Burgess, *The Politics of the Ancient Constitution*, 19).

5 Harold J. Berman, *Law and Revolution* (Cambridge: Harvard University Press, 1983).

(1) how the contending movements of contestation and appropriation of Elizabeth I's body and behaviour were settled and composed through the medium of intellectual traditions of thought;
(2) how this cunning negotiation provoked and incited theoretical discussions on the nature and the extent of authority;
(3) how the "Elizabethan issue" was at the heart of legal and ecclesiastical antiquarianism, the scholarly movement which, in substance, constructed the legal and narrative plot of Ancient Constitutionalism.

All of these questions are strongly related to the seminal arguments debated by Pocock and Burgess, insofar as they argue for a deeper investigation of the entangled structure of the common law mind, in order to uncover its unspoken implications in relation to the morphology of the English system. At the same time, they embrace the mutual relationship between rival languages (conceived as a *mentalité*) and the conflict of traditions (considered as willed and intentional, repositories of monuments and ideas) as the constitutive components of every legal system. In this respect, Elizabethan public life displayed itself by means of different discourses, each one having its own terms and concepts; for example, the discourse of the law, which used terms like custom, prerogatives, liberties, precedent, rights; the discourse of theology, which introduced words like God, providence, order, grace; the language inherited from the Classics and, in homeopathic doses, to quote Holdsworth's witty sentence, from Roman Law, that became the privileged way of expression of a nationalistic kind of neo-humanism.[6] This polyglot framework was also enriched by a variety of sub-discourses, such as idioms, rhetoric, distinguishable language games, each with its own rules, preconditions and implications, tone and style. My purpose here is to understand how these multifarious discourses were combined into the structure of a tradition, and how this process involved a degree of theoretically implicit intellectual endeavour. In my view, the emphasis must be placed on a hybrid "master discourse," implied in the organisation of professional corporations (respectively legal, literary, theological and ecclesiastical) capable of articulating the practices, which authorised and legitimised their language and placed them in a social and cultural hierarchy. These leading groups endowed historical facts with aesthetic forms; they participated actively in a battle of memories; they fought against the arch-enemy of temporal oblivion; they provided English

6 "We have received Roman Law, but we have received it in small homeopathic doses, at different periods and as and when required. It has acted as a tonic to our native legal system, and not as a drug or poison"; William Searle Holdsworth, *A History of English Law* (7th ed.), eds. Arthur Lehman Goodheart and Harold Greville Hanbuy (London: Methuen, 1956–1966), 293.

audiences with genealogies; they mingled educational with propaganda; and above all, they devised a ritual of commemoration. Basically, they projected the repetition of a selected past into a codified and legitimated present.

2 Representation and Cultural Negotiations. The Onto-Juridical Threshold Between Elizabeth's Flesh and the Body of Sovereignty

The approach I have proposed will involve the interpretation of the visibility of Elizabeth I, the public fascination that it generated, and the pivotal role played by this mythologised figure in giving an emblematic substance to English memory. In order to do so, I will emphasise two key concepts: firstly, the concept of representation and its powerful social, political and cultural effects, and secondly, the link between Elizabeth's flesh and the body of sovereignty, whose governance and disposition come to be a cultural device able to capture and articulate the numerous tensions existing across different fields of historical experience. In Tudor times and especially during Elizabeth's reign, the subtle nexus between representation and corporeality is the main issue to consider when approaching the construction of English public identity and, consequently, the juridical imagination of a national past. According to this perspective, on the one hand, Elizabeth's Flesh, that is her natural, physical, female and even sexual body, is the medium through which the words and terms I mentioned above, originally intrinsic to different, relatively autonomous discursive fields, are mingled, projected, transposed and transferred from one to another, and specifically from Theology to Law, assisted by the mediation of literary texts. On the other hand, the embodiment of Elizabeth's flesh, or the secular transfiguration of the feminine physique into the body of sovereignty, is shaped, refined and fashioned in dialogue with contending political and theological interests. The transubstantiation of the Flesh into the Body of Sovereignty, which recalls the Christian dogma, is the essential subject matter of representation: more precisely, it traces the line of a possible division between self-presentation (that is the ways in which Royalty and Queenship were portrayed and promoted by sovereignty itself and by the Elizabethan aristocratic court) and re-presentation (that is the figurative and narrative *presentification* of the image of authority proposed and vigorously exhibited in different contexts), consequently producing the emergence of a public space where perceptions and reactions are located. Moreover, it discloses the combination of the acts of repetition and remembering in the making of political legitimation and it facilitates the complete communicability of a "mysterious majesty." In this way, the body, as something more and other than natural flesh, might be viewed as the privileged site of a competition for representation and counter-presentation. Moreover, its controlled public exposure marks the limits of revelation, establishing what can be revealed as ostensible, manifest, visible and perceptible, on the one hand, and what, on the other hand, has to remain secret, and not open to public scrutiny. This argument is of particular importance for the proper comprehension of legal traditions in general, and of the English Legal Tradition in particular, insofar as it deals with an ontological structural excess, that lies behind the phenomenological appearance of every legal system. Furthermore, it justifies and supports the conventional statement according to which Elizabeth has become an icon, or rather *the* icon of the Nation that endlessly renews itself. In fact, what is under investigation here is the metaphysical nature of the icon, the typical device, and the critical means by which it becomes possible to penetrate what otherwise remains invisible. As Jean-Luc Marian has observed, "[t]he icon does not result from a vision, but provokes one. The invisible seems in a semblance which however never reduces the invisible to the slackened wave of the visible."[7] The icon breaks with the figured allocation of the visible in the perceptible face of the invisible. My inquiry into the liminal, onto-juridical threshold between Elizabeth's flesh and the body of sovereignty is therefore strongly related to a specific methodological approach that I have introduced in the field of comparative law. In this regard, my concern is to combine the historical perspective and the connected narratological accounts with the symbolic morphogenesis of a given system of law: the genealogical and archaeological perspectives are mutually interwoven with the aesthetic dimension, in order to discover the heterogeneous forms of *presentification* selected in diverse times and spaces; their correspondence or their fracture; and finally the aesthetic traces of resemblance or difference. This view is also oriented to expose the relics of the "unmasterable past," that is the past that does not pass away because it has not been either comprehended nor exorcized, and whose *presentification* has consequently been denied.

7 "L'icône ne résulte pas d'une vision mais la provoque [..] Tandis que l'idole résulte du regard qui la vise, l'icône convoque la vue, en laissant le visible peu à peu se saturer d'invisible. L'invisible semble, apparaît dans une semblance (*eiko / *eoika)" (Jean-Luc Marion, *Dieu sans l'être* (Paris: PUF, 2002), 28).

3 The English *Katéchon*. The Oppositional Ways of Salvation as Systematic Markers Within the Boundaries of the Western Legal Tradition

Moving from the premises that I have developed above, I would like to emphasize the discontinuity between Elizabeth's self-perception and self-presentation, based on her constancy and immutability and stigmatized in the motto taken from her mother "*Semper eadem*" (Always the same) on the one hand, and the multiple, even contrastive public representations of the figure of the Queen on the other hand. As Helen Hackett has noted "Elizabeth acquired different aspects as she was required to fulfil various symbolic needs, both spiritual and political."[8] This sort of gap or dissociation lays at the heart of a narrative that is both ambiguous and contestatory, that could be defined as the law of the narrative of the English Legal Tradition (a hybrid discourse composed of Literature, Law, Iconography and Arts). A rhetoric of stability, permanence and steadiness was counterbalanced by a rhetoric of erratic, alterable irresolutions and projections replete with their own symbolizations.

My aim is to analyse the impact of the complex performance of Regality and Sovereignty within the structure of English Literature and English Law. Through the means of an interdisciplinary approach, it is possible to appreciate a chiasmic epilogue for the morphological perceptibility of these two fields. In particular, the administration of what I have called the onto-juridical threshold between Elizabeth's flesh (as the objective correlative of self-perception) and the body of sovereignty (as the objective correlative of external representation), on the one hand, contributed to individuate, define and articulate different literary genres; on the other hand, it was politically managed in order to assert an undisputable and unitary order, personified by one and only one central authority. While Literature occasionally mirrored antagonistic views through the polymorphous strategies of literary composition, Law staked its claim for unity, uniformity and consistency. Therefore the juridical elites, along with the representatives of legal antiquarianism as a cultural movement were responsible for the selective shaping of practices and discourses into a coherent framework. Literature did not solve conflicts and rivalries, quarrels and dissensions; on the contrary, Law – or rather legal thought – presented an univocal portrait through a process of mythologisation. From this point of view, we can say that Literature partially

8 Helen Hackett, *Virgin Mother Maiden Queen. Elizabeth I and the Cult of Virgin Mary* (New York: St. Martin's Press, 1995), 164.

unsealed the ontological, and consequently, the representational excess that existed within the discourse of the Law. In one of its manifestations, and following a number of Classical precedents, the radical interrogation of sovereignty gave birth to satire, as a genre that became popular in the later years of Elizabeth's reign. The public theatre was an institution for the staging of cultural anxieties and for the creation of an embodied mediation, considered as a transaction from physical bodies (including the Queen's Body) to aural representations, from fantasmatic characters to corporeal beings. The theatre was the site par excellence, where through the medium of actors, the presence of an absence was performed. Moreover, the poetics of Gloriana, Astrea, Cynthia and Belphoebe did not eradicate a darker discourse of disrespect and dissent, deliberately provocative if not outrageous: the godly purity of a Virgin Queen was undermined by a pornographic literature,[9] and the textual exposure of sexual desire or of the female genitalia of Queen Elizabeth functioned to demystify and undermine the mystical secret defended by the royal body.

In the domain of Law, the omnipresent and celebrated cult of the Virgin Queen was the strategic means through which its jurisdictional elements were definitively regulated. It was fundamental to the fulfilment of Elizabeth I's father Henry VIII's programme, and was especially central to the assertion of national independence from the authority of the Roman Church. In relation to the process of the English Reformation, I will introduce an original characterization of Elizabeth in terms of "*Katechontic* Elizabeth," in order to present the legal understanding of Elizabethan Queenship according to the approach of political theology. In this context I will consider three main issues:

(1) the insertion of theological arguments into the legal and political domain to re-signify Elizabethan virginity;
(2) the hermeneutic revolution provoked by Reformation and, as its specific effect, the new explication of the act of representing;
(3) the contending strategies deployed by the Roman and Anglican Church to settle the relationship between a Sovereign Authority (secular, theological or hybrid) and the Authority of the Sacred Book. Here it will be interesting to note the mutual composition of the places assigned respectively to different kind of *corpora* within a theo-juridical order: a physical body, that is a vested human flesh, or a material body, that is a book.

9 Jeroen Deploige, Gita Deneckere, *Mystifying the Monarch: Studies on Discourse, Power and History* (Amsterdam: Amsterdam University Press, 2006), 105.

All these arguments serve to justify the syntagm I have introduced as the main core of my paper, "*Katechontic* Elizabeth," which is based on the adjectival use of the word *katéchon*, with its strong theological implications, in order to qualify the theo-political transubstantiation of Elizabethan Flesh into a doubled Sovereign Body. From this perspective, it is possible to produce a more considered reflection on Kantorowicz's theory of the king's two bodies[10] and a more incisive account of the peculiarities of English Majesty.

Within this theoretical framework it is important to keep in mind that Elizabethan ecclesiology provided one of the most significant foundations of the English Ancient Constitutionalism; the most notable common lawyers were clearly associated with the most famous theologians in the process that led to the assertion of English autonomy from Rome. John Guy has brilliantly observed that "St. German did for English Common Law what, a generation or so later, John Jewel and Richard Hooker did for Anglican Church."[11] In this framework I will reflect on the multifarious devices used to substantiate the Cult of the Virgin Queen or, more incisively, to transform virginal flesh into a body of salvation, and evocatively, into a *katechontic* body. Fundamentally, these devices involved the following: an apocalyptic narrative, an apologetic plot, the projection of a millenaristic order, and a redundant iconography.

First of all, the historical autonomy of England in religious affairs was asserted by means of the construction of a national apocalyptic moment.[12] In the intellectual tradition of ecclesiastical antiquarianism apocalyptic thought acquired a political dimension that supported the break with Rome. The main issue was to select evidences of the early Christianization of Britain in order to establish a pedigree for the Church of England that antedated the growth of the Holy See. John Bale, Matthew Parker, John Foxe and John Jewel, among others, were the authors of a new, reformed history of a correspondingly re-founded nation. Britain, as the genealogical ancestor of England, was properly Christianized as a part of the true, primitive church. This pristine, perfect state was gradually altered and destroyed by the illegitimate usurpations of the figure of the Bishop of Rome, the Catholic Pope, who extended both his power and his clerical jurisdiction at the expense of the English Crown. This master-narrative was, from an English point of view, instrumental to the rejection of the Catholic claim that the Church of England was in a state of schism from the true church, and to

10 Ernst Hartwig Kantorowicz, *The King's Two Bodies. A Study in Medieval Political Theology* (Princeton: Princeton University Press, 1957).

11 Alistair Fox and John Alexander Guy, *Reassessing the Henrician Age. Humanism, Politics and Reform 1500–1550* (Oxford: Blackwell, 1986), 101–103.

12 Pocock, *The Machiavellian Moment*, 341.

the identification of the Roman Pope with the Antichrist. The proofs of such onto-metaphysical correspondence were recognized in the Pope's defiance of Christ's teaching and, in particular, in the temporal ambitions of the papacy, in its scandalous behaviour and in the falsity of its magisterial doctrines. According to the main tenets of the apocalyptic story, the Reformation was interpreted as the struggle between good and evil, Christ and Antichrist, holy martyrs and satanic persecutors. As a consequence, England was construed as the new Israel, as the new paradigm of the Elect Nation, as a sacralised, redeemed, godly nation.[13] It could be declared that Israel was viewed as the prefigurement of England, its destiny finding resolution in the destiny of England. In the same narrative and legitimating context, English monarchs personified ancient prophets and patriarchs: Henry VIII was recognized as a new Hezekiah, Edward as a new Josiah and Elizabeth as a new Deborah.

According to English Apocalypticism, Elizabeth was depicted as the godly force providentially destined to fight the Antichrist. John Aylmer spoke of Elizabeth as an apocalyptic agent, who "may many years carry the sword of our defence and therewith cut off the head of the Hydra, the Antichrist of Rome in such sort that it may never grow again in this realm of England."[14] In the last speech of John Bale's *King John*, while Nobility claims that Elizabeth is the Apocalyptic angel, the character of Civil Order manifests her wishes for Elizabeth's long reign with these words "Pray unto the lord that her grace may continue / The days of Nestor to our souls' consolation, / and that her offspring may live also to subdue / the Antichrist, with his whole generation / in Elias' spirit to the comfort of this nation, / also to preserve her most honourable council / to the praise of God and glory to the Gospel."[15] In his *The Shepheard's Garland*, Drayton presents Elizabeth as the biblical Eve who defied the snake, and as the Apocalyptic woman who conquered the dragon with seven heads. Thomas Becon calls Elizabeth the noble conqueror of the Antichrist.[16] These textual portraits, wholly considered, transformed Elizabeth into the literal figuration of the Redeemer, whose kingdom was a millenarian paradise on earth.

---

13 John W. McKenna, "How God became an Englishman," in *Tudor Rule and Revolution: Essays for G.R. Elton,* eds. Delloyd J. Guth and John W. McKenna (Cambridge: Cambridge University Press, 1982): 25–44.
14 John Aylmer, *A Harbor for Faithful and True Subjects* (London: printed by John Day, 1559).
15 John Bale, *The Dramatic Writings of John Bale, Bishop of Ossory* (Rockville: Wildside Press, 2008), 294.
16 Quoted in Richard Bauckham, *Tudor Apocalypse* (Oxford: Sutton Courtenay Press, 1978), 128.

From this point of view, Elizabeth's natural and physical body was transfigured not only into a sovereign political body, but also into a theological *katéchon*. This word refers to a controvesial figure whom we find in the New Testament book of Thessalonians II, where Paul announces that Christ's imminent coming will be preceded by signs. More precisely, Christ will come again only after the Antichrist has usurped God's place in the Temple. Since the precise time of Christ's coming is not known, Paul introduces the figure of the *katéchon*, a sort of delayer or restrainer, whose mission is to defer the unbinding of the Antichrist, in order to prevent the arrival of Evil. The difficulty in interpreting 2 Thessalonians lies in the fact that the same word is used in two different forms and to refer to two different genders: in verse 6, it is used in the neutral form, as a kind of impersonal power (what is restraining); whereas in the following verse it is conjugated as a verbal form, as the present participle of the verb *katécho*, (masculine gender), to denote "he" who now is the restraining force. From a theological perspective, it has been argued that the neuter could be referred to the word of God, while the masculine form could be used to denote the Holy Spirit: the former could be the means through which the latter, as an agent, performs his task, or his proper mission and ministry. But, from the very origins of the intellectual debate on the possible meanings of this word, the figure evoked has been endowed with a political connotation. Tertullian was the first to identify the *katéchon* with the Roman Empire and the Roman Emperor; at a later period, John of Damascus confirms this interpretation (trad. "*The withholding power means Roman Empire. When that is finished, Antichrist will come*"). In this way, the secular space of the Political as such is shaped as a 'steered space,' as a space intrinsically designed to prevent the Antichrist's reign and consequently the end of the material world. Throughout the centuries this was the preferred view, which had generated, I suggest, a *katechontic* structure of history. To mention the most famous adaptation in modern times, in the writings of the juridical theorist Carl Schmitt, even the definition of the state of exception as *Frist* is a function of his arch-Catholic conception of the *katéchon*, a pattern in which history takes place in the space of time between the present and the coming of the Antichrist: without the *katéchon* time itself would long ago have come to an end. These arguments prompt a more considered reflection on the theological foundation of the Western Legal Tradition, extending H.J. Berman's analysis. In fact, in addition to claims for jurisdiction, that followed the so called Papal Revolution which established the modern form of the Western Church (as a visible, corporate and legal structure) and its relation to the secular authority, and also, in addition to the mutual borrowings of terms, concepts and practices, I think it is of particular importance to pay attention to the the soteriolgical dimension, to the various interpretations which have been given to the interface between history and salvation. As it has been brilliantly pointed out by Reinheart Koselleck, "[t]he history of Christianity is a history of expectations, or more exactly the constant anticipation of the End of the World on the one hand and the continual deferment of the End on the other. While the materiality of such expectations varied from one situation to another, the basic figure of the End remained constant."[17] In a systematic perspective, and as one of the sub-disciplines of comparative law, it could be of direct relevance to understand how the legal order reacted to the theological promise of human salvation, and in what ways the different legal systems coalesced into the supposed unitary Western Legal Tradition, confronted with the mysteries of the End Times. Moreover, the oppositional instruments implicit in the narrative of salvation and the subject of political propaganda can be viewed as markers that will allow us to trace differences and dissimilarities within the boundaries of the Western Legal Tradition. In this regard, Koselleck's account of the strategic use of the lecture on history offered by the Church, and on its internal critical self-awareness, is illuminating:

> The Church utilized the imminent – but future End of the World as a means of stabilization, finding an equilibrium between the threat of the End on the one hand and the hope of Parousia on the other. The unknown Eschaton must be understood as one of the Church's integrating factors, enabling its self-constitution as world and as institutions. The Church itself is eschatological. But the moment the figures of the Apocalypse are applied to concrete events or instances, the eschatology has disintegrative effects. The End of the World is only an integrating factor so long as its politico-historical meaning remains indeterminate.[18]

The mythical investment in the Apocalypse was thus historically adapted to different situations. According to this approach, the literary representation of Elizabeth as the force destined to resist and to wage war against the Antichrist allows us to identify the Queen as the English *katéchon*. This trans-historical equation was supported by an apologetic deification of Elizabeth's carnal virginity, implemented through the means of a new concept of representation introduced by the Reformers, and it gave new shape to geopolitical assets.

Initially, the celebration of virginity associated with Reformist doctrines served to re-legitimise the overall combination of references to emblematic figures of godly and faithful women used from medieval times. Marian typology was invoked to justify the secular power of the figure of the queens and it was

---

17 Reinhart Koselleck, "Modernity and the Plans of Historicity," in *Futures Past: On the Semantics of Historical Time*, ed. Reinhart Koselleck (Cambridge: MIT Press, 1985), 5–7.
18 Koselleck, *Modernity*, 13.

coherent with the conception of the time, insofar as they were primarily consorts who never ruled in their own right; they were, therefore, considered royal mediators, like the Blessed Virgin, who governed only indirectly by means of mercy or maternal love.[19] The urgent need to present Elizabeth as an independent monarch forced a reformulation of this Marian veneration and was nourished by the Protestant belief according to which Christ is the sole intercessor between the Human and the Divine. As a result, the attention paid to the sexual and natural status of Elizabeth's flesh (that is her virginity) produced a dislocation of the sacred prototypes of Christianity. While the Virgin's epithets (for ex. Virgin, Mother, Bride, Queen), as traditional devotional forms, were used to support Elizabeth's regime, Elizabeth's identification with godly women was moulded, recalling other scriptural models, such as the Virtuous Woman of the Proverbs, the Five Wise Virgins and the Woman Clothed with the Sun. Royal narratives and royal iconography were totally refurbished. John N. King properly remarked that

> Tudor apologists skilfully concealed or transformed a complex relationship to imagery associated with the Virgin Mary as Queen of Heaven when they addressed the unprecedented problem of defending the authority of a regnant queen. Because Elizabeth's virginity further complicated an already difficult political problem, apologists adapted late medieval iconography, which hailed queens consort as intercessors with imperious husband-kings, to offer instead emblematic variations that praised Elizabeth as a powerful monarch who could govern in the absence of any consort.[20]

This process culminated in the theological diversion from Marian typology to a Christological model. Indeed, since Elizabeth was both the only Godly Ruler of the Secular Reign and the Head of the Church of England, she was considered an earthly figuration of Christ, as John Foxe's *Introduction* to the second Edition of the *Acts and Monuments* clearly testifies. We can argue that the passage from the symbolization of the first edition of Foxe's *Book of Martyr*, where Elizabeth is presented as a new Constantine, to the allegorical meaning of the second one, where she is blessed as a new Christ, marks the literary and iconographic connection between the themes of *katéchon*, in its classical interpretation, and the time of the Second Coming.

As I have suggested, the original view of a "*Katechontic* Elizabeth" is a means that will allow us to address the new concepts of Representation introduced by

19 Edward P. Sri, *Queen Mother: A Biblical Theology of Mary's Queenship* (Steubenville: Emmaus Road Pub, 2005); David L. Jeffrey, *A Dictionary of Biblical Tradition in English Literature* (Grand Rapids: W.B. Eerdmans, 1992).

20 John N. King, "The Godly Woman in Elizabethan Iconography," *Renaissance Quarterly*, 38.1 (1985): 41–84, 42.

the Reformation. The main determination of the Reformers was the sacramental replacement of physical divine presence that mounted a strong challenge to the literalization of Christ's metaphor as it was institutionalised by the Roman Church. Papal tyranny collapsed the distinction between signifier and signified, in order to assert God's real presence in Eucharistic liturgy through the process of trans-substantiation. However, the figurative reading of the words "*hoc est corpus meum*" (in the proper sense "*hoc significat corpus meum*") became the main concern of the Reformers with an explicit, political intent, in order to dismantle the monopoly in interpretation asserted by the Church of Rome. The decline of the transubstantiatory doctrine, and its replacement by the protestant alternative of 'consubstantiation' introduced a new plurality of the different meanings of the act of representing, and especially between representation as *presentification* of an absence in onto-theological terms (make visible and existent what is invisible and absent), and representation as repetition and remembrance. Sacraments were considered as symbols, as significant covenantal stories whose truth is evidenced through repetition and reception:

> the bodily incarnation of Christ was relocated not in the elements, but in the community of believers that partook of them interpretatively [...] Remembrance, faith and thanksgiving – all enjoined of each individual participant at the very moment of reception – replace divine immanence as the essence of the Eucharist.[21]

In this renewed framework the contending meanings of representation could be viewed not only as the *clivage* within the theological matrix of Western Legal Tradition, but also as a source of the historical complexity of English Legal Tradition. The cult of Elizabeth absorbed the first concept of representation, introducing the Eucharistic dynamic into the field of Politics, and thus, the immanent power of the medieval eucharistic sign was desacralized in the theological domain and simultaneously re-sacralized in the political field. Moreover the Reformation produced an asymmetric relation among the *corpora* of authority, conceived as an opposition between two pairs: the Pope and the Bible, on the one hand, and Elizabeth and the reformed Bible to which was annexed the Book of Common Prayer, on the other hand, each of them with their own aesthetics. The first was based upon the central role of the Roman Catholic Pope as the sovereign who decides the authentic interpretation of the Sacred Book, and was aesthetically communicated through the proclaimed *unknowability* of God's Word. For this reason it was expressed through the medium of a hieratical

---

21 Timothy Rosendale, *Liturgy and Literature in the Making of Protestant England* (Cambridge: Cambridge University Press, 2007), 115.

Latin. Such closed and reserved forms of liturgcal expression, performed exclusively by clergy and choir and excluding the congregation, underlined the importance of the mediating institution, which historically can be shown to have had the effect of reinforcing the absolute difference between Divine and Human, in order to actualize only one form of possible relation. The protestant alternative was based on individual access to Scripture and correlatively on the subjective task of interpreting the Sacred Word and it was aesthetically communicated through a programmatic structure of worship. The result was a polemical choice expressed as a desire for the vernacular with the linguistic shift from Latin to English, and with equal fair access to liturgy for everyone. The complete eradication of extra-national jurisdictions and the renunciation of Roman authority were clearly illustrated by the iconographical title pages of Henrician and Elizabethan Bibles. The inclusive depiction of the Sovereign Body within the pages of the Book marked the undivided and unbroken integrity of the two *corpora iuris* (the secular and the divine law) as the main figuration or guise of the English Tradition.

There is another corollary that derives from this reading of Elizabeth as "*Katechontic* Elizabeth." It entails the history of geopolitical traditions. First of all, the providential mission of Elizabeth as historical restrainer transformed the space of England into a geographically bounded space of salvation. The theological perspective was, once again, transposed and located at a different level, specifically at a geopolitical level. The onto-theological fight against the Antichrist was at the same time a geographical and political fight against the assumed universality of the Catholic Church; the soteriological discourse thus provided a pattern for English nationhood. In this regard Pocock's arguments are clarifying and evocative:

> The vision of England as occupying a moment of apocalyptic election entailed the vision of England discharging a special role – largely identical with the maintenance of an autonomous jurisdiction – throughout church history. Archbishop Parker, as well as John Foxe, labored to recover the details of this history, in which Joseph of Arimathea, Constantine, King John, Wyclif, and Elizabeth all played important parts; and the idea of England's uniqueness in sacred history culminates in Milton's much quoted remark that God revealed himself, as his manner is, first to his Englishmen.[22]

The history of the Common Law Jurisdiction was transfigured into a nationalized sacred ontology. This was the intellectual and political process that metamor-

22 Pocock, *The Machiavellian Moment*, 344. Milton's quotation is referred to *Areopagitica*, *Works*, IV (New York: Columbia University Press, 1931), 340.

phosed theological tenets and assumptions and fashioned what I would like to call the "English canon." At the same time the Anti-Catholic stereotype became the criterion used to measure and to set and evaluate the boundaries of the new paradigm of Protestant orthodoxy. In this way the line between 'friend' and 'enemy' was both internalized and nationalized, and the antagonism with respect to canonical orthodoxy was the traditional means used to stigmatize an "internal other," who had been born and lived in England.

4 Contentious Traditions. Divested Symbols and Reformed Iconographic Frameworks

The appellation of Queen Elizabeth's sovereign body as the English *katéchon* can also be justified through the examination of visual representations. At this level of inquiry I would like to select those iconographic signs, symbols and icons which were associated with different traditions, with the aim of analysing their strategic and cultural signification. As I have argued elsewhere, the body of law is shaped by an indissoluble concurrence of ontological questions, aesthetical responses and narrative accounts.[23] Therefore the issue is how the politics of Revelation and the apocalyptic ascendancy of Queen Elizabeth were framed in images and communicated to subjects by the means of pictorial and contextual metaphors.

First, John Foxe's presentation of Elizabeth, in the dedicatory *Introduction* of his *Book of Martyrs*, provides an inescapable reference point. In the first edition (1563), Elizabeth is viewed as the figurative fulfilment of a divine plan. After suffering as a potential martyr for her Protestantism under Mary I, Elizabeth came to the English throne and restored the true faith and religion. For these reasons Foxe associates her with Constantine, the Emperor who established the union of Church and Empire in the name of the true Christianity. The dedicatory Epistle begins with an ornamental, great C, as the beginning of the word Constantine, and with the inscribed body of Elizabeth portrayed as the "Queen enthroned," who dominates the defeated body of the Roman Pope. More specifically, Elizabethan flesh, transfigured into the body of Sovereignty, surmounts the nullified body of the Bishop of Rome, who is entwined with demonic serpents beneath her feet. The celebrated victory of the Woman of Faith against the Antichrist is

23 Cristina Costantini and Lucia Morra, "Representing Sovereignty in Renaissance England: Pictorial Metaphors and the Visibility of Law," in *Law, Culture and Visual Studies*, eds. Anna Wagner and Richard K. Sherwin (Heidelberg-London-New York: Springer, 2014): 79–104, 80.

depicted through the battles among their respective emblems of power: the English Crown, supported by the sword and the sphere of dominium, wins over Tiara, and the annihilation of papal tyranny is testified by the break of St. Peter's keys. At the same time the assertion of royal authority over Church and State is expressed by mixing the traditional meaning of the sword of Justice with the theological image of the divine Word, conceived as the sword of the Spirit. The signs and symbols iconographically condensed into the initial 'C' of the Book of Martyrs expands to became a figural canon. The theological foundations of Elizabethan queenship is even more sumptuously exhibited in the title page woodcut of John Dee's *General and Rare Memorials Pertayning to the Perfect Arte of Navigation* (1577). In this representational context, Queen Elizabeth commands a ship identified as Europe by its Greek inscription and the mythical figure of Europa riding the bull. Two personified characters come to signify Elizabeth's voyage: St. Michael, the apocalyptic angel, descending from Heaven with the Protestant emblems of the sword of justice and the shield of faith, and Occasion, who stands on a fortress. In the upper right corner of the image, the Tetragrammaton bestows divine blessings on the ship, illuminating Elizabeth as the Governor of the Imperial Ship of Christendom.

Other relevant insights are offered by the title pages of the *Bishop's Bible*, which appeared in 1568 in a magnificent folio volume and that displaced the Great Bible as the official Bible of the English Church. In the woodcut frontispiece of the first edition, an enthroned Elizabeth is represented between the female personifications of Faith and Charity. Few words are added to the image: they reproduce the epigraph from Romans 1:16 ("*Non me pudet Evangelii Christi. Virtus enim Dei est ad salutem omni credenti*" – "For I am not ashamed of the gospel; it is the power of God for salvation to everyone who has faith") with the specific intent of making clear that the Queen is elected to complete St. Paul's triad of Theological Virtues by personifying the Hope brought by the Gospel faith. In the following edition (dated 1569), Elizabeth incarnates once again the Woman of Faith with the royalist emblems of the Sword and the Book and is the clear summation of the Virtues standing in the corners of the woodcut: Justice, Mercy, Prudence and Fortitude.

The most important aspect, from a systemological point of view, is the reappraisal of images and symbols derived from other traditions, namely from the Classical (Latin and Greek) tradition and from the Christian tradition. The figural devices used to project a specific representation of English sovereignty were the same, but their amalgamation and the objectives to be defended were substantially reversed. As Kevin Sharpe argued: "Memory, like tradition, involved invention as well as selection; the repositories of memory combined history and invention to validate present persons and policies through representations and performances that connected the present to an actual and imagined past."[24] What I have argued is also demonstrated by the analysis of the '*Sieve Portrait*'. Here the sieve, as the symbol of the vestal virgin Tuccia, denotes the device used to separate wheat from chaff, and hence, allegorically, Good from Bad and becomes the symbol of judgement and discrimination. If we consider that in some emblem literature the sieve represented the Last Judgement and the separating out of the elect from the damned, its attribution to Elizabeth could be interpreted as another propagandist presentation of a *katechontic* body. The wise and learned composition of claims and pretensions forged a new order (both political and juridical) by heralding Elizabeth as a godly champion, defender of the nation and founder of the English Empire, within whose boundaries the theatricalization of monarchy was combined with a history of salvation.

24 Kevin Sharpe, *Selling the Tudor Monarchy. Authority and Image in Sixteenth Century England* (New Haven: Yale University Press, 2009), 13.

Sidia Fiorato

Anna of Denmark and the Performance of the Queen Consort's Sovereignty

1 The Queen Consort

The cultural atmosphere of the first decade of the Stuart period is dominated by the figure of the queen consort Anna of Denmark. James I's accession after the long period of sovereign rule of the unwed Elizabeth I implied a royal duality, and the consequent possibility of the existence of two separate courts.

Legally, the figure of the queen consort is defined in the following terms:

> the queen consort is the wife of the reigning king; and she by virtue of her marriage is participant of diverse prerogatives above other women. [...] first, she is a public person, exempt and distinct from the king; [...] The queen of England has separate courts and officers distinct from the king's, not only in matters of ceremony, but even of law; [...] she is in all legal proceedings looked upon as a *feme sole*, and not as a *feme covert*; as a single, not as a married woman.[1]

The figure of the queen consort introduced a royal "other" in the monarchical constituency; actually, she enjoyed an ambiguous status being part of the Crown and demanded the same kind, if not the same degree, of obedience but at the same time occupying a dependent and subject position in relation to the king: "In general, unless where the law has expressly declared her exempted, [the queen] is upon the same footing with other subjects; being to all intents and purposes the king's subject, and not his equal."[2] Anna of Denmark was King James's wife and, according to the patriarchal institution of marriage, she was designated as the body or 'person' subordinate to her husband as head, owing him submission within the royal household; moreover, she was at the same time a subject and owed James homage as her king.[3] The royal marriage implied a doubling of the royal prerogative and thus opened up the possibility for the wife's insubordination and assertion of her own position and political aspira-

---

1 William Blackstone, *Commentaries on the Laws of England* (Chicago: The University of Chicago Press, 1979), Book I, ch 4. Of the King's Royal Family, 212–213.

2 Blackstone, *Commentaries on the Laws of England*, Book I, ch 4, 213.

3 See Sophie Tomlinson, *Women on Stage in Stuart Drama* (Cambridge: Cambridge University Press, 2005), 3 and Leeds Barroll, *Anna of Denmark, Queen of England. A Cultural Biography* (Philadelphia: University of Pennsylvania Press, 2001), 5.

tions. For this reason, King James's policy proposed a control of women through incorporation; in particular, James's conceptualisation of his kingship as what can be defined as a "patriarchal body politics" conjoined both roles of the queen. The monarch was regarded as the head of a body politic composed of many members and, at the same time, the ruler was presented as the spouse of the state, conceived of as an independent body.[4] During his speech to Parliament upon his accession in 1603, James declared "I am the husband and the whole island is my lawful wife: I am the head, and it is my body."[5]

A queen consort effectively and potentially incorporated several *personae*. In the case of Anna of Denmark, her own father had been a king; when she arrived in England she had already been King James's queen consort in Scotland for 13 years (from 1590 to 1603) with all the prerogatives and prestige that such role implied, and she was the mother of the royal heir, Prince Henry, born in 1594. As it can easily be seen, the body of the queen is subject to a codification that incorporates her into the monarchical political ideology, but at the same time it reduces her to a gendered dimension: "[i]ts [the queen's body's] political strength seems to require the proximity of a male body – as the consort of the king, the mother of future sovereigns, the widow and preserver of the royal or dynastic legacy."[6] However, Anna appears as a multiple persona, able to subvert this context in order to gain authority from all these codifications of her identity during the many times she redefined her role and her position in the course of her life. She proved to be a self-assured and self-assertive woman, well aware of the different contexts in which she found herself and also aware of the iconology of power and the related strategies for her own self-presentation in order to achieve her political ends. In this connection it is worth mentioning her two crowning ceremonies, in which her strong personality emerged and that demonstrate

4 See Martha Kalnin Diede, *Shakespeare's Knowledgeable Body* (New York: Peter Lang, 2008), p. 1.

5 *Political Works of James I*, ed. C.H. McIlwain (Cambridge MA: Harvard University Press, 1918), 272, quoted in Stephen Orgel, *Spectacular Performances. Essays on Theatre, Imagery, Books and Selves in Early Modern England* (Manchester: Manchester University Press, 2011), 67.

6 Regina Schulte, "Introduction. Conceptual Approaches to the Queen's Body," in *The Body of the Queen. Gender and Rule in the Courtly World, 1500–2000*, ed. Regina Schulte (Berghahn Books, 2006): 1–15, 1. With regard to this, see also Martin Butler, *The Stuart Court Masque and Political Culture*, Cambridge University Press, 2008, 24: "the wife's fate was always to be positioned as the subordinated partner, her gender difference testifying to her consort's superiority." However, "the notion of the husband's legal right to a woman's body and mind was being contested in the [Early Modern] period" (Kim Walker, *Women Writers of the English Renaissance* (New York: Twayne, 1996), 138).

her awareness and clever use of her own royal body to assert her presence and her role/status.

As McManus points out, the 1590 Scottish coronation relied upon the body of the queen consort for its ritual meaning and at the same time it marked Anna's own performance in an established court ritual. The ceremony represented the "public display of the legal fact of [her] queenship," an ambiguous position as it was at the same time "necessary but unacknowledgeable [... because it] threatened the conceptual base of James's power";[7] for this reason the ritual emphasised the legal implications of marriage and the subordinate status of a wife to her husband. Anna's sovereignty was staged as dependent upon that of the king by making the crown and sceptre pass from the king himself to all the representatives of antecedent male power structures before being bestowed upon her and thus sanctioning her new solemn status. Moreover, the enactment of Anna's spousal significance as queen consort underlined her being "one flesh" with the king.[8] In this ceremony we witness a transfiguration of the queen's body natural and her becoming part of the king's public body (and of his body politic):

> Her subsumption in his person through marriage brought human frailty and weakness within the orbit of the king (without of course undermining his quasi-divinity), while the coronation ritual imbued her with something of his charisma, thus elevating her beyond the ranks of ordinary women. Encased in her office, the queen functioned as an integral part of the king's public body.[9]

Actually, during her entry into Edinburgh, the pageant spectacles emphasized Anna's dependence on James but also interestingly acknowledged the queen consort's power; the speeches addressed to the new queen actually contained allusions to "her own royalty and her responsibilities within the contract of rule with the city."[10]

Another aspect of the Scottish coronation ritual that needs to be underlined is that King James had prevailed upon the Scottish clergy for the sacramental anointing of the queen, in order to underline royal divine right, while the clergy had insisted on the omission of this ritual's accompanying prayers in order to undermine what would be regarded as its sacramental significance. This situation reinforced Anna's "corpo-reality" as her passive body became the site for

---

7 Claire McManus, *Women on the Renaissance Stage. Anna of Denmark and Female Masquing in the Stuart Court 1590–1619* (Manchester : Manchester University Press, 2002), 70.

8 See Barroll, *Anna of Denmark, Queen of England*, 106.

9 Anne McLaren, "Queenship in Early Modern England and Scotland," *The History Journal*, 49. 3 (2006): 935–952, 941.

10 McManus, *Women on the Renaissance Stage*, 74.

ideological dispute and most importantly the site for the performance of the king's royal will: the baring of her skin thus acquired an eroticized dimension and "destabilized the coronation's idealization of the crowned queen [...] complicat[ing] any simplistic reading of Anna's representation in the ritual."[11] It must also be observed that Anna had not embraced religious conformity but was silently acquiescencent to the coronation oath, a passive (and corporeal) submission to the royal and religious written law.

Her subsequent coronation in England took place in 1603; by that time she had been Queen of Scotland for thirteen years, and therefore she was more self-assured and conscious of her position as well as of the iconological means to sustain it. Once again she remained passive and silent during the coronation; her stillness once again empowered her body, by underlining her voluntary physical withholding of complicity in the coronation ritual itself, while at the same time managing to make "her presence felt within its parameters."[12] Her autonomous immobility fostered the bodily impact of her presence at the centre of attention; she transformed the physical expressivity of stillness into non-movement/non-performance, and thus rendered her passive reification an act of her own will.

The two coronation scenes underline the manner in which Anna refused to subject herself to the normative image of the queen consort and turned it into an instrument for her own assertion. She demonstrated a deep awareness of the fact that

> [a]t its strongest, the legal definition of the person (*ius personarum*) is determined by the theory of images as the form of human appearance, of human presence. The legal person is a mask (*persona*) and that mask is governed in its representation – so also in its rights and capabilities – by the law of the image (*ius imaginum*) and the drama of masks [...].[13]

By staging the image of her bodily presence from within the domain of patriarchal ritual, she entered the discourse of the law in order to acquire a position from which she could then claim her own autonomous status: "to enter the realm of law it is necessary to be a legal subject and that is by definition a question of being both already a subject of law and of wearing the mask, the sign, of

11 McManus, *Women on the Renaissance Stage*, 71–72. With regard to this, McManus observes how "[i]In the baring of Anna's skin the coronation's gendered vision of sanctified queenship prefigured the definition of the female masquers through their eroticized bodies, and through a display of their sexuality." (McManus, *Women on the Renaissance Stage*, 71)

12 McManus, *Women on the Renaissance Stage*, 94.

13 Peter Goodrich, "Specula Laws: Image, Aesthetic and the Common Law," *Law and Critique*, 2.2 (1991): 233–254, 233.

the legal institution."[14] The coronation ceremony was the "primal scene" of monarchical self-representation and conferred full legal status upon the monarch.[15]

2 The Masque Form

In Scotland Queen Anna had managed to exploit the factions that divided the Scottish court for her own purposes, whereas in England the situation was more settled. Indeed, the choice of James VI as Elizabeth's successor had been almost unanimous and had emphasized a consensus among the English nobility, rather than "the kind of rampant divisiveness that Anna seems to have exploited so effectively in Scotland."[16] Moreover, as the king had experienced the Queen's strong influence and impact on matters of politics and government, as well as her drive for self-assertion, he had isolated her from her Scottish supporters, and assigned her only trusted English advisers as members of her court, while he had allowed his own loyal Scottish courtiers to move to England.

In this situation of patriarchal constraint, Anna found a new way to construct another kind of visibility and establish her royal identity through the masque form. Until then a marginalized court recreation dominated by male performers which displayed and enhanced social and political court relations, the masque became the means for a conscious self-presentation of the Queen consort and the establishment of her court and signaled an appropriation of the stage by women performers.[17] In this way, Anna refused a purely symbolic role and by appropriating an artistic genre focussed on the codification of the

14 Goodrich, "Specula Laws," 244.

15 See Janette Dillon, "The Monarch as Represented in the Ceremony of Coronation," in *Representations of Elizabeth I in Early Modern Culture*, eds. Alessandra Petrina, Laura Tosi (Houndmills: Palgrave Macmillan, 2011): 125–139, 125 and 126.

16 Barroll, *Anna of Denmark, Queen of England*, 36. See also Kenneth Olwig, *Landscape, Nature and the Body Politic* (Madison: University of Wisconsin Press, 2002), 63: "James' ascendancy to the English throne had been carefully planned by Queen Elizabeth's influential chief minister Robert Cecil, who [...] long used his influence to develop the ideological foundations for a unified Britain."

17 See Barroll, *Anna of Denmark, Queen of England*, 10 and 98: Inaugurated in the first Christmas season of the Stuart reign, Anna's masques need to be envisaged as court spectacles that for the first time in over forty years showcased a queen consort. Actually other masques were staged in the same period of Anna's ones (written by Jonson and Campion), however, they did not possess the same resonance for various reasons: they did not stage royalty, were all-male masques for the celebration of weddings, and they were performed for a restricted and less prestigious audience.

body, she managed to disembody herself from her imposed royal character; within this context, first she explicitly contravened the rules for female decorum in performance and established her own artistic tenets, and secondly she articulated her own concept of queenship.

All the different aspects of the masque form, its visual and kinetic elements, are "condensed and absorbed into the body and make their address through it."[18] Therefore, once again by exploiting the power of her bodily presence, Anna managed to escape a liminal condition at court and intervene in the cultural politics of the new monarchy: "by developing elaborate royal masques as her occasional signature events at Christmas, [she] seems to have created *ab ovo* a complex ceremonial featuring female courtiers, male courtiers and foreign ambassadors to which she alone was the key."[19] Anna understood the political potential of the masque form to "resonate with meanings other than the legitimation of male monarchy"[20] and focussed the spectacles upon herself for the acknowledgement of her position at court.

Anna[21] seemed to understand more deeply than her spouse[22] the dependence of power and social status upon display and the implications of such relationships. In Early Modern society "the power of sovereignty work[ed] primarily

---

18 Tom Bishop, "The Gingerbread Host: Tradition and Novelty in the Jacobean Masque," in *The Politics of the Courtly Stuart Masque*, eds. David Bevington, Peter Holbrook (Cambridge: Cambridge University Press, 2006): 88–120, 98.

19 Barroll, *Anna of Denmark, Queen of England*, 111. See also *Women and Politics in Early Modern England, 1450–1700*, ed. James Daybell (Aldershot: Ashgate, 2004), 188: "For the ambassadors, invitations to the masques, especially the Queen's, became the occasion for bitter fights over precedence." In this context, Anna could interfere in courtly diplomacy; in the case of *The Masque of the Twelve Goddesses*, the invitation of the Spanish ambassador and the exclusion of the French one put James in the unpleasant position to make amends. This was Anna's first political interference in the affairs of state, an attitude unprecedented from a queen consort. (See Botonaki, "Anne of Denmark and the Court Masque," 140).

20 Tomlinson, *Women on Stage in Stuart Drama*, 18.

21 Anna came from a court in which women actively engaged in courtly entertainment. Her family "patronized the most recent innovations in learning and the arts in Renaissance Europe." (Mara Wade, "The Queen's Courts: Anna of Denmark and her Royal Sisters: Cultural Agency at Four Northern European Courts in the Sixteenth and Seventeenth Centuries," in *Women and Culture at the Courts of the Stuart Queens*, ed. Claire McManus (Houndmills: Palgrave Macmillan, 2003): 49–80, 59.

22 While in Scotland, James participated in masque festivals, but in England, he was reluctant to engage in masques as a performer; therefore, during the early Stuart masques he was not in control of the representation of his own royal selfhood.

by making itself visible"[23]; the age was characterized by an "increased self-consciousness about the fashioning of human identity as a manipulable, artful process"; the verb "to fashion" indicates the forming of a self, and also implies the imposition of a form, or "a distinctive personality, a characteristic address to the world, a consistent mode of perceiving and behaving."[24] During the first Jacobean decade, the masque became the means for the queen consort's social and political self-fashioning, a forum for ideological statement which contested the King's court's gender ideology. In other words, it undermined the period's concept of a monolithic power opening it to negotiation and producing "a stir to the mind" through the *energia* of aesthetic empowerment. As Greenblatt points out, "We identify *energia* only indirectly, by its effects: it is manifested in the capacity of certain verbal aura, and visual traces to produce, shape and organize collective physical and mental experiences."[25] Instead of offering a mirror of power, the early masques opened themselves to cultural exchanges which followed multiple modalities by employing language and gesture, as well as "metaphors, ceremonies, dance, emblems, items of clothing, well-worn stories" that were continually renegotiated.[26] Only later will the form acquire its normative form as a Neoplatonic celebration of the king's sovereignty and power (thanks to the artistic codification by Jonson and Jones); the early Jacobean masques testify to "the Queen's dominant presence as planner, promoter, performer and first audience."[27]

Masques were dynamic artistic forms whose essence was in the performance; their printed text was first a pre-text containing scant indications for the action and later a sort of journalistic record of the event, a narrative account of the effect and meaning of the spectacle.[28] Jonson himself recognized the ephemeral character of this art form and the impossibility of recapturing its effect through words; as he observed, "Such was the exquisite performance, as

23 Richard Halpern, *The Poetics of Primitive Accumulation: English Renaissance Culture and the Genealogy of Capital* (Ithaca: Cornell University Press, 1981), 3, quoted in *The Politics of the Stuart Court Masque*, eds. Bevington, Holbrook, 3.

24 Stephen Greenblatt, *Renaissance Self-Fashioning. From More to Shakespeare* (Chicago and London: The University of Chicago Press, 1980), 2.

25 Stephen Greenblatt, *Shakespearean Negotiations* (Oxford: Clarendon Press, 1988), 6.

26 See Greenblatt, *Shakespearean Negotiations*, 8.

27 Barbara Kiefer Lewalski, "Anne of Denmark and the Subversion of Masquing," *Criticism*, 35.3 (1993): 341–355, 342.

28 See Alison Findlay, Stephanie Hodgson-Wright, Introduction to *Women and Dramatic Production 1550–1700*, eds. Alison Findlay, Stephanie Hodgson-Wright, Gweno Williams (Harlow: Longman, 2000): 1–14, 7, and Jerzy Limon, *The Masque of Stuart Culture* (Newark: University of Delaware Press, 1990), 18.

that alone (had all else been absent) was of power to surprise with Delight, and steale the Spectators from themselves only the envie was, that it lasted not still, or (now it is past) cannot by Imagination much less description, be recover'd to a part of that Spirit, it had in the gliding by."[29] This observation, which Jonson intended for a diversification between the two different parts of the masque (what he terms the "carcass," i.e., scenery, music and dance, and the "design," i.e., the text and its allegorical meaning, and its superior importance), actually attunes with contemporary critical discussions: "performance cannot be [...] documented or otherwise participate in the circulation of representations: once it does so, it becomes something other than performance [...] it betrays and lessens the promise of its own ontology."[30] Actually, Jonson identified the potential for these accounts to become different kinds of texts, almost to the point of suggesting a new genre; the literary masque as distinguished from the masque-in-performance offers a narrative reconstruction of the spectacle, but at the same time codifies its reception. By explaining its symbolism, by giving verbal expression to non-verbal spectacle it could modify, soften and/or readjust its real impact, and likewise silence subversive elements. The masquers' bodies represented the "unique fleeting materiality of the performance,"[31] their moving bodies represented a site of unstable legibility whose kinetic effect could undermine the court's control of expression and meaning: "No matter how accurately and in how much detail Early Modern dancing masters formalized a step, these descriptions were, and still are, always open to, and challenged by, their physical interpretation. [...] There is no way of fixing a choreography to the point of eliminating the individual dancer's creativity"[32] and the empowering impact of his/her physical presence on stage. Therefore, Jonson's innovation in this sense was represented by the controlled

29 Ben Jonson, *Hymenaei*, 1606, quoted in Limon, *The Masque of Stuart Culture*, 23.

30 Peggy Phelan, *Unmarked: The Politics of Performance* (New York: Routledge, 1993), 146.

31 Erika Fischer-Lichte, *The Transformative Power of Performance: A New Aesthetics* (New York: Routledge, 2008), 33.

32 Barbara Ravelhofer, *The Early Stuart Masque. Dance, Costume and Music* (Oxford: Oxford University Press, 2006), 100. Dance occupied more time than what could appear from the masque text. Actually, no textual representation was offered for the physical aspect of the masque, that is for music, the movement of the body, both danced and unchoreographed, scenery and costume. As far as dance is concerned, contemporary manuals depicted it from the male perspective only, while women were excluded or attributed only a marginal and physical presence. This was due to the difficulty of codifying the moving body's potentiality of expression (with regard to this, see *The Politics of the Stuart Court Masque*, eds. Bevington, Holbrook,14, and Sidia Fiorato, "Choreographing the Elizabethan and the Jacobean Age: A Self-Fashioning in Dance," *Il Lettore di Provincia*, 38.129 (2008): 71–86, 83.

textualization of the spectacle after its performance, a subjection of movement to the linguistic demands of accepted and pre-existing meaning.

The masque's structure was composed of five stages; after an initial symbolic performance for mere purposes of display, the masquers started phase two, "the measures," that is, slow and stately dances, aimed at proving their command of movement. Although they were same-sex dances, the gender differentiation required by the form was respected in their execution in couples. During the third phase, "the ordinary measures," the masquers invited persons of the opposite sex from the audience to dance, in the process known as "taking out" and in the fourth phase each one of the invited auditors, along with the masquers themselves, proceeded to a second "taking out." The general dancing was then interrupted and only the masquers performed a final dance which culminated in their exit, unmasking and joining of the courtly audience for the remainder of the evening's celebrations.[33]

The court masque was a form of elite social ritual, a politicized rather than a theatrical performance, and was an extension of the daily fashioning of identity in a court where status depended upon display. Participation in the masque allowed the creation, maintenance and strengthening of courtly identity through bodily performance. A threefold reciprocal relationship united the court, the masque and the dance (its fundamental element), which explicated itself in the shared importance of the performing aristocratic body in the full respect of gender dynamics, gender decorum and patriarchal authority. In the climactic and concluding moment represented by the final revels, when the masquers danced with members of the audience, they included the spectators/courtiers in the performance: "what they watched they ultimately became."[34] The masque's stage action became a social action: "[t]he masque world became a society as the dancers acknowledged their partners."[35] Women were allowed to perform in the masque's final revels (but, by contrast, in no other contemporary form of courtly or public theatre); however, their participation was strongly subjected to gendered performative codes in order to control their potential signification and were presented as bearers and not creators of allegorical significance. Dance played a substantial role in the masque (being instrumental both to the perform-

---

33 See Barroll, *Anna of Denmark, Queen of England*, 84–87.

34 Stephen Orgel, *The Illusion of Power* (Berkeley: University of California Press, 1975), 39 and Stephen Orgel, *The Jonsonian Masque* (Cambridge MA: Harvard University Press, 1967), 7.

35 Orgel, *The Jonsonian Masque*, 187. See also *The Politics of The Stuart Court Masque*, eds. Bevington, Holbrook, 97, and Fiorato, "Choreographing the Elizabethan and Jacobean Age," 80: "the dance steps represented a social code which proved and confirmed or conferred the status of being part of the court."

ance of the courtier's identity and to the celebration of the court's harmony); for this reason female participation strengthened the danger of potential disruption directly from the heart of the masque form itself, provoking a potential shift in its meaning from monarchical celebration to a statement of female agency.

3 Queen Anna's Masques

During the 1603–1604 Christmas revels, the masque's traditional structure underwent a radical change: Queen Anna's first masque was performed by royalty, who brought to the form the codification of their status. Authored by Samuel Daniel and performed in the Great Hall at Hampton Court, *The Vision of the Twelve Goddesses* (Twelfth Night, 1604) set the model for Anna's new conception of queenship and focussed on her own power as well as on the king's. The masque featured women[36] instead of men and increased the number of dancers from eight to twelve; moreover, instead of the traditional beginning which presented a homage to the king with the opening procession of the masquers, here the goddesses entered the scene and approached the temple of peace, thus rendering James an external observer of the spectacle, a condition that resulted from the scenery being dispersed around the room. Thus the introduction of the prospective stage did not support the king's elevated commanding position as both spectator and part of the spectacle). The women performers were married to the most powerful noblemen of the kingdom; however, during the first taking out they did not invite their own husbands, which would have represented a gesture of submission to patriarchal authority, but gentlemen of the court. This act established new court dynamics as it underlined the existence of the queen's court within the patriarchal context of the royal court and assigned/acknowledged power of action to women.[37] The traditional feminine position was thus reversed: instead of passively waiting to be invited to take part in the masque as a hierarchi-

---

36 See Clare McManus, "When is a Woman not a Woman? Or, Jacobean Fantasies of Female Performance (1606–1611)," *Modern Philology*, 105. 3 (2008): 437–474, 452: "Anna's arrival in 1603 transformed the court masque genre through a paradigm of women's participation that was [...] alien to the English court." However, as Barroll a.o. underlines, "despite male monopoly, noblewomen in England before 1603 had not been strangers to masquing. They seem to have organized such shows as private, patriarchally supervised entertainment." (Barroll, *Anna of Denmark, Queen of England*, 76)

37 See Barroll, *Anna of Denmark, Queen of England*, 98: "Instead of being asked to take part in the masque during the taking out by for example the men of James' Bed Chamber, they asserted their role in bestowing such honour to male members of the court."

cally gendered dance, they invited men, thus inverting the patriarchal gendered code.

This subversive action was disguised in the celebration of the Stuart succession (a central theme of the early Stuart masques); the goddesses' descent from the mountain mimed the journey of the king from Scotland to England and their gifts and blessings to the monarch sanctioned his legitimation and the passage of power from one royal dynasty to another. The main action of the masque consisted in the goddesses' gifts to James of those qualities useful to govern his kingdom; in this way, a seeming homage could imply the king's lack of such qualities. Moreover, the goddesses (for example, Diana, Astrea, Thetys) recalled Queen Elizabeth's celebratory identifications and her own chosen roles in the staging of her own sovereign person, thus recalling a female lineage of power. Significantly, Queen Anna did not represent Juno, the symbol of the queen consort, but rather Pallas, the virgin warrior symbol of Queen Elizabeth and of "the two key monarchical qualities of wisdom and military prowess."[38] In this way she implicitly distinguished her own position from that of her husband as a sovereign figure, but also from his domestic policy.

The performers used the former Queen's dresses as costumes, thus signaling an appropriation of her courtly body through the appropriation and adaptation of her royal clothes.[39] It is interesting to note here Anna's appropriation of Elizabeth's 'body politic' through a juxtaposition of their bodies natural. Actually, Anna's costumes for *The Vision* were shortened to reveal her feet and legs. As Sir Dudley Carleton remarked, the goddesses'

> attire was alike, loose mantles and petticoats, but of different colors, the stuffs embroidered satins and cloth of gold and silver [...] Their heads by their dressing did only distinguish the difference of the goddesses they did represent. Only Pallas had a trick by herself; for her clothes were not so much below the knee but that we might see a woman had both feet and legs, which I never knew before.[40]

---

38 Stephanie Hodgson-Wright, "Beauty, Chastity and Wit: Feminising the Centre-stage," in *Women and Dramatic Production*, eds. Finlay, Hodgdson-Wright, Williams, 44.
39 See Butler, *The Stuart Court Masque and Political Culture*, 101, and McManus, *Women on the Renaissance Stage*, 107. See also Alison Findley, *Playing Spaces in Early Women's Drama* (Cambridge: Cambridge University Press, 2006), 120–121: "Unlike Elizabeth's parliamentary robes, those made for Anna as queen consort did not invest her with ruling power. However, [in the context of the masque] Elizabeth's garments could be deployed to invoke queenly authority."
40 Quoted in Effie Botonaki, "Anne of Denmark and the Court Masque: Displaying and Authoring Queenship," in *The Emblematic Queen: Extra-Literary Representation*, ed. Debra Barret-Graves: 133–154, 139.

Masquers were mute throughout the performance, so their significance and their related qualities had to be expressed symbolically by their clothes, jewelry, and other accessories. Anna's appearance embodied her defiance of the court etiquette, theatrical conventions, and gender norms. "Unlike the enclosed body of Elizabethan entertainments, which presents a figure of chastity, absoluteness, and separateness from the contagion of physical defilement,"[41] Anna strengthened the physicality of her appearance rendering it the means for the expression of her independent subjectivity as a Queen Consort with equal status and rights to the king, thus actualising a normative and aesthetical subversion, particularly evident in her next masque.

Authored by Ben Jonson, *The Masque of Blackness* (1605) once more seemingly asserted James's centrality to the spectacle, but by staging powerful female figures it finally subverted the dominant court ideology from different perspectives. Jonson explicitly credits the Queen with the masque's governing idea of having blackamoors as its primary figures.[42] The main action is represented by the quest of the 12 daughters of the river Niger, who seek perfection, i.e. white complexions, from Albion-James, the sun king of Britannia, "whose beames [...] are of force / To blanch an Aethiope, and revive a Cor's."[43] As often pointed

---

41 Hardin Aasand, "'To blanch an Ethiop, and revive a corse': Queen Anne and The Masque of Blackness," *SEL* 32.2 (1992): 271–285, 273.

42 Anna's wish to introduce blackamoors in the masque may have been influenced by the staging of Shakespeare's Othello a few months earlier at James' court, a tragedy which presents a subversion of aesthetic tenets (from the beautiful to the ethical) in portraying the possibility for Desdemona, a Venetian noblewoman, to fall in love with a Moor (with regard to this, see Daniela Carpi, "Law and Aesthetics in *Othello*," in *Le cabinet du curieux*, eds. Witold Pietrzak, Magdalena Kozluk (Paris: Classiques Garnier, 2013), 79–89). Moreover, at the Scottish court representations of blacks as well as actual blacks were present during King James VI's court entertainments, and during his wedding pageant he had four negroes dancing in front of the royal carriage. However, "Blackness was unproblematic when associated with the body of the lower-class performers, but was subversive when assumed by the female aristocratic body." (McManus, *Women on the Renaissance Stage*, 78) As Botonaki points out, at the court of James IV of Scotland, a black lady had been an emblem of royal power by presiding over the ceremonies of the 1507–1508 tournament; however, presenting himself as her knight, the king had in a way subsumed her in himself, as his double and opposite, and had thus contained the potential power of her alien femininity. In the case of Anna, by assuming herself the black lady's identity, she claims royal power and presents herself as an unassimilable part of monarchy. (See Su Fang Ng, *Literature and the Politics of Family in Seventeenth-Century England* (Cambridge: Cambridge University Press, 2009), 38)

43 This expression means that the king is capable of accomplishing the impossible, but the expression contains also a linguistic pun with legal overtones/implications; "As a Scottish legal term, "blanching" refers to the king's ability to transform a subject's material debt to the crown into a merely ceremonial display of allegiance. Scottish law also allows the king to "blackout in the course of the present essay, "[f]emale masquers were on the whole granted access to expression only through make-up, costume, dance and gesture; through the physicality of the body within which they were confined."[44] The Queen and her ladies appeared wearing black make-up on their faces, and their arms were bare up to the elbows;[45] moreover, their short costumes revealed their legs and feet, thus evoking a dangerous and open sexuality. Contrary to the Renaissance ideal that fused the two concepts of "fair" and "beauty," and contrary also to her own embodiment of such ideal (as it had been underlined during her marriage),[46] Anna contravened conventional symbolism regarding the presentation of royalty to such an extent that some critics have compared the impact to a carnivalesque expression, with the Queen as the Lady of Misrule.[47] By unconventionally staining her face, arms and legs with black make-up in a deliberate act of self-fashioning, Anna subverted the decorous and chaste symbolism of fairness for a blackness which the Renaissance period regarded as connected to sexual energy and spiritual depravity. The audience of the period was not accustomed to consider blackness as beauty; although royalty, the fe-

en" or "black-ward" a Scotsman into military duty. [...] This transfer of debt from ward to blanch is akin to a civilizing process as well. [...] Jonson's praise of the new King of England's power to revive a corpse applies to James's intention to revive a body of laws [the Scottish one], as well as revive the ancient dignity of Britannia" through the union of England and Scotland (see Mary Floyd Wilson, "Temperature, Temperance, and Racial Difference in Ben Jonson's *The Masque of Blackness*," *English Literary Renaissance*, 28 (1998): 183–209, 191, 192).

44 McManus, *Women on the Renaissance Stage*, 10.

45 Prior to this masque, which records the first use of blackening to darken the skin of the masquers, Moors were staged wearing vizards or later also through black velvet (See Bernadette Andrea, "Black Skin, the Queen's Masques: Africanist Ambivalences and Feminine Author(ity) in the Masques of Blackness and Beauty," *English Literary Renaissance*, 29.3 (1999): 246–281, 264, and Andrea Ria Stevens, *Inventions of the Skin. The Painted Body in Early English Drama 1400–1642* (Edinburgh: Edinburgh University Press, 2013),91.)

46 Andrea points out how Anna during her journey to Scotland was constructed as a "fair" queen, in the context of the emerging counterposition between blackness and beauty; beauty converged into fairness, which in its turn, was defined as whiteness. Anna embodied such ideal, with her golden hair, blue eyes and ivory skin. However the residual model of black beauty emerges in Anna's own masques and the ongoing presence of black women in Early Modern cultural production. (See Andrea, "Black Skin, the Queen's Masques," 256–257). In *The Masque of Blackness* the character of Niger denounces the codification of English poets which celebrates white beauty and presents black beauty as inferior. Actually Moors were not excluded from beauty, as the "paradox of black beauty [was] often referenced in Early Modern drama as well as reflected in the recipe manuals of the period, which offer suggestion for dying the hair, brows and even skin black." (Farah Karim-Cooper, *Cosmetics in Shakespearean and Renaissance Drama* (Edinburgh: Edinburgh University Press [2006], 2012), 8).

47 See a.o. Aasand, "'To blanch an Ethiop, and revive a corse'," 272.

male masquers seemed whorish[48] and challenged norms of feminine modesty. As Sir Dudley Carleton famously reported,

> [t]heir Apparell was rich, but too light and Curtizan-like for such great ones. Instead of Vizzards, their Faces and Arms up to the Elbows, were painted black, which was disguise sufficient, for they were hard to be known; but it became them nothing so well as their red and white, and you cannot imagine a more ugly sight, then a troop of lean-cheek'd Moors.[49]

The courtier's remarks about Queen Anna's body were "a cultural reading of her social form – the garments and cosmetics which adhere to her physical body and to the body politic;"[50] ladies customarily used white makeup on the exposed parts of their bodies (face, bosom, hands and forearms) and Queen Elizabeth herself used cosmetics as an instrument of aesthetic empowerment. However, if the latter "carv[ed] herself out as a featureless icon hidden behind a cosmetic mask [... which] acted as a barrier between the untouchable queen and her subjects [...] in a theatrical proclamation of royal prerogative,"[51] Queen Anna exploited cosmetics in order to foreground her corporeality and sexuality. As Orgel underlines, "[t]he real innovation in the costumes for Blackness, indeed, was probably the fact that cosmetics were being allowed to do the work of clothing," thus allowing for bodily expressivity: "the ladies were not masked and had bare forearms and sheer overmantles that revealed their upper arms."[52] Carleton's negative reaction therefore endorses his refusal to countenance an innovatory aesthetics.[53]

Through blackness Anna wore the "identity of foreign royal woman [...] on her own body,"[54] she consciously enacted her estrangement from her English

---

48 With regard to this, see Tomlinson, *Women on Stage in Stuart Drama*, 25: "Black skin and face-painting were associated in Renaissance culture with "potentially unsettling figures, the African and the courtesan. The links between the masque and the courtesan were precariously close: each was inherently seductive, each employed painting and artful discovery; moreover, the masque drew its very name from the courtesan symbol."

49 Stephen Orgel, *Ben Jonson. The Complete Masques* (New Haven and London: Yale University Press, 1975), 19.

50 Aasand, "'To blanch an Ethiop, and revive a corse'," 273.

51 See Karim-Cooper, *Cosmetics in Shakespearean and Renaissance Drama*, 59 and 63.

52 Stephen Orgel, "Marginal Jonson," in *The Politics of the Stuart Court Masque* eds. Bevington, Holbrook: 144–175, 146

53 Aasand, "'To blanch an Ethiop, and revive a corse'," 273: Anne [...] is a royal grotesquerie, a figure blackened by heat and latent with an ethnic sexuality ("Curtizan-like") that disturbs established social and political order.

54 Clare McManus, "When is a Woman not a Woman?," 453. See also Wilson, "Temperature, Temperance, and Racial Difference," 199, footnote 50: According to Early Modern historiogra-

context and this in turn "constru[cted] her as an unassimilable part of monarchy"[55]; through her aesthetic transgression "she proudly paraded her ethnic, cultural, and personal differences as well as her indifference to the stereotypes that rendered her blackness immoral and unacceptable."[56] In this sense, this masque is unique because through bodily means, "it records indirectly [...] the public utterance of her voice."[57]

Moreover, the queen was six months' pregnant at the time, so, therefore, she represented the "Consort, Spouse and Progenitrix," as well as the embodiment of consummated sexual passion. By displaying her black limbs, as well as her advanced pregnancy, Anne presented herself as a sexually potent woman who consciously rejected the European codes of feminine decorum. Therefore, the queen employed black(ened) femininity as a "polysemic site of resistance."[58] This subversion of the feminine aesthetic tenets of representation became even more unsettling during the final revels; at this point in the masque, "the Queen and her ladies implicate the King and his men in the discourse of black beauty as they reach out and draw the male spectators into the final dance. Instead of washing the Ethiopian daughters white, the King risks being similarly blackened."[59] The masque exposes the king's failure to contain the Queen's self-assertive acts; this demonstrates how Anna always remained less of a wife and more of a rival sovereign to James. Actually only a queen who felt powerful would have dared to contravene female tenets in what can be considered a proto-feminist claim to author(ity).[60]

Even if the subversive potential of the masque seems to have been contained by the black princesses's voluntary submission to the English King, implying the acknowledgement of his power, as well as of the patriarchal order he symbolized, the transformation of the African nymphs into white stereotypical beauties does not take place during the action nor at the end of it. This was motivated by a practical difficulty, the impossibility of a quick make up removal, but its effect was to undermine the conception of the king's powers. Actually, the transformation will be achieved through feminine forces (in particular, through the Moon

phy, the Scots descended from the Egyptians and were considered black, therefore the make up connected the queen once more to the powerful position she had enjoyed in Scotland.

55 Su Fang Ng, *Literature and the Politics of Family*, 38.

56 Botonaki, "Anne of Denmark and the Court Masque," 142–143.

57 Aasand, "'To blanch an Ethiop, and revive a corse'," 277.

58 Andrea, "Black Skin, the Queen's Masques," 281.

59 Andrea, "Black Skin, the Queen's Masques," 274

60 See Aasand, "'To blanch an Ethiop, and revive a corse'," 279, and Botonaki, "Anne of Denmark and the Court Masque," 143.

Goddess Aethiopia, who recalls Queen Elizabeth as Cynthia and therefore once again strengthens the concept of female power) and the nymph's own ancestor, thus celebrating a power other than James's.

In 1609, *The Masque of Queens* continued the articulation of a new model of femininity. The central concept involved the celebration in the House of Fame of the twelve greatest Queens of history. Jonson's text credits Anna with the chief literary innovation of the work, the antimasque: "her Majestie (best knowing that a principall part of life in these spectacles lay in their variety) had commaunded mee to think on some Daunce, or shew, that might praecede hers, and have the place of a foyle, or false Masque."[61] In the antimasque, twelve witches openly threaten to undermine James's patriarchal government; their subversive action expresses itself with a disorderly performance encompassing appearance, language, movement and sound, and aiming at subverting the aesthetic order of the traditional masque ritual. The antimasque configured itself as complementary to the masque proper, inasmuch as it staged disorder and at the same time confined it into a limited expression. In this way, social and political anxieties remained contained in a liminal space and were vanquished with the appearance of legitimate order. The witches were impersonated by professional actors[62] who, in Jonson's intentions, represented the antithesis of courtly femininity and enacted all negative aspects of female agency and expression. In particular, the excessive and perverted femininity of the witches, with its stereotyped associate crimes of vocality and sexuality, was associated with the performing woman. During the masque's action, the appearance of the stately Queens, symbolising the proper values of the court, dispelled the witches in fear, and represented, always in Jonson's intentions, the courtly masquing woman taming the physicality and demonized image of the female performer.

However, as has been emphasised in the course of the present essay, despite all the attempts at control, the body on stage escapes strict codification and acquires a kinetic expressivity and significance of its own. Actually, the Queens are martial women, like the Amazon Queen Penthesilea, who overturn gender norms and achieve sovereignty by displacing men, a feature they share with the witches, who open the stage action by threatening to overcome a male-dominat-

61 Lewalski, "Anne of Denmark and the Subversion of Masquing," 346.

62 Hugh Craig, "Jonson, the Antimasque and the 'Rules of Flattery'," in *The Politics of the Stuart Court Masque*, eds. Bevington, Holbrook: 176–196, 181: "Professional actors originally took the roles of the antimasquers; courtiers undertook roles in the main action. The more decorous roles of the masque proper required no memorizing of lines while conversely maximizing opportunity for dancing and visual display."

ed world.[63] Moreover, they are equal in number and the leading witch appeared naked-armed and bare-footed, recalling Anna's undecorous appearance in her first two masques. The masque and antimasque therefore aimed at opposing two symbols of female power, but the final result in performance seemed to be assimilation.[64]

The witches are dispelled by the mere apparition of the twelve queens positioned on the façade of the House of Fame; at its apex was seated the classical hero Perseus. Jonson intended that Perseus should represent the slayer of Medusa (symbol of the quintessential female power) thus epitomizing the victory over dangerous and destructive women (once again a symbol of the patriarchal control of women); however, on the other hand, Perseus's strength depends on the goddess Pallas, thus resurrecting a female source of power, intertextually/"inter-performance-ly" linked to Anna herself, in her first impersonation in *The Vision of the Twelve Goddesses*. In this masque, Anna did not represent any historical female, but staged herself as Bel-Anna, thus creating a contemporary myth: "for the first time she employed the court masque not to symbolize but to signify her queenship."[65] Anna appeared as last and remained at the top of the pyramid, thus emphasizing her position of honour, once again at the centre of the masque, both as its protagonist and as the primary object of praise. The final songs celebrate the Queens and especially Queen Anna, their worthy sovereign, by asserting that it is their, and her, fame and virtue that exalt the age "How happier is that Age, can give / A Queene, in whome all they do live." (747–748)[66] Through echoes of her previous images and impersonations Anna manages to extend the threat to patriarchy of the antimasque beyond its site of containment and to stage a spectacle of female empowerment by symbolically establishing her own queenship.

63 Botonaki, "Anne of Denmark and the Court Masque," 147: "The Queens' fame is founded upon male defeat and female domination, both of which have been achieved through their fierceness and fearlessness – qualities that the queens' opposites, the hags of the antimasque, previously displayed." See also Kevin Curran, *Marriage, Performance and Politics at the Jacobean Court* (Farnham: Ashgate, 2009), 34, where the association of African women with the Amazon is pointed out, revealing an inter-performatively connection among the masques' characters.
64 See Kathryn Schwarz, "Amazon Reflections in the Jacobean Queen's Masque," *Studies in English Literature 1500–1900*, 35 (1995): 293–319, 308. The witches represented a Renaissance literary topos for man's fears about women's potentialities (See Daniela Carpi, *Sintomi di Modernità* (Bologna: Editrice Compositori, 1990), XVIII).

65 Barroll, *Anna of Denmark, Queen of England*, 113.

66 Ben Jonson, *The Masque of Queens*, in *Ben Jonson. The Complete Masques*, ed. Orgel:122–141.

The Masque of Beauty, performed during the Christmas season 1607–1608 (1608) as a sequel to *The Masque of Blackness*, precedes *Masque of Queens* and represents already a first full celebration of female sovereignty, though in a more harmonic way. The action opens by lamenting the condition of the Nigerian nymphs, who, once having attained their white complexions, are prevented from coming back to England to pay homage to King James; they are in fact held prisoners by Black Night on a floating island together with four more of their siblings, who likewise wished to attain whiteness. They are then freed by the intervention of their Queen, the Moon Goddess Aethiopia, and finally reach Britain on the floating island itself. By coming to Britain, the women seemingly wish to renounce their previous transgressive image of femininity, and finally adapt "what is alien and threatening in female beauty and sexuality to the norms of Jacobean culture."[67] However, the spectacle becomes, in fact, a celebration of a self-contained and harmonious form of female government. The princesses enter seated on the Throne of Beauty, at whose top is positioned Queen Anna, personating Harmonia ruling over the fruitful land. "The design of the masque relocates the power from the king's chair of State [upon which the King's body natural is reduced to the eye of his controlling gaze over the spectacle] to the [moving] body politic of the Queen's court in the setting."[68] The wisdom and peaceful government of Anna's feminine world criticises also Jacobean misogynist prejudices such as the wantonness connected to beautiful women in public life, and the vacuity of mind traditionally connected to beauty, and it finally declares women as "the souls of men." Beauty becomes synonymous with female virtue in a shift from visual to cultural qualities which are presented as innate to the female; in this way, beauty becomes a site of political contestation.[69] The *Masque of Beauty* ultimately suggests that "power is located just as much with the Queen and that body politic, as with the King."[70]

Tethys' Festival (1610) celebrated Anna as the mother of the future king of England, and therefore as the mother of the nation.[71] In the course of the masque

---

67 Lewalski, "Anne of Denmark and the Subversion of Masquing," 345.
68 Alison Findlay, *Playing Spaces*, 126.
69 Hodgson-Wright "Beauty, Chastity and Wit," 46.
70 Findlay, *Playing Spaces*, 126.
71 See Barroll, *Anna of Denmark, Queen of England*, 130 and 134: the masque symbolized the alliance between Anna and her son, Prince Henry. As the future king's influence at court increased, Anna started paying public deference to him, while he, in his turn, openly recognized his queen mother's royalty. Henry's sudden death in 1612 marked the end for Anna of any emerging court influence which was based on the heir apparent's prestige and support. See also James Knowles, "'To Enlight the Darksome Night, Pale Cynthia Doth Arise': Anna of Denmark, Elizabeth I and the Images of Royalty," in *Women and Culture*, ed. McManus, 21–48, 42.

action Anna presents James with a trident, metaphor of the sceptre of power; actually, on the stage the trident is the recurrent symbol of her own throne, and therefore it also represents her own sovereignty. Anna's offering of the trident to James, with all its metaphorical significance, is presented as a willful act of love, not deriving from compulsion, and more than a renunciation of her sovereign position, it symbolizes a concord and alliance between the two sovereign spouses. Anna took part in the masque action, but after the masque's dances she sat on her stage throne thus changing her role and becoming a primary spectator, thus mirroring James's own position as privileged spectator. "By thus positioning the queen, the masque makes clear the doubled nature of the audience, usually idealized as one, and therefore the duality of monarchy."[72] This image embodies the symbolic aspiration of Queen Anna of seeing her status at court acknowledged and in her 1617 masque she finally achieved the sanctioning of her role, albeit still within the context of the masque.

Cupid's Banishment (1617) was the last masque which saw the participation of Queen Anna as main spectator and contained a unique instance of female masquing speech (possible also because of a blurring of the formerly strict distinction between acting and masquing). The masque sanctioned the existence of a separate Queen's court at Greenwich and the creation of identity through performance, the two main aims of Anna's artistic project. Over time, Anna "interrogated the very notion of the masque as court masque [...] the nature of the court and of those who claimed membership of such an institution for themselves"[73] through her own liminality and appropriation of courtliness itself. The staging at Greenwich marks a shift in the locus of courtly power (Whitehall was the centre for James I's male favourites' productions). Actually the King was not present during the masque, as he was journeying to Scotland, so Anna assumed the focus of power and was the addressee of the courtly ceremonial, the only occurrence in which the figure of privileged spectator was somebody other than the king. The bodily absence of the male monarch, who was always a strong ideological symbol of his kingdom, was obscured by the presence of the queen consort's body. "Anna's assumption of the role is a telling gesture, the symbolic enactment of the political engagement which she had attempted

72 Su Fang Ng, *Literature and the Politics of Family*, 37. Moreover, Anna staged the separatedness and femaleness of her court as she sat enthroned with her daughter Elizabeth at her feet, in a mirror-image of James and Henry (See Stephanie Hodgson-Wright, "Beauty, Chastity and Wit: Feminising the Centre-stage," pp. 42–67, 42.

73 McManus, "Memorialising Anna of Denmark's Court: Cupid's Banishment at Greenwich Palace," in *Women and Culture*, ed. McManus: 81–99, 83.

in Jacobean society."[74] Conscious of her own status as queen, as the subject who shares the sovereign's authority, Anna had attempted to appropriate for herself the regency during James's absence, seeing it as an extension of her own role as queen consort. Indeed, by "occupying the physical space left by James, Anna appropriated the monarch's authority [at least] in the duplication of male state ritual."[75] In this way, she also staged a questioning of the absent king's authority and of the gendered structures of power, and established, although temporarily, a female court. "By enthroning herself as privileged spectator, Anna simultaneously stepped back from active performance and stepped up to James's quasi divine position as a complementary spectacle to the masque stage itself."[76] Surprisingly, as McManus remarks, there was no response to Anna's action, which appears almost as a mutiny against patriarchal royal power. The queen managed to enact and appropriate sovereign identity through physical performance, by staging her own enthronement no longer on stage but as privileged spectator and addressee of the masque. With regard to this, it must be noticed that the queen's name was staged in the graphic dance of the female masquers, and it represented the first recorded female name to be danced in an English masque before those of her husband and son. Within the context of this masque, female rule is established and the Queen and her court are shown to form an independent body politic.

4 The Performance of the Queenly Body

As it has often been emphasised in the course of the present essay, Queen Anna transformed the stage into a forum for the performance of her 'self' as royal consort; in particular, she used the effect of her body natural as a woman performer to define and establish her own body politic.[77] In this she proved to be well

74 McManus, "Memorialising Anna of Denmark's Court," 85
75 McManus, "Memorialising Anna of Denmark's Court," 89
76 McManus, "Memorialising Anna of Denmark's Court," 89
77 See Edmund Plowden, *Commentaries or Reports* (London 1816), 2123, quoted in Ernst Hartwig Kantorowicz, *The King's Two Bodies: A Study in Medieval Political Theology* (Princeton: Princeton University Press, 1997), 7, 9. "[T]he King has in him two Bodies, viz., a Body natural, and a Body politic. His Body natural [...] is a Body mortal [...] his Body politic [...] cannot be seen or handled, consisting of Policy and Government [...] these two Bodies are incorporated in one Person [Plowden, Reports 213] [and form] one unit indivisibile, each being fully contained in the other."

ahead of her time, aware of the empowering impact of performance and its focus on the body. As Lepecki points out, when discussing dance and performance theory, the discourse spontaneously focusses on the concepts of "presence" and "body" as "complicated sites where subjectivity challenges subjection [... and] resistance initiates its moves."[78] Anna proved able to connect the period's conception of the articulation of power through its privileged visibility and the combination of iconophilic and iconoclastic traditions in the construction of subjectivity.

> Subjectivity is created in the field of vision, to be a self is to be seen. I look from one position but I am looked at from everywhere. The 'social gaze' looks back at me from the place of the others and inscribes otherness in the midst of self. It is not the look of any particular other, but the visual, photographic action of otherness which places me within a field of vision as I turn towards others and look at them.[79]

Douzinas continues,

> The operation of normative systems (religion, morality, increasingly law) interposes a 'legal screen' between the subject and the social gaze, filtering the objects of vision and determining the way in which we see and are given to the world to be seen. The screen is a collection of authoritative images and material practices which offer a repertory of approved representations through which social identity is inscribed. It determines how each of us is given to the world to be seen [...] imagistic regimes bring together the fleshy body and approved imagery and create what can be called the 'normative' body of the individual.[80]

Anna managed to break the legal screen between the subject and the social gaze by subverting the normative vision through an alternative one which she staged with all the force of bodily presence and the empowering effect of performance. In such action, all meanings and implications of performance converged: "On the one hand, performance describes certain embodied acts, in specific sites, witnessed by others (and/or the watching self). On the other hand, it is the thing done, the completed event framed in time and space and remembered, misremembered, interpreted, and passionately revisited across a pre-existing discur-

---

78 André Lepecki, "Presence and Body in Dance and Performance Theory," in *Of the Presence of the Body. Essays on Dance and Performance Theory*, André Lepecki, ed. (Middletown: Wesleyan University Press, 2004), 2.
79 Costas Douzinas, "Sublime Law: On Legal and Aesthetic Judgments," *Parallax*, 14.4 (2008): 18–29, 18.
80 Costas Douzinas, "Sublime Law," 18.

sive field."[81] Moreover, according to Schechner, performance is a showing doing,[82] the accent therefore lying on the impact of the overall effect of such action, or in Greenblatt's terms, on its *energia*. Schechner's theory aptly describes public life at the Elizabethan and Stuart court, which followed a "rhetorical imperative of performance. *Esse sequitur operare:* identity was to be derived from behavior. [...] status [...] had become not a matter of being but of doing, and so of showing."[83] Within this context, the body is positioned centre stage both as the ideological focus of the articulation of power and, at the same time, as a repertoire of infinite (cultural and historical) possibilities. Anna exploited the fact that once on stage, the silent (and often immobile) female body became an expressive force, capable of affecting the process of meaning-creation. "Apparently constrained to submission within their physicality, the masquers in fact occupied an ambiguous, liminal position, [and could] transfor[m] apparent tools of constraint into the means for near-autonomous self-fashioning."[84]

Performance emerges as a cultural practice that "conservatively reinscribe[s] or passionately reinvent[s] the ideas, symbols and gestures that shape social life. Such reinscriptions or reinventions are, inevitably, negotiations with regimes of power, be they proscriptive conventions of gender and bodily display"[85] or resistance acts expressed through the polymorphous body of the performer. Anna articulated her own stance on the nature of consortship through the interpretation of courtly aesthetics and exploiting the ritual of sovereignty. She fashioned her own role and her own court necessarily in relation to the king's court and through constant negotiation. But she did so by appropriating masculine courtly practices, in particular the royal ceremonial (which proved to be available to those other than the king). Her women likewise appropriated masculine markers of courtliness and of courtly identity "privileging class over gender to form a par-

81 Elin Diamond, "Introduction" to *Performance and Cultural Politics* ed. Elin Diamond (New York: Routledge, 1996), 1.

82 See Schechner, *Performance Studies. An Introduction* [2002](New York and London: Routledge, 2006), 28: Schechner asserts that performance can be understood in relation to being, doing, showing doing and explaining showing doing and in relation to this he explains that ""Being" is existence itself. "Doing" is the activity of all that exists [...] "Showing doing is performing: pointing to, underlining and displaying doing. "Explaining showing doing" is the work of the performance studies."

83 Frank Whigham, "Interpretation at Court: Courtesy and the Performer-Audience Dialectic," *New Literary History, Renaissance Literature and Contemporary Theory,* 14.3 (1983): 623–639, 625.

84 McManus,*Women on the Renaissance Stage*, 11.

85 Diamond, *Performance and Cultural Politics*, 2.

ticular kind of institutional self-hood."[86] In this "dissident performance"[87] gender tenets were challenged and refashioned mostly by exploiting the centrality of the female body, and in particular the female body in movement.

The term "performative" was introduced in linguistic philosophy to indicate those utterances that are "self-referential and constitutive in so far as they [in specific circumstances] bring forth the social reality they are referring to."[88] Judith Butler then connected this concept to specific bodily acts in her performative theory of identity and this applies to Anna's context:

> Bodily performative acts do not express a pre-existing identity but engender identity through these very acts. [...] The specific materiality of the body emerges out of the repetition of certain gestures and movements; these acts generate the body as individually, sexually, ethnically, and culturally marked. Performative acts are thus of crucial importance in constituting bodily as well as social identity.[89]

On the one hand, we see Elizabethan and Jacobean society violating the integrity of individual bodies by imposing performative acts upon them that constitute gender and identity. On the other hand, performative acts offer individuals the possibility to embody themselves, and create identities that might deviate from dominant norms.

As a performer Anna proved able to unite the qualities of the masquer and the actor and to transcend both roles. As Orgel insists, masquers were not actors and were subject to courtly protocol. The concept of masquing distinguished itself from acting, as it did not imply the adoption of an alternative identity. "A masquer's disguise did not obscure the representation of the courtier beneath. He retained his primary persona and hence his position in the social hierarchy. His audience affirms his equality with them by consenting to join the dance."[90] His unmasking extends the significance of the masque beyond the boundary of the stage into the real world. A professional actor, on the contrary can assume all personae because he has none of his own; "his persona is not a representation of the reality beneath but the reality itself."[91] In his unmasking, the dramatic illusion collapses; the person who emerges does not see his social role confirmed, as

86 McManus, *Women and Culture at the Courts of the Stuart Queens*, 2.
87 McManus, *Women on the Renaissance Stage*, 203.
88 Erika Fischer-Lichte, *The Transformative Power of Performance* (New York: Routledge, 2008 [2004]), 24.
89 Fischer-Lichte, *The Transformative Power of Performance*, 27.
90 Orgel, *The Illusion of Power*, 39.
91 Stephen Orgel, *The Jonsonian Masque* (Cambridge: Harvard University Press, 1965), 117–118.

he has been performing an impersonation. The actor's identity has meaning only on the stage because his/her persona identity exists only in the theatre. Anna used the acknowledgement of the status given by the masquer's role in her staging of queenly sovereignty and extended it beyond the stage making it resonate within the context of the patriarchal court by becoming a performer. The performer's identity is always present in dramatic performance both in connection and in disjunction with their impersonation. Anna asserted her sovereign role by personating royal and divine female figures and presenting her obedience and apparent conformity to James's power as an act of consent rather than submission. After her unmasking she wished to see the confirmation of her royal status as a sovereign, as she had represented it in a shifting of planes between art and reality. Queen Elizabeth conceived of herself as an actor and she consciously staged her royal presence; however her political role as a monarch remained stable and visible in all her appearances. Queen Anna however, grounded her political role as a queen consort in her appearance, in the awareness that the theatricalization of Renaissance power actually thematized, enacted (and created) it; power was the object and enabling condition of representation itself.[92]

As Botonaki remarks, Anna's appearance as a masquer was in itself an act of defiance, a bold assertion of her difference from the queens who had preceded her[93] who were set at one remove from royal authority and exercised little or no political power. They were constrained in that "complex network of hierarchical relationships which governed and determined the whole fabric of society."[94]

Anna invested all the elements of masque production (speeches, costume, body language) "with her own individual energy; in a sense by fighting for her role, as the embodiment of a particular woman enclosed in a narrative that pretends to be universal."[95] Her subversion proceeded through images, first to displace the dominant aesthetics of the female model and then by proposing the image of her own sovereignty:

> Images give visual form to the invisible and make present what is absent. But the image does not represent the absent, it presents it. [...] The image unveils the thing for us, assem-

---

92 See Martin Butler, "Courtly Negotiations," in *The Politics of the Stuart Court Masque*, eds. Bevington, Holbrook: 20–40, 20.

93 See Botonaki, "Anne of Denmark and the Court Masque," 141, and Greenblatt, *Shakespearean Negotiations*, 2.

94 Lisa Hopkins, *Women Who Would Be Kings. Female Rulers of the Sixteenth Century* (London: Vision Press, 1991), 8.

95 Penny Gay "The History of Shakespeare's Unruly Women," in *The Routledge Reader in Gender in Performance*, eds. Lizbeth Goodman, Jane de Gay : (New York: Routledge, 1998): 41–46, 42.

> bles it for our eyes and thus brings it into being. The image poses the thing for a subject. In this 'presencing' the thing is assembled into being.[96]

What Anna achieved was the "pres-entification," in Costantini's terms, of her sovereign role by giving concrete expression to an ontological category she herself created, i.e. the sovereign queen consort. As such, she could only exist through embodiments or incarnations within a network of cultural images and performances, which she in-formed and circulated (as Greenblatt's social energy) in a definite spatial dimension.[97]

Anna's artistic engagement was a bold declaration of her stance in a contemporary patriarchal context. First of all she defied courtly opinion by assuming a role that was dangerously close to that of an actress, and thus subverted the tenets of female decorum. Moreover, as queen she could assume no other role except that of the key masquer, thus deflecting attention from King James and at the same time becoming the most exposed among her fellow women performers. She managed to turn such conditions to her own advantage and render the masques a site for contesting the King's gender ideology; actually she organized a reverse image of James' body politic by staging the power of women's bodies to produce queenly presence through space and assimilating them into her own body politic. "Physical movement figured the ways Anna and her ladies shaped the changing social dynamics of the Court."[98] Surely, the image Queen Anna tried to project upon herself was the result of multiple negotiations (with generic conventions, gender rules, royal obligations, political circumstances, masque author's intentions); she could not concretely alter her nominal position within King James's court, nor could she pursue political objectives in a sustained and systematic way. However, she managed to appropriate the ideological power of these masques in order to assert her own difference.[99] Her artistic achievements foregrounded the development of female and professional performance in the Caroline Court through the engagement in this sense of Queen Henrietta Maria.

---

96 Douzinas, "Sublime Law," 21.

97 See Cristina Costantini, *La Legge e il tempio* (Roma: Carocci, 2007).

98 Findlay, *Playing Spaces*, 122.

99 Stevenson defines Anna as "strong-willed and fiercely determined to have what she saw as her rights recognized" (David Stevenson, *Scotland's Last Royal Wedding* (Edinburgh: John Donald Publishers Limited, 1997), 64).

Aspasia Velissariou

The *Body Politic*, Female Transgression and Punishment in Jacobean Tragedy

1 Jacobean Sexual Politics and Tragedy

Evadne's execution of her royal lover while having sex with him and her suicide in Francis Beaumont and John Fletcher's *The Maid's Tragedy*, Tamyra's adultery and her torture by her husband in George Chapman's *Bussy D'Ambois*, the titular heroine's private marriage with an inferior man and her physical and mental torments until her execution in John Webster's *The Duchess of Malfi*, and the wilful transgression of Beatrice-Joanna in Middleton and Rowley's *The Changeling* are all extreme paradigms of female sexual transgression and subsequent punishment placed at the centre of many Jacobean tragedies. The heroines' desires spoil the training in subjection that the deployment of alliance performs, where alliance signifies "a system of marriage, of fixation and development of kinship ties, of transmission of names and possessions."[1] This system lays a heavy emphasis on the rules dictating the forbidden and the illicit and their opposites and on the pairing of the partners on the basis of "definite statutes" insofar as alliance is the main engine of the circulation of wealth.[2]

Socioeconomic changes and shifts in political dependencies in the early seventeenth century generated overwhelming anxiety and insecurity with regard to the subject's connection with and positioning within hierarchical power. To these "structures of feeling"[3] the sexual control of women was central insofar as it was felt to be an imperative for the maintenance of social order and vice versa. In the tragedies of the period the gendering of the resistant subject as female and the foregrounding of the suffering body as punishment for desire, the theoretical and political conflicts over political power are transposed onto the discourses of sex. On the other hand, the sexualisation of the political relations of subjection and resistance is dramatised as being predicated on physical pleas-

---

1 Michel Foucault, *The History of Sexuality: An Introduction* [1976], trans. Robert Hurley (London: Allen Lane, 1978), 106.

2 Foucault, *The History of Sexuality*, 106.

3 I draw on Raymond Williams' concept whereby "feeling" is different from "ideology" in that, while taking into consideration formal beliefs, it exceeds them because it is a lived experience of values and meanings. "Structure" refers to "a set, with specific internal relations, at once interlocking and in tension." *Marxism and Literature* (Oxford: Oxford UP, 1977), 132.

ure. As Michel Foucault argues, "a problematic of the 'flesh,' that is, of the body, sensation, the nature of pleasure"[4] became central to the deployment of sexuality that since the seventeenth century was gradually superimposed on that of alliance, without however supplanting it. The family, instead of being expelled by the development of this dynamic, became the terrain of the interplay between sexuality and alliance, in which the feminine body played a pivotal role.

Jacobean tragedies (as in Webster, Chapman, Middleton, Beaumont and Fletcher and others) offer an as yet premature instance of the emergence of female pleasure from within the system of alliance as a threatening, because potentially independent, force. That female desire is perceived as downright destructive of the patriarchal law that works on the basis of the analogy between the family and the state, the father/husband and the king is clear from the exemplary punishment of the desiring subjects. The danger embodied in active female sexuality is particularly grave for the maintenance of the hierarchical system intrinsic to this analogy especially when the King's body is consumed by a woman, Evadne, or the husband's body as the king's surrogate is sexually betrayed, as Montsurry is by Tamyra. Because of the symbiotic relationship between king and kingdom,[5] and husband and household, desire, by challenging the authority of the head, destroys the body. Most importantly, it arises as an acute political problem that strikes at the heart of the *body politic* when the latter is literally embodied in *the body natural* of a woman such as the Duchess of Malfi. The complexities involved in the position of a desiring female sovereign increase insofar as her sexual pleasure with her husband, Antonio, surfaces at the intersection of the deployment of alliance with the emergent system of sexuality. In this sense, as I shall argue, Webster adumbrates an Early Modern family on the basis of the companionate marriage emerging precisely from the uneasy coexistence of sexuality and alliance. The interplay, however, could only cease in the violent death of the transgressive female and the smashing of the newly formed system by her brothers, the perpetrators *par excellence* of the psychologically perverse patriarchal rules of alliance.

The fear of the feminine as, by definition, the unruly body turns into a wish for its objectification that is crystallised in its death. The corpse of the raped wife of Antonio on the stage, Gloriana's skull in *The Revenger's Tragedy*, the Duchess

4 Foucault, *The History of Sexuality*, 108. Also see Maurizio Calbi, *Approximate Bodies: Gender and Power in Early Modern Drama and Anatomy* (London: Routledge, 2005), n 122, 117.

5 For this symbiotic relationship see Catherine Belsey, "Desire's Excess and the English Renaissance Theatre: *Edward III, Troilus and Cressida, Othello*," in *Erotic Politics: Desire on the Renaissance Stage*, ed. Susan Zimmerman (New York: Routledge, 1992): 84–102, 86–87.

as a "figure cut in alabaster"[6] and a disembodied echo, along with the Tyrant's necrophilia in Thomas Middleton's *The Second Maiden's Tragedy*, all offer instances of the most shocking expression of the male fantasy of the woman's utter passivity. Because the health of the state mirrors and is mirrored in the well-being of the family and both apparatuses fear women's unregulated reproductive capacity they are heavily dependent for their smooth function on the surveillance of the female body. As Peter Stallybrass argues, surveillance is intensely focused on the female orifices, especially the mouth and the vagina, precisely because what is mapped in and through the chaste woman's body is the integrity of the state: "The state, like a virgin, was a *hortus conclusus*, an enclosed garden walled off from enemies."[7] Of vital importance is that the virginal hymen has to be ruptured by the "appropriate" phallus for the preservation of order. The question is what if the "appropriate" phallus is rejected for a different or better one? In other words, what if pleasure and not duty comprises the female drive? I shall attempt to show that, in the context of the static social body safeguarded by alliance, the mobility and penetrability of female desire turns into a treacherous force because it can easily open the gates of the state to the enemy from without, while at the same time, as in *The Changeling*, it identifies the enemy within. Therefore, sexual transgression, far from being perceived as a private vice, is considered a public crime, the equivalent of petty treason with torture, confinement and death constituting the means whereby the appropriate phallic order is reinstated.

Evadne and the Duchess of Malfi relate to political power in a peculiar manner. The former performs a singularly unfeminine act because she commits tyrannicide on stage. The latter, royal heir and dowager of the dukedom of Amalfi, is a female sovereign (and a widow) and therefore by nature an anomalous being, the very image of disorder. Evadne as a female avenger and the Duchess as a prince inscribe the problematical idea of female power. On the one hand, the social challenge of this improperly placed power is safely co-opted because it is conceptualised as sexual transgression. Evadne's fornication and subsequent adultery with the King, and the Duchess's marital choice of her steward, Antonio, reinscribe the masculine terror of a female sexuality turned loose, which dictates the structure of feeling in Jacobean tragedy (*The Changeling*, *The White*

6 John Webster, *The Duchess of Malfi* in *John Webster: Three Plays*, ed. David Charles Gunby (Harmondsworth: Penguin, 1977), 1.2.374: further references in the text to act, scene and line, abbreviated as DM.

7 Peter Stallybrass, "Patriarchal Territories: The Body Enclosed," in *Rewriting the Renaissance: The Discourses of Sexual Difference in Early Modern Europe*, eds. Margaret Ferguson, Maureen Quilligan and Nancy Vickers (Chicago: Chicago UP, 1986): 123–142, 129.

Devil, Women Beware Women, The Insatiate Countess and others). On the other hand, by the very same token in their choice of partners both heroines are ascribed with agency insofar as they are the ones to choose who will rupture their hymen (Evadne) or enter their vagina (The Duchess). The Duchess's transgression, however, is far more dangerous to the male order that Webster criticises. As a widow she is a sexually experienced woman ascribed by the patriarchal myth with insatiable desire, a force which threatens the core of patrilineality. I contend therefore that *sexual transgression as agency* serves as a Jacobean theatrical convention through which the dramatists interrogate and resist the dominant practices of subjection that is also a process of "subjectivation."[8] Resistance to patriarchal absolutism, however short-lived, constructs the common ground for the dramatists' critique of the hegemonic ideology that conceives of the body of the king as "the social plenum"[9] that provides dependency and incorporation as the subjects' only available positions.

In *Basilikon Doron* James I draws attention to the political urgency of the king's exemplary nature, as indicated by his being on public display:

> It is a trew old saying, That a King is as one set on a stage, whose smallest actions and gestures, all the people gazingly doe behold ... and according to the outward appearance, if his behauiour bee light or dissolute, will conceiue prae-occupied conceits of the Kings inward intention ... and praeiudged conceits will ... breed contempt, the mother of rebellion and disorder.[10]

Webster and Beaumont and Fletcher set on stage the body, the gestures, and the small actions of the sovereign for the spectators to behold, but the spectacle is rather peculiar. What is exposed in *The Duchess of Malfi* is the body of a pregnant woman, whose symptoms of pregnancy are described by the malcontent, Bosola, as physically revolting. In *The Maid's Tragedy* the King is shown to be asleep. On waking up, and while blissfully expecting a novel sexual experience, he is tied to his bed by Evadne who sadistically carves him to death. The King is not only murdered on stage but his death is displayed in the context of sadomasochistic

8 See Judith Butler's reading of the Foucauldian notion of subjectivation which is "bound up with subjection" as a process that, however, allows "resistance to regulation or to the form of subjection that regulation takes." Judith Butler, "Competing Universalities," in *Contingency, Hegemony, Universality: Contemporary Dialogues on the Left*, eds. Judith Butler, Ernesto Laclau and Slavoj Žižek (London: Verso, 2000): 136–181, 151.

9 Francis Barker, *The Tremulous Private Body: Essays on Subjection* [1997] (Ann Arbor: U of Michigan Press, 2000), 28.

10 James I, "*Basilikon Doron*," in *King James VI and I: Political Writings*, ed. Johann P. Sommerville (Cambridge: CUP, 1994): 1–61, 49.

foreplay. Considering the concept of the king's two bodies, a *body natural* and a *body politic*, the question that these tragedies pose is what happens when of the sovereign's two bodies the physical one, as with all other human bodies, is shown to be either disgusting or foul while the metaphorical transcendent body is deemed infallible and immortal. Beaumont and Fletcher offer an intense dramatisation of the issue of the subject's position in the face of this glaring dissymmetry between the king's two bodies, which sets him/her before the dilemma of either to submit or resist. The spectacular murder of the King's body in bed by a woman's hand serves as the corporeal transcription of the collapse of the boundaries between the sovereign and the (female) subject who, significantly, constructs herself as an avenger. By turning the King's outward appearance and his dissolute conduct into a wretched spectacle the dramatists show how contempt by the tyrant for his subjects does indeed breed rebellion.

In *The Duchess of Malfi* the orthodox reading of the *body politic* is inverted insofar as in the place of a prince/mind, who should rule over his people/body, there is a woman who is, according to the stereotype, the irrational sex *par excellence*. The Duchess's sexual choice of her steward and her marriage to him fully articulates the frightening vision of women on top, intensified by yet another grave inversion whereby in the state's mirror structure, that is, the family, the husband must be the head to woman/body. Interestingly, what connects the aberrant femininity in the figure of the Duchess with the King in *The Maid's Tragedy* is "unbridled" sexual desire that overrules reason. Although usually identified with the female body, excessive appetite does not necessarily coincide with it as in the case of the lustful nature of the tyrant that has defined the type since Plato. The King flagrantly violates the law and morality in order to accommodate his desire for Evadne. By opting for a private marriage with an inferior and raising a family in secret the Duchess as an independently sovereign figure implicitly performs a similar function. Rebecca Bushnell observes the explosive political nature of the collapse of the two bodies into one:

> Insofar as the 'natural' or physical body of the monarch stood for the mystical 'corporation' of the body politic, the unity of the natural and mystical bodies of a king posed a danger to the state: the identification of the two implied the disintegration of the body politic with the vulnerability of the king's natural body.[11]

11 Rebecca Bushnell, *Tragedies of Tyrants: Political Thought and Theatre in the English Renaissance* (Ithaca: Cornell UP, 1990), 38–39. Bushnell draws particular attention to the association between tyranny and effeminacy (63–69).

Both tragedies dramatise precisely the identification of what ought to remain distinct and separate, that is, the *body politic* is required to remain distinct from the *body natural*. In *The Maid's Tragedy* Evadne's body is the terrain where the King is revealed to be essentially only a physical being, something that paves the way to succession by his brother, Lysippus, a better man. Although the King's *body natural*, subject to sexual perversion, is butchered by a woman on stage, the *body politic* survives intact through his successor. In fact, the spectacle of the dead royal body becomes the presupposition for the continuation of the *body politic*: regicide neither causes divine wrath nor does it upset the natural order.[12] *The Duchess of Malfi*, on the other hand, questions long-ingrained assumptions about women's rule as naturally tyrannical, and women's desire as insatiable, embedded in the supposed feebleness, changeability and vulnerability of the female body.[13] Webster constructs a female aristocrat whose desire in violation of social status and traditional gender position disempowers her politically and renders her a private person. However, by shifting the connection between tyranny and emotional and physical excess from the Duchess to the real tyrant, her brother, Ferdinand, the text performs a subversive gesture. The *body politic* is not simply sick but in the Aragonian brother's lycanthropia inscribes in a paradigmatic manner the psychological bestiality that is the absolute mark of tyranny. Ferdinand's incestuous desire for his sister, that is the underside of his patriarchal authority, and the Tyrant's necrophilia in *The Second Maiden's Tragedy* are certainly the most perverse instances of a dramatic politics that sexualises the problem of subjection and resistance to royal absolutism.

Beaumont and Fletcher turn the tyrant's death into a public spectacle by sensationally exposing it on stage, and in *The Tragedy of Valentinian* John Fletcher exhibits the painful symptoms of poisoning while his eponymous protagonist is dying. James I's argument against "monstrous and vnnaturall rebellions" in the eventuality of "intolerable abominations a souereigne prince commit"[14] is that the latter will eventually be punished in heaven; hence the king's injunction to his subjects to suffer in patience tyrannical abuse. In flagrant challenge of this dogma these tragedies stage the murder of the tyrant by the resistant subject. By the same token, they foreground the corruptibility

12 William Shullenberger, "'This For the Most Wrong'd of Women:' A Reappraisal of *The Maid's Tragedy*," *Renaissance Drama* 13 (1982): 131–156, 151.

13 According to John Knox once women become rulers their "natural" weaknesses turn into those vices that typify the tyrant, such as, for example, irrationality, cruelty and instability. Bushnell, *Tragedies of Tyrants*, 65.

14 James I, "The Trew Law of Free Monarchies," in King James VI and I, *Political Writings*, ed. Johann P. Sommerville (Cambridge: Cambridge University Press, 1995): 62–84, 83.

of *the body natural* and its absolute desecration. *The Maid's Tragedy* is particularly interesting in another respect, too in that it inscribes the shift in the concerns of tragedy "from military to sexual honour"[15] politicising therefore female honour by differentiating it from its prevalent identification with chastity. In her dual capacity Evadne embodies at once the hero of the tyrannicide tradition and the sexually wronged woman who turns avenger in the name of her lost honour. This is a rather singular instance in a genre where women figure as the instigators of revenge as, for example, Charlotte, sister of Bussy, in George Chapman's *The Revenge of Bussy D'Ambois,* but not as *perpetrators.* Or where the chaste body of a woman who decided to take her own life rather than submit to a lustful male, functions stereotypically as the engine for male honourable revenge, as exemplified by Gloriana in *The Revenger's Tragedy,* the Lady in *The Second Maiden's Tragedy,* Lucina in *The Tragedy of Valentinian* among others.

In *Bussy D'Ambois* female adultery is politicised albeit in manner different from *The Maid's Tragedy.* Tamyra is not the protagonist but Bussy, who, feeling his freedom curtailed by the increasing concentration of power in the court, becomes the spokesman for the inherent rights of man; hence he is part of the republican tradition of antiquity, as represented by Brutus and Cassius.[16] However, Tamyra is important insofar as her adultery with Bussy and her subsequent torture at the hands of her husband, Montsurry, forcefully inscribe not only the analogy between the state and the family but also their collapse into each other, thus offering a conceptual foundation for Chapman's problematics of subjection. In this sense, her sexual transgression is central to the dramatic action because it turns the adulterous wife from being a subject to her husband and the monarch to the subject of resistance against her double subjection. Although she does not physically kill Montsurry, she sexually betrays him, thereby symbolically cutting off the head of the conjugal body assumed to be the husband.[17] Her sexual offence far from being private lies at the core of the above political analogy: for this reason she is arraigned for treason, and a justification is given for her torture on the rack which would be the same as any other enemy of the state.

---

15 Kathleen McLuskie, *Renaissance Dramatists* (Hemel Hempstead: Harvester-Wheatsheaf, 1989), 157.

16 As J. W. Lever argues in *The Tragedy of State: A Study of Jacobean Drama* (London: Methuen, 1980), 43. Bussy "looks ahead to the stand of John Lilburne and his Levellers in the English Revolution that lay forty years ahead."

17 For the issue of "male headship" in marriage see Frances E. Dolan, *Marriage and Violence: The Early Modern Legacy* (Philadelphia: University of Pennsylvania Press, 2008), 26–27.

2 The *Body Politic* on Stage

Webster significantly chooses as the opening speech of *The Duchess of Malfi* Antonio's description of the ideal *body politic* in France:

> In seeking to reduce both State and people
> To a fix'd order, their judicious King
> Begins at home. Quits first his royal palace
> Of flatt'ring sycophants, of dissolute,
> And infamous persons, which he sweetly terms
> His Master's master-piece, the work of Heaven,
> Consid'ring duly, that a Prince's court
> Is like a common fountain, whence should flow
> Pure silver-drops in general. But if't chance
> Some curs'd example poison't near the head,
> *Death and diseases through the whole land spread.*
> (DM, 1.1.5–15)

Although Antonio makes it clear that he exempts the Duchess from his indictment, his admiration for her is expressed in clearly personal terms: he simply idealises her as a woman without mentioning any public quality that would recommend her as his ideal superior. However, for Webster there had been a recent paradigm of an exemplary female monarch and that was Elizabeth whose sexual politics nonetheless were the exact opposite of his heroine's. The English queen made her *body natural* serve her *body politic* in accordance with the Tudor dogma of the immutability of the monarch, while at the same time resolving the oxymoron of a female sovereign. This Elizabeth accomplished by remaining a virgin, that is, by sealing the orifices of her body from male penetration and by simulating in her own physicality the immutability and impenetrability of the *body politic*. Her dexterous handling of her sexual [non]availability consolidated her rule through a uniquely hegemonic gesture that was entirely hers: "she redefined the concept of the female body politic [...] through her uniting her natural and political bodies."[18] In this case the identification of the two bodies, far from signifying the tyranny of desire over the intellect, marks its opposite. Insofar as the female body is insulated and absolutely closed upon itself, the state remains safe and healthy. By the same token it is masculinised because it was not legally penetrable.

18 Theodora A. Jankowski, *Women in Power in the Early Modern Drama* (Urbana and Chicago: Illinois UP, 1992), 64. Interestingly John Knox uses the image of "a corrupted fountain" for the female rule (quoted in Jankowski 63).

By contrast the Duchess's body is open and therefore her sovereignty is morally and politically ambiguous. As Antonio tells Delio "The common rabble do directly say / She is a strumpet" (DM, 3.1.25–26) precisely because she conflates the two bodies by having sex with an inferior; her changing pregnant body inscribes her fundamental fluidity and instability. The Duchess's *body natural* therefore deceives her people because it is pregnant with secrets: her private marriage and the raising of a family constructs a shadowy *body politic* that improperly duplicates the proper one since it coincides with her bedroom and with the night, where the husband rules, as Antonio claims, "only in the night" (DM, 3.2.8). The vision of an ideal commonweal such as the French kingdom evaporates when the Duchess's initial pose of rank superiority, in her wooing of Antonio, gives way to her famous appeal to him few lines later: "This is flesh, and blood, sir, / 'Tis not the figure cut in alabaster / Kneels at my husband's tomb" (DM, 1.2.372–374). In this scene the Duchess dispenses with her widowhood in that she now forsakes mourning and her link with a marital past. The key line in the whole play is "flesh and blood" because it is the crux of Webster's state politics. His heroine's emphatic corporeality, her pregnancy and pleasure in married sex, are presented as an early attempt to adumbrate the private sphere as constitutive of subjectivity and vice versa; as such it is pitted against the sick patriarchal apparatuses of the church and state embodied in the Cardinal and the Duke Ferdinand. The Duchess bleeds as a woman and a mother, blood signifying her femaleness and sexual desire. Blood is the life-asserting principle of a young woman who refuses to remain "widowed" by being turned into a statue, to which she was condemned by the Aragonian patriarchy. From the text arises the Duchess's "personal" adherence to flesh/blood as the founding principle of a new organisation of sexuality identified with reproduction where pregnancy and marital sexual pleasure turn the family into the locus of desire and bliss. As Judith Haber acutely observes, "the association of pregnancy here with sexual pleasure and bodily excess on the one hand, and with female sociality on the other, make it potentially threatening to a patriarchal order in ways that have been lost ... in its current desexualized and medicalized form."[19]

My argument is that the privileging of flesh in the play appears as an emergent form of the deployment of sexuality. Central to this is precisely the redefinition of blood outside and against the deployment of alliance whose logic is projected in the Aragonian brothers' obsessive valorisation of the purity of patriarchal blood. On hearing that the Duchess has given birth to a son the Cardinal

---

19 Judith Haber, *Desire and Dramatic Form in Early Modern England* (Cambridge: CUP, 2009), 85–86.

wonders, "Shall our blood? / The royal blood of Aragon and Castile, / Be thus attainted?" (DM, 2.5.22–24), while Ferdinand wants to find a "desperate physic" (DM, 2.5.25) that would "purge infected blood, such blood as hers" (DM, 2.5.26). Because Ferdinand perceives his twin sister's body as a mirror image of his own, in which his own aristocratic blood flows untainted, class-endogamy verging on incest "naturally" emerges as the aristocracy's defence mechanism from alien intrusion from inferior ranks. Even more so, when this intrusion is felt as an essentially sexual offence against Ferdinand himself insofar as his sister's body "functions as a specular image, conferring an 'ideal unity' also on *his* body."[20] However, this "ideal unity" is the spectral image of a sick patriarchal apparatus that suffers from "lycanthropia" (DM, 5.2.6), Ferdinand's disease. To common blood ties dictating positionality in the context of alliance that consolidates and reproduces inheritance and dynastic interests Webster juxtaposes the blood of the Duchess's independent female corporeality.

Central to affective bonds generated by her maternal and sexual femininity, an attractive alternative to the hierarchical subjection that describes alliance, is the image of the womb and the pregnant body in particular. Bosola's obsessively misogynist gynaecological discourse in its compulsive disclosure of female interiority constructs the Duchess's pregnancy as sickness (DM, 2.1.67–70). Her pregnant body is inscribed as grotesque in the system of patriarchal alliances, falling woefully short of the "classical body" which is "[n]ot to be eaten, not to be entered."[21] But this very same image is pitted against the beauty of fecundity that lies precisely in a body to be eaten as in Antonio's proud remark: "She's an excellent / Feeder of pedigrees" (DM, 3.1.5–6). At the end however, the Duchess's flesh will turn into a prey for her lycanthropic brother in the same way that her blood will seal her martyred femininity. The Duchess returns from the grave as an immaterial voice, "a thing of sorrow" (DM, 5.3.24), echoing significantly her husband's words. Idealised as a suffering, almost saintly, femininity she is finally meant to reinscribe the physical abnegation, a position to which she was culturally relegated and that she has fought against. On dying, she is turned into "some reverend monument" (DM, 4.2.33), an eternal object. Significantly, however, the vision of a new healthy *body politic* closes the play in Antonio's and her own son, the offspring precisely of class adulteration who will succeed the dead

---

20 Calbi, *Approximate Bodies*, 28.

21 Peter Stallybrass, "Reading the Body and the Jacobean Theatre of Consumption: *The Revenge Tragedy* (1606)," in *Staging the Renaissance: Reinterpretations of Elizabethan and Jacobean Drama*, eds. David Scott Kastan and Peter Stallybrass (New York: Routledge, 1991): 210–220, 214.

aristocrats. "These wretched eminent things" (DM, 5.5.113) now, in the voice of the dying Cardinal, plead to be erased from history.

In direct contrast with Elizabeth the Duchess is subjectivated by refusing her impenetrability and by "choosing instead who may 'enter' her."[22] However, *The Maid's Tragedy* inscribes a more extreme instance of female subjectivation though the sexual act. Evadne chooses the reverse: she is the one who penetrates the male body by symbolically raping and killing the King. On her wedding night she repells her husband's advances, and when he takes her conduct as maidenly bashfulness, she scornfully remarks: "A maidenhead Amintor at my years?"[23] Furthermore, she deals a final blow to his masculinity in her boastful declaration: "I doe enjoy the best" (MT, 2.1.327) implying that he is second. Evadne's sexual ascendancy over Amintor relegates him to a "feminine" position but so does his passive endurance of his cuckolding by the tyrannical king. The tragedy equates non-resistance to tyranny with a stereotyped femininity: the subject who suffers patiently the sovereign's injustice is a feminised subject.

The King's interrogation of Amintor on his wedding night expresses the great pleasure he takes in the young man's emasculation, while his kissing Evadne in front of him marks her as royal property. When she plainly declares to Amintor her adulterous affair in front of the King it is only then that he cries "Y'are a tirant" (MT, 3.1.252) and fantasises himself as a violent regicide. He would dismember the King's body and scatter his limbs all over the land.[24] It is precisely the illicit sexual act that the King performs from which emerges Amintor's instantaneous recognition that the sovereign is "meere man" (MT, 3.1.263), and the transgressive female body serves as the terrain upon which this ideological disenchantment takes place. Thus, he would disfigure the King's *body natural* so that the *body politic* would survive and regenerate itself for ever. However, to the King's challenge to draw his sword Amintor stops his "treacherous hand" from touching "holy things!" (MT 3.2.280–281). In a militarist world full of brandishing swords Amintor, in a telling gesture of self-emasculation, drops his sword before the King's holy body. In this sense, his initial advice to his wife concerning the King's offence, "let us / Suffer, and waite" (MT, 2.1.346–347), anticipates his future submission in its articulation of the discourse of Jacobean monarchy on

22 Haber, *Desire and Dramatic Form*, 76.

23 Francis Beaumont and John Fletcher, *The Maid's Tragedy*, ed. Andrew Gurr (Edinburgh: Oliver and Boyd, 1969), 2.1.220: further references to acts, scenes and lines in the text, abbreviated as MT.

24 See Gurr's note for Amintor's threat that he would "send [the King's] *lives* through all the land" (MT, 3.1.260), in which he notes many editors' acceptance of Theobald's emendation "your lims" (115), which I also accept.

the wronged subject's position in the face of the sovereign's abusive power. He reiterates it later in his injunction to Melantius, who wishes to take revenge for his wronged honour, "rather live / And suffer with me" (3.2.276–277) in a language that rephrases James's command to the subjects of tyrannical rule.

But there is no exit for the King insofar as "the image of the body politic is vitiated by its participation in a duality, caught between the singularity of royalty and the commonality of the visceral body."[25] In other words, the *body politic* has by definition collapsed into the *body natural* of the tyrant which, shown to be exclusively "visceral," causes the pollution of the former. The one who definitely "strikes" is Evadne, both convinced and coerced by her brother Melantius to take revenge upon the King. Melantius draws his sword on her and forces her to the ground: "speake, you whore, speake truth, / Or by the deare soule of thy sleeping father / This sword shall be thy lover" (MT, 4.1.108–110). In disciplining the sexually unruly woman Melantius threatens to penetrate his sister's already penetrated body by means of his phallic sword while standing on top of her in a symbolical display of patriarchal superiority.[26] As William Shullenberger incisively remarks "[t]he claim of family, that primary organization of psychic energy [...] is the snare in which Melantius catches his sister. He couples his death threat with the spectre of their blood father to tear Evadne from her liaison with the king."[27] Thoroughly disciplined she will be sacrificed by her brother in a coldly premeditated act, her tyrannicide appearing as obedience to male command.

However compelled into revenge, it is through this act that Evadne constructs her subjectivity by resisting patriarchal regulation. This process of subjectivation, although fragile and short-term, is what enables her to recognise the exact form of subjection that patriarchal regulation takes. Significantly her position in the court as the King's lover, which she had perceived as empowerment before realising her disposability, is precisely what genders her sense of injustice as "the most wrong'd of women" (MT, 5.1.127). That this awareness is articulated in the misogynist terms voiced by her brother anticipates her eventual gender coopting but at the same time it enables her to turn her personal plight into a cath-

25 Jason R. Denman, "Anatomizing the Body Politic: Corporeal Rhetoric in *The Maid's Tragedy*," *Philological Quarterly*, 84.3 (2005): 311–31, 314.

26 Although Melantius's phallic aggression is reminiscent of Ferdinand who threatens the Duchess with their father's poniard, here there is no trace of incestuous desire. The sexual undertones inscribe the powerful homoeroticism exhibited in the friendship of Amintor and Melantius. The latter's excessive grief for the death of his friend is contrasted with his total indifference towards his slain sister. To him Amintor was his "Sister, Father, Brother, Sonne" (MT, 5.3.287).

27 Shullenberger, "'This For the Most Wrong'd of Women'," 148–149.

olic demand for justice: the King is "such a tyrant / That for his lust would sell away his subjects" (MT, 5.1.103–104). As a rebellious subject, an avenger who could paraphrase Vindice's self-assertion in *The Revenger's Tragedy* into "'Tis I, 'tis Evadne, 'tis I," she takes revenge for all the victims of tyranny. Finding the King asleep in his bed she decides not to kill him while he is sleeping but to confront him with his "sicke conscience" (MT, 5.1.35) articulating thus the heroic ethos of the typical avenger. Because the whole act is seen by the King as a "pretty new device" (MT, 5.1.47), put up in order to arouse him, her medicalised linguistic violence targets his body: "You are too hot, and I have brought you physicke, / To temper your high veines" (MT, 5.1.56–57). The royal lover misreads "physicke" as implying her body but Evadne hastens to restore meaning: "I know you have a surfeited foule body, / And you must bleed" (MT, 5.1.60–61). She will make the king's "foule" *body natural* bleed by stabbing it to death in order to heal the sick *body politic* through a restorative blood-letting. In an effort to retrieve his power he commands her by re-registering his position as "thy King," but he soon gives way to the emergent subject of resistance whom he implores to pity him.

At the end of the tragedy the dramatic politics transcribe the extreme radicalism of tyrannicide as a passionate act done by a woman for a man's love. In a spectacular reversal Evadne is the one to implore Amintor to have sex with her. This happens after showing her repentance in a familiar recuperation of female resistance in Jacobean drama: "My whole life is so leprous it infects / All my repentance" (MT, 4.1.223–224).[28] Here the female tyrannicide turns her phallic knife against herself because she is sexually rejected by her husband. In this sense, she duplicates Aspatia, the wronged virgin, who dies by her beloved Amintor's sword that is thrust into her in a displaced form of coitus. The female body on stage, whether fully penetrated or obsessively closed up, is finally entered and thus symbolically reinstated as a fissured thing in the patriarchal order. However, there is a residue left. Upon discovering the King's dead body one of his attendants wonders "who can beleeve / A woman could doe this?" (MT, 5.1.143–144) This simple statement ironically sums up the dramatists' strategy of resistance which is not obfuscated by the final verdict that typically denies female agency by registering it simply as a means to a patriarchal end.

In Chapman, Bussy's liaison with Tamyra represents the trespassing into Montsurry's fenced-in enclosure by a low-born agent and the symbolic confer-

28 The infection of the body politic by female sexual transgression also marks *The Changeling* which ironically echoes Evadne's eventual position by having Beatrice-Joanna admit to her father that she "bleeds" for his, and the citadel's "better health."

ring on him of a class-privilege to which he is not entitled. The threat that Bussy's sexual desire poses to the aristocratic body on the whole is explicit in Montsurry's initial suspicion that the upstart might have "privy access" to the Duke of Guise's wife.[29] The opening up of the enclosed elite to the upward mobile intruder is dangerous because of the possible dilution of aristocratic blood through the prospect of illicit offspring. This is an essentially political problem insofar as it disrupts the patriarchal inheritance of property and power. Interestingly, adultery emerges as a class-contingent offence as is obvious from Montsurry's toleration of Monsieur's advances to Tamyra because he is a prince. In a constitutional language he shows how the princes' prerogative cancels the law represented by Parliament and their adherence to law is therefore a pure formality (BD, 22.118–123). To this political realism verging on cynicism Tamyra juxtaposes her right of resistance. She correctly discerns that her compliance with the prince's immodest proposal would be tantamount to political subjection. To Monsieur's threat that he has "power t'advance and pull down any" (BD, 2.2.54), should she not submit to him, she responds by politicising an essentially sexual offence in a language that emphasises the subject's emergent demand for self-determination: "Mine honour's in mine own hands, spite of Kings" (BD, 2.2.59).

Chapman foregrounds the heroine's choice of Bussy as a double assault on socio-political order: first, on the patriarchal power of the husband and, second, on the political power of the prince. Her sexual desire for Bussy designates her new obedience to an alternative hierarchical system, ruled by "blood" as synonymous with passion, directly inimical to the state-family analogical structures and the values invested in them. Her subjectivation is constructed in and through adultery insofar as she will use her submission to marital legality as a tool for her new subjection to the law of passion this time, something construed as typical female hypocrisy. Montsurry voices the misogynist topos of women's sexual agency as monstrous, and wonders "with what monsters women's imaginations engross them / when they are once enamoured" (BD, 3.2.280–281). Later on he uses the Copernican image of the reversal of order in order to underscore women's transgression as a rebellion against all hierarchical gradations of family and state alike. In a typical hegemonic gesture the state apparatuses are naturalised as cosmic order, so Tamyra's shifting out of her place is tantamount to her shifting out of the order of Creation (BD, 5.1.150–157). She must be thoroughly disciplined in order to accept subjection as the only position that these structures analogical to patriarchy afford her.

---

29 George Chapman, *Bussy D'Ambois*, ed. Nicholas Brooke, *The Revels Plays* (London: Methuen, 1964), 3.2.221–222: further reference to act, scene and line in the text, abbreviated as BD.

Montsury uses torture to interrogate Tamyra by stretching her on the rack and stabbing her arms repeatedly. With the exception of this scene, the rack, "that potent symbol of the state's compulsion to wring truth from the subject,"[30] but also a gratuitous marker of its power, does not appear on the Renaissance stage that nonetheless displays other extreme forms of corporeal violence. Consequently the staging of the officially sanctioned form of violence that only the state is allowed to inflict on offenders, and *not* husbands on adulterous wives, is precisely what differentiates this tragedy from others. Montsurry uses the rack in order not to extract the truth about Tamyra's adultery, which he already knows, but to force her to write a letter as a bait to her lover so that, caught in the trap, he could be murdered, something that eventually happens at the end. But this does not adequately justify the form of torture. Most emphatically the choice of the rack as an instrument of state torture signifies the essentially political nature of the offence against the husband who is also the lord and head of the conjugal body. Tamyra under torture exclaims: "O who is turn'd into my Lord and husband? / Husband? My Lord? None but my Lord and husband" (BD, 5.1.143–144). The lord-husband, as the microcosmic replica of the sovereign, stages "private" punishment as a state spectacle in the context of a text that consistently underscores the structural continuity between the state and the family; indeed, both are deemed instrumental in the notion of order that it interrogates. Tamyra's tortured corporeality inscribes the gendering of the resistant subject while, at the same time, it serves as a paradigm of state violence exercised on the body of the rebel. Chapman specifies the character "of the vexed relation between the subject and the early modern state"[31] from the point of view of the subject's subjection to violence. While being stabbed Tamyra emerges as victim of Montsurry's tyranny: "[F]eel, O feel / how you are turn'd to stone; with my heart blood. / Dissolve yourself again, or you will grow / Into the image of all Tyranny" (BD, 5.1.129–131). He impressively collapses the tyrannical state into sadistic masculinity in the figure of the husband-torturer: "Now break [my arms] as you please, and all the bounds / Of manhood, noblesse, and religion" (BD, 5.1.119–120).

State violence extracts the truth from the body of the criminal, which at the same time it constructs as the physical imprint of a visible and spectacular power. In Foucault's theory of the shift from the violence performed on the body to the knowledge of the soul from the Classical Age onwards, torture is crucial because it reveals the operations of power:

30 Elizabeth Hanson, *Discovering the Subject in Renaissance England* (Cambridge: CUP, 1998), 55.

31 Hanson, *Discovering*, 56.

> [I]t made it possible to reproduce the crime on the visible body of the criminal; in the same horror, the crime had to be manifested and annulled. It also made the body of the condemned man the place where the vengeance of the sovereign was applied, the anchoring point for a manifestation of power, an opportunity of affirming the dissymmetry of forces.[32]

Montsurry physically inscribes on the material surface of Tamyra's body his vengeance as a sovereign, thus visibly reasserting "the dissymmetry of forces." He sculpts his wife's body by literally re-inscribing it with his own male "characters" (alphabet) in a language strongly reminiscent of Melantius' threat to write his male alphabet on Evadne's flesh: "Till thou writ'st / I'll write in wounds (my wrongs' fit characters) / Thy right of sufferance. Write" (BD, 5.1.124–126). The script is monotonous, and consists of a single word, "whore," but writing reasserts masculinity and restores destabilised order. At the same time, by cutting openings on her body, Montsurry symbolically duplicates the specific form that adultery has taken, namely, Bussy's illicit sexual penetration of the aristocratic body. In this sense, he re-enacts the crime in the criminal's corporeality turning his wife's punishment into a spectacle that foregrounds and reconfirms official disciplinary practices.

Bussy D'Ambois "appropriately" closes with Tamyra's reversion to the position of a masochistic femininity, reminiscent of Evadne, in her declaration to her husband that she loves her wounds "[b]eing open'd by your hands." (BA, 5.3.240) However, this conventional gesture of co-opting is undercut by Chapman's refusal to offer the couple's reconciliation as a closure. They can forgive but not reunite, their separation underscored by the direction "*exeunt severally.*" In the sequel to the play, *The Revenge of Bussy D'Ambois*, Tamyra strikes back, conspiring in her husband's death with Clermont who will take revenge upon Montsurry for the murder of his brother Bussy. Chapman, like Webster and Beaumont and Fletcher, genders the subject of resistance as a sexually aberrant woman in order to question the ideological and material workings of state power. Central to this essentially dissenting practice is the female body through which the disintegration of the *body politic* is staged in ways that only seemingly reconfirm the dominant narrative of subjection. In this sense, these tragedies and others despite their ambiguities and ambivalences, or thanks to them, offer complex and essentially radical readings of the problem of power and the subject's position in the face of it.

32 Michel Foucault, *Discipline and Punish: The Birth of the Prison* [1975], trans. Alan Sheridan (Middlesex: Penguin, 1979), 55.

Contributors

Heinz Antor is Chair of English Literatures and Head of the Department of English at the University of Cologne (Germany). He has taught at the Universities of Würzburg, Düsseldorf, and Bremen as well as at George Mason University (Fairfax, VA). Antor is editor of the journal *Anglistik: International Journal of English Studies*. He has published on anglophone literatures from the early modern period to the 21st century, postcolonial, inter- and transcultural studies, Canadian and Australian literature, and literary pattern-building. Among his books are *The Bloomsbury Group*, 1986; *Die Narrativik der Angry Young Men*, 1989; *Text – Culture – Reception. Cross-Cultural Aspects of English Studies*, 1992; *Der englische Universitätsroman*, 1996; *Intercultural Encounters – Studies in English Literatures*, 1999; *English Literatures in International Contexts*, 2000; *Refractions of Germany in Canadian Literature and Culture*, 2003; *Refractions of Canada in European Literature and Culture*, 2005; *Inter- und Transkulturelle Studien*, 2006, *Fremde Kulturen verstehen – fremde Kulturen lehren: Theorie und Praxis der Vermittlung interkultureller Kompetenz*, 2007; and *From Interculturalism to Transculturalism: Mediating Encounters in Cosmopolitan Contexts*, 2010.

Riccardo Baldissone is Visiting Scholar at the University of Westminster, London, for the academic year 2015–16. His previous research project aimed at reconsidering human rights discourse in the broader context of the modern theoretical framework. He is now taking further his genealogical commitment in narrations that link the process of construction of the logic of identity in classical ontology with the medieval emergence of conceptual discourse and the transformations of modern naturalism, in the perspective of the overcoming of the double Western straitjacket of entities and representations. Among his publications, "The Costs of Paradise: Temporalisations of Place in Pasargadae," in *World Heritage in Iran: Perspectives on Pasargadae*, Ali Mozaffari ed. (London: Ashgate, 2015); "I and Another: Rethinking the Subject of Human Rights with Dostoyevsky, Bakhtin and Simondon," in *Literature and Human Rights: The Law, the Language and the Limitations of Human Rights Discourse*, Ian Ward ed. (Berlin: De Gruyter, 2015); "Non Giudicheremo gli Angeli: Dalle Biopolitiche alle Polibiotiche," in *Differenze Italiane. Politica e Filosofia: Mappe e Sconfinamenti*, Dario Gentili and Elettra Stimilli eds. (Roma: DeriveApprodi, 2015); "Speech and *Graphomena:* The Power of Apuleius' Words in Court and in Translation," *Pólemos*, 9.2 (2015): 441–456.

Daniela Carpi is Full Professor of English Literature at the Department of Foreign Literatures and Languages of the University of Verona. Her fields of research are: Renaissance theatre, critical theory, postmodernism, law and literature, literature and science, literature and visual arts. She is in the scientific board of the journals *Symbolism: a Journal of Critical Aesthetics* (New York), *Anglistik* (Heidelberg), *La torre di Babele* (Parma), *Law and Humanities* (Warwick), *Cardozo Law Bulletin* (University of Trento), *COSMO Comparative Studies in Modernism* (Torino). She is a member of Academia Europaea, ESSE, AIA. She is the president of AIDEL (Associazione Italiana di Diritto e Letteratura) and a member of the Advisory Board of the series "Edinburgh Critical Studies in Law, Literature and the Humanities"; she edits the series "Law and Literature" and the journal *Pólemos* for DeGruyter.

Cristina Costantini is Associate Professor of Private Comparative Law at the University of Perugia. She is member of AIDC (Associazione Italiana di Diritto Comparato), AIDEL (Associazione Italiana di Diritto e Letteratura), Selden Society (Faculty of Law, Queen and Westfield College, London), ESSE (The European Society for the Study of English) and AIA (Associazione Italiana di Anglistica). Her main fields of research are the history of the English legal system, the construction of legal traditions, the intellectual assessment of the liminal thresholds within Humanities (Law and Literature, Law and Philosophy, Law and Religion). Among her publications, "Representing Law. Narrative Practices, Poetic Devices, Visual Signs and the Aesthetics of the Common Law Mind", in *Liminal Discourses. Subliminal Tensions in Law and Literature*, eds. Daniela Carpi, Jeanne Gaakeer (Berlin: DeGruyter, 2013): 27–36, "The Keepers of Traditions. The English Common Lawyers and the Presence of Law", *Comparative Law Review* (2010): 1–12; *La Legge e il Tempio* (Roma: Carocci, 2007).

Raffaele Cutolo holds a PhD in English Studies from the University of Verona and the title of Doctor Europaeus. His fields of research include law and literature, food studies, queer theory, the performing arts, and the fairy tale. He has held a Research Associate position in Health Communication at the Department of Translational and Molecular Medicine at the University of Brescia, where he has also been Adjunct Professor of English. His monograph *Into the Woods of Wicked Wonderland* (Winter, 2014) has proved a valuable contribution to the field of the fairy tale studies. He has also published essays on contemporary British literature.

Roxanne Barbara Doerr is Adjunct Professor at the Universities of Milano, Padova, Verona (English language) and Modena (English literature). She holds a PhD in English Studies from the University of Verona, the title of Dr. Phil. from the University of Köln, and the title of Doctor Europaeus for an international co-tutored doctoral thesis entitled *The Debate Between the Concepts of Justice and Equity in the XX century Anglo-Saxon Legal Thriller.* Her areas of research and publication include language of new and social media, workplace communication, distance learning, multiculturalism, English for specific purposes, law and visual arts, law and literature, law and culture, the legal thriller, postmodern and contemporary literature.

John Drakakis is Emeritus Professor of English Studies at the University of Stirling and Visiting Pofessor at the University of Lincoln. He is the editor of *Alternative Shakespeares* (1985), *Shakespearean Tragedy* (1992), *Tragedy* (1994) with Naomi Liebler, and the Arden 3 edition of Shakespeare's *The Merchant of Venice* (2012). He is the general editor of the Routledge New Critical Idiom series, and he is the general editor and contributing editor of the revision of Geoffrey Bullough's *Narrative and Dramatic Sources of Shakespeare* (forthcoming). He has contributed numerous book chapters and learned articles on Shakespeare, Literary Theory, and Renaissance culture, and he guest edited journals such as the *ESSE Journal*, and (jointly with Monika Fludernik) *Poetics Today.*

Sidia Fiorato is Researcher of English Literature at the University of Verona. Her fields of Research include detective fiction and the legal thriller, law, literature and culture, literature and the Performing Arts, Shakespeare Studies, the Fairy Tale. Among her publications *Il Gioco con l'ombra. Ambiguità e metanarrazioni nella narrativa di Peter Ackroyd* (Verona, Fiorini, 2003), *The Relationship Between Literature and Science in John Banville's Scientific Tetralogy* (Berlin, Peter Lang, 2007), essays on the contemporary novel, Shakespearian adaptations, Victorian Literature.

Beate Neumeier is Professor and Chair of English at the University of Cologne. Her research interests and publications are in the fields of gender studies and postcolonial studies pertaining to drama, theatre and fiction from the English Renaissance to the present time, with a specific focus on aspects of otherness (madness, the monstrous, the gothic). She is editor of the e-journal *genderforum* and *GenderInn, a Gender Studies data base.* Her most recent publications are with Kay Schaffer, *Decolonizing the Landscape: Indigenous Cultures in Australia* (Amsterdam: Rodopi, 2014) and with Elisabeth Bronfen, *Gothic Renaissance* (Manchester UP, 2014).

Paul Raffield is Professor of Law at the University of Warwick, where he teaches Tort Law, Origins of English Law, and Shakespeare and the Law. After graduating from Cardiff University with a degree in Law, Paul went to drama school and subsequently worked for twenty-five years as an actor, prior to his appointment at Warwick. While an actor, Paul studied for a PhD at Birkbeck Law School. He has subsequently published extensively in the fields of Law and Literature and Legal History. In 2007, he co-organised an international conference at Warwick on Shakespeare and the Law, which attracted leading Shakespearean and legal scholars. The papers were published in an edited collection: *Shakespeare and the Law*, eds. Paul Raffield and Gary Watt (Oxford: Hart Publishing, 2008). He is the author of *Shakespeare's Imaginary Constitution: Late Elizabethan Politics and the Theatre of Law* (Oxford: Hart Publishing, 2010) and *Images and Cultures of Law in Early Modern England: Justice and Political Power, 1558–1660* (Cambridge: Cambridge University Press, 2004). His forthcoming monograph, *The Art of Law in Shakespeare*, will be published by Hart/Bloomsbury in 2017. He is founding co-editor-in-chief of the journal *Law and Humanities*, and a member of AIDEL (Associazione Italiana Diritto e Letteratura). Paul is a National Teaching Fellow, a Fellow of the UK Higher Education Academy, and a recipient of the Warwick Award for Teaching Excellence.

Mariangela Tempera was Professor of English Language and Literature at the Department of Human Sciences of the University of Ferrara. Besides dealing with British Renaissance Theatre and Shakespeare in particular, she wrote extensively on popular literature and film versions of Shakespeare with a specific interest also on Shakespearean references in Italian cinema. She was chief editor of the series "Shakespeare from Page to Stage" (published by Clueb, Bologna). In 1992, following an agreement between Ferrara City Council and the University of Ferrara, she founded the "Shakesperean Centre" which she directed. Among her publications, "Giorgio Strehler's La Tempesta, from Stage to (Comic) Screen", in *Shakespeare in Performance*, eds. Eric C. Brown and Estelle Rivier (Cambridge: Cambridge Scholars Press, 2013), and the edited volume *Richard II. Dal testo alla scena* (Emil, Bologna, 2015).

Aspasia Velissariou is Professor of English Literature and Culture and Head of the Postgraduate Studies Programme in the Department of English Language at the University of Athens, Greece. She is the author of *Discourses of Power and Truth in Wycherley's Drama* (1991), *Congreve and the Politics of Comedy* (1997) and *Female Sexual Transgression in Jacobean Tragedy* (2002). She has published widely on Restoration literature and seventeenth-century theoretical discourses with a special emphasis on John Locke, Jacobean tragedy, as well as on formations of gender in English drama.

Ian Ward is currently Professor of Law at Newcastle University. His research is focused on the intersection of law, literature and history. He has published a number of books and articles in this area including *Law and Literature: Possibilities and Perspectives* (Cambridge: Cambridge UP, 1995), *Shakespeare and the Legal Imagination* (London: Butterworths/CUP, 1999) and more recently *Law and the Brontës* (Basingstoke: Palgrave Macmillan, 2012) and *Sex, Crime and Literature in Victorian England* (Hart/Bloomsbury, 2014).

Index

Bei Fragen zur Produktsicherheit wenden Sie sich bitte an:
If you have any questions regarding product safety,
please contact:

Walter de Gruyter GmbH
Genthiner Straße 13
10785 Berlin
productsafety@degruyterbrill.com